SILICON VALLEY NORTH

A HIGH-TECH CLUSTER OF INNOVATION AND ENTREPRENEURSHIP

TECHNOLOGY, INNOVATION, ENTREPRENEURSHIP AND COMPETITIVE STRATEGY SERIES

Series Editors: **John McGee and Howard Thomas**

Published
STEFFENS
Newgames — Strategic Competition in the PC Revolution

BULL, THOMAS & WILLARD
Entrepreneurship: Perspectives on Theory Building

SANCHEZ, HEENE & THOMAS
Dynamics of Competence-Based Competition

DAI
Corporate Strategy, Public Policy and New Technologies

BOGNER
Drugs to Market

SUSMAN & O'KEEFE
The Defense Industry in the Post-Cold War Era

NORDBERG
The Strategic Management of High Technology Contracts: The Case of CERN

SCHULZ & HOFER
Creating Value with Entrepreneurial Leadership and Skill-Based Strategies

Forthcoming title
PORAC & VENTRESCA
Constructing Industries and Markets

Other titles of interest
DURING, OAKEY & KAUSER
New Technology-Based Firms in the New Millennium, Volume III

HOSNI
Management of Technology: Internet Economy

KATZ
Advances in Entrepreneurship, Firm Emergence and Growth, Volume 7: Corporate Entrepreneurship

LIBECAP
Advances in the Study of Entrepreneurship, Innovation and Economic Growth, Volume 15: Intellectual Property and Entrepreneurship

Related journals — sample copies available online at www.sciencedirect.com

Journal of Business Venturing
Journal of Engineering and Technology Management
Journal of High Technology Management Research
Technological Forecasting and Social Change
Technovation

SILICON VALLEY NORTH

A HIGH-TECH CLUSTER OF INNOVATION AND ENTREPRENEURSHIP

EDITED BY

LARISA V. SHAVININA

Département des Sciences Administratives, Université du Québec en Outaouais, Canada

2004

ELSEVIER

Amsterdam – Boston – Heidelberg – London – New York – Oxford
Paris – San Diego – San Francisco – Singapore – Sydney – Tokyo

ELSEVIER B.V.	ELSEVIER Inc.	**ELSEVIER Ltd**	ELSEVIER Ltd
Sara Burgerhartstraat 25	525 B Street, Suite 1900	**The Boulevard, Langford**	84 Theobalds Road
P.O. Box 211	San Diego	**Lane, Kidlington**	London
1000 AE Amsterdam	CA 92101-4495	**Oxford OX5 1GB**	WC1X 8RR
The Netherlands	USA	**UK**	UK

First edition 2004

Library of Congress Cataloging in Publication Data
A catalog record is available from the Library of Congress.

British Library Cataloguing in Publication Data
A catalogue record is available from the British Library.

ISBN: 0-08-044457-1
ISSN: 1479-067X (Series)

⊗ The paper used in this publication meets the requirements of ANSI/NISO Z39.48-1992 (Permanence of Paper). Printed in The Netherlands.

To Evgueni and Alexander

Contents

Part III: Conclusion

About the Authors

Robert Armit is a professional economist and consultant in Technology Business Development. Prior to establishing his consultancy in 1998, Robert Armit served as Director of the Technology Transfer Centre at OCRI in Ottawa and as Director of Technology Transfer at both the University of Alberta in Edmonton and Carleton University in Ottawa. While at Carleton, for three years he served laterally as Vice-President (Technology) of the Carleton University Development Corporation where he developed the concept for the technology initiative at the base of the Carleton Technology and Training Centre. Robert Armit was a member of the Board of Directors of the Association of University Related Research Parks in the USA and was Secretary-Treasurer of the Canadian Research Management Association.

Antonio J. Bailetti holds a faculty appointment in both the Department of Systems and Computer Engineering and in the Eric Sprott School of Business at Carleton University, Ottawa, Canada. Professor Bailetti has been the Director of the M.Eng. in Telecommunications Technology Management program since 1998. He was the Director of Carleton University's School of Business from 1981 to 1988 and a Director at Bell-Northern Research (today a part of Nortel Networks) from 1988 to 1992. Professor Bailetti's work has been published in engineering management journals such as *IEEE Transactions on Engineering Management*, *Journal of Product Innovation Management*, *Research Policy*, and *R&D Management*.

François Brouard is a faculty member in the Eric Sprott School of Business at Carleton University in Ottawa, Canada, where he teaches Accounting and Taxation. A Chartered Accountant, François earned a doctorate in business administration (DBA) from Université du Québec à Trois-Rivières. He develops a diagnostic tool for environmental scanning practices in small and medium-sized enterprises (SME).

John Callahan is cross-appointed in both the Department of Systems and Computer Engineering and the Sprott School of Business at Carleton University, Ottawa, Canada. He teaches graduate courses and supervises graduate research in telecommunications and product development management in Engineering, and in R&D management in the Sprott School of Business. He has published in journals such as *Management Science, Research Policy, IEEE Transactions on Engineering Management, Technovation and R&D Management*. Professor Callahan graduated from Carleton University with a B.Sc. (Hon) in Mathematics and Physics. He then did an MA in Applied Mathematics and a Ph.D. in Industrial Engineering at the University of Toronto.

Tyler Chamberlin is a faculty member in the School of Management at the University of Ottawa, Canada where he teaches International Business and Technology Management. Tyler is a researcher with the Program of Research on Innovation Management and Economy (PRIME) where he has been active in the research of Ottawa's technology clusters as part of a major national study of industrial clusters. He is also a doctoral candidate at the University of Manchester's ESRC Centre for Research on Innovation and Competition (CRIC) in the United Kingdom where his dissertation work investigates the acquisition strategies of firms in technologically intensive industries.

Ken Charbonneau is a partner and team leader at KPMG who specializes in assisting technology companies with business strategies and models, raising financing and financial reporting. Ken has over 25 years of business experience, including the two years ended February 2000, as CFO of an international software development company where he gained industry experience. As a CFO and company Director, Ken was involved in a wide range of activities including managing and completing a $5 million venture capital financing and the acquisition of two businesses. He also negotiated various bank credit facilities; implemented a comprehensive business planning and budgeting process; developed international transfer pricing models; implemented an employee stock option plan; and negotiated various software sale, royalty and escrow agreements.

Arvind Chhatbar is President & CEO of Vitesse Re-Skilling Canada Inc. — an organization he founded in 1998. He is also the Director of National Research Council of Canada's Regional Innovation Centre and the Executive Director of the Regional Innovation Forum. Apart from founding Vitesse, Mr. Chhatbar has founded a number of other companies. He has been a pioneer in creating NRC's first and eight other spin-off companies that provided the basis for the launching of NRC's Entrepreneurship Program. His insight and pioneering role in the creation of NRC's first and well received Regional Innovation Office led to NRC later adopting Regional Innovation as primary policy and vision plank that helped the organization to expand regional operations all across the country and establishing a presence in all of the provinces.

David C. Coll is Professor Emeritus of Systems and Computer Engineering at Carleton University and President of DCC Informatics, a consulting firm offering professional engineering services in Information Technology. He is a Life Fellow of the IEEE, and a Fellow of the Canadian Academy of Engineering. Dr. Coll was with the Defence Research Board of Canada from 1956 to 1967, where he worked in communications and signal processing. He joined the Department of Systems and Computer Engineering at Carleton University, where he was Chairman of the Department from 1975 to 1978 and again in 1988/1989. At the time of his retirement in 1998, he was the Director of the M.Eng. Program in Telecommunications Technology Management.

Jérôme Doutriaux (Dipl.Ing., M.Sc., Ph.D. (Carnegie-Mellon)), is Full Professor and Vice-Dean in the School of Management at the University of Ottawa. University-industry technology transfer, technology incubation, high-technology entrepreneurship and regional development have been the main thrusts of his research activities for many years. Professor Doutriaux has published several books in applied economics, a monograph on university-industry linkages in Canada, and many articles in academic and professional journals such as *IEEE Transactions on Engineering Management, the Journal of Business Venturing, Industry and Higher Education, the Revue Internationale des PMEs, the Canadian Journal of Development Studies, Canadian Public Policy.*

Linda Duxbury is a Professor at the Sprott School of Business, Carleton University. Within the past decade she has completed major studies on balancing work and family, management support and career development in the public and high tech sectors. Dr. Duxbury has published widely in both the academic and practitioner literatures in the area of work-family conflict, supportive work environments, stress, telework, and supportive management. Dr. Duxbury held the Imperial Life Chair in Women and Management from 1992 to 1996. In May 2000, Dr. Duxbury was awarded the Public Service Citation from the Association of Public Service Executives for her work on supportive work environments.

Lorraine Dyke is an Associate Professor in the School of Business at Carleton University where she teaches courses in Management and Organizational Behaviour, Workforce Diversity and Interpersonal Skills. Dr. Dyke is the founder and current Director of the Centre for Research and Education on Women and Work and the Management Development Program for Women at Carleton. Dr. Dyke is the author of numerous articles and has received extensive funding for her research on careers, mentoring, gender issues and workforce diversity. Her recent monographs include a cross-cultural study of attitudes towards women in management, a study on career development in the federal public service and a study of career issues in the high tech sector. She is the recipient of two Best Paper Awards from the Academy of Management.

Jocelyn Ghent Mallett earned a Ph.D. in History and International Affairs from the University of Illinois in 1976, and has since enjoyed a career spanning the academic, public and private sectors. She has held a variety of senior positions in the Canadian government and gained broad experience in areas of technology policy, international trade, and industrial and economic policy. In 1995, she established Rippon Associates Inc., an Ottawa consulting service specializing in strategic public policy analysis and organizational development issues affecting the growth of high tech firms. She served for five years as a member of the Chairman's Executive Council at Newbridge Networks Corporation, and has been active on many private and public sector boards. She has been a member of Carleton University's Board of Governors since 1996, and currently serves as its Chair.

George H. Haines Jr. is a Professor of Marketing at the School of Business, Carleton University, in Ottawa, Ontario, Canada. He is the author or co-author of over one hundred refereed publications, two monographs, and was editor of two published books. He received his Ph.D. in Economics from Carnegie Institute of Technology, Pittsburgh, PA, USA. He has taught at Carnegie Institute of Technology, UCLA, University of Rochester, University of Toronto, McMaster University, and Queen's University. His professional duties have included serving as Treasurer for the Association for Consumer Research, as an elected member of the Council of The Institute of Management Sciences, and as the Vice-Chairman of the Institute of Management Sciences' College on Innovation Management and Entrepreneurship.

Edward T. Jackson is Chair of the Centre for the Study of Training, Investment and Economic Restructuring, and Associate Professor of Public Administration and

International Affairs, at Carleton University of Ottawa. Cofounder of the nationwide Community Economic Development Technical Assistance Program, he is one of Canada's leading authorities on local and regional development, advising foundations, governments, development agencies, non-profits, labour and business. His research interests include local governance and poverty reduction, knowledge management, financing civil society, and citizen-directed evaluation.

Rahil Khan is Research Associate with the Centre for the Study of Training, Investment and Economic Restructuring at Carleton University. A graduate of Carleton's School of Public Policy and Administration, he has researched and written extensively on technology and regional development.

Natalie Lam is an Associate Professor in the School of Management at the University of Ottawa, Ottawa, Canada. She teaches in the areas of organizational behavior, human resources management and performance management. Dr. Lam holds a Ph.D. from the University of California at Berkeley and has extensive consulting experience with local and international companies in the area of management training. Her research, which has been published in international journals, includes work on cross-cultural management, career development, women and work, and human/organizational aspects of operations management.

Judith Madill (Ph.D. from the Ivey School of Business, University of Western Ontario, 1985) is currently Associate Professor of Marketing and Coordinator of the Marketing Area in the Eric Sprott School of Business, Carleton University. Dr. Madill has authored over 40 papers and reports in the marketing field, including a recent paper on networks and linkages among firms in the Ottawa technology cluster, as well as papers on managing relationships in marketing, and financing small and medium size business.

Franco Materazzi holds a Masters in Economics from McGill University. He initially was employed with federal government. He then worked for 15 years with the Société d'aménagement de l'Outaouais, a unique regional development agency in Quebec dedicated to the economic development of the Quebec part of the National Capital of Canada. In that capacity he started in the late 1980s one of the first incubation centers in Canada, as well as participated in the launching of one of the first regional venture capital funds. Since 1992 he provides consulting services to start ups and growing technology firms, as well as to governments. He presently sits on the board of Innovatech du Grand Montreal one of the biggest Canadian venture capital fund that supports the high technology industries.

John de la Mothe is a Professor, Canada Research Chair on Innovation Strategy, and the Director of the Program of Research on Innovation Management and Economy (PRIME) in the School of Management at the University of Ottawa. Professor de la Mothe has taught at Harvard, Yale and most recently is cross-appointed to the University College of London, UK. Dr. de la Mothe's work looks at issues of science, technology, innovation and strategies. His most recent books include: *Networks, Alliance and Partnerships in the Economic Process*, edited with Albert Link, and *Science, Technology and Governance*.

Alan O'Sullivan gained his Ph.D. from McGill University and is an Assistant Professor at the University of Ottawa in Ottawa, Canada, where he teaches MBA courses in strategy and innovation. His research investigates multilateral (or, extended-enterprise) organizing in the development of complex products. Virtual collaboration, network-based learning, and inter-firm power relationships are all topics addressed through his research. He has published in the *Journal of Engineering and Technology Management*, and book chapters in JAI Press and Sage publications.

Gilles Paquet is Professor Emeritus at the University of Ottawa in Ottawa, Canada, where he also served as Dean of the Faculty of Administration and Founding Director of the Centre on Governance. He has been Editor-in-Chief of *Optimum* (later www.optimumonline.ca), a most influential journal of public management, and has published extensively in the fields of industrial organization, regional development, knowledge management, and governance. He has been elected a Fellow of the Royal Society of Arts (London) and made a member of the Order of Canada. He has recently been appointed President of the Royal Society of Canada (2003–2005).

Allan Riding is a Professor of Finance and coordinator of the Finance Division at the School of Business, Carleton University, in Ottawa, Ontario. He received his Ph.D. in Finance from McGill University in 1983. He is the author or co-author of 26 peer-reviewed publications, more than 30 articles presented at peer-reviewed conferences, three books, and numerous consulting reports for government and industry. His research on small business finance has received both national and international attention. The quality of his research is witnessed by 10 peer-adjudged awards from academic and professional organizations including the *Toronto Society of Financial Analysts, the Administrative Sciences Association of Canada, the International Council for Small Business*, and the *Canadian Council for Small Business and Entrepreneurship*.

Jeffrey Roy is an Associate Professor of Governance and Management at the University of Ottawa in Ottawa, Canada, specializing in collaborative models of economic development and e-governance. Dr. Roy served as Managing Director of the Centre on Governance in 2001–2002. In 2002 he was a Canadian consultant to the Organization for Economic Cooperation and Development (OECD) on two international studies: the governance of border-regions in Europe and North America and the emerging governance challenges of digital government. In 2003 he was a visiting Scholar in the School of Public Administration and Urban Planning at San Diego State University. He is also a regular contributor to *CIO Government's Review*, a Canadian publication devoted to better understanding the nexus between technology and government.

Larisa V. Shavinina is a Professor in the Department of Administrative Sciences at the Université du Québec en Outaouais, Gatineau, Québec, and an Adjunct Research Professor at the Eric Sprott School of Business, Carleton University, Ottawa, Canada. Originally focusing on psychology of high abilities (i.e., talent, giftedness, creativity), Dr. Shavinina's research has expanded to encompass innovation. She is engaged in research aimed at unifying the field of innovation, that is, to merge psychological, management, and business perspectives together. Her publications have appeared in the *Review of General Psychology, New Ideas in Psychology, Creativity Research Journal*, and others. She edited *The International Handbook on Innovation* (Elsevier Science 2003) and co-edited *CyberEducation* (Libert 2001) and *Beyond Knowledge* (Erlbaum 2004).

Warren Thorngate is a Professor in the Psychology Department of Carleton University, specializing in research on human decision-making, social and organizational psychology, the economics of attention, the ecology of problems, and social issues of computing. He has taught at several universities around the world, including Carnegie Mellon University and the universities of St. Petersburg, Warsaw, Havana and Tehran. He has also worked for 15 years to adapt computer and communication technologies for educational projects in the Third World. He is a founder of the National Capital FreeNet (Ottawa), a founding member of the Human Oriented Technology Laboratory at Carleton University, and currently a member of the Board of Directors of the Society for Judgment and Decision Making.

Christopher Wilson is the managing partner of Invéniré 4, an Ottawa-based consulting company. He has been a Senior Research Fellow with the Centre on Governance at the University of Ottawa since 1997. He is the team leader for SmartResults, an evaluation and assessment project of SmartCapital, Ottawa's not-for-profit Smart Community Demonstration Project. Mr. Wilson is also Co-Chair of the Steering Committee for SmartSites, a not-for-profit organization that coordinates public Internet access for Ottawa residents. He was a principal author of *Ottawa Works: A Mosaic of Ottawa's Economic and Workforce Landscape* prepared for TalentWorks. Mr. Wilson is also a lecturer in both the School of Management and the Faculty of Social Science at the University of Ottawa.

Preface

Silicon Valley North: A High-Tech Cluster of Innovation and Entrepreneurship is an edited volume about the Canadian Silicon Valley, that is, Canada's National Capital Region (Ottawa-Gatineau). Although much is written about Silicon Valley in California and other Silicon regions around the world, and high technology entrepreneurial clusters are actively discussed by scholars and policy makers alike, the Silicon Valley North was not a subject of a special book. It was a combination of my interest in this topic with my vision of it as lacking an important component — a comprehensive cover of the Canadian Silicon Valley — that encouraged me to initiate the present project. I came to believe that the time was ripe for such a book, which would further advance the scientific understanding of economic clusters worldwide and fill an apparent niche in the literature on the topic.

I am grateful to many people who helped to bring this book to fruition. Most important are definitely the authors: I thank them for their willingness to undertake the difficult and challenging task of contributing chapters and investing time in this endeavour. I am particularly grateful to Jean Vaillancourt, the Dean of Research at the Université du Québec en Outaouais, who has been very supportive of this project in many ways. I am also grateful to my editors at Elsevier — Catherine Hutchinson and Becky Lewsey — for the right blend of freedom, encouragement, and guidance needed for successful completion of the project.

I also wish to acknowledge my debt of gratitude to my husband, Evgueni Ponomarev, and our four-year-old son, Alexander. In countless ways, Evgueni has been an advisor, critic, and friend throughout the project. As always, he provided the moral and technical support, and — more importantly — the time I needed to complete this project. He did so by performing numerous tasks, from reminding me about deadlines to cooking and administering PC problems when I worked at nights and to assuming the lion's share (and the lioness's, too) of child care for our Alexander. I owe my biggest debt of gratitude to Alexander for his amazing understanding that mommy needed time and silence to work on the book. I thank them both for their patience with me.

Larisa V. Shavinina

Part I

Introduction

Chapter 1

Silicon Phenomenon: Introduction to Some Important Issues

Larisa V. Shavinina

Abstract

This introductory chapter presents a new perspective on understanding the phenomenon of Silicon Valley. In light of this perspective, Silicon Valley is a region of excellence, where all key players tried to do their very best, sometimes surpassing themselves, or they compensated for a lack of excellence in something. Regions of excellence will succeed in the future, and this is exactly what the knowledge economy needs. This introduction also provides an overview of the book by summarizing the main contents of each chapter.

Introduction

The Silicon phenomenon was, is, and will be an extremely important phenomenon in the accelerated technological, scientific, and economic development of countries and regions. The success of the American Silicon Valley inspires governments all around the world to establish Silicon Valleys, Alleys, and Islands in their own countries. Today people increasingly realize that the Silicon phenomenon is even more important than in the past. The New Economy is a knowledge-based economy and new ideas are beginning to rule the global economy. Successful, innovative ideas, with money making potential produced by companies in Silicon regions generate long term, sustainable economic prosperity. Due to this, the Silicon phenomenon has been receiving considerable attention from management and business scholars, innovation researchers, economists, urban planners, sociologists, psychologists, geographers, policy decision makers, and futurists. A lot of literature on the topic describes Silicon Valley in the USA, Silicon Islands in Asia, and so on.

The Ottawa-based high tech cluster — one of the globally competitive technology clusters — plays an exceptionally important role in making Canada a highly innovative economy. By bringing together a critical mass of talented people, expertise, venture capital, and entrepreneurial drive, and by giving birth to many internationally recognized companies (e.g. Corel, Nortel Networks, JDS Uniphase, Cognos, just to mention a few), the cluster thus contributes to a higher quality of life for the community, the region, the country, and the world as a whole. As a result, this high tech cluster is known worldwide as Silicon Valley North or Canadian Silicon Valley. Despite the quite evident importance of Silicon Valley North for the local, national, and international technological developments (especially when Nortel Networks and JDS Uniphase became global leaders in their fields and expanded in explosive fashion), this phenomenon is far from being well understood. Because of this, a book on the Canadian Silicon Valley is an exceptionally timely endeavour. Therefore, the book further advances the scientific understanding of the Silicon phenomenon by presenting in detail the Ottawa case, or Silicon Valley North.

Before briefly discussing the main contents of each chapter included in the book, I would like to address an issue of exceptional importance, namely: What is so exceptional about the American Silicon Valley that stimulates many countries to follow it as a prototypical model? The next section of the chapter deals with this.

The American Silicon Valley as a Prototypical Model of the Silicon Phenomenon: Hidden Mechanisms

In fact, the ultimate answer to the above question, what is so exceptional about the American Silicon Valley, is more or less known: This is the Silicon Valley's phenomenal capacity to generate and nurture technological innovations leading to the birth of dozens of the world's most successful high-technology companies, such as Hewlett-Packard, Apple Computers, Intel, Sun Microsystems, Cisco, Conner Peripherals, Cypress Semiconductor, Silicon Graphics, and many others. Its general success formula is also known: entrepreneurship, relatively easily accessible venture capital, institutions of higher education, which supply talented employees and conduct research; and social and technical networks (Kenney 2000; Porter 1998; Saxenian 1994). However, this is not the whole story. This section proposes a new perspective on the success of the Silicon Valley. Specifically, the account discusses those less evident ingredients of the region's triumph, which might be referred to as hidden mechanisms. The word "hidden" does not mean that these facts and aspects described below were not mentioned in the literature; they were. But they were not considered as essential factors when compared to venture capital, entrepreneurship, universities, social and technical networks, and so on. Instead, I will argue that these hidden mechanisms were equally important in building the success story of Silicon Valley. And this is the real novelty of the proposed explanation.[1]

---

[1] In my discussion below I will mainly rely on Saxenian's (1994) book, which so far is the most comprehensive account available on Silicon Valley. Although I agree with her entirely that Silicon Valley success was the result of a complex social and technical networks rooted in an industrial community, my explanation focuses more on *human* side of the region.

The first and the foremost of such mechanisms, which is responsible for the Silicon Valley's success, is *excellence*. Virtually every generation[2] of the Silicon Valley's entrepreneurs, as well as companies that they founded and headed, have been constantly demonstrating excellence and strive for excellence in almost every aspect of their business activity. As many of them did not have managerial backgrounds, their understanding of excellence was often based on a simple, uncompromising edict: do your best. And they really tried to do their best, sometimes surpassing themselves. It looks like they were internally motivated to make every effort to achieve excellence. There are certainly many manifestations of their excellence. I would identify the following.

(1) Entrepreneurs in Silicon Valley highly valued excellence as a worthy goal per se. As one semiconductor executive who has worked in Silicon Valley for three decades told in an interview with Saxenian (1994: 36), "Here in Silicon Valley there is far greater loyalty to one's craft than to one's company. A company is just a vehicle, which allows you to work. If you are a circuit designer it is important for you to do *excellent* work. If you cannot in one firm, you will move on to another one" (italics added). This is why they frequently changed jobs, and high job mobility was the norm, not the exception. Intel, for instance, was known for its encouragement of excellence through competitive achievement. Silicon Valley companies relied, to a significant extent, on external suppliers, which acquired a great deal of expertise in developing certain products or processes. Relying on best experts and top talents in the field means nothing else than relying on excellence. Saxenian (1994) concluded that shared commitment to *technological excellence* unified Silicon Valley's industrial community even under persistent competitive pressure.

(2) Businessmen in the Silicon Valley created an exceptionally *democratic atmosphere or humanistic culture* in the companies, rejecting the idea of a social hierarchy and any social distinctions. They did their best in eliminating the usual boundaries between employers and employees and between corporate functions within the company. They always refused such things as executive offices, special parking lots, executive dining rooms, and other privileges for top management. As Robert Noyce, one of the founders of Intel, pointed out, "If Intel were divided into workers and bosses, with the implication that each side had to squeeze its money out of the hides of the other, the enterprise would be finished. Motivation would no longer be internal; it would be objectified in the deadly form of work rules and grievance procedures" (quoted in Saxenian 1994: 56).

It is important to emphasize that they not simply initiated the democratic atmosphere in their companies; the Silicon Valley's businessmen were excellent in supporting this atmosphere in all its possible manifestations. Thus, they treated people fairly, trusting them and in their ability to produce innovative ideas, and granting them an exceptionally high extent of professional freedom to execute on these ideas, all while rewarding their work generously. In fact, they intuitively applied a common sense wisdom known for centuries: treat all as you want to be treated. Specifically, they did their best in promoting a sense of teamwork, open and informal communication, initiative, and a participative style well

---

[2] "Virtually all generations" refers to early semiconductor companies like Hewlett-Packard, semiconductor companies of the 1960s–1970s, semiconductor equipment companies of the 1980s, and the 1980s-generation computer firms.

before experts on project team management figured out that these are the optimal conditions for successfully realizing projects and crucial factors for high performance teams (Bennis & Biederman 1997; Hershock *et al.* 1994; Katzenbach & Smith, D. K. 1993; Leavitt & Lipman-Blumen 1995; Smith, D. C. *et al.* 2000). As one of the Silicon Valley's executives pointed out, "The most important communications that occur in our company are *informal*, the ad hoc meetings that occur when we walk around the plant. Structured meetings held between 2:30 and 3:30 P.M. on specific topics really are atypical" (quoted in Saxenian 1994: 54; italics added). In other words, Silicon Valley's entrepreneurs successfully managed not only technological innovations in their companies; they also did their best in managing people, the human — and critically important — side of any business (Katz 1997).

The obvious consequence of the democratic atmosphere was not just a group of people working together in the same company, but a *community* with the common objectives and team spirit, and passionate employee with a commitment to company goals. Only in such an informal and decentralized environment employees could do their best: be excellent in their respective roles, and outperform themselves by constantly producing creative new product ideas and working long hours to implement those ideas. It was a chain reaction: the excellence in one direction initiated by top management led to excellence in many other directions, vital for the company's prosperity. The rule was simple: if top management did its best (from the viewpoint of common sense), employees did their best, too.

Another consequence of the democratic atmosphere or the humanistic culture in Silicon Valley's companies was enhanced motivation or enthusiasm in employees. As one engineer told in an interview with Saxenian (1994: 55), ". . . We were all treated well, and there was a sense that everyone knew what was going on and everyone could get a piece of the wealth through stock options. Our attitude was 'we are all in this together, so let us work hard and let us play hard.' "

(3) Entrepreneurs in Silicon Valley were also *excellent in creating decentralized organizations*, which were particularly suitable for rewarding individual initiative and creativity and keeping the focus and responsiveness of start-up companies. For example, Cypress Semiconductor demonstrated an exceptionally innovative approach. When it reached $100 million in sales, the company adopted a venture capital model. Its CEO, T. J. Rodgers, saw his goal to "become a $1 billion company made up of ten loosely linked $100 million subsidiaries. The four subsidiaries . . . receive cash, management advice, and contacts (as in traditional venture capital arrangement), as well as access to one another's sales and distribution channels and fabrication facilities" (Saxenian 1994: 196). Such excellence in decentralization of their companies allowed them to develop and introduce new products faster than their more integrated, large competitors. For instance, Cirrus Logic and Chips and Technologies shortened their development times to 9 months in comparison to more than 2 years, the normal new-product lead time in the industry of the day (Saxenian 1994).

Similarly, when Sun became a $3.5 billion company in 1990, the company broke itself into five companies. The idea behind such decentralization was to bring the market "inside the company." The management of each company or "planet" were granted full responsibility for profit and loss and their own independent sales force. Interestingly, these five companies were stimulated to look for business opportunities even if their actions might harm another Sun planet. Saxenian (1994) provided real examples of how Sun companies worked in this direction. In doing so, Sun successfully followed common sense wisdom, namely:

customers would better identify than managers as to where Sun was competitive and really added value, and where it was not and should therefore rely on external partners to continue to be a radically innovative company. These examples show a real impact of decentralized organizational structures on the company's ability to produce technological breakthroughs. This is why one CEO in Silicon Valley advised: "Avoid vertical integration like the plague. Vertical integration forces a company to build in a high fixed cost, which assures loss of profitability when volume drops . . ." (quoted in Saxenian 1994: 125).

(4) Businessmen in the Silicon Valley were excellent in developing *intensive informal communication networks*, which supported collaboration and stimulated experimentation (e.g. creativity), that transcending company boundaries. For instance, they openly communicated with competitors. As one experienced CEO said in an interview with Saxenian (1994: 33), "This is a culture in which people talk to their competitors. If I had a problem in a certain area, I felt no hesitation to call another CEO and ask about the problem — even if I did not know him . . ." Another executive added, ". . . I have senior engineers who are constantly on the phone and sharing information with our competitors. I know what my competitors say in their speeches and they know what I say in private conversations" (Saxenian 1994: 36–37). Frequent face-to-face communication is needed to sustain successful collaboration.

(5) Open informal communication led to *high-trust* business relationships, which, in turn, resulted into *accelerated speed of information exchange*. As one manager at Apple noted, "We have found you do not always need a formal contract . . . If you develop *trust* with your suppliers, you do not need armies of attorneys" (quoted in Saxenian 1994: 149). They were *excellent in making quick decisions*. One observer emphasized "intuitive, quick-fire approach" in Silicon Valley, pointing out that "tactical decisions that take six weeks in Boston can take anywhere from six days to six nanoseconds in Cupertino . . ." (quoted in Saxenian 1994: 68). One venture capitalist noted, "Somehow, companies in California *get things done faster, deals go down faster* . . . they seem to *run with technology faster*; each year *we are spending money faster* there" (quoted in Saxenian 1994: 105; italics added). It is interesting to note that a quick and accurate decision-making process, or speed of human information processing, is considered as one of the distinguishing characteristics of highly intellectual individuals (Shavinina & Kholodnaya 1996).

One can therefore see the chain reaction again: The timely new information received from reliable personal networks was definitely more important in fast changing industry than conventional, but less timely professional journals and meetings at conferences. As one Silicon Valley executive observed, "There is an absolute desire to be *highly informal* on the West Coast. Individuals find it easy to *communicate quickly*. This *informality* allows us to share consensus and *move rapidly*" (quoted in Saxenian 1994: 54; italics added). This quick decision-making process led to the general fast pace of business activity in Silicon Valley.

(6) They were *excellent in cooperation*, in developing habits of informal cooperation and a wide range of cooperative practices. It was their way of life: their way to successful continuous innovations in an environment of high technological volatility. As Silicon Graphics CEO told in an interview with Saxenian (1994: 150), "Our engineers *jointly design products with other companies*. We do not worry if they go and sell them to our competitors. Our whole style is not to compete defensively, but to take the offensive.

The world is changing too fast to just try to defend your position. In order to keep up with change, you have to be on the offensive all the time . . . The key is to have products that are good" (italics added). They did not want to collaborate for the sake of it; they wished to gain the best from cooperation. And this strive for excellence strategy rewarded all players involved in collaboration. Companies in Silicon Valley participated in joint problem solving and were mutually interested in one another's success.

(7) They were extremely *excellent in creating an open business environment*, both inside and outside their companies, that accelerated the exchange of know-what and know-how. It manifested itself, for example, in open communication that guaranteed open knowledge sharing and fast exchange of information and in openness to risk-taking, both at the levels of individual company and technological community. Thus, at Intel, Robert Noyce and Gordon Moore had lunch every Thursday with a random group of employees. Employees were encouraged to "say whatever they think." For example, a new engineer was supposed to challenge Noyce or other engineers with differing ideas. Another executive compared the business environment in Silicon Valley with that of other regions in the following way: "The communication patterns are clearly different in Silicon Valley. There is *far more openness* and much less worrying about whether someone goes around you. There is not only a tendency not to follow channels, there is a deliberate attempt to stimulate a wide variety of ideas. Innovations bubble up in unexpected places. Champions receive support from unexpected sponsors . . ." (quoted in Saxenian 1994: 54; italics added).

(8) These intensive informal communication networks, democratic atmosphere or humanistic culture, and open business environment provided a strong foundation for *excellent flourishing of creativity*. As one executive noted, ". . . a management style that permits *geniuses* to contribute is important. If you were to look at why GE and RCA have failed [in semiconductors], it is because their *organization was too disciplined* and *unable to respond quickly to true innovation*" (quoted in Saxenian 1994: 82; italics added). True creativity, which leads to innovations, cannot prosper in highly disciplined environment (Amabile 1998; Kiely 1993; Lehr 1979; Mumford 2000). Saxenian (1994) pointed out that such a decentralized and fluid social climate accelerated the diffusion of new technological knowledge with amazing speed within the Silicon Valley industrial community. What was not explicitly emphasised is the fact that the diffused knowledge was re-combined, modified, and elaborated by its receivers in multiple ways into new ideas; and this is the essence of creativity. It is not therefore surprising that Silicon Valley experienced multiple trajectories of technological development simultaneously, that resulted into a wide range of cutting edge new products, which were often rapidly introduced to the marketplace. This is a reason why businessmen in Silicon Valley were very good in sensing new market opportunities, new technological trends, and new product developments. As a result, Silicon Valley as a whole was able to continuously create new markets and industrial sectors. The end of the 1980s particularly demonstrated that competition was increasingly based on creativity, that is, on companies' ability to add value (i.e. to see new applications and improvements in performance, quality, and service) rather than simply on lowering costs.

The ease of new firm formation (e.g. easy access to venture capitalists, which were mainly former entrepreneurs themselves) also contributed to pursuing multiple paths of technological development.

In discussing creativity at the regional level the most important factor was that Silicon Valley entrepreneurs were mostly highly creative people, whose internal or intrinsic motivation to create — new products, new companies, and so on — was behind their success. This motivation to create was a driving force for them; and this is one key to their excellence. As with all creative people, engineers in Silicon Valley often experienced frustration, disappointment, and similar feelings when they were unable to develop and implement their ideas in the current workplace. One Silicon Valley venture capitalist concluded, "The presumption is that employees of the big companies leave and go to venture companies to found start-ups to make more money. That is not the way. Andy Grove, Bob Noyce and others left Fairchild to found Intel, not to make more money. They left to make a product that Fairchild was either unable or unwilling to make or, for whatever reason, did not get around to making. That is why ventures are started: from lack of responsiveness in big companies . . . *The only reason good people leave is because they become frustrated. They want to do something they cannot do in their present environment*" (quoted in Saxenian 1994: 112–113; italics added). Careers of T. J. Rodgers of Cypress Semiconductors and Gordon Campbell of Chips and Technologies also support this observation. They both left jobs at large semiconductor companies being frustrated by their employers' growing isolation from customers and unwillingness to assimilate new ideas and inability to sense new market opportunities.

It is important to emphasize that every manifestation of the Silicon Valley entrepreneurs' excellence has many sub-manifestations, all of which I will not be able to mention here. It is also true that many various factors contributed to the appearance of every manifestation of their excellence. In this respect Ray's course on creativity (Ray & Myers 1989) offered by the Stanford University School of Business played a certain role in developing creativity in Silicon Valley, although creativity experts can definitely debate the content of this course.

(9) Entrepreneurs in the Silicon Valley did their best *in tolerating failures*. Not all Silicon Valley start-ups became successful ventures, some of them failed. Understanding that failure is an integral part of risk-taking, failures were socially acceptable in Silicon Valley. As one expert noted, "In Silicon Valley, failure is an accepted way of life, unlike the East where failure is viewed as a death sentence . . ." (quoted in Saxenian 1994: 68). In fact, the Silicon Valley businessmen intuitively followed dialectical nature of risk-taking, namely: if you are open to and highly encourage risk-taking, you have to be equally open to its consequences, one of which is failure. The positive side of failure is definitely its contribution to learning and developing professional experience. One executive pointed out, "Everybody knows that some of the best presidents in the Valley are people that have stumbled" (quoted in Saxenian 1994: 111–112). John Sculley, the Apple Computer CEO, told in an interview with McKenna, "In Silicon Valley, if someone fails, we know they are in all likelihood going to reappear in some other company in a matter of months" (quoted in Saxenian 1994: 111). They were excellent in understanding how failure is important, both for personal and regional successes. Success by learning from failure was the norm for Silicon Valley entrepreneurs. As one executive noted, "Unless failure is possible, no learning is possible . . . in the realm of ideas, unless falsification is possible, learning is not possible. As a matter of fact, in information theory, no information is transmitted unless negation is possible, and so the tolerance of failure is absolutely critical to the success of Silicon Valley. If you do not

tolerate failure, you cannot permit success. The successful people have a lot more failures than the failures do" (quoted in Saxenian 1994: 112). Such excellence in failure tolerance was the norm in Silicon Valley well before management scholars, business consultants, and practitioners highlighted it as a desirable leadership style (Deschamps 2003; Farson & Keyes 2002; Lehr 1979).

(10) In a highly competitive business environment characterized by shorter product cycles and accelerating technological change, they were *excellent in applying common sense and intuition*. Thus, when Sun Microsystems was working on its first product, the founders, all in their twenties, decided to adopt the Unix operating system developed by AT&T because they felt that the market would never accept a workstation custom designed by four graduate students. Sun also used standard, readily available components by relying on outside suppliers. A consequence was that the Sun products were cheaper to produce and lower priced than that of competitors (Saxenian 1994). Sun was therefore a pioneer in recognizing customers' preferences for standard operating systems.

Another manifestation of Sun's ability to excel in applying common sense wisdom was already mentioned above when Sun broke itself into five quasi-independent companies allowing them, for instance, to sell their products even to competitors. The common sense in this case was to mainly let customers — not Sun's managers — to identify where Sun was or was not competitive.

Usually, Silicon Valley start-ups were founded by a group of engineers — friends and/or former colleagues — who developed a certain deal of expertise working in other companies and who had an innovative idea, which they could not realize in their current workplace (Saxenian 1994). And, they deliberately avoided hiring professional managers. Thus, Robert Noyce, one of the founders of Intel, preferred to recruit recent graduates of schools of engineering rather than experienced managers. Interestingly, many of Silicon Valley entrepreneurs did not have any managerial background. They just did their best in applying common sense to managing their companies; they relied on intuition. As one executive noted, ". . . In semiconductors, it turned out that it was better to have a new industry filled with young people who did not know much about how you were supposed to do business" (quoted in Saxenian 1994: 81). It was definitely good from the viewpoint of excellence: minds of young Silicon Valley entrepreneurs were not restricted by certain norms imposed by traditional theories of management and business schools. As a result, they were able to actively experiment with organizational alternatives in addition to multiple technological innovations. In other words, their open minds were sensitive to any creative ideas. Later business scholars studied managerial styles of Silicon Valley entrepreneurs as exemplary ones. For example, the Harvard Business School prepared a special case about Hewlett-Packard way. They were simply excellent in using common sense and intuition. Excellence is not equal to knowledge of how to do business or to university degrees. It is something above that, as well as above any other attributes of conventional wisdom associated with successful business development. It is worth noting that a highly intuitive decision-making process is one of the essential characteristics of creative people (Shavinina 2003; Shavinina & Ferrari 2004). Interestingly, when some executives compared Silicon Valley business culture with that of the large East Coast companies, they noted the formality of the communication process, emphasizing that "there is so much staff work done before top managers see anything, so much report generation that you are not really involved *intuitively* in key decisions..." (quoted in Saxenian 1994: 54; italic added). Silicon Valley entrepreneurs' "intuitive, quick-fire approach" to decision making was already mentioned above.

Similarly, they intuitively realize the importance of positive emotions — of having fun — for high performance of truly innovative technological projects. For instance, while the traditional American corporations of the East Coast enforced a dress code, Sun Microsystems's employees showed up in gorilla suits on Halloween. Everything was natural in Silicon Valley companies in this respect. They followed their common sense well before management scholars found that fun is one of the distinguishing characteristics of effective teams (Smith, D. C. *et al.* 2000).

(11) They were excellent not only in anticipating new market opportunities and promising technological advances; they were equally *excellent in developing new products*, many of which turned out to be breakthrough innovations. It looks like they did not simply want new products, they wanted *excellent, the best possible products*, products at the cutting edge of that day's technology. The case in point is Sun Microsystems. Thus, rather than manufacturing the new chip itself for its workstations, or subcontracting it to a single maker, the company set up collaboration with *five* semiconductor manufacturers. Each manufacturer used its own technological process to develop the required microprocessor. The final chips were common in design, but had different speed and price. It looks like the Sun Microsystems strategy was to choose the best from the best. Interestingly enough that after receiving the chips, Sun Microsystems encouraged these manufacturers to sell the chips to its competitors. This allowed Sun Microsystems to expand acceptance of its architecture that led to increasing market share. As Saxenian (1994) concluded, Silicon Valley companies competed by rapidly introducing differentiated and high-value-added products.

(12) Likewise, Silicon Valley entrepreneurs were *excellent in reducing time-to-market process*, in rapid introduction of new and differentiated designs of best products. Thus, an executive at 3Com told in an interview with Saxenian (1994: 114), "One of the things that Silicon Valley lets you do is *minimize the costs associated with getting from idea to product*. Vendors here can handle everything. If you specify something ... you can get hardware back so fast that your *time-to-market is incredibly short*" (italics added). The presence of a wide range of sophisticated local customers was important in this respect and this eventually led to success of many start-ups. As one executive at a semiconductor company told in an interview with Saxenian (1994: 114), "When we come out with the specs for a new product, we take them to a series of companies that we have relations with ... and they will give us feedback on the features they like and do not like. It is an iterative process: we define a product, we get feedback and improve it, we refine it and develop associated products. The process feeds on itself. And the fact that these customers are nearby means that the iterations are faster; *rapid communication is absolutely critical to ensuring fast time-to-market*" (italics added). Another executive concluded, "... The key to winning is [not cost or price, but] getting close to the customer" (Saxenian 1994: 120).

(13) Taking into account the outstanding role played by Stanford University in developing Silicon Valley, it should be stressed that its *professors did their best in encouraging the engineering students to start up new companies* and commercialize their ideas embedded in new products. The case in point is definitely exemplified in Frederick Terman, an electrical engineering professor, who encouraged his graduate students Bill Hewlett and David

Packard to commercialize an audio-oscillator that Bill Hewlett had designed while working on his master's thesis. Terman lent Bill and David "$538 to start producing the machine, he helped them find work to finance their initial experiments, and he arranged a loan from a Palo Alto bank, which allowed them to begin commercial production" (Saxenian 1994: 20). Obviously, Terman's exceptional support of his students significantly exceeded the usual limits of traditional professorial encouragement. Later, when Terman was Dean of Engineering at Stanford University, he extended the scope of his support to start-ups and entrepreneurs in Silicon Valley by establishing and promoting the Stanford Research Institute, the Honors Cooperative Program, and the Stanford Industrial Park. It is safe to assert that professors at Stanford University were excellent in stimulating the development of local industry.

(14) Silicon Valley venture capitalists (usually former entrepreneurs and engineers themselves) were *excellent in moving very rapidly on promising opportunities, in believing in new entrepreneurs, and in making fast decisions*. Saxenian (1994) provided many examples demonstrating that for many entrepreneurs, it took only a few days or even minutes to finance their start-ups. Thus, the founder of a successful computer company recalled, "When I started Convergent, I got commitments for $2.5 million in 20 minutes from three people over lunch who saw me write the business plan on the back of a napkin. *They believed in me* ..." (quoted in Saxenian 1994: 65; italics added).

The second mechanism in building the success story of Silicon Valley is the conscious or unconscious use of *compensatory mechanisms*. Its essence is straightforward: if you are not exceedingly excellent in some aspects of your activity, then compensate for that. To put it even more briefly: be excellent in compensating for your lack of excellence in something. The case in point is Sun Microsystems. Whether its founders realized it or not, but they did their best in using compensatory mechanisms. The above-mentioned examples demonstrate that Sun Microsystems continually evaluated its "points of excellence" (i.e. those products and processes in which it could add value) and tried to develop them. Alternatively, Sun Microsystems subcontracted [to other specialized companies] those components [of their workstations] in which it did' not have a great expertise. Sun Microsystems therefore understood and successfully applied the simple rule of compensatory mechanisms: if you are not competitive — that is, if you are not excellent — rely on partners and/or suppliers who are.

Sun Microsystems was not the exception in Silicon Valley. The computer producers MIPS, Pyramid, Tandem, and Silicon Graphics all relied to a great extent on networks of external suppliers. Thus, Silicon Graphics CEO pointed out that his company largely relied on "*interdisciplinary teams* that focus on bringing new products to market fast" (quoted in Saxenian 1994: 143; italics added). By extending the definition of an interdisciplinary team (Katzenbach & Smith, D. K. 1993), I would say that this is a group of people with complementary knowledge bases and skills that allows its members to *compensate* for a particular lack of certain kinds of expertise at the team level.

Moreover, it looks like the entire way of doing business in Silicon Valley consciously or unconsciously applied compensatory mechanisms. For example, the typical Silicon Valley start-up usually included talented people from a range of companies and industries, which therefore represented a combination of technical and corporate competencies. Managerial and engineering teams were consequently ready to compensate for a lack of excellence in something just from the beginning. Thus, Eisenhardt & Schoonhoven's (1990) research showed that the heterogeneity of past professional experiences among founders of semi-conductor start-ups was correlated with higher growth.

In order to be highly profitable and compete with large companies which produced memory and other commodity devices, the new semiconductor companies of the 1980s successfully compensated for usual weaknesses of start-ups. They created a new market of high value-added chips by relying heavily on the proximity of customers, engineering talent, specialized suppliers, and fast information exchange via social networks. As Weitek founder and CEO told in an interview with Saxenian (1994: 121), "Contrast commodity products which have no engineering content and are priced at cost with Weitek chips which have high engineering content, small output, and high value-added. This is a talent-leveraged business, which is highly competitive but not capital intensive. The key to winning is [not cost or price, but] getting close to the customer." This compensatory strategy turned out to be successful: the new companies were highly profitable and fast growing. While large companies — National Semiconductor or AMD — struggled to stay in business, many of the 1980s start-ups experienced growth rates of 45–50% a year (Saxenian 1994).

Everything said above here does not definitely mean that Silicon Valley entrepreneurs were always excellent; as well as they were not excellent in absolutely all aspects of business activity. They made mistakes, too. But this only confirms the general rule of excellence: as soon as they stopped to be excellent, to do their best — at some point in their development — they began to fail. Thus, they missed a series of key markets and technological opportunities, such as "the return to semi-custom and application-specific integrated circuits (ASICs), the complementary metal-oxide semiconductor (CMOS) process, and chip sets . . . It took a new generation of start-ups in the 1980s to commercialize these technologies" (Saxenian 1994: 93).

Apple Computer's failure to open up the proprietary architecture for its Macintosh personal computers is another example. Protecting itself in such a way, Apple turned out to be in isolation from the computer industry, and, as a result, lost market share. The similar case is when some leading Silicon Valley companies — National Semiconductor, Intel, and AMD sacrificed their organizational flexibility in order to become the "big three" of the semiconductor industry. They built bureaucratic companies that centralized authority and limited the autonomy of formerly independent business divisions (Saxenian 1994). At the level of the region as a whole, Silicon Valley businessmen failed to acknowledge the significance of the social networks of informal communication and collaboration they had created in their own success. Saxenian (1994) concluded that entrepreneurs' individualistic view of themselves and their successes as independent of the Silicon Valley and a variety of its relationships have limited their ability to respond collectively to challenges. The examples of such failures in excellence can be continued. However, the general imperative is clear: if you want to succeed, you have to be excellent in as many facets of your activity as possible, or compensate for a lack of excellence. Otherwise, you will fail.

To sum-up, this section proposed a new perspective on the success of Silicon Valley, which deepens the existing explanations of the Silicon phenomenon. Definitely, this interpretation does not account for all possible facets of the Valley's advanced technological development, and sometimes it is both vague and speculative in its formulations. However, it provides a useful attempt to further understand more how the human side contributes to the prosperity of the region. At the first glance, it looks very obvious: do your exceptionally best, surpass yourself, and know when, where and how to compensate for those things in which you are not excellent. But this rule might not be so easily implemented in other regions, because human understanding of excellence and its fulfilment, as well as the use of compensatory mechanisms, will be different. Due to numerous individual differences, people vary significantly. Other regions have other people. Human side matters, because this is the most important carrier or provider of excellence.

The proposed perspective sheds additional light on a very important issue of why the success of Silicon Valley cannot be easily replicated around the world. Academics and policy decision-makers actively discuss how to do that the Silicon Valley model could be reproduced in other regions and countries. Some researchers point out that this is totally impossible (Menon 2001), others assert that this is possible to a certain extent. In the first case it will be imitation, at best. In the second case the result will be of limited success. For example, analyses of science parks show their low success rates (Phillimore & Joseph 2003), in spite of the availability of all the traditional components needed for successful technological growth, such as entrepreneurship, available venture capital, research universities, and highly qualified labour markets. However, many of them (e.g. Cambridge, U.K.) cannot be named "the second Silicon Valley." A reasonable question therefore is, Why? Saxenian (1994) would say that a variety of social and technical networks were not developed at that regional level. I would add that this is because those regions are not regions of excellence.

Nobody can motivate people (for example, in start-ups in those regions) to really do their best, to surpass themselves. It is mainly because only individuals themselves know what they can and cannot do, that is, their existing abilities. Moreover, often even people themselves do not know the limits of their excellence, that is, their hidden or potential abilities. How can we measure unborn creative ideas, which could lead to innovative technologies and highly profitable start-ups? Also, nobody can encourage people to create their own companies if they are frustrated in the current workplace by inability to realize their innovative ideas. They may find another employer. Equally, nobody can inspire professors in local universities to encourage students in such a way as Frederick Terman did it. Policymakers cannot do everything.

Silicon Valley is not simply a learning region, this is a region of excellence. Some researchers assert that learning regions will succeed in knowledge economy (Florida 1995). From my point of view, this is relatively a simplistic way of thinking about industrial or entrepreneurial clusters. Regions of excellence will thrive in the future, and this is exactly what the knowledge economy needs. This book presents one of such region of excellence: Canada's National Capital Region (Ottawa-Gatineau) or Silicon Valley North. The next section below briefly outlines each chapter included in the book. It will allow readers to gain an insight on what to expect.

The Ottawa Case: Canadian Silicon Valley

The proposed book is devoted to the multidimensional and multifaceted nature of Silicon Valley North, its history, current state and future developments. Silicon Valley North is the high tech capital of Canada, the nation's most developed and dynamic technology sector, which includes multiple clusters in telecommunications, software, photonics, and life sciences. It gave birth to many well-known companies such as Cognos, Corel, JDS Uniphase, Mitel, Newbridge Networks, Nortel Networks, Digital Equipment of Canada, just to mention a few. The purpose of the book is to present the Canadian Silicon Valley from the viewpoints of various disciplines, that is, technology, engineering, business, management, economics, psychology, sociology, and history. The book will accomplish this purpose by enlisting chapters from engineers, technologists, management and business scholars, economists, sociologists, and psychologists.

This book hopes to accomplish at least two things. First, to provide expert insight into what Silicon Valley North is all about, by presenting its many aspects, including high tech development, entrepreneurship, the role of venture capitalists in its development, the role of local universities, and so on. This breadth will allow the reader to acquire a comprehensive and "panoramic picture" of the nature of Canadian Silicon Valley within a single book. Second, and perhaps most importantly, the reader will be able to apply the ideas and findings in this book to critically consider how best to foster the development of his or her unique region.

The book is divided into three (III) parts. The first part, consisting of three chapters, provides both general and historical introduction to the work discussed in the book. Part II, consisting of 12 chapters, discuss various, although sometimes overlapping, aspects of the Ottawa high tech region. The third and final part integrates all these facets.

Part I comprises three chapters, which provides various introductory elements to the topic of the book. Chapter 1 sets the stage for understanding the American Silicon Valley as a region of excellence. This chapter also briefly describes the facets of the Canadian Silicon Valley examined by authors of the book by summarizing the main contents of each chapter.

In Chapter 2 of the Part I, *Silicon Valley North: The Formation of the Ottawa Innovation Cluster*, Jocelyn Ghent Mallett analyses the process of building of the Canadian Silicon Valley. Specifically, she focuses on five components, which led to the appearance of the Ottawa high tech cluster: access to technology and technical know-how; availability of highly qualified people; visionary entrepreneurship; access to venture capital; and networks and linkages, that is, a closely networked community of high tech business leaders. One of Dr. Ghent Mallett's important conclusions is that the "overnight success" of the Silicon Valley North took 50 years to build. Interestingly, she refers to the Ottawa high tech cluster as the Ottawa *innovation* cluster that emphasizes the role of local companies in developing cutting edge innovative products.

Chapter 3 of the Part I, *Yesterday's Adventures with Today's Technology: Carleton University's Wired City Simulation Laboratory*, by David C. Coll, provides a historical introduction to technological advances made in the Canadian Silicon Valley. He describes the creation and functioning of the Wired City Simulation Laboratory at Carleton University, Ottawa, aimed at conducting innovative research on emerging technologies. Thus, this laboratory pioneered investigations at the intersection of telecommunications and the computer that were apparent in the early 1970s. Dr. Coll also underlines the efforts of federal government in supporting studies on new technologies, such as policies issues, research grants, government laboratories, just mention a few. The result of the joint university-government collaboration was an impressive list of technological breakthroughs invented in Canada, which David C. Coll mentions in his chapter.

In Chapter 4 of the Part II, *Firm Demographics in Silicon Valley North*, François Brouard, Tyler Chamberlin, Jérôme Doutriaux, and John de la Mothe analyze clusters of companies in Silicon Valley North. They identify five clusters, namely: telecommunications, photonics, microelectronics, software, and life sciences. The authors also compare these clusters with similar clusters in other Silicon regions around the world such as Silicon Valley in California and Oxfordshire in the U.K.

Chapter 5 of the Part II, *A Tale of One City: The Ottawa Technology Cluster*, by Judith J. Madill, George H. Haines Jr., and Allan L. Riding, examines in detail the Ottawa high tech cluster, particularly its recent past, that is, the economic downturn. They discuss the origins of the firms in the cluster, describe a profile of both businesses and founders of these firms, and identify sources of knowledge and capital. The authors concluded that these firms are not "overnight successes," nor are they "fly by night" businesses. Rather, the firms are solidly anchored in the local community with informal investors who supply financing, as well as significant non-financial inputs to the firms in the cluster. An important finding of Drs. Madill, Haines, and Riding's research is that the non-financial contributions from informal investors, along with networks and contacts maintained by these investors, comprise much of the "glue" that holds intact the fabric of the Ottawa cluster. The authors also found that a high percentage of firms survived the economic downturn.

In Chapter 6 of the Part II, *The National Capital Region's Product Leadership Cluster*, Antonio J. Bailetti identifies the product leadership cluster in Silicon Valley North and describes its distinguishing characteristics. It is very interesting to emphasize that the author discusses cluster of innovative companies. Dr. Bailetti presents a model explaining how the product leadership cluster may influence regional performance.

Chapter 7 of the Part II, *How Technology-Intensive Clusters are Organized in the Ottawa Region*, by Alan O'Sullivan, analyzes the locational advantages associated with clustering and how they are created by inter-firm interactions. According to the author, these interactions have both horizontal and vertical dimensions. Dr. O'Sullivan describes how clusters in technology-intensive industries in the Ottawa area are organized in terms of these dimensions.

In Chapter 8 of the Part II, *The Role of Venture Capital in Building Technology Companies in the Ottawa Region*, John Callahan and Ken Charbonneau provide a comprehensive review of how venture capital contributes to developing Silicon Valley North. The important role of venture capital in high tech innovation is widely recognized by both innovation scholars and experts on economic clusters. The authors identified four distinct periods of venture capital in the region, which are relatively distinct in terms of the investors present in the market, the companies seeking capital, the investment climate, the terms and instruments used, and the contribution made by venture capital to business development.

Chapter 9 of the Part II, *The Role of Universities in Developing Canadian Silicon Valley*, by Robert Armit, examines the role of the University of Ottawa and Carleton University in the advanced technological growth of the Ottawa region. Universities are exceptionally important in developing the regional economy, as sources for both new research and highly qualified people. Dr. Armit analyzes in detail technology transfer in both universities. He concluded that Silicon Valley North is a story of industry, government and universities growing and changing in tandem and developing a successful regional economy in Ottawa.

In Chapter 10 of the Part II, *The River Runs Through It: The Case for Collaborative Governance in the National Capital Region*, Gilles Paquet, Jeffrey Roy, and Chris Wilson discuss the issues of the local governance in Canadian Silicon Valley. Chapter 11 of the Part II, *Technological Development in Gatineau, the Quebec Sector of Silicon Valley North*, by Franco Materazzi, analyzes the contribution of the Quebec side's companies to the advancement of Canadian Silicon Valley.

In Chapter 12 of the Part II, *Developing Knowledge Workers in Silicon Valley North: It Is Not Just About Training*, Lorraine Dyke, Linda Duxbury, and Natalie Lam examine a critical aspect of Silicon Valley North: its talent management or people related issues, that is, how to develop knowledge workers in the turbulent environment of the Ottawa cluster. As high tech industry is in constant change by experiencing cycles of boom and bust, the Canadian Silicon Valley is a highly stressful competitive milieu for employees of local companies. The new global business environment of stronger competition, downsizing, customers requiring new levels of quality, and reduced product cycle times are challenges for both corporate management and employees. Specifically, challenges for talent management include selecting, developing and retaining a workforce that can meet constantly changing requirements while sustaining the company's market or its culture. The authors analyze this range of issues by using findings from interviews with 110 key personnel and surveys completed by 1509 knowledge workers in Silicon Valley North.

Chapter 13 of the Part II, *Can Technology Clusters Deliver Sustainable Livelihoods? Constructing a Role for Community Economic Development*, by Edward T. Jackson and Rahil Khan, discusses the potential for community economic development (CED) in the Ottawa region to "deal in" those on the outside of the sector and also help knowledge workers themselves cope with the inevitable volatility of clusters. Digital-divide bridging, customized training, work-life programs, mobilizing private philanthropy, multi-sector leadership structures, and community-owned science facilities are among the CED strategies, which Drs. Jackson and Khan consider.

In Chapter 14 of the Part II, *An Innovative Model For Skill Development in Silicon Valley North: O-Vitesse*, Arvind Chhatbar describes a new approach to talent management. Aimed at addressing the fast changing requirements of the Ottawa high tech cluster, this project, O-Vitesse, is a success story in rapidly re-skilling highly qualified professionals to meet the demands for new skills, particularly when business cycles become shorter and new technologies are rapidly introduced into society. In light of these challenges and increased global competition, companies in Silicon Valley North have to be able to meet new skills needs in compressed timeframes. The Vitesse Re-Skilling model helps both companies and employees to gain this goal.

Chapter 15 of the Part II, *Ottawa's TalentWorks — Regional Learning & Collaborative Governance for a Knowledge Age*, by Gilles Paquet, Jeffrey Roy and Chris Wilson, examines another project for workforce development: TalentWorks. Aimed at orchestrating an integrative strategy for talent development at the regional level, TalentWorks is an important initiative and a revealing case study on the challenges of building collaborative governance.

Part III, *Conclusions*, contains a single chapter by Warren Thorngate, which serves to integrate the various aspects discussed in the chapters of the book into a more coherent framework.

The chapters of this book therefore cover a wide range of issues and various facets of Silicon Valley North. The main goal of the book is to present the existing research on this high tech region. In order to achieve this goal, the book includes chapters by leading specialists responsible for much of the current research in the area. This is an academic book based mainly on research findings and supplemented by the opinions of the authors who are chief experts in the field. The book thus provides what is perhaps the most comprehensive account available of what Silicon Valley North is, how it was developed, how it functions, and how it affects the business world.

Acknowledgments

I thank Warren Thorngate and Louis Albert for comments on earlier versions of the chapter. The editorial assistance of Louis Albert and the Université du Québec en Outaouais financial support for his work are also gratefully acknowledged.

References

Amabile, T. M. (1998). How to kill creativity. *Harvard Business Review* (September–October), 76–87.

Bennis, W., & Biederman, P. (1997). *Organizing genius: The secrets of creative collaboration.* Reading, MA: Addison-Wesley.

Deschamps, J. P. (2003). Innovation and leadership. In: L. V. Shavinina (Ed.), *International handbook on innovation* (pp. 815–831). Oxford, UK: Elsevier.

Eisenhardt, K. M., & Schoonhoven, C. B. (1990). Organizational growth: Linking founding team strategy, environment, and growth among U.S. semiconductor ventures 1978–1988. *Administrative Sciences Quarterly, 35*(3), 504–529.

Farson, R., & Keyes, R. (2002). The failure-tolerant leader. *Harvard Business Review, 80*(8).

Florida, R. (1995). Toward the learning region. *Futures, 27*(5), 527–536.

Hershock, R. J., Cowman, C. D., & Peters, D. (1994). From experience: Actions teams that work. *Journal of Product Innovation Management, 11*, 95–104.

Katz, R. (Ed.) (1997). *The human side of managing technological innovation.* New York: Oxford University Press.

Katzenbach, J. R., & Smith, D. K. (1993). *The wisdom of teams: Creating the high-performance organization.* Boston, MA: Harvard Business School Press.

Kenney, M. (Ed.) (2000). *Understanding Silicon Valley: The anatomy of an entrepreneurial region.* Palo Alto, CA: Stanford University Press.

Kiely, T. (1993). The idea makers. *Technology review* (January), 33–40. Reprinted in R. Katz (Ed.), *The human side of managing technological innovation* (pp. 60–67). New York: Oxford University Press.

Leavitt, H. J., & Lipman-Blumen, J. (1995, July). Hot groups. *Harvard Business Review, 73*, 109–116.

Lehr, L. W. (1979). Stimulating technological innovation — The role of top management. *Research Management* (November), 23–25.

Menon, M. G. K. (2001). The characteristics and promotion of innovation. In: OECD (Ed.), *Social sciences and innovation* (pp. 77–87). Paris, France: OECD.

Mumford, M. (2000). Managing creative people: Strategies and tactics for innovation. *Human Resource Management Review, 10*(3), 313–351.

Phillimore, J., & Joseph, R. (2003). Science parks: A triumph of hype over experience? In: L. V. Shavinina (Ed.), *International handbook on innovation* (pp. 750–757). Oxford, UK: Elsevier.

Porter, M. (1998). Clusters and the new economics of competition. *Harvard Business Review* (November–December), 77–90.

Ray, M., & Myers, R. (1989). *Creativity in business based on the famed Stanford University course that has revolutionized the art of success.* New York: Doubleday.

Saxenian, A. (1994). *Regional advantage: Culture and competition in Silicon Valley and route 128.* Cambridge, MA: Harvard University Press.

Shavinina, L. V. (2003). Understanding scientific innovation: The case of Nobel Laureates. In: L. V. Shavinina (Ed.), *International handbook on innovation* (pp. 445–457). Oxford, UK: Elsevier.

Shavinina, L. V., & Ferrari, M. (Eds) (2004). *Beyond knowledge: Extracognitive aspects of developing high ability.* Mahwah, NJ: Erlbaum.

Shavinina, L. V., & Kholodnaya, M. A. (1996). The cognitive experience as a psychological basis of intellectual giftedness. *Journal for the Education of the Gifted, 20*(1), 3–35.

Smith, D.C., Harris, M., Myersclough, P., & Wood, A. (2000). Building highly effective information systems project teams: An exploratory study. *Proceedings of PMI (Project Management Institute) Research Conference 2000* (pp. 419–429). Paris, France: 21–24 June.

Chapter 2

Silicon Valley North: The Formation of the Ottawa Innovation Cluster

Jocelyn Ghent Mallett

Abstract

This chapter examines the formation of the Silicon Valley North. Five elements are identified that were crucial in the development of the Ottawa high technology cluster: (1) access to technology and technical know-how; (2) availability of highly qualified people; (3) visionary entrepreneurship; (4) access to venture capital; and (5) networks and linkages. The latter element refers to a closely networked community of high technology business leaders. I conclude that the "overnight success" of the Canadian Silicon Valley took 50 years to build.

Introduction

Community leaders and governments at every level have long been fascinated by the question of how to grow a successful high-tech cluster. Why do some flourish while others fade? Is there a recipe and, if so, what are the magic ingredients? Many consultants make a very good living advising municipalities and regions on the steps they need to take to transform themselves into an Austin (Texas, USA), a San Jose (California, USA) or a Singapore. Numerous community-sponsored conferences, business media reports and scholarly books and articles have also examined the issue and produced multiple analyses and/or generic recommendations. Although cluster formation is still imperfectly understood, the results of all this attention generally boil down to a focus on five elements considered essential to success:

- access to technology and technical know-how;
- availability of highly qualified people;
- visionary entrepreneurship;
- access to venture capital;
- networks and linkages.

The purpose of this chapter is to take an historical look at the functional significance of each of these elements in the growth of the Ottawa technology cluster and to draw from the Ottawa story a clearer understanding of how and why clusters really form. Ottawa was chosen as an appropriate case study because the city represents Canada's best example of a mature cluster — one with deep roots and a development pattern that by the 1990s, earned it the title of fastest growing high tech community in Canada. Ottawa in the 1990s actually grew at a rate faster than that of its model, Silicon Valley, California.

Access to Technology: Ottawa's Scientific Research Strength

Ottawa's strong R&D emphasis is regarded as unusual among comparable clusters in North America. Measured on a per capita basis, Ottawa in the late 1990s was doing three times the R&D of other Canadian cities. The region's powerful research strengths have twin roots. The first lies in the growth after World War II of public scientific research labs, including the National Research Council (NRC), the Defence Research Establishment, the Communications Research Centre (CRC) and later, the Atomic Energy of Canada Laboratory (AECL). The second root lies in a decision taken in the late 1950s by Northern Electric (now Nortel) to choose Ottawa as the site for its small but rapidly growing R&D operation.

Public Sector R&D Institutions

During the war, NRC built the foundation for its development into a world-class research institution, developing expertise in fields like chemistry, communications, engineering, information systems and later biotechnology. The origins of more than 60 technology-based companies can be traced back to NRC, beginning in 1950 with Computing Devices (CDC, now General Dynamics Canada). CDC started with the development of a navigational aid for aircraft and grew into a major technology player making a wide range of highly sophisticated military products.

As viewed by high-tech pioneer Denzil Doyle, "if Ottawa had not been blessed with government laboratories such as the National Research Council and the Defence Research Board at the end of World War II, firms like Computing Devices of Canada and Leigh Instruments would not have been created" (Doyle 2000: 47). By attracting talent and developing a range of new technologies, these entities in turn supported the start up of at least another dozen firms, Dy 4 and Lumonics among them.

Through the 1960s, 1970s and 1980s, the federal government continued to influence the development of the Ottawa cluster. By the mid-1990s, federal R&D expenditure had risen to $5 billion annually and about 30% of that amount was concentrated on activities in Ottawa. In strategic collaboration with local companies, NRC's institutes and CRC's labs supported innovative developments in communications, microelectronics, software and later photonics technologies, and provided incubator facilities to sponsor early stage growth. In the 1960s and 1970s, the federal government also used its mainframe computer purchasing requirements to encourage multinationals to establish R&D and manufacturing facilities in Canada. Digital's establishment in Ottawa, which eventually produced a number of spin-offs, and the IBM origins of Ottawa-born SHL Systemhouse, are two examples of the kind of development that was stimulated by the investment of foreign corporations during that early pre-NAFTA period.

Linkages also developed among public research institutes, the education sector and local business. As they expanded through the 1970s and 1980s, universities and colleges in Ottawa became important R&D players. The Doyletech genealogy of high-tech companies credits one local university — Carleton — with influencing the start-up of some 50 firms via the research and training functions of its engineering and science faculties (Doyletech Corporation 2002). Ottawa also attracted a provincial Centre of Excellence, Communications and Information Technology Ontario (CITO), as well as federally funded, industry-led consortia like CANARIE (see also the chapter by Coll, this volume). All of this activity furnished the region with a public sector R&D infrastructure second to none in the country.

Private Sector R&D Institutions

The greatest single influence on the development of the Ottawa cluster, however, was the decision by Northern Electric (Nortel) to concentrate its R&D activity in the nation's capital via two subsidiaries — Bell Northern Research (BNR) and Microsystems International. BNR's labs and test facilities seeded the development of Ottawa's telecom expertise with research focused on the use of computers in electronic switching. Microsystems was an early developer of semi-conductor technology and, although it was shut down in the mid-1970s, it attracted many highly skilled and entrepreneurial engineers and scientists to Ottawa. Some of these later joined BNR, helping to spur Nortel's research operation into one of the most powerful and innovative R&D centers in the world — one which spent billions of dollars, employed thousands of highly skilled people, and spun off several dozens of companies, including future fibre-optics powerhouse JDS.

Others from the Microsystems family went on to start their own firms. One of these was Calian, and its President, Larry O'Brien, recalled how the number of spin-offs directly related to Microsystems eventually generated in Ottawa billions of dollars in annual revenues. "It is just absolutely phenomenal," he declared, ". . . Newbridge, Mitel, Corel, Mosaid, Calian . . . they just go on and on." Organizations of the scope and size of Microsystems, he added, "act as a major technology engine," fuelling not only spin-offs, but also "capability development, other companies of the same type, support companies and service suppliers . . ." — in other words, the foundation of a cluster (Ghent Mallett 2002c).

The Ottawa story emphasizes the critical importance in cluster development of deeply rooted R&D strength. It also clearly underscores the fact that access to technology demands the presence of world-class scientific research institutions. Only through the combined impact of local public and private sector institutional research activity could Ottawa have spawned its own homegrown high-tech industry.

Capitalizing on the talent and funding available in the region, the 1970s start-ups like Mitel, Gandalf, SHL Systemhouse and Quasar (now Cognos) grew steadily into the early 1980s, when they were joined by other Nortel- or CDC- and Leigh-inspired spin-offs. These companies and others developed a strong track record as a result of working with local institutions to commercialize new discoveries and of converting their R&D investments into products and services for a global market. It took decades, but by the mid-1980s, when the controlling interest in Mitel had been sold to British Telecom and Mitel's co-founders had moved on to start Corel and Newbridge, the Ottawa cluster began to take off.

Some of Ottawa's early innovators believe that the take-off in telecom would have happened a lot sooner if the domestic environment had been more competitive. Bell, the major procurer in Canada of leading edge telecom product, favored its BNR partner Nortel as a supplier, particularly in the 1960s and 1970s, thus handicapping the efforts of smaller firms to demonstrate their technology and to develop their initial export markets. Small firms countered by extensive recruiting of BNR personnel, with the net result that BNR acted as a recruiting and training vehicle for local companies — overall, a plus in growing the cluster.

In any case, by the early 1990s, the companies in the region had achieved critical mass. This phenomenon and the business opportunities it presented acted in turn as a magnet for large foreign corporations like Alcatel, Cadence, Cisco, Nokia and Siemens. These firms and other world players moved in with major R&D investments, aggressively seeking the partnerships, skilled personnel and innovative environment they needed to support their own corporate expansions. By the end of 2000, the region was home to over 1000 technology companies, employing approximately 75,000 people.

Availability of Highly Qualified People: Ottawa's Competitive Advantage

As in the case of its R&D strengths, the genesis of the region's skilled workforce goes back to the presence of world-class research institutions in Ottawa. In the immediate post-war environment, NRC and the Defense Research Establishment attracted people from around the world. In the late 1940s, hundreds of British scientists and engineers who had worked in the defense sector found themselves without employment and decided to emigrate to Canada. Similarly, many highly skilled people from continental Europe left their war-torn homelands and/or Soviet-occupied countries to find challenging work and a new life in Canada. Nortel's decision to locate BNR and Microsystems International in Ottawa was based in part on the availability of talented people who might be lured out of federal labs to work in the private sector.

Thanks largely to the presence of NRC, CRC and especially BNR, which flowed research dollars and many gifted scientific and engineering minds to Ottawa, the number of private sector high-tech workers in the region gradually multiplied from about 200 in 1950 (mostly in CDC) to 1500 in 1965. In the 1970s and 1980s, as Nortel continued to expand its research activities and companies like Mitel, Newbridge, Corel and JDS were founded, the demand for brainpower, credentials and certified competence intensified. The region's three universities and two technical colleges graduated increasing numbers of science, engineering and other technical graduates, many thousands of whom found employment and some, entrepreneurial opportunity, in the emerging cluster. Increasingly, the region tended to create its own workforce. By 1995, the number of high-tech workers reached 35,000 and within five years, that number had doubled (see also the chapter by Armit, this volume).

Ottawa's workforce grew to become the most educated in Canada. Of the population aged 25–64, close to 30% had a university degree, compared to the national average of 17%. In 2000, 7% of the population was comprised of scientists and engineers, compared to 3% nationally. Managerial talent also began to flourish in the dynamic environment of Silicon Valley North. The opportunity to develop skills in a variety of both successful and less successful high-tech businesses developed CEOs with experience and battle scars, making them more able to provide the strategic focus, cash consciousness, customer orientation and pragmatism needed to lead and run start-ups.

Ottawa's highly educated and talented labour pool had also become a saleable commodity in the attraction of new investment. In explaining, for example, why California-based Premisys Communications had chosen Ottawa in 1997 over several other cities as the location for a new R&D operation, the Senior VP of Engineering observed that a critical mass of workers meant lower risk for start-ups and for expanding companies. Other sites in Canada and the U.S. did not have "a high enough concentration" of talent (Landriault 1998: 1 & 14). Ottawa's cadre of highly qualified people had become an important competitive advantage.

Visionary Entrepreneurship: The Ottawa Model

Ottawa benefited from the entrepreneurial vision of many of the scientists and engineers who were attracted to the city by the opportunities presented by BNR and Microsystems International, the companies set up by Nortel in the mid-1960s. One of these engineers, Terence Matthews, borrowed $4000 from the Bank of Nova Scotia in 1972 and founded Advanced Devices Consultants of Canada. Telling a true tale that is now part of Ottawa folklore, Matthews recalled how he and Michael Cowpland, another U.K. émigré he had met while at Microsystems, then adopted the name Mitel (Mike and Terry's Lawnmower Company). "We never did well with lawnmowers, but we did really well with the design and introduction of a new type of Touch Tone receiver. This is what really started up the company" (Ghent Mallett 2002a). Matthews sold these receivers to switch manufacturers all over the world and followed this success with the introduction of a family of microprocessor-controlled PABXs, all of which grew Mitel from a small Canadian company to a world leader in telecommunications.

In 1984, Copeland went on to start Corel, which grew within a decade to become the largest software company in Canada. In 1985, Matthews incorporated Newbridge, acquired fifteen years later by Alcatel for $7.1 B (U.S.) in stock. The importance of these two legendary entrepreneurs and of others who co-founded some of Ottawa's bigger high-tech enterprises (e.g. Jozef Straus, JDS; Rod Bryden, Systemhouse; Michael Potter, Cognos) lies less in the wealth and the technology they generated than in their inspirational impact on the development of other startups. By the mid-1990s, Ottawa had the highest per capita percentage of owner-operated high-tech companies in the world.

Matthews, especially, played a seminal role. In the early 1990s, he initiated the Newbridge Affiliates Program, a novel approach to spinning off companies led primarily by ex-Newbridge senior managers, in technology areas that were non-core yet still related to Newbridge's telecom equipment market. Crosskeys (now Orchestream), Tundra,

Timestep (now part of Alcatel), Bridgewater, Vienna Systems (sold to Nokia), Spacebridge, Telexis (now part of March Networks) and Cambrian (sold to Nortel) were among the Ottawa/Gatineau-based companies that Newbridge spun off. Others were headquartered in Halifax, Waterloo, Vancouver and California.

In return for an investment in kind (e.g. administrative support, temporary office space, R&D assistance), Newbridge gained an equity position in the company. Several affiliates developed advanced applications that could ride on Newbridge product (e.g. video conferencing and surveillance, voice carried on Internet), and benefited in selling their products from the parent's marketing strength. Others developed new technologies, like Cambrian's wave division multiplexing, or Tundra's bus-bridge semiconductors. Sheltered by the Newbridge umbrella, and counseled by Matthews as well as by his experienced senior staff who sat on the affiliates' Boards of Directors, the Newbridge spin-offs were given the kind of quick leg up not normally available to other start-ups (see also the chapter by Callahan *et al.* this volume).

Matthews, either personally as an angel investor, or through his venture capital company Celtic Investments, also financed or helped to finance numerous other startups like Skystone (sold for almost $60M) and Extreme Packet Devices (sold for over $400M) — events that helped to confirm Ottawa's prominence on the world's high-tech map. The investments made by Newbridge and Matthews were not all winners, but more than enough are succeeding to influence the continuing growth of the cluster. The model also inspired the development of other in-house incubators, or "intrapreneurship" programs such as Nortel's Business Ventures Group, which spun off NetActive (formerly Channelware) in 1999, a company that went on to raise — independently — nearly $30M in venture capital.

As Denzil Doyle observed, any community that thinks it can build a high-tech industry with an importation strategy has "not taken the time to look at how successful clusters have been built, not just in Canada, but also throughout the world. They have nearly all been homegrown by local entrepreneurs who were determined to survive through good times and bad. By contrast, branch plants have a way of disappearing overnight, not because they are not successful, but because something changed at head office" (Doyle 2001: B8).

Access to Venture Capital: The Ottawa Challenge

Canada has always lagged the U.S. in the availability of start-up capital, and in the formation of the Ottawa cluster this problem was particularly acute. Until the late 1990s, relatively little institutional venture financing was available to Ottawa's technology firms. Before then, entrepreneurs seeking to set up or expand a company, were dependent on traditional debt financing provided by banks and government agencies, as well as on equity financing available from personal funds, friends and family, employee share payments, and/or private investments by high net worth individuals. Mitel grew, Terry Matthews recalled, "on the basis of sweat equity and a $120K loan which we repaid in two years" (Ghent Mallett 2002a).

In the late 1970s and through the 1980s, governments at all levels developed R&D assistance programs for high-tech firms. The availability of repayable contributions from the federal Defense Industry Productivity Program (DIPP) or the Microelectronics

Systems and Development Program (MSDP), to name just two federal initiatives, helped to support the growth of the Ottawa cluster. Newbridge, for example, at a critical point in its expansion, benefited hugely from $15M in MSDP money to fund the development of Asynchronous Transfer Mode (ATM) technology, the basis for its family of innovative ATM switches. With the onset of government cutbacks in the early 1990s, these and other sources dried up — unfortunately just at the point when the number of high tech firms in Ottawa had begun to explode and access to capital had become an even more critical issue.

The activities of venture capitalists are part of the social structure of innovation. "Vencap" firms typically counsel entrepreneurs on business plans and marketing strategies, help them find additional financing, assist in recruiting the right management and serve on Boards of Directors. Independent venture capital firms raise 95% of all the start-up capital in the United States and so perform these roles for start-up American firms. Without similar forms of funding assistance and management guidance, companies in Ottawa were obviously disadvantaged. In 1990, the Ottawa Economic Development Corporation started to try and plug the gap. As Denzil Doyle recalled, a successful investment matching service was developed — the Ottawa Capital Network, "aimed at helping young entrepreneurs network themselves to sources of risk capital, particularly the local angel community" (Doyle 2001: B8). Ottawa companies needing the service usually sought early stage financing of between $150K and $1M. Within a few years of its initiation, the Ottawa Capital Network had facilitated around $25M in investment.

More institutional venture capital became available in the mid-1990s, once Matthews' Celtic Investments and an Ottawa-based labour-sponsored fund — Capital Alliance Ventures — began operations. The angel community also expanded, as new millionaires sprouted from the innovative successes of a growing cluster. In the late 1990s, venture capital began to flood the region from large pension and labour-sponsored funds in Canada and, more and more, from financiers in the U.S. New Ottawa-based venture firms like Skypoint also contributed. Just in the year 2000, Ottawa high-tech firms attracted over $1B in investment capital, with one company alone (Innovance) securing a record-breaking $115M in second-round financing from California-based vencap firms.

Yet early stage financing remained a challenge even in the mature cluster. Analyses of venture capital investment in the 1997–2001 period revealed that the biggest share, by far, went to high-tech companies preparing for an Initial Public Offering (IPO). There had been little growth in deals of less than $5M, indicating that sophisticated investors — understandably preferring the lower risk and more assured exit strategies inherent in near-IPO investments — were not being attracted to smaller, earlier-stage deals (see also the chapter by Callahan *et al.* this volume).

Clearly, access to venture capital, and in particular to early stage financing, was problematic in the early Ottawa experience (see also the chapter by Madill *et al.* this volume). However, it was not a significant factor in the formation of the Ottawa cluster. Other factors — visionary entrepreneurship combined with a strong network of business relationships — provided the force to overcome this obstacle. The evidence demonstrates that Ottawa had reached critical mass before seeing any large infusion of institutional financing: the Silicon Valley North entrepreneurial community had already taken shape before the availability of early stage venture capital. In fact, the absence of venture capital acted as a liability — one that individual entrepreneurs and the community were able to overcome. In Canada's

Silicon Valley, the entrepreneurs were out in front of the angel investors and/or venture capitalists. The Ottawa high tech cluster is a testament to their vision and resolve.

Networks and Linkages: Ottawa's Technology Community Culture

Networks and linkages are necessary to the development of successful clusters because innovation is an active social process. Community networks speed up innovation by connecting people across boundaries and by accelerating collective learning. The set of relationships that linked institutional researchers, entrepreneurs, financiers, technology workers, lawyers, consultants, marketers and others in Silicon Valley, California, has often been called the "real secret" of that region's stunning success.

Different assets and different conditions in Ottawa led to a less company-centric and more partnership-based set of relationships. In the case of Silicon Valley North, the existence of a strong research and educational infrastructure (see also the chapter by Armit, this volume), the impact of catalytic entrepreneurs and the economic development interests of municipal governments combined into a unique approach to building local community networks. But looking at both Silicon Valleys, it is clear that a tremendous local capacity for, and dedicated commitment to, collaboration was the critical factor they had in common.

As the fledgling Ottawa high sector developed in the late 1970s, leaders from the business, university and federal research communities began to see a need for some kind of collaborative research and commercialization effort. Andy Haydon, then Chair of the Regional Municipality of Ottawa-Carleton rammed the financial support through the Regional Council. The result was the 1983 founding of OCRI — the not-for-profit Ottawa Carleton Research Institute (subsequently renamed the Ottawa Centre for Research and Innovation) — that became the primary vehicle for the convergence of Ottawa's high-tech development efforts (see also the chapter by O'Sullivan, this volume). As former OCRI President Bill Collins noted in an interview with *Time*, the new organization was tasked with a mandate to foster research cooperation, but its real job was to build a technology community (Jerabec 2001).

From modest beginnings, OCRI paralleled Ottawa's expansion and in less than two decades, had 600 members who included a diverse range of large and small companies, individuals, school boards, universities, and other research institutions. Initially seeded by $200K in municipal funding and an equivalent amount in membership fees from its nine original business partners, OCRI's budget doubled to $10M following its merger with the Ottawa Economic Development Corporation. The history of OCRI's membership-driven advance shows the influence it had on the growth of the cluster through its building of linkages between firms, and among firms and educational institutions. OCRI grew thanks to the on-going commitment of its founders, its members and the organizations's own success at building key collaborative relationships.

For example, one of the organization's more significant initiatives was the launch of OCRINet, a research partnership that showcased local expertise and developed local R&D infrastructure by connecting, electronically, some of Ottawa's leading high-tech firms with universities and federal research labs. Over time, OCRINet evolved into a fibre-based broadband network connected to CANARIE, the national optical infrastructure (see also the chapter by Materazzi, this volume). OCRINet was also the genesis for the SmartCapital initiative, a plan to provide broadband connectivity for the whole community. OCRI's success in harnessing energies across the community to create this physical network, symbolized in very real terms the organization's vision of linking together people, ideas and technology to strengthen Ottawa's knowledge base and to enhance its quality of life.

OCRI developed as a grassroots organization, acting as a facilitator or as a broker of cost-shared new initiatives wherever these activities served to advance the broader interests of the technology community. Hence OCRI became the rallying point for the overt development of a community technology culture. This culture embraced not only innovative new research partnerships, but education partnerships at all levels, and business learning services that encouraged a collective shift toward a more knowledge-based community, while also helping Ottawa companies to thrive.

Tony Stansby, a former Chair of one of the early OCRI Boards, thought the dynamics of Board meetings "were quite unusual and wholly fascinating. Despite the diverse backgrounds, viewpoints and vocabulary of the industrial, academic and government board members, the sense of excitement was palpable. It was as if each, in his or her own way, was seeing a way to advance through collaboration, some cherished community goal that had hitherto seemed unattainable" (Ghent Mallett 2002b).

Beyond OCRI's monthly High-Tech Breakfasts, the Tech Rocks concerts, and other outreach programs, something else was at play, something less tangible and more difficult to describe. In the 1980s and early 1990s, as the cluster worked its way to maturity, a remarkable kinship or what OCRI's Bill Collins would later describe as a "real feeling of family" began to develop. One indicator lay in the willingness of competing companies to work closely with each other, and with similarly competitive institutional partners towards a common community goal. Another lay in the shared conviction that the region would achieve world-class distinction as a center for advanced technologies, and that efforts to foster collaboration and learning would result in significant pay-offs. A collective pride in what the community had already accomplished, and an enthusiastic, resolute faith in the future generally defined the mood.

Even now, despite the severity of the technology downturn, the high-tech community's continuing confidence in its future is barely rattled. Rather, the downturn is viewed as a temporary breathing space, allowing the community time to address problems that in the last few years had been threatening to limit Ottawa's growth — i.e. shortages of highly qualified people, and inadequate physical infrastructure. In fact, many expect the re-distribution of talent accompanying the shake-up to have a positive long-term effect on the business vitality and diversity of the region — much like the impact of the mid-1970s shutdown of Microsystems International.

Conclusion

Building a technology cluster is the work of decades. To the outside world in the mid-1990s, Ottawa looked like an overnight success story. But the groundwork had actually been laid 20, 30, 40 and even 50 years earlier. "Just setting up a cluster in Timbuktu won't work,"

Terry Matthews noted. "You have to build a nucleus around something deep-rooted" (Ghent Mallett 2002a). *Time Magazine* echoed his thought in a March 2001 report, concluding that Ottawa represented no dot-com bubble: the city's high tech industry has long, deep roots that are not likely to be torn up in a single market storm (Jerabec 2001).

The Ottawa high tech cluster shows that R&D strength is the most important factor in the formation of a cluster, not only because it spurs a collective capacity to generate innovative ideas for commercial application, but also because creative and talented people go where there is technological challenge and excitement. Thanks to local world-class research institutions like NRC and BNR, which provided access to technology while attracting bright, highly qualified and entrepreneurial people, Ottawa was able to capture quickly three of the five essential elements deemed necessary to the foundation of a globally competitive technology cluster.

With its R&D base, pool of skilled labour and, especially, the vision, drive and persistence of its local entrepreneurs, Ottawa was also able to transcend its one real disadvantage — the availability of early stage financing. Access to venture capital never played a significant role in the formation of the Ottawa cluster, which suggests that this element may be a less critical factor in cluster formation when the other elements — in particular, the entrepreneurial element, are there. Ottawa's visionary enterprises created new models to finance and mentor start-ups, while also stimulating and supporting the development of a powerful community technology culture. This culture — driven by the expansion of linkages among business, government and education players — helped to provide the infrastructure needed for innovative success.

The way Ottawa blended four of the five ingredients deemed necessary to cluster development (as well as the way it survived the absence of the fifth ingredient), might be unique. But the central importance of the three interdependent elements of research strength, talented people and visionary entrepreneurship is by no means original to the Ottawa cluster.

The R&D strengths of the University of Waterloo, Ontario, Canada, for example, have been credited with giving Canada its foothold in the software industry, and with producing not only gifted scientists and engineers, but also entrepreneurs like RIM co-founder Mike Lazaridis, Cyberplex co-founder Dean Hopkins and Pixstream's Stephen Basco. In 1994, the University's Research Office profiled 100 homegrown companies that had been spun off. Over the next several years, the momentum increased. The high-tech industry in Waterloo, recognizing the similarity of their cluster development with Ottawa's, and the value of the networks and linkages that had been created in Silicon Valley North, set about to create their own technology culture by founding Communitech, an industry/government/education partnership openly modeled on OCRI.

In summary, technology clusters are started and achieved when the fundamentals are right. The presence of a world-class research institution, with its innovative capacities and its magnetic attraction for highly talented people — including visionary entrepreneurs — is the essential condition.

The question for policy makers is, can this experience be reproduced. World class research institutions exist elsewhere in Canada and in the world. So does a supply of smart graduates from good universities. And institutional financing is more ready than it was. But visionary entrepreneurs and closely-knit, entrepreneurial communities are much more difficult to foster.

Acknowledgments

Financial support from the Information Technology Association of Canada (ITAC) for the conduct of this study is gratefully acknowledged. The research assistance of Diana Shapirkina and the Université du Québec en Outaouais' support for her work are also appreciated.

References

Doyle, D. (2000). Was that a federal push in the right direction or a kick in the pants? *Silicon Valley North*, 5(11), 47.
Doyle, D. (2001). Branding cities — technically — doesn't work. *Silicon Valley North*, 6(9), B8.
Doyletech Corporation (2002). *A family tree of home grown Ottawa-Gatineau high technology companies*. http://www.doyletechcorp.com/pubs.htm.
Ghent Mallett, J. (2002a, September 25). *Personal communication*. Ottawa, Ontario, Canada.
Ghent Mallett, J. (2002b, September 26). *Personal communication*. Ottawa, Ontario, Canada.
Ghent Mallett, J. (2002c, September 27). *Personal communication*. Ottawa, Ontario, Canada.
Jerabec, A. (2001). The morphing of Ottawa: Special report. *Time Magazine*, *157*(10), 38–44.
Landriault, G. (1998). It is not exactly an invasion, but it is a good start. *Silicon Valley North*, 3(5), 1 & 14.

Chapter 3

Yesterday's Adventures with Today's Technology: Carleton University's Wired City Simulation Laboratory

David C. Coll

Abstract

In response to new possibilities arising from the marriage of telecommunications and the computer that were apparent in the early 1970s, the Carleton University Wired City Simulation Laboratory undertook a prescient series of investigations of the technology, applications, and social psychology of multi-node, broadband, multimedia teleconferencing. Experiments were conducted in television-based small group discussions and other mediated communications; the design of conferencing terminals; the use of television as a computer display in the classroom, computer-aided public touch-tone information retrieval over cable television; remote teaching including course exchanges between Carleton University and Stanford University via real-time digital television.

Introduction

In the late 1950s, it became apparent to many involved with information technology that the computer, coupled with data communications, was going to play a large role in society. The extent of the economic and social impact and of the technological advances to come, of course, could not even be imagined at that time. Likewise, the extent of the lack of adequate systems engineering models for the technology was not appreciated, and is still not totally understood.

While the author was a graduate student at MIT, his supervisor insisted that he and his classmates take a course on computer programming. The programming language was FORTRAN and the computer was the IBM 704. The course was taken in the year in which FORTRAN was released and IBM's first commercial scientific computer, the 704, was installed. The author was also associated at MIT with early data transmission trials on

Silicon Valley North: A High-Tech Cluster of Innovation and Entrepreneurship
Copyright © 2004 by Elsevier Ltd.
All rights of reproduction in any form reserved
ISBN: 0-08-044457-1

telephone lines. The data was transmitted from northern radar sites to the experimental SAGE control center at MIT Lincoln Laboratories. This was the same year that the artificial intelligence laboratory was created at MIT. Sputnik was launched that fall; and satellite communications was being discussed.

The supervisor was R. M. Fano, who was the leader of the Information Theory Group at MIT at that time. Dr. Fano had recognized that the computer was destined to play a large role in communications. He went on to create project MAC, Multiple Access Computing, MIT's program in time-shared computers.

D. A. George, the principal investigator in the Carleton University Wired City Simulation Laboratory, was also a graduate student at MIT at the same time. He was studying in the Statistical Communications Theory Group. The two groups in the MIT Research Laboratory for Electronics (RLE), that is Information Theory and Communication Theory, whose genesis was the World War II-era Radiation Laboratory (RLE 1991), were the cradle of the theoretical foundations of the communications revolution that we are still experiencing.

Ideas expressed by J. C. R. Licklider in 1960 on man-computer symbiosis and the computer as a communications device laid the foundation for our modern use of the computer in those ways (Hewlett-Packard 1990). Needless to say, it wasn't long before the social impact of the interaction between computers and communications was being studied. By the end of the 1960s, digital communications systems had been introduced, the computer was well established, and it was clear that we were entering an era of enhanced broadband communications.

About this time the Canadian government undertook a series of studies of telecommunications in Canada. The studies took the form of what were called TeleCommissions — committees of experts who gathered opinions on the state of telecommunications in Canada — in many diverse fields such as the structure of the industry, the state of the technology, the probable directions in which it would go, and the economical, social and legal impacts of the computer and data communications on Canadian society. The TeleCommissions led to the formation of a Department of Communications. One of the first publications of the new Department was a report called Instant World, a summary of the TeleCommission reports (Department of Communications 1971).

In this era of the Internet we tend to take world-wide multimedia connectivity and the universal access to information it provides through the World Wide Web for granted. The studies that led to Instant World not only recognized the role that communications had played in the creation and continuing maintainance of the Canadian nation, they also forecast the role that the marriage of communications and computers would play in the future.

While recognizing that communications play a large role in all modern societies, they are particularly important to Canada. With Canada's population spreads across 6,000 km from sea to sea to sea, communications are one of the threads holding this country together; and communications are also among Canada's major industries. Canadian geography and population distribution have always required effective communication systems. Communications have always played a large role in Canadian affairs. We have excellent communications. The telegraph, the telephone, radio and television broadcasting are all well developed. Our communication systems have grown and now include satellite communications, national data networks, optical fibre networks, cellular telephones and a host of other communication-based services. Canada has one of the world's highest levels of universal telephone service, cable television access, internet connectivity, and domestic satellite service.

Instant World was among the first, but certainly not the last, studies that established and justified the Canadian government's commitment to telecommunications as an essential part of their policy. The Telecommission studies were concerned with the social impact of telecommunications and foretold that foreseeable developments in the technology of telecommunications and computers hold possibilities of a more convenient and satisfying way of life, the satisfaction being measured in spiritual as well as material terms. New and emerging techniques will offer access to information on a scale hitherto unimaginable, together with opportunities for a much wider participation in community affairs and the democratic process. The report also predicted that the emerging technology of telecommunications offers the possibility of an eventual network affording universal access to the means of transmitting and receiving information in virtually any conceivable form. It referred to the impending possibility of virtually instantaneous transfer of information in any form between all parts of the country helps to reduce absolute distance, reduces regional disparities and develops the North.

Instant World made it clear that the technologies of telecommunications and computers used effectively in combination could make a striking contribution to the economic prosperity and the general quality of life in Canada.

The capability of information technology, both the equipment (hardware) and the ability to make it do whatever we desire (software), has progressed enormously since Instant World was published. Computer power (processor speeds, memory sizes, cost, size, energy consumption, networking, graphics, printing, etc.) has evolved at exponential rates.[1] It is noteworthy as an indication of how much has changed since 1971 to realize that the personal computer revolution did not occur until ten years later. Digital transmission and data computer networks are now the norm. Digital audio and television broadcasting has commenced; digital channels are available on many cable and satellite systems. Fibre optic transmission is now the routine mode of connection in long distance networks; and it is also used throughout urban distribution networks. Email and facsimile are everywhere and personal radio communications (pagers and cellphones) are the fastest growing sector of the industry. Multimedia computer communications are now part of common operating systems.[2] The integration of Global Positioning information and Geographical Information Systems has produced a variety of new services such as GM OnStar[3] and 911-caller location. So-called e-commerce, with universal secure on-line access to shopping, financial services including ubiquitous point-of-sale terminals, credit authorization and banking, all manner of reservation and ticketing services, and so on, is now the heart and soul of

---

[1] The rate of growth of computer power is typically referred to as Moore's Law, the observation made in 1965 by Gordon Moore, co-founder of *Intel*, according to which the number of *transistors* per square inch on *integrated circuits* had doubled every year since the integrated circuit was invented. (http://www.webopedia.com/TERM/M/Moores_Law.html).

[2] For example, NetMeeting, audio-video teleconferencing, is an integral part of Windows and supported by machine language instructions for digital signal processing and graphics that are part of the Intel Pentium processor.

[3] OnStar Canada web site: http://www.onstar.com/canada_english/jsp/whatisonstar/whatisonstar.jsp.

our economy. In fact, communications are as much a part of the infrastructure of modern society as water and sewer, electrical power and natural gas. In fact, communication facilities are included routinely, like any other utility, in new construction.

Canada has been consistently in the forefront of communications technology (Binder 2003; Coll URL1; Collins 1997; Department of Communications 1971; Hill & Hill URL1; Teracom URL1). The first Trans-Atlantic radio transmission was received in Newfoundland. Canada had the world's first commercial telephone system and North America's first mobile telecommunications system. The first commercial meteor-burst communication system was Canadian. Canada had the Western world's first domestic satellite communications system. Canada had the world's first nation-wide digital data network. Canada has the world's largest contiguous cellular telephone network. Canadians have greater access to cable television service than the people of any other nation. Canada now has nation-wide fibre optic links. The government of Canada is commitment to be the most electronically connected government in the world to its citizens by 2005 (Government of Canada 2003).

Telecommunication systems, and the information that flows through them, are the nervous system of the modern world. International trade and finance, cooperation and conflict all depend on communications. Communications hold the "global village" together. Radio and satellite links, terrestrial and undersea coaxial and fibre optic cables connect Canada to other countries throughout the world.

Plans for future development by the Canadian telecommunications industry tended to focus on similar ideas. This was emphasized by the formation of a corporation devoted to promotion of a vision for Canada's communications industry. The vision came about through industry — government cooperation. In 1989, Communications Canada gathered together the leaders of Canada's telecommunications community from industry, government and academia. The outcome of meetings held that year in St. Saveur, Quebec and Kananaskis, Alberta was the formation of an organization called Vision 2000 Incorporated.

Vision 2000 was charged with the mission of preparing briefings for provincial and federal politicians to inform them of the belief that universal, ubiquitous, broadband communications were an essential component of modern economies. The organization focussed on advanced personal communications as an identifiable objective, and adopted multimedia-enhanced facsimile as a practical route to the multimedia future.[4]

The position taken was that advanced personal communications would enhance productivity in the workplace. They would increase enjoyment of leisure time; improve the efficiency of social services, and help people share ideas, values and experiences. The telecommunications industry committed itself to developing personal communication technologies, systems, services and applications through research and development and innovative applications of existing technologies. It focussed on creating a policy, regulatory, standards and spectrum environment that would encourage the rapid development and diffusion of personal communication systems. According to the Vision 2000 Inc. report

---

[4] Personal communications was chosen by Vision 2000 as the general focus of future communication developments, to a large extent because of the anticipation of substantial interest and support for emerging PCS (Personal Communication Systems). Vision 2000 identified enhanced facsimile as the basic technology.

(Vision 2000 Inc. 2000), knowledge-based innovation is the key to the competitive advantage of companies and nations.

While Vision 2000 was incorporated with substantial industrial and government funding, it never did achieve its objective. The exercise, however, developed and focused the knowledge that laid the foundation for the implementation of Canada's broadband national research network — CANARIE, the Information Highway Task Force, and several provincial studies.

Canada's concern with telecommunications was reinforced with the 1992 publication of "Telecommunications: Enabling Ontario's Future" (The Advisory Committee 1992). This report to the Minister of Culture and Communications from the Advisory Committee on a Telecommunications Strategy for the Province of Ontario echoes Instant World in many ways. The Committee was comprised of members representing all sectors of Ontario society. It is not surprising that, aware of what they termed the "convergence of computing and telecommunications" they took a broad view of the term telecommunications, discussing opportunities, barriers and directions for telecommunications as part of information technology. The committee was concerned with human as well as technological issues. As described in their report, their vision was "that through the enabling effect of telecommunications, Ontario, and in turn Canada, will be the best place in the world to work, learn and do business." They presented four goals for the province: a telecommunications infrastructure, a dynamic telecommunications sector, enhancement of the quality of life, and strategic application of telecommunications by the Ontario government. There was a very clear recognition that economic prosperity lies in a knowledge-based economy, and that the foundation for this new economy are information in general and information technology in particular.

The recognition of telecommunications as an essential component of the infrastructure of modern societies by governments and industry has continued. The convergence of telecommunications and computing and the advent of broadband multimedia networks led the Government of Canada to create a small, blue-ribbon panel, called the Information Highway Advisory Council in 1994 with the mandate to determine how the country should proceed along the Information Highway. The Council's 1995 report, *The Challenge of the Information Highway: Final Report of the Information Highway Advisory Council* (Information Highway Advisory Council 1995), and the 1997 follow-up *Preparing Canada For A Digital World: Final Report of the Information Highway Advisory Council* (Information Highway Advisory Council 1997), describe (once again) the importance of the Information Highway and related technologies in all aspects of Canadian life, including education and training.

Following up, in January 2001 the Government of Canada established the National Broadband Task Force to map out a strategy for achieving the Government of Canada's goal of ensuring that broadband services are available to businesses and residents in every Canadian community by 2004.

The Task Force was founded to create a plan for providing all Canadians with access to broadband network services. The idea, following in the familiar footsteps of previous administrations that had seen the social potential of communications, was to allow citizens to live and prosper in any part of the land and have equal access to high levels of education, health, cultural and economic opportunities. The Task Force was to provide plans for a high-capacity, two-way link between end user and access network suppliers capable of supporting full-motion interactive video applications. This service was to be delivered to all Canadians on terms comparable to those available in urban markets. In their report (Johnson 2000; National Broadband Task Force 2000, 2001), the Task Force defines broadband service as: "A minimum symmetrical speed of 1.5 Mbps . . . currently required, increasing to the 4–6 Mbps range — more in public and commercial facilities."

Beginnings of the Wired City Simulation Laboratory

It is apparent that universal, ubiquitous, broadband communications is not a new idea. However, as we will see, the activities of a small group of researchers at Carleton University developed and demonstrated many of the themes and applications that are still foreseen today as part of the future promise of computer communications.

In the late 1960s, Professors B. A. Bowen and D. C. Coll of the Department of Systems and Computer Engineering at Carleton University developed the concept of what they called "The National Information Bus"[5]: a wideband communications trunk linking all parts of the country, providing universal access to persons and information. The National Information Bus was to be based on cable television; and, while computer-to-computer communications was part of it, the majority of the traffic was considered to be television-based teleconferencing. It was conjectured that such a facility would support *telesynesis*, the ability to work together at a distance — something that today might be called a collaborative space.

Because no one had ever experienced an environment like the National Information Bus, no one knew really what the research questions were. A number of persons, including the author, had suggested that test facilities should be established so that some experience could be gathered. For example, a former colleague of the author, Mr. E. A. Walker, of the Communications Research Laboratory of DOC, had suggested a "high-speed" digital communications system be installed at the Shirley Bay site of what is now the Communications Research Centre, so that experience with the technology could be acquired. The concept was not accepted — such an idea was not considered "research."

At the end of 1969 (December 30th, to be exact), the author wrote a memorandum (Coll 1969) to the Dean of Engineering (D. A. George), the Electrical Engineering faculty, and to others in Architecture, Visual Aids, Psychology, and Journalism at Carleton University inviting them to meet to discuss experiments "leading to the development of a conference room in which the 'presence' of a remote participant can be maximized in some way." This memorandum followed discussions between Carleton and Queen's Universities on the creation of a Joint Institute in Communications and Electronics with Queen's University in Kingston.

One of the aspects of the proposed cooperation with Queen's that was discussed in the memorandum was the establishment of those types of communications between Ottawa and Kingston that would best serve such a program. As defined in the memorandum, the goal of the communications was to "put in each other's offices: to achieve the same sort of

---

[5] *Bus* is technical term for energy or information carrying conduits used in electronic circuits and computers.

'presence' that exists when one drops into a colleague's office, uses his board, and works with him over a drawing or document on his desk." The facilities envisaged included real-time telecommunications made up of "hard-copy" devices such as teleprinter, scratch-pad, facsimile, and graphical (computer) display; audio such as voice-grade telephone, open-line voice, hi-fi quality telephone, and stereo all-round sound; and video including slow-scan TV, standard Closed Circuit TV, holographic images, multiple-image TV, and 3-D TV, colour with wall size displays. The experimental program included examining questions regarding the acoustical design of the conference room; and the décor, furnishings and comfort to enhance face-to-face communications in the room and investigating the effectiveness of voice, graphical, and video communications; the effect of communication channel limitations on hope of success; the type of audio and video systems that could be achieved with reasonable cost; and the criteria that could be used to measure the quality of "presence."

Concurrently, Bowen, Coll and George, with colleagues from the Department of Psychology and the School of Journalism, made a proposal for the establishment of a multidisciplinary communications laboratory and research program built around a communications link between Carleton and Queen's University in Kingston, Ontario. This link was to have provided continuous wideband two-way communications with like-minded colleagues in the Department of Electrical Engineering at Queen's. The concept was to provide an open window into each other's workspace, a process that was termed "*telepresence.*" The proposal was presented to the National Research Council (then the prime granting agency for scientific research in Canada)[6] in the form of what was called a Negotiated Development Grant. The proposal was not funded, due in large part to the speculative nature of the proposed research[7], but also because of the multi-disciplinary nature of the research program: the visiting assessment team had substantial difficulty believing that engineers and social scientists could manage a project and work together without strictly defined protocols. It has always been the author's opinion, and remains so to this day, that the consequences of hitherto unavailable communication modes (and information technology) are unknown and overly formal research plans are bound to be incorrect.

Undeterred by the lack of support from the traditional funding sources, Coll, Bowen and George together with some colleagues from the School of Journalism decided to explore the basic concept of multi-node, broadband communications in the summer of 1971. A three-node network was set up in a drafting room in the Faculty of Engineering using closed-circuit television equipment. Each node comprised two cameras, one focused on the participant, and one on his or hers "writing space," i.e. looking over the participant's shoulder at a pad of paper. Full audio was provided, using headsets to avoid feedback problems. The set-up worked! Experiments on the effectiveness of the arrangement were carried out with the assistance of personnel with a background in social psychology.

---

[6] At present, NSERC, SSHRC, and NRC are the federal prime granting agencies in Canada.

[7] The basic premise of the research was that because no one had ever experienced the proposed environment, a working environment was required before research questions could be properly formulated, and certainly before experiments could be designed and specified.

The Wired City Simulation Laboratory

The author and his colleague, Dr. D. A. George, took advantage of the experience gained from the ad hoc video conferencing experiment and the fortuitous formation of the Department of Communications and in a collaboration that lasted until the late 1970s, formed what they called "The Wired City Simulation Laboratory" in the Faculty of Engineering at Carleton University.

The Laboratory grew out of a proposal developed as the result of a 1971 study conducted for the Department of Communications study entitled "The Wired Scientific City" (Bowen *et al.* 1971). The proposal was to interconnect the research centers in the Ottawa area with a broadband communications network designed to achieve an enhancement of successful communications within a restricted, yet diverse, technically aware community. The basic medium was to be multi-channel, full bandwidth, analog television. The centers to be connected were the DOC laboratories at Shirley's Bay (the present Communications Research Centre), the near-by Bell-Northern Research Laboratories at Crystal Beach, Carleton University, the University of Ottawa, the Department of Communications headquarters in downtown Ottawa, and the National Research Centre in east-end Ottawa. Physically, the connections were to be via microwave radio — all sites are visible from the top of the Dunton Tower at Carleton University. Logically, the network was specified as a ring network.

The Wired Scientific City was seen as a way to bring the potential of the "wired city" within the reach of other Canadian users and experimenters in as useful a way as possible, to develop realistic applications of information technology in a Canadian urban environment in a multi-user, multipurpose facility.

The Wired Scientific City network was to operate in three modes:

- The one-to-many mode, with a limited "talkback" capability; to provide for conventional lecture series and seminars.
- The one-to-one mode, to provide for discussions and working sessions between collaborating individuals, or two small groups.
- The many-to-many mode, to provide group discussions: to bring all participants into a "common space" to support the following functions:
  - Lectures and seminars;
  - Collaborations, and resource sharing; and
  - Conferences and discussions.

While human-human communications were stressed initially, it was understood that both man-machine and machine-machine communications would play a significant role in the "Wired Scientific City." In the "Wired Scientific City" project, with its emphasis on the experimental development of suitable facilities and procedures for use by a much wider community than that involved in a pilot project, it went without saying that computer access, aids to communication, control of the network, data transmission, and other automated features were to be included in the evolutionary development of the network.

The activities to be supported were:

- joint, inter-institutional seminars;
- the linking of teaching institutions with each other and off-campus students, as recommended for study by "The Ring of Iron"[8]
- joint meetings of small groups of people, working as a committee;
- close collaborative work between physically separated individuals; provision of a common working space;
- the expanded opportunity for members of this community to meet together on an informal basis to exchange information, problems, ideas, etc., and to stimulate creativity.

The points of contact at each institution were to be those individuals identified as "gate-keepers" in the sense that they were engaged actively in collaboration with a number of other individuals in other institutions. Specific experiments that were suggested included:

- The implementation of an information system to enable efficient and convenient use of the networks.
- The dissemination of selected graduate courses from Carleton and Ottawa Universities.
- The presentation of courses given by sessional lecturers employed in governmental laboratories, from their place of employment.
- The presentations of seminars given at the Communications Research Centre, Bell-Northern, Carleton University, the University of Ottawa, Department of Communications, and the National Research Council.
- The day-to-day administrative and technical communications between the Department of Communications and the Communications Research Centre.
- The installation of terminals of the National Research Council Computer Aided Learning system at the nodes of the network.
- The interconnection of the Low Energy Nuclear Physics group, whose mebers were scattered about the Ottawa area.
- The operation of the diabetic metabolism cooperative experiment between Carleton University and the Ottawa Civic Hospital.[9]
- The extension of the Project 91 evaluation experiments and the Carleton University teleconferencing experiments.[10]
- The development of management information systems activities by interconnection of the informal Ottawa group spanning Bell-Northern, Carleton University, and the Departments of Communications and Defence.

While the Wired Scientific City implementation project itself was not funded by DOC, substantial support was provided for what became the Wired City Simulation Laboratory.

---

[8] "The Iron Ring" was a report written in 1971 by Dr. P. A. Lapp on the engineering educational programs in Ontario universities. He identified a major portion of Carleton's Electrical Engineering program as actually being what he termed Information Engineering. The Faculty of Engineering never did declare it so in public, although many faculty still consider it to be exactly that.

[9] In this experiment, a Digital PDP-8 mini-computer at Carleton was used as the real-time controller of a glucose injection system at the Ottawa Civic Hospital, connected over telephone line.

[10] Project 91 was a videophone experiment carried out at Bell Northern Laboratories in Ottawa by C. A. Billows.

This laboratory and the initial research program carried out in it were described in Coll *et al.* (1975).

The Wired City Lab was developed within the C. J. Mackenzie Engineering Building at Carleton University. Three teleconference stations, several offices and classrooms were connected to a switching centre in a central laboratory. Coaxial and audio cabling providing for five-way conferences connected each conferencing node. The conferencing consoles in each station each originated two video signals (a view of the participant and a view of the writing space). Interconnections were made by manual patch cords in the central laboratory. Facilities were incorporated for video recording, remote camera control, single frame storage and retrieval. Then, in 1976, direct two-way connections to the Stanford University Bay Area Teaching Network were established via the CTS (Hermes) satellite to the NASA Ames Research Center at Moffat Field and thence by a terrestrial microwave link to Stanford University.

During the period from 1971 to 1978, a wide variety of experiments were carried out. Both technical and psychological studies were performed, and several prescient innovative applications were developed and tested. The key personnel involved were D. A. George, the principal investigator; the author, principal co-investigator; L. H. Strickland, of the Department of Psychology at Carleton University, principal social psychology investigator; S. A. Paterson, Laboratory Manager; and P. D. Guild, evaluation investigator.

The development of the facilities and the experiments that were conducted are described in a series of reports to the Department of Communications (Coll 1973; Coll *et al.* 1974a, b; George *et al.* 1975).

The experiments fell into a number of categories. Many experiments were carried out using one or more of the teleconferencing nodes. These included social psychology experiments, technical development and demonstrations. Among the social psychological experiments were:

- Prof. Jay Weston of the Carleton University School of Journalism conducted an investigation of mediated course discussion group meetings, with three students at one node and three at another. The sessions were videotaped with a three-way vertical split, showing each group in one split and pertinent information in the third.
- The effectiveness of remote collaborative problem solving was tested in one-to-one experiments with one student at one node with the colour-coded plans for a Tinker Toy model communicating with the "constructor" at another node over black-and-white television.
- Simulated Disarmament Negotiations were evaluated under the direction of Prof. Lloyd Strickland of the Psychology Department.
- The effect of telecommunications mediation on the "risky-shift" phenomenon was investigated.[11]
- Students from the Urban Planning program at the University of Toronto used the Wired City Simulation Laboratory to investigate the potential use of multi-point video

---

[11] The "risky-shift" phenomenon is the tendency of small groups to become carried away with enthusiasm created by the synergy of the moment when developing a solution to a problem, thereby arriving at a solution that would not normally be chosen.

conferencing for distributed planning sessions, as between the constituent parts of Metropolitan Toronto (when it had such parts) (Dakin 1974).

Among the technical developments and demonstrations were:

- The design and test of a command and control system for the Laboratory based on character-oriented data communications (Potvin 1976). This system was based on a loop network of programmable Network Interface Units (NIU). The NIUs consisted of serial communications modules, analog and digital inputs and outputs, A/D and D/A converters, and a micro-controller based processing unit. A message system was designed to allow communications between a central computer and the NIUs. Text messages, commands, and data could be exchanged. A basic instruction set was designed for the NIUs, allowing them to control output devices and to read inputs. The NIUs were interconnected with character-oriented communications on a serial bus. Each NIU had a distinct address and, when its own address was detected it read the attached message, and acted according to its contents; otherwise it regenerated the message and sent it on. The NIUs were implemented using a set of basic modules, containing microcontrollers. The modules were in the form of integrated circuit printed circuit cards that were designed and fabricated. A complete software system for central computer control from a mini-computer was developed.[12]
- One of the major "understandings" of mediated communications at the time (and still is), was that eye contact in addition to a wide range of visual cues, are essential for effective interpersonal communications.[13] As a result, a number of trials were conducted of the use of half-silvered mirrors in the sight path between the user and the main viewing monitor. With this arrangement the user, when looking at the monitor, was looking directly into the camera. To the remote viewer, the user was staring directly into his eyes at all times — a most unsettling situation. In a multi-user situation, the user appeared to be looking directly at each and every viewer — a situation that all viewers knew to be false — creating a sensation of total impersonality to the communication, destroying any illusion of intimacy. As a result, the point was not pursued. All other studies conducted in the Wired City laboratory tended to indicate that the mode of video conferencing used created an intimate and intense communication environment, even though the users understood full well that it was (physically) not so.
- Rideau Microwave Inc. demonstrated the feasibility of short path video communications in the urban environment in a study. An 11.2 GHz microwave link was tested on the Carleton University campus, which led the conclusion that "when a clear line of sight existed between the antennae, little difficulty as encountered in obtaining very good

---

[12] Development of the NIUs preceded the introduction of the microprocessor by many years. It is interesting that use of such devices did not become widespread even with the availability of the microprocessor and the PC, particularly in domestic applications. Unfortunately, the NIUs were not developed into a product. It was not until the relatively recent popularity of the Internet Protocol and universal IP addresses that such applications seemed to be on the verge of acceptance. However, they are still not commonplace. The author notes that the concept of 'smart' devices incorporating a communications module and a controller module is the basis of the Global Information Infrastructure model, and of course is an integral concept in a universe of addressable devices.

[13] See, for example, http://www.cs.unc.edu/~ryang/publications/ECCV-camready.pdf; http://www.virtue.eu.com/, or http://www-hsd.worldbank.org/symposium/427-2-ivancevich.htm.

transmission" which often paraphrased in the Laboratory as "if you can see the other end, you can transmit video" (McKillican 1973).

- The data communication requirements necessary to support the real-time digital transmission of handwriting were measured (McDonald 1972).
- The storage and transmission of documentary information, stored as video pages, was investigated, using a digitally controlled analog video frame-grabber and addressable memory (Coll & Mahmoud 1976).
- The concept of increased channel utilization by time-division multiplexing of video frames was explored in some detail. An individual video signal was re-constituted by showing each "live" frame as it is received, and storing it in a video memory from which it is repeated until the next live frame is received[14] (Coll 1980; George & Coll 1978; Roddick 1980). Each individual video signal looks to its observer as reduced frame rate video. The *activity*, or amount of change, in the video signal determines the fidelity of the reduced rate TV (Coll & Choma 1976). Image activity measurement showed that a TV channel could be shared by two signals without much perceived distortion; and, three or four was very acceptable with certain types of television programming — such as "talking heads." In a surveillance situation, only changed frames need to be transmitted, so the channel utilization could be greatly enhanced for this application.[15]
- A major multimedia system demonstration involved the use of a minicomputer, touch-tone signalling, video frame retrieval from the video memory, and the local Ottawa-area cable TV networks. Subscribers (persons equipped with touch-tone dialing and cable TV) could call a telephone number and, using their touch-tone pad, enter the number of a frame they wished to see. The selected frame was retrieved from the video store and transmitted (as an analog video signal) to the head-end of the local cable TV networks, where it was broadcast on their community channel. This system, informally called *PhoneInfo*, was in operation for a month during 1974. The data was supplied by participating organizations, and up-dated as received. One of the interesting observations was that the system was accessed most heavily when school let out in the afternoon, displaying such information as the skating conditions on the Rideau Canal, liquor store opening hours, theatre offerings, etc.
- Professor Peter Fried of the Carleton University Psychology Department examined the feasibility of utilizing physiological signals to indicate user interest in a commissioned study (Fried 1973).

The Educational Communications Project

The Wired City Laboratory equipment was used in a number of educational applications (Coll & Paterson 1975; George *et al.* 1976; Guild *et al.* 1975a), supported by the Educational Communications Program of the Department of Communications.

---

[14] This work took place in the late 1970s, before practical time-domain interpolation was even conceivable.

[15] The development of high-speed digital video signal processing has made these early ideas manageable. In fact, the incorporation of the underlying digital signal processing instructions into common CPU's (the MMX instruction set on the Pentium chip) has made video conferencing, literally, a machine language instruction.

In the Fall of 1974, the research program in the Wired City Laboratory began to focus on what became to be called the Educational Communications Project (ECP). The research continued to be funded by Communications Canada, specifically by the Educational Technology Branch, with Dr. J. de Mercado as its Director General. From the Wired City Laboratory point of view, the application of enhanced multimedia communications in education and collaborative research had always been a cornerstone of its philosophy. Thus, to apply this technology in an educational environment was a natural progression.

The first stage of the ECP was to experiment with audio-video communication systems for educational purposes within the existing facilities of the Carleton University Wired City Laboratory; that is, within the C. J. Mackenzie Building. The emphasis was on developing the physical technological elements and developing and evaluating teaching and learning applications for them.

The second phase was seen as a realization of the Wired Scientific City. That is, it was to be an extension of the facility into the Carleton University campus and into the Ottawa community. Technical resources such as the Wired City Laboratory, the Carleton University Television production and broadcasting facilities, the Ottawa cablevision networks, Bell Canada video conferencing facilities, Communications Canada, and other institutions in Ottawa were mentioned as possible components of a future educational communications network. The third phase of the ECP was to be an extension to an inter-university service, specifically curriculum sharing between Carleton University and Stanford University via satellite communications.

The experiments in Phase 1 started with a specially equipped lecture theatre with a seating capacity of 120, connected to the four interactive teleconferencing nodes of the Wired City Laboratory. Two of the monitors were located at the front of the room and two more about half-way towards the back, both pairs at the side of the room. A fifth monitor was located in the lecturer's console. The console was equipped with an overhead TV camera focused on the surface of the lecturer's console, providing a televised image of any graphical or pictorial information as well as objects placed in its field of view. The lecturer could select the field of view between $3'' \times 4''$ and $12'' \times 15''$. The latest data transmission systems were used: the university computer time-sharing system could be accessed through an acoustic telephone coupler at 300 bit per second, or the Systems Engineering computer could be accessed over a direct line at 2400 bits per second! Using a video switch, the lecturer could select the computer display, the overhead camera, or a superposition of the two. Any object could be displayed; however, the normal mode of operation was to display a small writing pad on which the lecturer wrote with a felt-tip pen, providing every student with exactly the same view of the written material that the instructor had. Computer output, converted to a television format, could be displayed; and superimposed or otherwise mixed with the live display. Of course, videotapes could be played, and the lecture could be recorded, or transmitted to a remote classroom. A video memory, capable of storing 1000 frames of broadcast quality video, was an integral part of the facility. The frames could be retrieved on a random-access basis by a touch-tone keypad.

In the classroom, the "document view" idea was used to display a $5''$ by $7''$ pad, on which the instructor wrote with a black felt-tip pen, in lieu of using the blackboard. The image was displayed on large monitors hung from pillars at the side of the classroom. This technique creates a unique environment, wherein the student is in precisely the same relationship to the written communication as the lecturer or tutor is. In some classroom instances, computer output text was converted in a graphics generator to a TV signal that was mixed with the document image — allowing the instructor to 'write' on the computer output — a multimedia display! e reaction to teaching using video as an overhead projector was assessed, in a series of courses, with the use of a list of polar adjectives. The results were unambiguously positive.[16]

The Télé-Prof Project, a major experiment in distance education, was conducted in support of the bilingual requirements of the Canadian Armed Forces. The Télé-Prof Project was carried out between College Militaire Royal (CMR), located in St. Jean, Quebec and the Royal Military College (RMC) in Kingston, Ontario during May 1975. The project was "a joint Department of Communications and Department of Defense project for the development of a capability to provide an interchange of courses and lectures between the Canadian Military Colleges by remote teaching methods using telecommunication interconnections" (Guild *et al.* 1975b). The objective of the trial was to investigate the use of multimode communications to provide equal access to courses delivered in French at CMR to students at RMC. A project was set up to determine the suitability of various telecommunications modes for use in remote teaching and to come up with an optimal combination to provide a system, and to evaluate its effectiveness.

The proposed system included a variety of communications equipment, including:

- a direct data and voice line between RMC and CMR;
- dial-up connections for voice and data;
- a government telephone network connection for voice and data;
- a Bell audio conference terminal;
- an experimental Bell-Northern "Daisy" voice-switched conference terminal;
- two different slow-scan television systems;
- an RCA slow-scan TV system using a silicon storage tube for data storage, used in a two-way link; and
- a Colorado Video Incorporated system using a rotating magnetic disk for storage, used in a one-way (CMR → RMC) mode;
- an alphanumeric video text generator/storage/display facility;
- closed-circuit television equipment for the local display of audio-visual support material and the output of the slow-scan TV;
- digital facsimile; and
- touch-tone key pads for student inputs and feedback.

The system was thoroughly examined in the Wired City Laboratory after which field trials were held and the technological and pedagogical effectiveness assessed. Trials of the system were conducted between the two colleges. In one group of trials tele-teaching was coupled with the simultaneous occurrence of a face-to-face lecture: the instructor lecturing

---

[16] According to the report on the experiment, "Rao's Canonical Factoring Method produced one potent factor accounting to 62% of the variance." Adjectives correlated over 0.7 with this factor were: cooperative, pleasant, satisfactory, agreeable, easy, wise, successful, sensitive, comfortable, understandable, inspiring, and (at 0.872) good.

to both local and remote students at the same time. The other group of trials involved an instructor at CMR with the students at RMC.

A variety of different configurations were evaluated over a one-week trial period. Three telephone lines were used, with audio always connected and the other equipment switched in as appropriate. It took the first day to introduce the instructors and the students to the equipment. Each of the subsequent lectures a single mode was used, while on the last day all technologies were connected with an operator in place to accomplish switching as needed.

The technical components of the tele-teaching connection were assessed on the basis of inflexibility in use, preparation time for effective use; delivery time between terminals; cost factor; and operational complexity. The assessment led to the recommendation that in any future tele-teaching system should comprise a good quality audio link, a combination of a writing tablet with video display and the alphanumeric data storage/retrieval system; and the digital (key-pad) feedback system.

The results of the experiment were mixed. The student attitudes towards this teaching method were found to be mildly positive: some were distinctly opposed to this type of educational innovation, while others accepted it. The conclusions of the brief trial were that teachers would have to learn to use the modality to advantage, to be aware of the "remote" students, and to use the focusing effect found in mediated communications to advantage. All of the students liked the anonymity of the digital feedback sub-system.

While evaluation of the technical modes used was the most salient feature of the trial, it revealed more about what was unknown about tele-teaching in this multimedia environment than what was known. In particular it identified the scope of uncertainties that affect teaching effectiveness in general, and which are still inherent in tele-teaching systems today.

The major experiment of the Wired City Simulation Laboratory, and its crowning achievement was the Carleton-Stanford Curriculum Sharing Project (Coll *et al.* 1974b; Down *et al.* 1976; Hofman & George 1977; Hudson *et al.* 1975; Lumb & Sites 1974). This was a joint U.S.-Canadian experiment utilizing the CTS (Communications Technology Satellite). The project was a cooperative effort involving Carleton University, the Department of Communications, NASA Ames Research Center and Stanford University. In essence, a direct two-way link was created between Carleton University and Stanford University via CTS. The satellite ground terminal at Carleton was on the roof of the C. J. Mackenzie Engineering Building. The satellite link was terminated in Moffat Field, California at the NASA Ames Research Center. The connection from Ames to Stanford was a terrestrial microwave connection into Stanford's Instructional Television System, which provided regular instructional TV to the San Francisco Bay area (television out — audio feedback). The communications system contained some very advanced equipment: the video was compressed using adaptive three dimensional Hadamard Transform Coding (Heller 1974). The data link used a 10 Mbps digital modem with convolutional error correcting coding using the Viterbi algorithm.[17] The link operated for some two hours a day, five days a week, for about nine months. Carleton students were able to register

---

[17] The success of the Stanford-Carleton Curriculum Sharing Project was aided by personal connections between the Carleton participants and a number of the U.S. contributors. The video compressor was designed at Ames and fabricated by Linkabit — a company founded by Irwin Jacobs, an MIT classmate of George and Coll. Andy Viterbi was a Vice-President at Linkabit.

for credit in Stanford courses and vice-versa. Stanford offerings included a graduate course in Research Management given by Hans Mark, Director of NASA Ames Research Center (and subsequently Associate Secretary of Defense), and a regular undergraduate computer science course whose instructor was Donald Knuth, a renowned Stanford professor often called "the Father of Computer Science." Carleton offered graduate courses in digital system design.

The Wind Up

The Carleton University Wired City Simulation Laboratory and the Educational Communications Program wound down towards 1978 or so. There were several reasons. For example, the effort involved in fund raising became an overwhelming burden. One problem was that many in the research community saw the activities as "mere technology" and not "academic research"; thus funding from the granting agencies was difficult to obtain. This attitude has persisted into the present time, even with the growth of applications of enhanced broadband multimedia networks, exemplified by the Internet and World Wide Web. Another major reason was that the principal investigators moved on to other domains where their interests in applications research could be more effectively pursued. For example, D. A. George became the Director of Instructional Development and utilized his expertise to support the growth of Carleton's Instructional Television Program. The author became Chair of the Department of Systems Engineering and Computer Science and applied his Wired City experience in consulting. He was the architect of the Atmospheric Environment Service's National Communication System that combined satellite communications and emerging data networks to facilitate the Canadian weather service multimedia forecasting system (Coll 1981). He was also involved in the conceptual design of the communications system of the North American Advanced Train Control System (Coll *et al.* 1990).

At about the time the Wired City Laboratory was winding down, a new technology, called teletext or videotext, emerged. Videotext allowed the transmission of coded digital information as part of the normal television signal to a decoder which could display the decoded information on the TV screen. The Canadian effort was called Telidon.[18] The Telidon project was Canada's response to the European systems: Prestel, Antiope and others.

Carleton University was involved with Telidon in a number of ways. With his Wired City experience with television technology and his understanding of the non-entertainment uses and their social impact, the author served on both technical and educational committees, and carried out associated research (Coll *et al.* 1981). Several former students were involved in Telidon; for example, the designer of the information coding system was a Carleton graduate student, and the original picture encoding instructions were part of his thesis (O'Brien 1975).

---

[18] A general description of Telidon may be found at http://www.friendsofcrc.ca/Telidon/Telidon.html.

Telidon was adopted as Canada's flagship information technology project, circa 1978. It exemplified the role that telecommunications could play in Canadian development, so eloquently stated in Instant World and subsequent government policy statements.

In Telidon, images were defined by Picture Description Instructions (PDI's). The PDI's were coded in a 7-bit teletype-compatible character format, decoded and displayed on a conventional raster-scanned TV set. In the teletext version, the PDI's were transmitted in the television signal's Video Blanking Interval (VBI). The PDI's were eventually enshrined as the North American Presentation Level Protocol (NAPLS).

By August 1981 the Government had created The Telidon Industry Stimulation Program, to provide 6,000 terminals to businesses. AT&T and CBS had adopted Telidon standards. 1,500 delegates attended Videotex '81 in Toronto, where there were 90 speeches in electronic publishing and 40 exhibits, and microprocessor-based terminals were exhibited. There were committees set up for every conceivable aspect of the project — for technology, social impact, educational applications and so on. The impact of this new information technology on society was a major concern during the early 1980s, and an industrial sector was being created.

The Telidon project was a mixed success for a number of reasons. The major reason for its demise was that the strategies for developing and marketing new information technology products just weren't there; nor were the resources adequate. Telidon was invented and developed by a small team of brilliant researchers at the Communications Research Centre. The team became involved in all aspects of the project: managing development contracts, standards setting, trials, evaluation, social impact, and marketing. As a result, development of the fundamental technology was not pursued with the intensity that the team was capable of. Telidon was developed at a time when the personal computer with its visual interface and computer graphics capability, computer graphics workstations and accompanying standards, data communication standards, and voiceband modems were all being developed. Telidon ignored these developments, in pursuit of a policy of establishing the Telidon standards as the mechanism to ensure — *a priori* — the acceptance of Telidon technology. The Telidon project starved as a result of this basic decision to devote almost all of the energy to establishment of a "safe" market environment through world-wide adoption of the Telidon videotex standard. The technology never really worked reliably — the VBI data modulation strained the capacity of the TV channel; a broadcast experiment at a Public Broadcasting station in Washington, D.C. required on-the-scene attention from a Ph.D. engineer troubleshooter; and so on. As well, the small team did not have the resources to keep up with technological progress: Telidon was not compatible with basic data communications, television, or computer graphics standards. A compiler or even an assembler was never developed to simplify page creation — all picture coding was in PDI "machine language." In addition, the personal computer was not seized upon as the basic implementation technology or "platform as we would call it today."

In spite of these failings, Telidon provided a glimpse of the future that would emerge through the Internet connection of personal computers and World Wide Web browsers. Eventually, Telidon itself was developed to a high state of performance. In the 1990s, Norpak (the originally designated contractor for development and production of Telidon equipment) had developed superb teletext and videotex equipment. They finally achieved the integration of high speed data communication and high quality television signals that was so lacking in the original Telidon development; but the world moved on.

The Wired City experiences and subsequent research with the Canadian cable television industry (Coll & Chrichlow 1980; Coll & Hancock 1980) enabled the author to predict that cable television networks would be used for the distribution of broadband services in the urban areas (Coll & Hancock 1985).

Starting in 1993, the author's TelePresence Laboratory[19] was the Carleton University connection to OCRINET, a 45 Mbps ATM optical fibre network connecting the major research establishments in Ottawa. OCRINET was created to establish video-based communications for distance educational and related purposes; and was administered by the Ottawa Carleton Research Institute (OCRI), now known as the Ottawa Centre for Research and Innovation. OCRI was established in 1983 to facilitate academic, industrial and governmental collaboration. OCRInet was a project of the Ottawa Carleton Research Institute (OCRI) initiated by Newbridge (through the personal initiative of Terry Matthews) and Bell Canada. Through OCRINET, Carleton, along with the University of Ottawa and Algonquin College, could be connected to the Communications Research Centre, Bell-Northern Research, Telesat, the National Research Council, and OCRI through broadband ATM circuits — designed for multimedia traffic. The similarity to the topology of the original Wired Scientific City network of 1971 was startling.

From 1994 to 1999 the author was the principal investigator in the TelePresence project of the TeleLearning Network of Centres of Excellence (TL-NCE). This research project was based on the use of OCRINET. The major research activity was the design and control of a teleteaching classroom. The facilities were used to "close the loop" on one aspect of distance education. D. A. George, after his term as Dean of Engineering expired in 1975, had become the Director of both Instructional Aids and Media Services, specifically to promote and develop mediated communications as an educational tool. Thus, when the Wired City Laboratory was terminated, much of the equipment was used to augment the Carleton University Instructional television (ITV) program. The Carleton model for ITV was the broadcast of live lectures on cable television; i.e. to provide viewers with the opportunity to attend lectures. This mode is still in place, and roughly 20% of all undergraduate course enrollments are in "video" sections. The TelePresence Laboratory with its broadband connections to the Internet was used to broadcast four ITV courses in the summer of 1997 (Coll *et al.* 1997; Pychyl 1997).

Experience with the Wired City and subsequent activities led to a study to analyze, assess, and forecast future network trends as they affect TeleLearning and TeleTeaching (Coll 2000). The report proposed a way in which the TeleLearning National Centre of Excellence could contribute to the development of a conceptual framework for the TeleLearning environment consisting of an architecture for a TeleLearning environment, comprising all of the means necessary and sufficient for the creation, delivery and support of TeleLearning and TeleTeaching systems. The dominant message of the report was that current trends in network development will inevitably provide network services that will allow the creation of compete, interactive, interoperable, distance education systems and

---

[19] TeleLearning Research Laboratory, http://www.sce.carleton.ca/faculty/coll/research.shtml.

their introduction into the learning process — providing an alternative to the focus on server-based self-learning software packages accessed through the WWW. The conclusion of the report was that the TL-NCE should aim its research towards a horizon of a richer, more useable, universal, distributed, intelligent, broadband, multimedia, communications environment, i.e. to make full use of the ability to actually communicate in real time with students to include teachers in the distance educational loop.

Conclusions

It appeared for a while that the community network proposed in The Wired Scientific City (Bowen *et al.* 1971) would be realized with OCRINET. This did not occur, even though it had the topology and characteristics required. In any event, the Wired City Simulation Laboratory served as the model for a number of subsequent attempts to "wire" the Ottawa region. These include the OCRI/Ottawa Valley Information Technology Alliance (OVITA) project established in 1996 (Markham 1996) and the Ottawa Community Network proposed in 1997 (Stewart 1977), as well as the more recent Smart Capital venture (Wilker & Sage 2002).

The major legacy of the Wired City Simulation Laboratory was the clear understanding that video-based communications was an effective medium for a variety of human interactions. Every researcher and student, who was associated with the Laboratory from 1971 to 1978, became aware of the exciting potential of the rapidly developing multimedia, broadband telecommunications technology and computer-controlled and enabled information processing (Coll 1994, 1997, 1998). Perhaps more importantly, they were also acutely aware of the immense difficulties of designing and implementing such complex systems.

As well, it has been a remarkable point from which to observe subsequent developments. In the same way that the possible uses of the telephone and its impact on society were forecast with eerie precision and foresight as early as 1910 (Casson 1910), the "new" applications of communication networks we see introduced almost daily were anticipated in one way or another in the Wired City Laboratory.

As Karr said,[20] "The more things change, the more they remain the same [Plus ça change, plus c'est la même chose].

References

Binder, M. (2003). *Think innovation — Canada in the network age: Building an infrastructure for innovation and inclusion.* Presentation to Bell University Labs Conference, Toronto, Ontario, Canada. November 20, http://broadband.gc.ca/pub/media/presentations/binder/index.html and http://smartcommunities.ic.gc.ca/binder/PTC-JUNE02.pdf.

Bowen, B. A., Coll, D. C., & George, D. A. (1971). *The wired scientific city.* Research Contract OIG. R.36100-1-0096. Department of Communications, November.

Casson, H. D. (1910). *The history of the telephone.* http://sailor.gutenberg.org/by-title/xx710.html.

---

[20] http://www.bartleby.com/66/88/32088.html.

Coll, D. C. (URL1) http://www.sce.carleton.ca/courses/96502/references/webrefs.htm.

Coll, D. C. (1969). Personal communication 1969.

Coll, D. C. (1973). *The wired city simulation laboratory: Phase 1*. DOC Research Contract Report, May.

Coll, D. C. (1980). *Technological inspirations for new services (frame memories)*. Presentation at the 23rd Annual Convention of the Canadian Cable Television Association. Vancouver, May, 1980.

Coll, D. C. (1981). *A future communication system for the Canadian atmospheric environment services*. March 1981. A SPAR/MDA/AES/P. A. Lapp Ltd. Report.

Coll, D. C. (1994). Commentary: How we can pick up speed on the information highway. *Equinox*, *xiii:2*(74), 13.

Coll, D. C. (1997). *Multimedia communications: Through the critical threshold*. Post2000, The Financial Post, October, 11.

Coll, D. C. (1998). Multimedia communications: Reaching a critical threshold. *Canadian Journal of Electrical and Computer Engineering*, 1–2.

Coll, D. C. (2000). *Trends in telecommunications and their impact on telelearning*. A report submitted to the telelearning network of centres of excellence, March 21. http://www.sce.carleton.ca/faculty/coll/TLNReportbody.htm#_Toc489784657.

Coll, D. C., & Choma, G. K. (1976). Image activity characteristics in broadcast television. *IEEE Transactions on Communications*.

Coll, D. C., & Chrichlow, G. (1980, December). *Field multiplex video teleconference system feasibility study*. Prepared for Premier Communications Ltd.

Coll, D. C., Diequez, E., & Strickland, L. H. (1981, March). *Development of guidelines for the evaluation of proposed TELIDON applications*. DOC/GTA Contract Report, DSS No.OSU81-00147.

Coll, D. C., George, D. A., Guild, P. D., & Paterson, S. A. (1975). Multidisciplinary applications of communication systems in teleconferencing and education. *IEEE Transactions on Communications*, 23(10).

Coll, D. C., George, D. A., & Strickland, L. H. (1974). *Studies in broadband interactive communications*. Proceedings of the National Telecommunications Conference, December.

Coll, D. C., George, D. A., Strickland, L. H., Paterson, S. A., Guild, P. D., & McEown, J. M. (1974, May). *The wired city laboratory: Studies in interactive broadband communications*. DOC Research Contract Report.

Coll, D. C., & Hancock, K. E. (1980). A study of the categorization of cable TV news services with particular reference to data transmission. A report prepared for Premier Communications Ltd., December.

Coll, D. C., & Hancock, K. E. (1985). A review of cable television: The urban distribution of broad-band visual signals. *Proceedings of IEEE*, 73(4), 773–788.

Coll, D. C., & Mahmoud, S. A. (1976, June). Introduction to still picture storage and retrieval in video communication systems. Presentation at the 8th Biennial Symposium on Communications. Queen's University, Kingston, Ontario.

Coll, D. C., Mohammed, L., & Shi, S. (1997, August). *MBone multicast of Carleton University instructional television courses on the Internet*. A Report for CANARIE (the Canadian Network for the Advancement of Research, Industry and Education). http://www.sce.carleton.ca/tln/ITVMBONE.htm.

Coll, D. C., & Paterson, S. A. (1975, April). *The application of communications technology to education*. Presentation at the APEO Annual Meeting, Toronto.

Coll, D. C., Sheikh, A. U. H., Ayers, R. G., & Bailey, J. H. (1990). The communications system architecture of the North American advanced train control system. *IEEE Transactions on Vehicular Technology*, 39(3), 244–255.

Collins, R. (1997). *A voice from afar: The history of telecommunications in Canada*. Toronto: McGraw-Hill Ryerson.

Dakin, J. (1974). *Telecommunications experiments in urban and regional planning.* Toronto: University of Toronto Press.

Department of Communications (1971). *Instant world: A report on telecommunications in Canada.* Ottawa: Information Canada.

Down, K. S., Sites, M. J., & Lumb, D. R. (1976). University resources sharing using the CTS. *Proceedings of the International Communications Conference.*

Fried, P. A. (1973, May). Is anyone out there paying attention? Appendix B in D. C. Coll (Ed.), *The Wired City Simulation Laboratory: Phase 1.* DOC Research Contract Report.

George D. A., & Coll, D. C. (1978, August). *Reduced frame rate television.* Presentation at the Ninth Biennial Symposium on Communications, Queen's University, Kingston, Ontario, Canada.

George, D. A., Coll, D. C., Strickland, L. H., Paterson, S. A., Guild, P. D., & McEown, J. M. (1975, May). *The wired city laboratory and educational communication project.* DOC Research Report.

George, D. A., Coll, D. C., Strickland, L. H., Paterson, S. A., & Guild, P. D. (1976, June). *Educational communications.* Presentation at the 2nd Canadian Conference on Instructional Technology, Quebec City, Quebec, Canada.

Government of Canada (2003). *Connecting Canadians.* http://www.connect.gc.ca/en/800-e.asp.

Guild, P. D., George, D. A., & Coll, D. C. (1975, June). *The Carleton university educational communications project.* Presentation at the University of Wisconsin Conference on University Applications of Satellite/Cable Technolog, Madison, Wisconsin, USA.

Guild, P. D., Henri, F., & Paterson, S. A. (1975, August). *Télé-Prof: Assessment of a remote teaching trial.* A Report to the Educational Technology Program, Department of Communications.

Heller, J. A. (1974). *A real time Hadamard transform video compression system using frame-to-frame differencing.* Records of National Telecommunications Conference.

Hewlett-Packard Laboratories (1990). *In memoriam: J. C. R. Licklider 1915–1990.* HP Labs Technical Reports, SRC-RR-61, August 7. http://www.hpl.hp.com/techreports/Compaq-DEC/SRC-RR-61.html.

Hill, C., & Hill, H. (url1). *Transatlantic cable communications: The original information highway.* Nova Scotia, Canada. http://collections.ic.gc.ca/canso/.

Hofman, L. B., & George, D. A. (1977). *Curriculum sharing by digital TV using Hermes.* Proceedings of the 20th Symposium of the Royal Society of Canada.

Hudson, H. D., Lumb, D. R., & Guild, P. D. (1975, July). *College curriculum sharing via CTS.* Presentation at the AIAA Conference on Communication Satellites, Denver, Colorado, USA.

Information Highway Advisory Council (1995). *The challenge of the information highway: Final report.* Ottawa, Canada: Government of Canada. [http://e-com.ic.gc.ca/english/strat/doc/september1995.pdf].

Information Highway Advisory Council (1997). *Preparing Canada for a digital world.* Ottawa, Canada: Government of Canada, September. [http://e-com.ic.gc.ca/english/strat/doc/september1997.pdf].

Johnson, D. (2000, October). *The new national dream: Networking the nation for broadband access.* http://ebusinessroundtable.ca/documents/johnston/sld001.htm.

Lumb, D. R., & Sites, M. J. (1974). *CTS digital video college curriculum-sharing experiment.* Proceedings of the National Telecommunications Conference.

Markham, J. (1996, 20 September). *The Ottawa Valley and the information technology and telecommunications industry.* http://www.bcctc.ca/conn18-4/ottawa.html.

McDonald, J. W. A. (1972). *Writing tablets for man-man telecommunications.* M. Eng. Thesis, Department of Systems and Computer Engineering, Carleton University, Ottawa, Ontario, Canada.

McKillican, R. W. (1973, May). A feasibility study for the design of short path video transmission systems in an urban environment. Appendix A in D. C. Coll (Ed.), *The Wired City Simulation Laboratory: Phase 1.* DOC Research Contract Report.

National Broadband Task Force (2000, 16 October). *Government of Canada announces commitment to bringing high-speed broadband internet services to all Canadian communities.* http://www.ic.gc.ca/cmb/welcomeic.nsf/0/85256779007b79ee8525697a00468c17?OpenDocument.

National Broadband Task Force (2001, 18 June). *Report of the national broadband task force: Telecom Update.* http://www.angustel.ca/update/up288.html#TASK%20FORCE%20RECOMMENDS%20CANADA-WIDE%20BROADBAND%20BY%202004.

O'Brien, C. D. (1975). *IMAGE — A language for the interactive manipulation of a graphics environment.* M. Eng. Thesis, Department of Systems and Computer Engineering, Carleton University, Ottawa, Ontario, Canada.

Potvin, L. (1976). *A microprogrammed communication interface unit.* M. Eng. Thesis, Department of Systems and Computer Engineering, Carleton University, Ottawa, Ontario, Canada.

Pychyl, T. (1997). *Instructional television (ITV): MBone broadcasting project.* http://www.carleton.ca/~tpychyl/mbone/.

RLE (1991). *RLE history: The radiation laboratory.* http://rleweb.mit.edu/radlab/radlab.htm, http://rleweb.mit.edu/Publications/currents/4-2cov.htm.

Roddick, P. A. (1980). *The frame repetition approach to redundancy reduction in television.* M. Eng. Thesis, Department of Systems and Computer Engineering, Carleton University, Ottawa, Ontario, Canada.

Stewart, W. (1977, 13 May). *The Ottawa community network.* http://www.city.ottawa.on.ca/calendar/ottawa/archives/rmoc/Corporate_Services_and_Economic_Development/20May97/Stewart.pdf.

Teracom Training Institute (url1). *Telecommunications in Canada: A reference source for the telecommunications community.* http://www.telecommunications.ca/index.htm.

The Advisory Committee on a Telecommunications Strategy for the Province of Ontario (1992, August). *Telecommunications: Enabling Ontario's future.* Report to the Minister of Culture and Communications. Toronto: The Queen's Printer for Ontario.

Vision 2000 Inc. (2000). *Vision 2000: Networking the global village.*

Wilker, P., & Sage, C. (2002). *The smart capital vision.* http://www.smartcapital.ca/aboutsmartcapital/smartcapital_overview.pdf.

Part II

Silicon Valley North: Its Recent Past, Current State, and Future

Chapter 4

Firm Demographics in Silicon Valley North

François Brouard, Tyler Chamberlin, Jérôme Doutriaux
and John de la Mothe

Abstract

Based on Ottawa Centre for Research and Innovation (OCRI) database, this chapter analyzes clusters of firms in Silicon Valley North (SVN) and compares them with other clusters in other Silicon areas like Oxfordshire, England, and Silicon Valley, USA. Specifically, the purpose of the chapter is to present some demographics data on firms in Silicon Valley North. Firms are divided into five clusters: telecommunications, photonics, microelectronics, software, and life sciences.

1. Introduction

Innovation is a key factor in the economic development of regions and countries. Reich (1991, 2003) insists on the competitive pressure for continuous innovation. The Government of Canada (2001, 2002) acknowledges the importance of innovation in the information-economy era and has developed an innovation strategy to attempt to reach a new level of innovation in this country.

Papadopoulos (1997) recognized the shift from a "local" economic development perspective to a "world city" point of view, where cities across the globe compete against each other to develop and prosper. A world city may be a "technology centre" if the city has a strong presence in the technologically intensive sectors of the knowledge-based economy. A quality economic foundation is also a must. The economic foundations consist of: the human resources, technology, financial capital, physical infrastructure, business climate and quality of life in a region (ICF Consulting 2000).

In a study for the City of Ottawa, ICF Consulting (2003b) proposes a framework for strategic decision making with respect to innovation for the City and the various stake-holders in the regions clusters. The innovation system could be divided into three strategic challenges: (1) the discovery of new knowledge by harnessing basic and applied science assets; (2) the development of that knowledge into new products and services by promoting a commercialization culture; and (3) the deployment of those products and services through new or expanded businesses by accelerating incubation and enabling the maturation and survival of firms.

Because of Ottawa's status as the nation's capital and the resulting concentration of national research centres, Ottawa's technology institutions are considered strong (ICF Consulting 2003a). We add to this the existence of two research-intensive universities and provincial research centres and programs. However, some problems are seen regarding the size of firms in Ottawa. To address these problems, Silicon Valley North (SVN) has created the Ottawa-Gatineau Commercialization Task Force (CTF) (Re$earch Money 2003). The objective of the CTF is to examine the apparent inability of Silicon Valley North firms to develop past the $5 million in annual sales level.

The CTF includes representatives from a variety of organizations such as the Canadian Advanced Technology Alliance, the City of Ottawa, the City of Gatineau, the Greater Ottawa Chamber of Commerce, the National Capital Institute of Telecommunications, the National Research Council, OrbitIQ, the Ottawa Centre for Research and Innovation, the Ottawa Life Sciences Council, The Ottawa Partnership, and representatives from the business schools and engineering faculties of both Carleton University and the University of Ottawa.

To help the CTF in this task of validating the anecdotal evidence that many of the members had contributed on the possible lack of commercialization in the region, a research team from both the local business schools (Carleton University's Eric Sprott School of Business and University of Ottawa's School of Management) was created. The first two phases of our research were: (1) to look at the distribution of firms based on size in the region; and (2) to compare Silicon Valley North to other technology regions. This study is a result of the collaboration between the two schools on behalf of the CTF.

The purpose of this chapter is to present some demographics data and analysis on firms in Silicon Valley North (SVN). Our research here focuses on five technologically intensive clusters (telecommunications, photonics, microelectronics, software, life sciences) paralleling previous studies of the broader technology sector in the city.

This chapter is organized as follows: first, this introduction has briefly presented some of the important contextual elements of the study. Then, Section 2 provides information regarding data used and definition of clusters. Section 3 presents data for the region as a whole and discusses each cluster. Section 4 compares Silicon Valley North data with other technology centers in the world. Finally, some concluding remarks are presented in Section 5.

2. Methodology and Data

2.1. Description of the OCRI Database

The Ottawa Centre for Research and Innovation (OCRI) is a partnership organization. The mission of OCRI is to be "the rallying point for business, education and government to advance Ottawa's globally competitive knowledge-based economy. With and through its members and partners, OCRI brings people, ideas and resources together — through connectivity — to build wealth and quality of life in Ottawa" (OCRI 2003; see also the chapters by Ghent Mallett and by O'Sullivan this volume).

As part of its mission, OCRI has developed and managed a database of technology firms in the Ottawa area. The database provides up-to-date listings of both public organizations and private firms in Ottawa's technology sector. The database is shared with the City of Ottawa (Ottawa Region 2003) and with the Ottawa Business Journal (2003). OCRI and the Ottawa Business Journal publish, on an annual basis The Ottawa Technology Industry Guide based on the information in this database. The data used in this study comes from the OCRI database updated as of June 2003.

2.2. Definition of Clusters

Silicon Valley North is a global technology centre, having strengths in a number of sectors. We have investigated five technologically intensive clusters in this study including: telecommunications, photonics, microelectronics, software, and life sciences (ICF Consulting 2000). In addition to these technology-intensive sectors, Silicon Valley North firms are supported by a strong professional services cluster. As Canada's capital, Ottawa has a dynamic tourism sector and is the seat of the federal parliament. The federal government, as a result, is the largest local employer with more than 92,000 employees in mid-2002 working in a variety of departments, agencies and institutions.

The telecommunications cluster in this study is defined as those firms engaged in, or linked to, the production of telecommunications equipment. It includes networking equipment, transmission systems, satellite/microwave equipment, communication interface devices, and similar technologies (ICF Consulting 2000). The telecommunications cluster has a strong research & development (R&D) emphasis and covers a wide range of technical activities from the assembly of basic telephone handsets to highly sophisticated digital switches.

Photonics could be defined as the field of science and engineering encompassing the physical phenomena and technologies associated with the generation, transmission, manipulation, detection, and utilization of light (OPC 2003). The photonics cluster includes an array of technologies related to the commercial application of light, including fibre optics, lasers, and optoelectronics, imaging, optical processing of information, and related applications (ICF Consulting 2000).

The microelectronics industry can be divided between semiconductor and electronic component design, system design, component manufacturing, component testing and design tools (CMC 2003). Ottawa's microelectronics cluster includes firms in all those industry groupings.

The software industry can be defined as an industry where firms primarily develop, sell, or support software products/systems, and Internet products/systems. Ottawa's software cluster encompasses an array of packaged software, software and information technology (IT) services, communications, Internet security, and remote sensing.

The life sciences industry can be divided between biotechnology, medical devices, pharmaceuticals, telehealth, health industries and health services. Ottawa's Life sciences cluster includes medical devices, biotechnology, stem cells research, medical diagnostic equipment, therapeutic equipment, implants/prostheses, and a range of electromedical applications (ICF Consulting 2000; OLSC 2003).

2.3. Challenges of the OCRI data

The OCRI database poses some challenges for the researchers. First, it is important to note that the purpose of the database is not academic research. An example of the challenges here includes the existence of incomplete data for some firms. Even if the objective of the researchers is to look at the distribution of firms based on size in the region, the database includes only the number of employees and the number of local employees. There are a very limited number of firms with revenue information. Secondly, it is up to the firms being surveyed to self-identify themselves for inclusion in one or more clusters. No specific or technical definition of the clusters is presented during the telephone interviews used to collect the data. Therefore, some firms are identified in multiple clusters (this is especially true for the largest firms in the region). This means that the data that is presented below for each of the individual clusters must be viewed in the context of the whole region. Totalling the number of firms identified within each of the clusters will result in double counting as some firms have identified themselves within multiple clusters. Finally, the data is updated on an on-going basis; hence there are no historical figures to compare to.

3. Silicon Valley North: History and Present Context

3.1. Canadian Silicon Valley: A High-Tech Region in the Making

The early development of Ottawa, or Bytown as it was known in the early 1800's, was related to the timber trade and large milling operations. Selected as capital of the Province of Canada in 1857 and capital of the Dominion of Canada in 1867, its dominant economic activity evolved from the timber trade and saw milling roots in the early 1800s, into pulp and paper which were the dominant industry in the early 1900s, to public services. The federal government of Canada became the dominant employer around 1940 (The Canadian Encyclopaedia 1988: 1595). In 1970, the Ottawa metropolitan area[1] had a population of slightly over 500,000 inhabitants and 33% of its workforce worked for the federal government. Since that time, population in the area has more than doubled to about 1,100,000 inhabitants, and in 2002 18% of the workforce (78,000 persons) was working for the federal government. High-Tech employment grew rapidly over the past 25 years, from 8,200 jobs in 160 firms in 1975, to a peak of 79,000 jobs in 1,300 firms 2000. Since that time, total employment in the sector is down slightly to about 70,000 jobs, based on a wide measure of employment generated by OCRI, albeit in 1,400 firms in early 2003. In 30 years, the local culture has changed from that of a sedate government town to that of an entrepreneurial and dynamic growth-oriented region. The main sectors of technology activity include telecommunications and microelectronics (40% of local high-tech jobs in 1999, a much lower percentage in 2002), software products (20% in 1999), software services, photonics, life sciences, and defence/aerospace. Ottawa has a well-educated labour force

[1] The "Ottawa" metropolitan area includes the city of Ottawa (currently about 800,000 inhabitants, in the province of Ontario) and of Gatineau (300,000 inhabitants, in the province of Quebec; see also the chapter by Materazzi this volume).

(28.1% of the population 20 years and older have a bachelor's degree or higher university degree, the highest in Canada, with Toronto at 24.9% and Calgary at 23.1%, ranking second and third respectively; Statistics Canada 2001), and a relatively wealthy population. The average annual household income in Ottawa was $62,800 with "very wealthy households" totalling 10.9%, compared to $68,400 and 14.8% respectively for Toronto, Canada's wealthiest metropolitan area in 2001 (FP Markets, Canadian Demographics 2001; Financial Post Publications 2001).

The development of Ottawa as a technology pole can be attributed to its solid research base and the existence of one large anchor private sector firm: large federal research laboratories such as the National Research Council (NRC, created in 1916), the Communication Research Center (CRC, created in late 1940s), and a very large private research laboratory, Bell Northern Research (the research arm of Northern Telecom, now Nortel), which was developed in Ottawa in 1960 to be close to the CRC. The failure of a small subsidiary of Northern Telecom in 1971 (Microsystems International) led a few local engineers to create several high-tech start-ups which did exceptionally well, and became role models for other would be entrepreneurs (see the chapter by Ghent Mallett this volume). They started the development of what was to become a very active entrepreneurial region. The creation, in 1983, of the Ottawa-Carleton Research Institute, a pro-active consortium of business, government and universities with the objective of developing business-university linkages, contributed significantly to the evolution of the region into a significant technology pole. Starting in the mid-1980s and accelerating in the 1990s, the sale of several successful start-ups created many instant millionaires who became active angel investors and led to the development of a very active venture capital industry (see also the chapter by Madill *et al.* this volume). Venture capital investment in the region peaked at $1.2 billion in 2000 (over a third of all venture capital investments in Canada) and has retreated to about $600 million annually since (see also the chapter by Callahan *et al.* this volume).

The region has often been described as a "home grown" technology pole. Until the mid-1990s, most technology enterprises were local start-ups. Only in the mid to late 1990s did multinationals create subsidiaries in Ottawa and foreign investors started to invest locally. For many years, new firm creation in telecommunications, microelectronics, software and photonics, occurred with no formal public technology incubation infrastructure and no direct university support. The region acted as a giant virtual incubator, with independent entrepreneurs finding advice and support through local networks and with former employees of the largest private firms (Nortel & Newbridge, for example) creating record numbers of spin-offs. In the mid-1990s, CRC opened a technology incubator and NRC started to provide advice to its own scientists on commercialization issues to spin-off firms, later followed by the opening of a technology incubator (Industry Partnership Facility). And more recently (2000), InnoCentre, an independent non-profit incubator, opened an office in Ottawa. To encourage the development of a life science sector to commercialize the research done in the field at both the NRC and at the University of Ottawa, the Provincial government created, in 1992, a provincially supported science park. The Ottawa Life Sciences Council, a not-for-profit consortium involving the government, local public organizations, private firms, the University of Ottawa, and the City of Ottawa manage this park. It was hoped that the park would attract more research organizations and private firms in the domain. Ten years later, that new "life science cluster" is slowly starting to emerge, with a second multi-tenant building being built in the science park and two biotechnology incubators having just been completed in 2001.

Until the mid 1980s, the two local universities were less than pro-active in supporting the technology development of the region except as suppliers to a well trained labour force. Through OCRI and other partnerships with the private sector, and through their own research activities including their own spin-offs, they have now become pro-active partners in that development (Doutriaux 2003; see also the chapter by Armit this volume).

Local telecom activities have been hard-hit by the industry meltdown that occurred in later part of 2000. Local entrepreneurial spirit is still very high with a very high rate of creation of new technology firms in telecom, photonics, software, and life sciences. Three major challenges for Ottawa at this time are: (1) a paucity of top managerial talent and leadership to grow local firms to world class status; (2) insufficient knowledge and skills in technology marketing and sales to develop and grow new markets; and (3) encouraging local telecom-minded angel investors and venture capital firms to invest in life sciences start-ups, a sector which is expected to lead the next technology cycle (profiting in many cases from the convergence of telecom-photonics and life sciences).

It may be helpful to break the development of Ottawa's Technology region into a chronological series of stages. We have chosen to divide this between six periods/stages that distinguish Ottawa's path to development. Only in stage three we do we see the emergence of specific actions designed to support the development of a technology cluster.

3.1.1. Stage one   A high level of government R&D and government procurements led to an environment conducive to research and innovation, technology commercialization and high-tech start-ups. This occurred through: (1) unsolicited proposals for applied research and development; (2) subcontracts with the government; and (3) access to government procurements (one of the most important success factor for Canadian start-ups in the 1970s — early 1980s; Doutriaux 1991). Creating a company during this stage was also relatively simple (few regulations, easy incorporation), even in the absence of local investment capital (see also the chapter by Madill *et al.* this volume).

3.1.2. Stage two   This stage is distinguished by the growth of BNR/Northern Telecom/Nortel, a large research and manufacturing telecommunications company, which developed its research laboratories in Ottawa to be close to government and its research laboratories and acted as a large private sector anchor organization, making the region more attractive to other private-sector ventures.

3.1.3. Stage three   This period is characterized by:

- slow growth of the local telecommunication, microelectronics, and software sectors;
- "home-grown" start-ups follow the steps of solid local role models such as Mitel and Mosaid;
- creation of OCRI, a private sector-universities-government consortium intent on developing successful business-university-government partnerships, and creating occasions

for active networking activities (Monthly Technology Executive Breakfasts, monthly Zone 5 meetings (technology marketing), etc);
- development of better communication links (direct flights to major U.S. cities),
- development of high-tech support services (precision machining, precision mouldings, and so on); and
- growth of angel networks (wealthy local entrepreneurs).

3.1.4. Stage four   This period is marked by:

- international recognition and high regional growth for Ottawa;
- development of local venture capital (VC);
- entry of U.S. VC following the highly visible purchases of local start-ups by large multi-nationals;
- some very successful IPOs;
- arrival in the region of external firms such as Cisco, Compaq, and Nokia.

3.1.5. Stage five   This period is distinguished by:

- second generation VCs;
- wealthy entrepreneurs start nurturing local firms;
- creation of public and private incubators;
- high rate of start-ups;
- growing interest for medical and health sciences (partnership of universities, NRC, and hospitals).

3.1.6. Stage six (post 2000)   This period is characterized by:

- relative regional slowdown with large layoffs by the largest corporations;
- high rate of start-ups by laid-off employees;
- drop in VC investment; creation of biotech incubators; and
- health sciences and biotechnology are considered as the next technology wave.

3.2. Ottawa's Technology Firms

The largest high-technology firms currently active in SVN are listed in Table 1. In addition, the *Ottawa Business Journal* has identified 46 public firms as local firms. These stocks are traded on the Toronto Stock Exchange (TSX), the TSX Venture Exchange (TSXV), the New York Stock Exchange (NYSE), and the NASDAQ. They are listed in Table 2.

The distribution by size (number of local employees) of all high-tech firms in the region listed in the OCRI database is given in Figure 1. That distribution shows that high-tech firms in the region are predominantly small, only 33 of 1,043 firms having more than 250 local employees. We will now consider the individual technology sectors (Figure 2).

Table 1: Major players in Ottawa by cluster(s).

	Number of Local Employees	Clusters				
		TE	PH	MI	SO	LS
Nortel Networks	6,000	x	x	x		
Alcatel Canada	2,000	x	x	x		
Mitel Networks	1,500	x				
Cognos Inc.	1,300				x	
Anjura Technology Corporation	950				x	
JDS Uniphase Corporation	860		x	x		
General Dynamics Canada	815	x				
MDS Nordion	800			x		x
IBM Canada Limited	700			x		
Corel Corporation	540				x	
Zomax Canada Company	526				x	
i-STAT Canada Ltd	520					x
Canadian Bank Note Company Limited	500				x	
BreconRidge Manufacturing Solutions	400	x		x		
Cisco Systems	400		x			
CRC — Communications Research Centre	400	x				
X-Wave	350	x			x	
DEW Engineering and Development Limited	300				x	x
Zarlink Semiconductor	300			x		

Note: TE = Telecommunications; PH = Photonics; MI = Microelectronics; SO = Software; LS = Life sciences.
Source: OCRI database.

3.3. Telecommunications

Understanding what the telecommunications industry was, what it is presently, and what it is going to be both with respect to products, customers, and industrial structure, is not easy. It is equally difficult to appreciate the rate of changes that have taken place over recent years. From a situation not long ago where firms were predominantly state protected monopolies and where services changed at a fairly slow speed we have now witnessed fundamental changes take place for telecommunications firms (for both operators or carriers, as they are most often called, and manufacturers). The kinds of services that firms provide to customers and the delivery channels that are available for those services (i.e. land-line vs. wireless) have been altered, as the result of radical technological developments (i.e. the movement to optical systems).

Speciality manufacturing firms were the first to change, around the 1970s, the result of the manufacturing and carrier businesses being separated from each other and the

Table 2: Publicly traded firms in Ottawa.

3M	JDS Uniphase
Adherex Technologies	Linmor
Adobe Systems	MDS
Alcatel Canada	MetaSolv
Avalon Works	Monolithic Systems
BCE	Mosaid Technologies
Beaufield Consolidated Res.	Nortel Networks
Calian Technology	Nuvo Network Management
Canadian Bank Note	O&Y Properties
C-Com Satellite Systems	Orezone Resources
CGI Group	Patrician Diamonds
Cisco Group	PharmaGap
Cognos	Phoenix Matachewan Mines
Electronic Data Systems	Plaintree Systems
EMS Technologies	PMC-Sierra
Entrust Technologies	Prospectus Group
Environmental Management Sol.	Seprotech Systems
Gennum Corp.	Solectron Corp.
GSI Lumonics	Thermal Energy
InBusiness Solutions	Tundra Semiconductor
International Datacasting	Workstream
In-Touch Survey	World Heart
I-STAT	Zarlink Semiconductor

willingness of governments to allow international competition for the specialized products that they sold. Telecommunication carriers were far slower to change as regulations continued to protect their regional markets from competition.

The movement towards deregulation, especially in Europe, and the creation of the Internet fundamentally altered the telecommunications industry. The potential of the Internet can still only be imagined, and yet it has already changed the nature of modern day work and life. For the industry, it represented a sales opportunity of epic proportions. While the initial timelines predicted for Internet traffic growth did not prove to be correct, the question of what the ultimate potential for the communications and computing medium could be remains an important motivator for firms and individuals alike. To reflect this motivating force, we now consider an Information and Communications Industry as a whole rather than telecommunications industry as a separate industry.

Ottawa has a rich tradition in the speciality manufacturing sector of the telecommunications industry. This industrial strength is the legacy of Northern Electric's decision in the late 1950s to locate substantial research facilities in the region, which was in part made because of the existing research strength of the city at that time (see also the chapter by Ghent Mallett this volume). This is also the result of research into communications technologies that

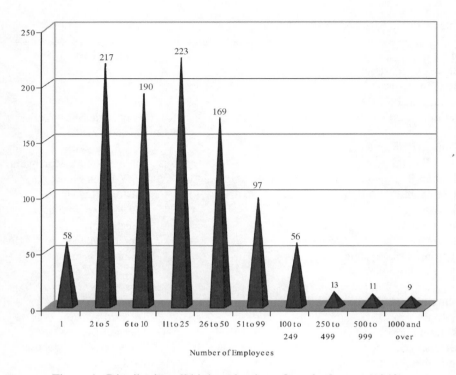

Figure 1: Distribution all high-technology firms in Ottawa (1043).

took place in Ottawa's dating back to the wartime efforts of the National Research Council (see also the chapter by Coll this volume). It was this sector that led the development of Ottawa's technological clusters. The explosive growth of Nortel and JDS Uniphase brought international attention to the region in the late 1990s. Nortel became the largest telecommunications firm in the world, while JDS Uniphase became a billion dollar (in sales) firm in record time.

The new millennium quickly brought with it major changes for the industry as a whole. Carriers, who had invested heavily in system upgrades to make the Internet a reality, became burdened with twin problems of heavy debt loads and excess capacity, both of which would come to hurt the specialty manufactures of the region. In 2000, it is estimated that internationally carriers spent $70 billion (U.S.). By 2003, this figure is estimated to have dropped to $20 billion (U.S.). The Ottawa-based telecommunications firms who counted international carriers as their most important customers did all they could to react to this almost unbelievable decline in customer sales, laying off thousands of workers and shutting down facilities as quickly as possible. Internationally, Nortel reduced its workforce by 60,000 with over 10,000 of those cuts taking place in Ottawa. This reduction was similar to those made internationally at Ericsson (54,000 world-wide) and Alcatel (60,000 world-wide), cuts that were very costly. The telecommunications industry in Ottawa is now fundamentally different than it was only three years ago. Total employment in all technological sectors

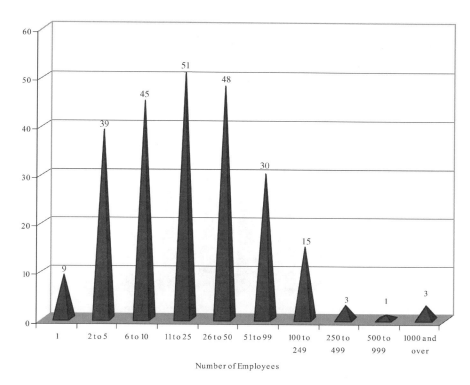

Figure 2: Distribution of telecommunications firms (total of 244 firms).

stands at approximately 51,000 in August of 2003, down by 18,000 jobs since its peak in March of 2001.

As Figure 1 has shown, Ottawa, as a technology region, is made up of mostly small firms, which is also the situation for the telecommunications sector in the region. On top of the dramatic declines in customer demands facing many of the telecommunications firms in the region, there has been an international redistribution of employment in the sector, with low-paying and relatively low-skilled manufacturing and assembly jobs being shifted from high-cost countries such as Canada and the United States to low labour cost regions such as South-East Asia (including China). JDS Uniphase, for example, has shifted almost all of it's manufacturing jobs that were previously located in Ottawa to Chinese facilities to save costs.

Even if we are to believe some of the more optimistic industry leaders, such as Ericsson CEO Carl-Henric Svanberg who has stated that "The industry is recovering" (BBC News 2003), the changes with respect to manufacturing are likely permanent and any future increases in employment in Ottawa's telecommunications sector will be dependent on the growth of highly-skilled and highly-paid jobs.

At the present time, we note that the number of firms with greater than 250 employees is only 7. These firms play an important role in the region as some of the only local customers of many of the smaller firms. Indeed, many of the smaller telecommunications firms are

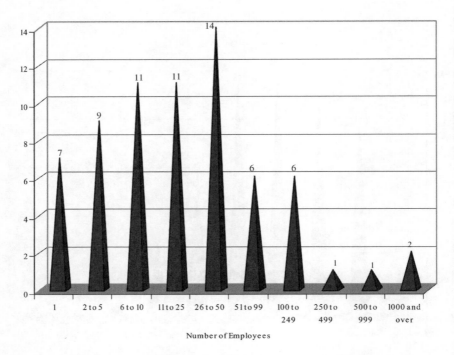

Figure 3: Distribution of photonics firms (total of 68 firms).

spin offs from the larger telecommunications firms, and some of the larger firms (Mitel, for example) are actually the result of previous rounds of downsizing and closures by Nortel (see also the chapter by Ghent Mallett this volume). There is therefore a symbiotic relationship between the large and small firms in Ottawa that was developed historically and we believe this will continue in the future. Stimulating the development of new firms, as well as the growth of existing medium-sized firms, is needed (Figure 2).

3.4. Photonics

The photonics sector, while presently the smallest sector in our study, is seen as containing great potential for future development (see Figure 3). However, this sector is not without its present challenges. First, it is important to comment that photonics is not presently a distinct sector so far as industrial classification systems are concerned. For example, there is no North American Standard Industrial Classification (NAICS) Code for photonics. The photonics sector in Ottawa has developed out of the telecommunications research and firms in the region, and the telecommunications industry continues to be important customer of photonics firms. The term "photonics," that is used to describe the sector, refers to technologies that are being utilized in the industry. As *The* Photonics Dictionary (2003) explains:

Photonics is the technology of generating and harnessing light and other forms of radiant energy whose quantum unit is the photon. The science includes light emission, transmission, deflection, amplification and detection by optical components and instruments, lasers and other light sources, fibre optics, electro-optical instrumentation, related hardware and electronics, and sophisticated systems. The range of applications of photonics extends from energy generation to detection to communications and information processing.

Viewing the photonics sector from this technological standpoint illustrates the potential of the industry. The parallel could then be made between photonics and semiconductors (a sector where Ottawa also has strengths and which will be discussed in our section on microelectronics): whereas photonics applications in telecommunications are already in practice, the potential applications of this light-based technology are only beginning to be understood with respect to the bio-technology/bio-medical sector. Semiconductors have been one of the driving technologies of Silicon Valley for decades, and while the sector has had a number of very pronounced downturns, the ubiquity of chips (as they are commonly called) has meant that new product markets have continued to be found for the base semiconductor technology. It is suggested that photonics could be a similar type of technology as semiconductors with early indications being the foray of photonics firms into aviation and aerospace sectors.

At a regional level, the Ottawa-based photonics firms have benefited greatly from venture capital investments over the past many years. These investments, often totally over $10 million per company, per round, have provided the fuel necessary for the industry to grow. The largest firms in this sector are in fact the same as in the telecommunications sector, the result of their operations in both areas.[2]

Acknowledging the potential of the sector, we must note that the current photonics applications, which are presently available for sale, are predominately telecommunications based. Fibre-optics cables have been laid across land and under water at an incredible rate, however this "long-haul" capacity greatly exceeds present demands. As a result, the long-haul telecommunications products developed by the photonics sector are suffering from poor demand. Finishing the "last mile" or within metropolitan regions remains an important step, however what is more important for the firms within Ottawa is to develop new products for other sectors.

3.5. Microelectronics

The microelectronics sector in Ottawa is also intimately connected to the telecommunications sector at least historically. The largest firms in the sector (see Figure 4) such as Nortel Networks, Alcatel, and JDS Uniphase are also the largest telecommunications and

---

[2] This might result in a double counting problem when looking at these sectors individually, but we noted in Figure 1 (total employment for the region) that each firm is counted only once. For example, to deny that Nortel Networks, Alcatel, and JDS Uniphase are in the photonics industry would be to ignore the reality of cross-sectoral business and their contribution to the region within each sector.

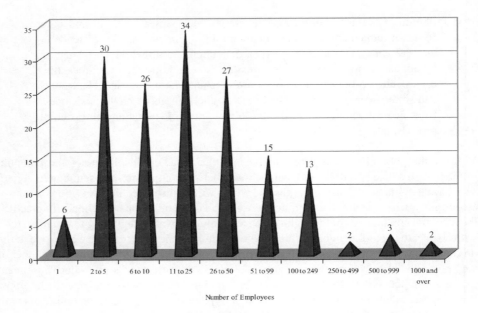

Figure 4: Distribution of microelectronics firms (total of 158 firms).

photonics firms. However, the firms that follow them (in terms of size) are an eclectic group of firms serving different sectors. MDS Nordion, for example, serves the health and life-sciences sector, while Dy-4 systems serves primarily the military and defences sectors, and IBM serves a variety of sectors including personal and industrial computing sectors.

Semiconductors, one of the product groups contained in this sector, have a particular international distribution of activities and significant employment. Ottawa-based semiconductor firms such, for example, as Tundra Semiconductors operate in a particular part of the industry, contributing design and development services to its customers. This places them in a high-valued position within the international semiconductor industry, where most employees are employed in highly paid research, design, and development positions. The largest semiconductor firms in the world, including Intel and Samsung, provide a full range of services and manufacturing. In order to be able to do this, they are required to build fabrication facilities that can cost in excess of $3 billion, which lose massive amounts of money if they are not kept at full capacity. Furthermore, the techniques for manufacturing the chips change periodically, the result of which has seen manufacturing move to Japan in the 1980s and then to other nations such as Singapore and perhaps with new manufacturing techniques, such as those used at IBM's East Fishkill facility in up-state New York, back to the United States. Competition in this part of the semiconductor industry is fierce and often influenced by government actions. As a result of these industrial realities, staying focused on niche markets may be optimal for firms in Ottawa. This does not, however, mean that they are unable to grow. Firms such as Tundra Semiconductors, Zarlink Semiconductors, and Dy-4 are excellent examples of what is possible. The market realities may limit the possibilities of growing many purely microelectronics firms into very large firms (i.e. greater than 1000 employees).

3.6. Software

Software is Ottawa's largest sector by number of firms (see Figure 5). This is a sector where the city has a small number of star firms including Corel and Cognos. The former of these firms attempted, ambitiously, to compete directly with Microsoft Corporation, an attempt that has been widely criticized but must be seen as bold, especially in the context of Canadian firms. The latter of these two firms, Cognos, is regarded by some as Canada's most successful technology company. Their success has recently provoked the likes of Microsoft to consider moving into that specialized niche of the software industry where Cognos and Corel operate.

Beyond these two firms, there are almost 500 small firms. It is interesting to note that when locally developed software firms do grow, they have often been the targets of acquisitions by larger, typically American, firms. JetForm is the classic example. It was taken-over by Adobe Systems of San Jose, California.

Microsoft Corporation, the world's largest software company employs over 54,000, including about 26,000 in Puget Sound, its Washington State Global campus. But considering

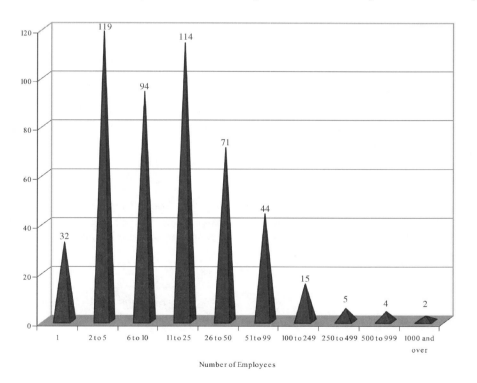

Figure 5: Distribution of software firms (total of 500 firms).

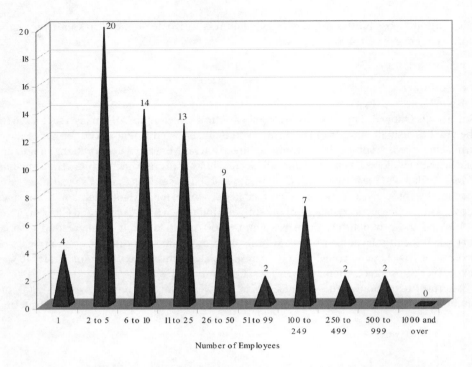

Figure 6: Distribution of life sciences firms (total 73 firms).

the dominance of this company in the many product and service markets that it serves, this total may appear small. Therefore, size in terms of employment in the software industry is less of an issue than in other industries such as telecommunications equipment manufacturing.

3.7. Life Sciences

Life sciences are a new emerging area of strength for Ottawa (see Figure 6).

This strength is spread amongst a number of different areas of life sciences, which were identified by the Ottawa Life Sciences Council and are summarized in Table 3.

Table 3: Regional research strengths in life sciences.

Ag-biotech	Biochips and Biosensors
Bioproducts and Materials	Clinical Trials
Diagnostics	Genomics and Proteomics
Information Technologies	Medical Devices and Imaging
Pharma, Biopharma and Biologics	Stem Cells and Cell Therapies

Source: Ottawa Life Science Council.

Total employment in life sciences firms is estimated at 3,700 and further 7,300 work in the field of life sciences in universities and hospitals. The private sector firms are estimated to earn $650 million a year in revenues. The strengths of the University of Ottawa's medical school (4th highest level of medical research in Canada), as well as two Biotechnology Incubation Facilities and existing government laboratories, create an excellent atmosphere for life sciences firms. This environment is needed in a sector where product development can be both very costly and time consuming (see also the chapter by Armit this volume).

MDS Nordion is the star in the local life sciences sector. The firm was created out of a series of crown corporations, including Atomic Energy of Canada Limited (AECL), to take advantage of the new medical applications of nuclear technologies that were then developed. This dates back to the mid-1940s and the firm has had roots in Ottawa ever since. Today it represents approximately 19% of the parent MDS Corporation's revenues ($1.8B in 2002).

Encouraging for the future development of the sector is the group of 7 firms with between 100 and 249 employees. Many of these firms develop and sell products into the life sciences sector. These firms include QNX Software, Fisher Scientific Limited and Med-Eng Systems. QNX develops software for a variety of industries including medical instrumentation. Fisher Scientific Limited, a Canadian subsidiary of Fisher Scientific International, provides a wide range of products including instruments and equipment for laboratories and clinics. Med-Eng develops and sells a wide range of human protective clothing including bio-chemical blast protection suits. These suits are used for a variety of purposes including police/military work. The firm has an active research program in Ottawa.

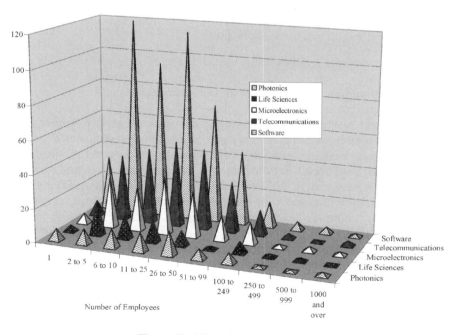

Figure 7: All technology sectors.

3.8. Intersectorial Comparisons

Figure 7 plots the size distributions of the various sectors against each other.

The size of the software industry, based on the number of employees is very distinct in this image. The maturity of the telecommunications and microelectronics sectors are also visible by their relative concentrations in larger sized firms. Finally, it is important to note that the size distributions are quite consistent across each of the sectors studied.

4. Comparison of Silicon Valley North with Other Countries and Regions

Are Silicon Valley North (SVN) firms very different from high-tech firms in other parts of the world? How do they compare in terms of size and size distribution? And, if there are significant differences, can they be attributed to easily identifiable causes? Answering those questions will provide a better idea of the positioning of SVN firms in a Canadian and an international context, information very relevant in a global world with increasing competition between world cities. As shown below, the largest Canadian firms tend to be significantly smaller than the largest firms in most developed countries, and the largest Canadian technology firms tend also to be significantly smaller than the largest technology firms in California. However, a comparison of SVN high-tech firms with Oxfordshire (UK) and with Silicon Valley (U.S.) high-tech firms shows that SVN firms tend to be larger on the average than high-tech firms in those two regions. What does that tell us about the Ottawa region and about Canadian firms in general?

4.1. Comparison with the Largest Canadian Corporations

Canadian firms tend to be relatively small by world standards. As shown in Table 4, Canada's largest firms, George Weston, ranks 269 among Fortune Magazine 500 Global firms (Fortune 2003), compared, for example, with rank 1 for Wal-Mart, the largest U.S. firm, and rank 4 for Shell, the largest Dutch/UK firm. Among Canadian firms, SVN firms tend also to be relatively small. As shown in Table 4, the largest firm with close links to Ottawa which appears on the list, Nortel Networks, is 11th in size in Canada and 470th in size in the world. Silicon Valley North firms are therefore small by world standards.

The largest firms listed in Tables 4 and 5 are either in the global retailing business (Wal-Mart), natural resources and energy (Shell, Total), manufacturing (Daimler Chrysler, Toyota), banking (Royal Bank, Scotia Bank), or are conglomerates spanning a number of sectors (George Weston, Power Corporation). Those are not the primary activities of SVN firms and therefore do not make for a fair comparison. Bombardier stands out as the largest Canadian "technology" firm, its size being driven by the nature of its business (transportation, aeronautics), again not representative of the Ottawa type of activity.

Table 4: Largest Canadian Corporations.

Company	Rank in Canada	Rank in the world	Revenues ($mUS)
George Weston	1	269	17,476.0
Bombardier	2	329	15,115.9
Royal Bank	3	337	14,771.7
Onex	4	344	14,424.1
BCE	5	390	13,020.7
Magna International	6	391	12,971.0
Alcan	7	402	12,540.0
Power Corporation	8	418	12,108.9
ScotiaBank	9	432	11,633.1
CIBC	10	464	10,835.8
Nortel Networks	11	470	10,701.0
Manulife	12	479	10,526.6

Source: Fortune (2003), Fortune Global 500.

4.2. Comparison with the Largest International Corporations

The second step is to position Canadian firms with respect to the largest firms from other countries. Table 5 provides a list of the largest firms from other countries from the 2003 edition of Fortune Magazine Global 500. The list includes the country, rank and annual revenues for each corporation.

Table 5: Largest firm from selected countries.

Company	Country	Rank in the world	Revenues ($mU.S.)
Wal-Mart	United States	1	246,525.0
Shell	Netherland /United Kingdom	4	179,631.0
Daimler Chrysler	Germany	7	141,421.1
Toyota	Japan	8	131,754.2
Total	France	14	96,944.9
Nestle	Switzerland	38	57,598.9
Assicurazioni	Italy	44	53,598.9
Samsung	Korea	59	47,605.6
China National Petroleum	China	69	44,864.4
:	:	:	:
George Weston	Canada	269	17,476.0

Source: Fortune (2003), Fortune Global 500.

Comparing Canadian firms with the largest firms from selected countries, it is possible to conclude that Canadian firms are smaller ones. The largest Canadian firm, George Weston, has annual revenues of $17,476 millions U.S. and ranks 269 in the world. It is therefore not surprising to find that Silicon Valley North firms are relatively small because this seems to be a Canadian characteristic.

4.3. *Comparison of Largest Canadian and Californian High-Tech Firms*

Canada and California have approximately the same population and well educated labour forces. Rather than comparing Canadian and SVN firms with the largest firms in the world, it may be more logical to compare Canadian high-tech firms with Californian high-tech firms due to similar sectors and state/country with similar populations.

As it appears from Table 6, Canadian technology firms tend to be much smaller than Californian technology firms. Whereas Californian firms tend to be U.S. multinationals headquartered in California, a number of Canada's largest high-tech firms are branches of foreign multinationals, some with significant presence in SVN. Only one large Canadian high-tech firm, Nortel Networks, has a significant presence in SVN.

SVN has a number of software firms who are world leaders in their market segment (Table 7). Those firms are however small (in terms of revenue) by world standards.

Table 6: Largest California and Canadian Technology Firms.

Californian Tech Firms (World-Wide Revenue)[a]		Canadian Tech Firms (World-Wide Revenue; Telecom Carriers Excluded)[b]	
Company	**Revenue ($mU.S.)**	**Company**	**Revenue ($mCDN)**
Hewlett-Packard	58,588	Bombardier	23,790
McKesson	50,006	Nortel	10,621
Intel	26,764	Celestica	8,289
Cisco Systems	18,915	General Electric Canada	3,379
Sun Microsystems	12,496	Siemens Canada	3,100
Solectron	12,276	Pratt and Witney Canada	2,600
Computer Sciences	11,426	H. P. Canada	1,800
Oracle	9,673	ATI Tech.	1,026
Science Application Int	6,104	Xerox Canada	1,519
Agilent	6,010	EDS	1,427
Apple Computer	5,742	Linamar	1,360
Amgen	5,523	Honeywell Canada	1,323

[a] Fortune 500 World largest firms 2003.
[b] ROB Top Tech 2003.

Table 7: Largest software firms in Ottawa (World Wide Revenue).

Company	Revenue ($mCDN)
Cognos	500.2
Corel	130.3
Pieta tech.	13.5
MXI	10.1
Autoskill	7.9
Watchfire	6.9
Hemera	5.7
TrueArc	5.2
FreeBalance	5.0
Taske Tech.	4.2
Data Kinetics	4.1
KOM Networks	4.1
Workstream	3.1

Source: Branham Group 2003.

4.4. High-Tech Firms in Silicon Valley North, Oxfordshire(UK) and Silicon Valley(U.S.)

We compared the distribution of SVN high-tech firms by size with that of firms in Oxford-shire and in Silicon Valley. Size is estimated by the level of local employment, a measure of a firm's contribution to local economic activity, local value added, rather than by sales level. Local employment has the advantage of being easily measured and of being publicly available whereas sales level is seldom publicly available for private firms and does not always represent fairly the firm's real contribution to economic activity (are Wal-Mart's sales really representative of its contribution to global wealth?).

Data was obtained for two high-tech regions, one in the United Kingdom (Oxfordshire) (Chadwick *et al.* 2003)[3] and one in the U.S. (Silicon Valley) (Zhang 2003). Oxfordshire, the region surrounding Oxford University in the United Kingdom, has a technology profile that is comparable to SVN: 1,400 high-tech firms[4] (including an estimated 60 university spin-offs) and 36,700 high-tech jobs in 2001, about three-quarters of the firms being home-grown, and about two-thirds having been founded since 1991 (Chadwick *et al.* 2003). In term of employment, the most important high-tech activities in Oxfordshire are R&D (8,200 jobs), software (4,300 jobs), web/internet and other computer-related services (3,650 jobs), precision instruments, medical and optical equipment (5,050 jobs), biotech,

---

[3] We are grateful to Professor Helen Lawton Smith who has facilitated our access to data prepared by the Oxford-shire Economic Observatory.

[4] In this chapter, we have to use the terms "firm" and "establishment" interchangeably in order to integrate the basic concepts used for analysis in the Oxfordshire report (Chadwick *et al.* 2003), the Silicon Valley report (Zhang 2003), and the OCRI data.

pharmaceuticals and medical diagnostics (3,250 jobs), technical consultancy and testing (3,250 jobs), computer equipment (1,850 jobs), electronic and communications equipment (1,550 jobs), telecommunications services (2,350 jobs), and motor-sports and automotive engineering/design (2,500 jobs; Chadwick *et al.* 2003). Silicon Valley, located not far from Stanford University in California, has been the role model for most high-tech regions and provides an interesting benchmark for comparative analyses. It is much larger than SVN, with 25,787 firms employing 672,825 persons in 2001 (Zhang 2003). Computers/communications is Silicon Valley's largest sector with 1,127 firms and 150,974 jobs, followed by software (4,505 firms, 114,639 jobs), innovation services (6,257 firms, 112,150 jobs), professional services (11,897 firms, 103,856 jobs), semiconductors (816 firms, 103,443 jobs), bioscience (847 firms, 51,854 jobs), and defence/aerospace and environmental with, jointly, 338 firms and 35,912 jobs (Zhang 2003).

The comparative analysis that follows includes all 25,787 Silicon Valley firms, the breakdown of the data by sector not being available. Silicon Valley data therefore include bioscience, computers/communications, defence/aerospace, environmental, semiconductor, software, professional services, and innovation services. To focus the analysis on firms operating in similar fields, only biotechnology, software, telecom services, computer equipment, electrical/electronic equipment, instruments, technical consulting and testing, other R&D, other computer services, and aerospace firms were retained for Oxforshire (a total of 1,095 firms). For SVN, telecommunication, microelectronics, photonics, software, and health sciences were kept for the comparative analysis (a total of 1,043 firms; Zhang 2003). It is clear that there is not a perfect match in terms of data for the three regions in our comparative analysis. However, the data retained for the analysis includes most high-tech firms in telecommunications, microelectronics, software, photonics, and bio/health sciences.

Data on the distribution of high-tech firms by size (number of local employees) in the three regions appears in Table 8.

That data was used to prepare three graphs (for Oxfordshire (see Figure 8), for Silicon Valley (see Figure 9), and for Ottawa (see Figure 1 presented earlier in this chapter) for a visual analysis of similarities and differences between regions.

Table 8: Comparing technology regions, all high-tech firms.

Oxfordshire (1,095 Firms)		Silicon Valley (25,787 Firms)		Ottawa (1,043 Firms)	
1–5	49.2%	0–4	62.0%	1–5	26.40%
6–10	16.7%	5–9	13.2%	6–10	18.20%
11–25	14.6%	10–19	9.2%	11–25	21.40%
26–50	8.8%	20–50	8.6%	26–50	16.20%
51–99	4.9%	51–100	3.2%	51–99	9.30%
100–249	3.3%	101–250	2.2%	100–249	5.40%
250–499	1.6%	251–500	0.8%	250–499	1.20%
500–999	0.4%	501–1,000	0.4%	500–999	1.10%
1000 and over	0.5%	1001–2,500	0.2%	1000 and over	0.9%
		Over 2,500	0.1%		

Sources: Ottawa (OCRI 2003), Silicon valley (Zhang 2003), Oxfordshire (Chadwick *et al.* 2003).

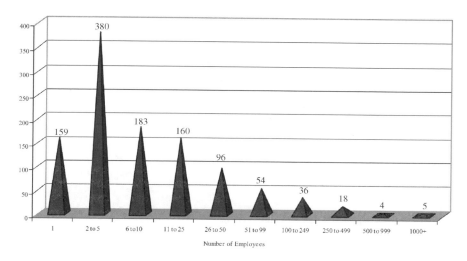

Figure 8: Distribution of firms in Oxfordshire (total 1,095).

As illustrated by the three distributions, the three regions have a high percentage of very small firms (0–4 or 5 employees) and very few firms with very large local employment, a distribution that reflects quite well the size distribution of all firms among all sectors in the British, Canadian, and American economies, which are dominated by very small and small firms. This is also representative of entrepreneurial milieus, with a high rate of firm creation

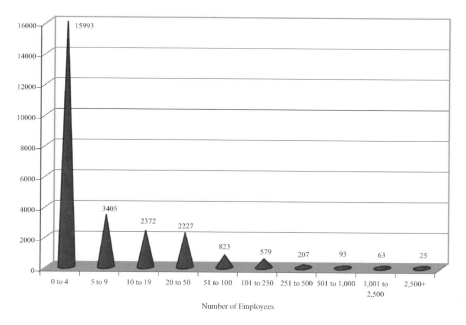

Figure 9: Distribution of firms in Silicon Valley (total 25,787).

Table 9: Comparing regions, all high-tech firms with 5 or 6 employees and greater.

Oxfordshire (624 Firms)		Silicon Valley (9,794 Firms)		Ottawa (768 Firms)	
6–10	32.9%	5–9	34.8%	6–10	24.7%
11–25	28.8%	10–19	24.2%	11–25	29.0%
26–50	17.3%	20–50	22.7%	26–50	22.0%
51–99	9.7%	51–100	8.4%	51–99	12.6%
100–249	6.5%	101–250	5.9%	100–249	7.3%
250–499	3.2%	251–500	2.1%	250–499	1.7%
500–999	0.7%	501–1,000	0.9%	500–999	1.4%
1,000 and over	0.9%	1,001 +	0.9%	1,000 and over	1.2%

Sources: Ottawa (OCRI 2003), Silicon valley (Zhang 2003), Oxfordshire (Chadwick *et al.* 2003).

and many small firms, and only a very small percentage of firms becoming large or very large. SVN has a smaller percentage of very small firms than the two other regions (26.4% of firms with 1–5 employees, compared with 49.2% in Oxfordshire (1–5 employees) and 62% in Silicon Valley (0–4 employees) and a larger percentage of mid-size and large firms. This observation could be skewed by the very large number of very small firms in Silicon Valley, either a special characteristic of that region, or a difference due to data collection. To correct for the potential bias due to the number of very small firms, another analysis was done, focusing on firms with 5 or 6 employees and more (see Table 9). We found that in SVN, 24.2% of those firms have 50 employees or more, and 2.6% have over 500 local employees, compared with 18.2% and 1.8% respectively in Silicon Valley, and 21% and 1.6% respectively in Oxfordshire.

Why does there seem to be less very small firms and more medium and large firms in SVN than in Oxfordshire and in Silicon Valley? The difference observed between SVN and the two other regions in this comparative study may be due to differences in data collection or differences in the sectors included in our study. SVN data comes from the annual Ottawa Centre for Research and Innovation survey, a self-reporting exercise, which almost certainly misses a significant number of self-employed consultants (Silicon Valley's "zero employee" firms) or very small firms. Oxfordshire data was developed from a number of public databases, firm selection and sectoral classification being based on scientific criteria (Chadwick *et al.* 2003). Silicon valleys data was based on the National Establishment Time-Series, a data set based on the Dun & Bradstreet data sets, and from the Venture One data set on venture-backed firms (Zhang 2003). As noted previously, even if the high-tech sectors included in our comparative analysis are similar, sect oral classifications and definitions were developed independently and may not be exactly similar. The differences observed may also be partly due to differences in regional environments and differences in individual firms strategies. Research on systems of innovation has clearly illustrated the relationship between national and regional characteristics and firm development. Regional culture, education, R&D activity, business and commercialization expertise, availability of informal and formal venture capital are some of the factors often considered in the analysis (Corona *et al.* 2003). In our case, the extraordinary influx of Venture Capital in SVN between 1999 and

2002 may explain in part the relatively larger size of firms in the region in comparison with the other regions. Firm size is also driven by firm strategy, a key element in the development of a business enterprise and in its growth. Individual strategies, in addition to regional factors, may also explain some of the differences observed between SVN, Silicon Valley, and Oxfordshire.

5. Conclusion: A "Glass Ceiling" for SVN High Tech Firms?

"Clusters" are a topic that have become of both analytic and political interest (recall, once again the Innovation Strategy of the Canadian federal government). The idea begins with the observation that economic growth is local. Cities and their communities drive the prosperity of nations. They attract, retain and transform foreign direct investment as well as creative, talented, people (de la Mothe & Mallory 2003). Institutions are key, such as the National Research Council of Canada. Firms are of course critical. Ottawa has a blend of at least 5 industrial clusters. Universities and colleges, such as the University of Ottawa, Carleton University, Université du Quebec en Outaouais, Cité Collégiale and Algonquin College, provide the region with highly skilled talent. Entrepreneurial financial institutions are critical, offering an industrial suave range, from love capital through equity and FDI. Moving up the later stages of capital, the roles of investment, tax and monetary policies is central, as is the opportunity to be involved with federal trade missions which open markets. The "environment" is also key. The availability of low crime rates, of cultural venues, of entertainment, of athletic facilities, including golf clubs, bike paths, running tracks, tennis clubs, and the like are essential.

Clusters — or taken down a level or two lower — communities and alliances have long been of importance to the understanding of firm behaviour and corporate strategy. In part this is because we understand that the etymological origins of the word "competition" do not emphasize conflict — as is often assumed in business schools — but instead means "to seek together." By "seeking together," a firm can effectively trade on its strengths —

Table 10: Forms of competition.

Old Competition	New Competition
Prices	*Re-Definitions of*
Costs	Core business
Productivity	Core competences
Capital and labour	Value added (from what you have to what to know and do)
Savings	Expanded value chain
Ownership	Social organization and innovation
	Notions of
	Access
	Lean production

be it in technology, capital or distribution channels — and shore-up its weaknesses, create synergies, moderate risk exposure, and access value chains. Much recent literature has begun to discuss this in terms of knowledge management (de la Mothe & Foray 2001; de la Mothe & Cimoli 2002) and in terms of networks (de la Mothe & Link 2002). Thus, the variety of forms of collaboration accurately underscores the importance of alliances as a means through which to create value and stimulate innovation. But alliances are not simply a feature of inter-firm relationships. They are not restricted to R&D consortia or to knowledge transfer relationships between private and public institutions. Indeed, increasingly alliances can help us understand the dynamics of larger innovative communities such as cities and indeed they are being used as strategies to achieve local growth. This is a far cry from the notion of industrial districts of the early 20th century and the Ricardian notion of comparative advantage. It shows even an important evolution from Porter's notion of competitive advantage towards his assessments of locations for innovation. Ottawa features many of these requisite advantages, as noted in Table 10.

This discussion of clusters, coupled with the research findings that we have presented in the chapter, provide us with some observations. Our first observation is that, it appears that SVN has proportionately less very small firms and more medium and large high-tech firms than Silicon Valley and Oxfordshire. Secondly, large Canadian high-tech firms tend to be small when compared with the largest high-tech firms in California, a State with a population similar to Canada's.

Acknowledgments

We would like to thank the Ottawa Centre for Research and Innovation (OCRI) for making this database available to us. We would also like to thank the members of the Ottawa Gatineau Commercialization Task Force for their helpful comments and suggestions on the early draft of this chapter.

References

BBC News (2003). World edition. *Ericsson returns to profit.* http://news.bbc.co.uk/2/hi/business/3226395.stm. Accessed on 30 October 2003.

Chadwick A., Glasson J., Lawton Smith H., Clark G, & Simmie J. (2003). *Enterprising Oxford. Volume 2: The anatomy of the Oxfordshire high-tech economy.* Oxford, UK: Oxfordshire Economic Observatory.

CMC (Canadian Microelectronics Corporation) (2003). http//:www.cmc.ca.

Corona, L., Doutriaux, J., & Mian, S. (2003). Regional innovation in NAFTA countries: Case studies of selected innovation poles. Pre-Publication Working Paper. University of Ottawa #03–53.

de la Mothe, J., & Cimoli, M. (2002). Technology, growth and development. In: J. de la Mothe (Ed.), *Science, technology and governance.* London, UK: Continuum.

de la Mothe, J., & Foray, D. (Eds) (2001). *Knowledge management in the innovation process.* Boston, MA: Kluwer.

de la Mothe, J., & Link, A. N. (Eds) (2002). *Networks, alliances and partnerships in the innovation process.* Boston, MA: Kluwer.

de la Mothe, J., & Mallory, G. (2003). Local knowledge and the strategy of constructed advantage: The role of community alliances. *International Journal of Technology Management*, December.

Doutriaux, J. (1991). High-tech start-ups, better off with government contracts than with subsidies. *IEEE Transactions on Engineering Management, 38*(2), 127–135.

Doutriaux, J. (2003). University-industry linkages and the development of knowledge clusters in Canada. *Local Economy, 18*(1), 63–79.

Fortune (2003). Fortune Global 500. *Fortune Magazine* (July 21, pp. 97–126).

Government of Canada (2001). *Achieving excellence: Investing in people, knowledge and opportunity.*

Government of Canada (2002). *Knowledge matters: Skills and learning for Canadians.*

ICF Consulting (2000). *Choosing a future: A new economic vision for Ottawa.* August.

ICF Consulting (2003a). *Innovation Ottawa: A strategy for sustaining economic generators — Executive summary.* January 14.

ICF Consulting (2003b). *Innovation Ottawa: A strategy for sustaining economic generators.* January 22.

OCRI (Ottawa Centre for Research and Innovation) (2003). http//:www.ocri.ca.

OLSC (Ottawa Life Sciences Council) (2003). http//:www.olsc.ca.

OPC (Ottawa Photonics Cluster) (2003). http//:www.ottawaphotonics.com.

Ottawa Region (2003). http//:www.ottawaregion.com.

Ottawa Business Journal (2003). http//:www.ottawabusinessjournal.com.

Papadopoulos, N. (1997). *Competitive profile of a world city: Ottawa-Carleton compared to leading technology centres in North America. A brief for the Ottawa-Carleton board of trade.* Ottawa, Ontario, Canada: IKON Research Group, School of Business, Carleton University, October.

Photonics Dictionary (2003). A Laurin Web Site, http://www.photonics.com/dictionary/lookup/XQ/ASP/url.lookup/entrynum.3996/letter.p/pu./QX/lookup.htm. Accessed on 28 November 2003.

Reich, R. (1991). *The work of nations: Preparing ourselves for 21st-century capitalism.* New York: Alfred A Knopf.

Reich, R. (2003). Jobless in America. *CIO Magazine* (Fall/Winter). http//:www.cio.com/archive/092203/reich.html.

Re$earch Money Inc. (2003). *Task force seeking answers on how to grow high-tech firms in era of global competition.*

Statistics Canada (2001). *Census.* Ottawa, Ontario, Canada: Statistics Canada.

The Canadian Encyclopaedia (2nd ed.) (1988). Edmonton, Alberta, Canada: Hurtig Publishers.

Zhang, J. (2003). *High-tech start-ups and industry dynamics in Silicon Valley.* San Francisco: Public Policy Institute of California.

Chapter 5

A Tale of One City:
The Ottawa Technology Cluster

Judith J. Madill, George H. Haines Jr. and Allan L. Riding

Abstract

This chapter documents the recent history of the Ottawa Technology Cluster. It describes the origins of the firms in the cluster, provides a profile of both businesses and founders of these firms, and identifies sources of knowledge and capital. These enterprises are not "overnight successes," nor are they "fly by night" businesses. They are solidly anchored in the local community with informal investors who supply financing as well as significant non-financial inputs to the firms in the cluster.

Introduction

Ottawa is one of Canada's foremost technology clusters and the home of such leading companies as Mitel, Corel, Cognos, and others. The Ottawa cluster appears to be unique in at least two important respects. First, it evolved in the absence of any local supplier of institutional venture capital for significant periods of time. Second, during the early development of the cluster in Ottawa, the firms did not, by and large, compete with each other in the product market — but did compete in the labour market. Recent years have witnessed considerable research on the development, evolution and contribution of technology clusters.[1] However, much of this writing focuses on clusters prior to the relatively recent technology sector recession. This recent so-called meltdown of technology sectors worldwide has posed challenges to the continued growth and prosperity of most

---

[1] A number of studies examine the development, extent and significance of regional clusters across North America and Europe (Capello 1999; de Bernardy 1999; Keeble *et al*. 1999; Lindholm Dahlstrand 1999; Longhi 1999; Pinch & Henry 1999; Saxenian 1994; Sternberg & Tamasy 1999). In the Ottawa context, Steed examined the origins of the Ottawa cluster in a series of papers in the early 1980s (Steed 1987; Steed & DeGenova 1983; Steed & Nichol 1985). Other authors analyzed the origins of the Ottawa cluster in the business media at around the same time (McDougal 1986; Mittelstaedt 1980; Sweetman 1982). Two early academic studies of this cluster were those performed by Callahan (1985) and Doutriaux (1984).

Silicon Valley North: A High-Tech Cluster of Innovation and Entrepreneurship
Copyright © 2004 by Elsevier Ltd.
All rights of reproduction in any form reserved
ISBN: 0-08-044457-1

clusters — Ottawa included — and to the communities in which these technology clusters are located. So, while there have been a number of early papers on the Ottawa cluster and recent interest on clusters worldwide, little has been written about the Ottawa cluster in current times.

This chapter presents a brief analysis of the origins of the Ottawa Technology Cluster, but focuses primarily on recent developments. In particular, the work examines:

(a) the networks and linkages that defined the cluster in the late 1990s and early in 2000 prior to the technology downturn;
(b) the role of business angels in supporting the development of the cluster; and
(c) the impact of the recent downturn on the economic environment for technology firms in the Ottawa cluster.

In examining the networks and linkages in the cluster as well as the role of business angels, the authors utilize data collected from surveys of cluster members by the authors in the year 2000. In assessing the impact of the recent downturn, the chapter presents an analysis of in-depth case histories conducted in 2002 that focus on how technology firms have weathered and adapted to the economic challenges of the past several years.

Previous studies on technology clusters (Keeble & Wilkinson 2000; and references cited therein) have generally been conceptual in nature. The empirical approach has, according to Cooper *et al.* (2001) been impoverished. Therefore, one of the goals of this chapter is to present empirical findings on the Ottawa regional technology cluster (parts of this longitudinal study have been conducted by Cooper *et al.* (2001) as well as Haines *et al.* (2002) and Madill *et al.* (2001). This cluster has not been the subject of detailed study since the early 1980s, except for an input-output study by Bathelt (1991). It was not until an unpublished Ph.D. Dissertation by Roy (1999) and a consultant's report (ICF 2000) commissioned by the local economic development agency (which was circulated primarily in the region itself), as well as the study upon which the current chapter is based, that the cluster became the focus of research once again. It is also currently included in a research project (http://www.utoronto.ca/isrn/clusters.htm) being undertaken through the University of Toronto.

Thus, it is hoped that one of the contributions that this chapter (and book) will make is to expand the geographical range of analyses of technology clusters. Much of the research on regional technology clusters has been undertaken in the United States, focusing on Silicon Valley. By providing a contemporary account of a Canadian technology cluster, the work enables comparison with similar regions in the USA and Europe and highlights aspects that may be unique. From a policy perspective, the results may be of interest to policy makers and agencies concerned with the development of regional and national innovation policies.

Previous Research

Findings of recent studies of successful regional technology clusters shows that key processes are: linkages and networking among firms and other organizations (Madill *et al.* 2001); flows of highly skilled workers within scientific and professional labour markets;

and spin-offs of new firms from existing organizations (Keeble & Wilkinson 1999b). Regional collective learning processes appear to play a central role in creating a capability for combining and reassembling knowledge to generate high rates of technological and product innovation (Lawson & Lorenz 1999). In turn, this leads to enterprise development and employment growth. These collective learning processes are underpinned by shared culturally based rules of behaviour. These rules establish the pre-conditions for learning by engendering the development of trust and co-operation in the context of an interlocking and integrated web of supportive organizations and institutions such as trade associations, chambers of commerce, financial institutions, local authorities and business service organizations, organizations that enhance collective learning capabilities.

Is Ottawa a Cluster?

There are a number of views about what constitutes a cluster. For example, Keeble & Wilkinson (2000: 1) state that "regional high technology clusters . . . are characterized by substantial numbers of small, new, and innovative enterprises engaged in technology-advanced manufacturing and service activities." Prevezer (1997 as reported in Cooper & Folta 2000) defines clusters as "groups of firms within one industry based in one geographical area." Porter (1998, as reported in Cooper & Folta 2000) defines clusters as "geographic concentrations of interconnected companies and institutions in a particular field." As Cooper & Folta (2000: 348) note, both these latter definitions suggest "a set of related firms in close geographic proximity," a concept also embraced by Keeble and Wilkinson's definition. Doyletech (2002) published a genealogy of firms in the Ottawa region that demonstrates that many Ottawa enterprises share common roots. Under any definition, therefore, the Ottawa grouping of technology-based firms fulfills the definition of an entrepreneurship and high-technology cluster.

The next sections of the chapter will review existing literature on what is known about clusters, the role of venture capital in clusters, and angel capital in the Ottawa cluster. This literature review continues with an investigation of the role of founders in clusters, networking in small and medium businesses, as well as strategies for successfully managing in tough economic times. Following this overview of previous research and writing, the authors move to present a baseline profile of the Ottawa Technology Cluster. This includes a brief introduction of the early days in Ottawa, then a focused examination of the cluster in 2000, including an assessment of business origins, sources of knowledge upon which businesses were built, as well as detailed discussions of the contributions of angel investors to the cluster and networking in the cluster in 2000. The chapter then shifts to a study of the impacts of the recent economic challenges facing the technology firms in the cluster. The chapter ends with a brief summary, discussion and conclusions section.

Clusters: What is Known?

Numerous studies have sought to assess how regional collective learning processes contribute to the success of various regional high technology clusters. Recent work in the

European context was published in a special edition of the scholarly journal, *Regional Studies* (Keeble & Wilkinson 1999a). This special issue included papers on Cambridge (Keeble *et al.* 1999), Sophia-Antipolis (Longhi 1999), Grenoble (de Bernardy 1999), Pisa, Piacenze and NE Milan (Capello 1999), Munich (Sternberg & Tamasy 1999) and Goteborg (Lindholm Dahlstrand 1999). Keeble & Wilkinson (2000) subsequently published later edited versions of these papers as well as further work by Lawson (2000). Pinch & Henry's (1999) analysis of the clustering of the British motor sports industry also draws heavily on concepts of regional collective learning. Perhaps the most influential seminal study, however, is Saxenian's comparison of Silicon Valley and Boston's Route 128 (Saxenian 1994).

Saxenian sought to explain the contrasts in the development of Silicon Valley and Route 128 during the early 1990s based on a framework that embraced three components.

- The first part of Saxenian's framework (1994: 7) comprised local institutions and culture, defined as "the shared understandings and practices that unify a community and define everything from labor market behavior to attitudes toward risk-sharing." This concept embraces non-firm entities such as educational and research institutions, business associations, local governments, and other formal and informal organizations that provide for local social integration.
- Second, Saxenian defines "industrial structure" as the degree of vertical integration linking firms in the community. This includes linkages among producers, suppliers, and customers and is, to a large extent, similar to the model postulated by Ryans *et al.* (2000). Saxenian, however, argues that industrial structure must be embedded within an overarching framework. The framework she proposed incorporates the three components mentioned previously.
- The third component of the Saxenian's model is "corporate organization," which she defines as "the degree of hierarchical or horizontal coordination, centralization or decentralization, and the allocations of responsibilities and specialization of tasks" within firms (Saxenian 1994: 8). According to Saxenian, the relative size of firms within their cluster is also an important element of this component.

Using this framework, Saxenian examines the origins of both the Silicon Valley and Route 128 technology clusters. Both areas had benefited from Federal government funding and university linkages (Stanford and San José State, MIT respectively). In both settings, key individuals provided starting points that led to both areas becoming renowned for electronics and computer-related industries during the 1970s. Saxenian describes Route 128's decline through the 1980s, relative to Silicon Valley, and attempts to infer lessons from this difference.

Saxenian concludes that local institutions and culture are important elements in fostering innovation and wealth creation. She reasons that within such a culture, a local economy built on flexible networks of firms of various sizes is more desirable than larger, more autonomously structured firms in terms of economic competitiveness and market responsiveness. In short, the East Coast setting was characterized, according to Saxenian, by relatively greater degrees of corporate secrecy, more conservative universities, and more independent and hierarchical firms. She maintains that in Silicon Valley a more open and entrepreneurial environment fostered a network-based region with a relatively greater capacity to innovate and share knowledge.

Roy (1999) argues that Saxenian's paradigm has considerable merit, but that it is mute with respect to the roles of various levels of government. He therefore expands Saxenian's model and defines a framework that he calls the "strategic localism" template. In this template, Roy hypothesizes three potential forms of local advantage:

- Competitive advantage is determined by the strength of market-driven linkages within clusters. This construct embraces Saxenian's concepts of industrial structure and corporate organization. This concept is also consistent with the market linkages described by Ryans *et al.* (2000).
- Innovative advantage reflects the knowledge infrastructure, as well as the intellectual and human capital sources in the region. This infrastructure construct includes knowledge-generating institutions such as universities, colleges, research institutes and laboratories, and various consortia or partnership arrangements among them. Innovative advantage includes the pool of human resources and skills.
- Collaborative advantage relates to the local capacity for cooperation and the efforts of organizations with a mandate to build collaborative capacities, particularly in the form of innovative initiatives that meld socio-economic sectors. This element of community culture provides a basis for the institutionalization of shared practices and beliefs that emphasize connectivity and reciprocity between members. This construct includes the potential roles of various levels of governments.

Roy (1999) investigated these issues on the basis of a series of interviews with key informants in the Ottawa region. He concluded that his paradigm is a useful extension of Saxenian's (1994) approach and that governments (especially local governments) and local trade associations can play a key role in cluster formation and development.

The Role of Venture Capital Investors in Clusters

Some accounts of technology clusters identify the importance of venture capital firms. For example, Florida & Kenney (1988: 43) refer to venture capital as being "an integral part of the well developed technology infrastructures," or "social structures of innovation" while Saxenian (1994: 39) notes the involvement of Silicon Valley's venture capitalists in the businesses they funded: "advising entrepreneurs on business plans and strategies, helping find co-investors, recruiting key managers, and serving on the board of directors."

Various studies have recognized that the contribution made by venture capital investors to the formation and growth of entrepreneurial ventures is "more than just money" (Van Osnabrugge & Robinson 2000). Bygrave & Timmons (1992), for example, describe these non-financial contributions as falling under three headings: strategic, networking and social/supportive. The entrepreneurship literature has confirmed that these contributions can be extremely valuable to the businesses. However, attempts to establish a causal relationship between this hands-on contribution and firm performance have been unsuccessful

(Barney *et al.* 1994), not least on account of methodological difficulties in measuring contributions and firm performance.

Studies of regional collective learning processes have recognized that the presence of venture capitalists contributes to the "institutional thickness" of regions. Florida & Kenney (1988: 43–44) highlight the role of venture capitalists as conduits of information through their position "at the centre of extended networks linking financiers, entrepreneurs, corporate executives, headhunters and consultants."

The Ottawa cluster may be unique in that very little institutional venture capital was available in the region until relatively recently. During the 1950s and 1960s, government laboratories, particularly those associated with the development of early Canadian satellites, (e.g. Alouette), supported much of the innovation that marked this early period of the Ottawa cluster. In addition, innovations were fostered and commercialized by larger businesses such as Bell-Northern Electric's Microsystems initiative and Control Data Corporation Ltd. (CDC). To some degree, many of the entrepreneurial firms that arose between the 1960s and 1980s were offshoots of these enterprises. Aside, however, from a venture capital subsidiary of Noranda Enterprises, little institutional venture capital was available in the Ottawa region. As noted by the Ottawa Carleton Research Institute (OCRI), following the closure in the early 90s of this venture capital subsidiary of Noranda Enterprises Ltd., no venture capital firms maintained a presence in Ottawa until 1995 (see also the chapter by Callahan *et al.* this volume). Accordingly, much of the development of these firms was attributable to angel investors (also known as business angels, informal investors, and private investors).

Because of this difference, the Ottawa region may be an important example of cluster development for other regions in which a venture capital infrastructure may be lacking. What occurred in Ottawa in the absence of venture capital was the development of a collection of sophisticated informal investors. However, very little research has addressed the contributions of informal angel investors to the development of technology clusters. The next section of this chapter will examine the role of these investors within the Ottawa region.

Angel Capital in the Ottawa Cluster

Typically, angels' investments are in sectors and stages that are complimentary to those in which institutional venture capital firms focus and are particularly important for start-ups and early-stage firms. According to Freear & Wetzel (1988).

(1) Angels concentrate on the provision of relatively small investments in the start-up and early stages, where the so-called "equity gap" is said to be most significant.
(2) Compared with the formal venture capital market, they are more accommodating to the needs of SME owners by having lower rejection rates, longer exit horizons (patient capital), and target rates of return that are similar to those of institutional venture capitalists even though they assume more risk.
(3) Third, unlike the formal venture capitalists who usually concentrate in a few core areas (both in terms of geographical area and investment sectors), informal investors usually invest in their local economies, thus helping to reduce regional and sectoral disparities.

The supply side of the informal market has been widely studied and a consistent picture of informal investors has emerged (for additional detail, see, in particular, Short & Riding (1987a, 1987b ,1989), Aboud (1998), and Haines *et al.* (2003):

- Informal investors are self-made, high income, well educated (normally hold a minimum of a college degree), and middle-aged.
- They are predominantly male and have substantial business experience. Most angels have entrepreneurial experience as owners or managers.
- They usually prefer investing within their localities. In Riding & Short (1987a), over 85% of the investments by the respondents had been limited to within 50 miles of Ottawa.
- Business angels are generally experienced investors confident about their ability to appraise investment opportunities and therefore do not typically rely on professionals.
- Their investment decisions are usually opportunistic (based on commercial intuition) rather than scientific (Mason & Harrison 1996).

The literature suggests that economic motives (particularly the opportunity for high capital appreciation) are primary reasons for informal investments. In addition to that, however, there are some significant non-economic motives (Haines *et al.* 2002). Many investors may also derive "psychic income" from the opportunity to play active roles in the entrepreneurial process (Sullivan & Miller 1996, refer to this as a "hedonistic motive"). Others invest on "moral" grounds. Most investors are former business owners who have succeeded through their own efforts or with the help of others. Many feel an obligation to give back to society, through investments in up and coming entrepreneurs, job creation in areas of high unemployment, ventures developing socially useful technology (e.g. medical or energy saving) and ventures created by minorities (Wetzel 1983). Sullivan & Miller (1996) refer to these as altruistic motives. Many investors are willing to trade-off economic returns to obtain these hedonistic and altruistic returns.

Aboud (1998) documented the financial impact of business angels in the Ottawa region. He showed that Ottawa angels made a strong impact both in terms of value and volume of investment. This is consistent with much of the previous research, which has documented attributes of business angels, their importance in terms of the financing they provide, and information about their decision processes and criteria. However, there is little that has identified the specific nature and the value of informal investors' non-financial contributions, especially as perceived by business owners. This chapter provides further evidence of the importance of angels in the context of the Ottawa region.

The evolution of regional technology clusters is inextricably linked with issues of entrepreneurship. The next sections of this examination of the literature will focus on the role of founding entrepreneurs in clusters and the role of networking in SME's.

The Role of Founders in Clusters

Entrepreneurs play critical roles by recognizing opportunity, by creating new ventures and fostering innovation within existing firms, and by helping to maintain the health and dynamism of technology-based complexes. Previous research has considered technical entrepreneurs and helped inform our understanding of their role in the processes of firm formation and growth (Cooper 1973; Roberts 1991). Also, public sector institutions, such as universities or government research centres, and other commercial organizations have been identified as principal sources of entrepreneurial spinouts (Oakey 1995). Research has revealed the tendency for many founders to establish firms in the same sector in which they worked immediately prior to start-up (Cooper 1998; Oakey 1995). Findings also indicate that the majority of founders set up firms in the locality in which they are living and working at startup (Markusen *et al.* 1986), a spin-off pattern which results in the reinforcement of a region's technology profile. Some entrepreneurs establish enterprises on their own, but the majority team up with others to form a business, pooling skills (Oakey *et al.* 1990).

Intuitively, when starting and growing a business, entrepreneurs will draw upon the whole of their "life's experience," both personal and professional. Therefore, the entire background of the entrepreneur should be viewed as influencing opportunities for learning and knowledge transfer. Anecdotal evidence suggests that some founders have very varied careers within a number of organizations prior to setting up their own firm, and by implication are exposed to a rich variety of learning environments. Moreover, these previous employers may not have been local. Some founders may have a long-term goal to establish their own business and will adopt a strategic approach to the acquisition of core skills and knowledge that will assist them with their new venture. Additionally, a focus on only the principal entrepreneur in multiple founder start-ups fails to take into account the valuable contributions of knowledge and skills of other team members.

Steed & Nichol's (1985) study of technology entrepreneurs in Ottawa reports that, on average, entrepreneurs had lived in Ottawa for eleven years before starting their firms (this ranged from eight months to 59 years), and 84% had held jobs outside Ottawa. Yet only 43% of the respondents identified their last employer (in most cases located in Ottawa) as providing the greatest impetus to entrepreneurship. Hence, collective learning that arises from the spin-off process need not be regional. Cooper (1998) confirms this by showing that while the majority of technology-based spin-offs are local, many founders are not born within the locality in which they set up their firms. People may move into or within a cluster for a variety of reasons: for further/higher education; as a result of promotion within a firm; to join a new organization; etc. Spatially mobile founders bring new ideas as well as different perspectives and knowledge of external networks that they may employ in developing their business. As yet, no research seems to have identified which types of learning and knowledge accumulation occur within a regional technology cluster and which are acquired elsewhere and imported via the inward movement of human capital. In the context of multiple founder starts, analysis of the histories of all team members is required to better understand the ways in which collective learning contributes to the establishment and development of businesses.

Networking and Small and Medium Sized Businesses

A developing body of literature, built on the foundations of the seminal studies of Granovetter (1973, 1985), is focused on networking in entrepreneurial firms (Chell & Baines 2000; Collinson, 2000; Freel 2000; George *et al.* 2001; Johannisson 1995a, 1995b, 1998,

2000; Katz & Williams 1997; Shane & Cable 2002; Vanhaverbeke 2001). Much academic literature argues that networking is a desirable activity for entrepreneurial firms — especially knowledge-based technology firms (Freel 2000; Ryans *et al.* 2000) leading to competitive advantages which in turn leads to increased performance.

Networking is often defined as the set of all links among people (Granovetter 1985; Katz & Williams 1997). This set of links comprises both strong and weak ties. There is considerable discussion about the value of both strong and weak ties in networking. Strong ties to family and close friends lead to trust as well as sharing of contacts and information (Chell & Baines 2000; George *et al.* 2001). The strength of weak ties (Granovetter 1973, 1985) allows individuals in business to draw upon information, advice and assistance from a large diverse pool of contacts with people.

There is some debate in the literature concerning the relationship between networking and success in entrepreneurial firms. The majority of the literature argues that weak tie networking is fundamental to success in entrepreneurial endeavors (Chell & Baines 2000; Freel 2000; George *et al.* 2001; Vanhaverbeke 2001). However, this view is not universally held. Johannisson's (1990) study of Swedish firms did not find networking related to success and Johannisson (1995a: 190) argues that a causal relationship is far from self evident: "That which is taken for granted, especially in American but also European network research, that networks enhance qualitative and quantitative growth, must be reconsidered."

According to Johannisson's later work (2000: 378), "an elaborate personal network appears to be a necessary, but not a sufficient, condition for entrepreneurial success." He notes that networking revolves around the founding entrepreneur (2000: 374) "as a set of interlocking ventures embedded in the personal network of the entrepreneur . . . [where the entrepreneur is shown . . . as being at the center of the personal network]." Johannisson also notes that networking is not necessarily undertaken with growth or performance of the firm as the prime reason.

While many, like Johannisson, postulate that networking is necessary to success, research by Curran *et al.* (1993) has shown that owners of small firms in the U.K. do not actively engage in networking activities with other business owners or organizations. Reasons for lack of networking include lack of time, lack of growth aspirations, as well as a reluctance to network arising from the entrepreneur's need for independence (Chell & Baines 2000; Johannisson *et al.* 1994). On the basis of 104 interviews with small business owners, Chell & Baines (2000) show that small businesses do use their trading links as sources of useful information. Customers were found to be the most important source (71% overall) while other business owner-managers were also important (57% overall). Chell & Baines (2000) also report on the frequency (not on value) of contact with more formal institutions showing that only slightly more than one-third of owner managers had had any contact during the previous three years with the Chamber of Commerce (38%), or professional or trade associations (35%).

The research literature also suggests that there may be sectoral differences in the extent and type of networking. Collinson (2000: 236) presents Scottish data to show that high technology firms utilize networks although "the kinds of interaction and interdependencies . . . in Scotland are certainly very different . . . from the Silicon Valley model." Ryans *et al.* (2000) argue that high technology firms *should* utilize networking in order to be successful. Freel's (2000) study of 228 U.K. manufacturers showed generally that innovators make greater use of external linkages, in particular, vertical value chain linkages. The most innovative firms are significantly more likely to be linked: (a) with their suppliers (51.5% compared to 37.2% of non-innovators); (b) with universities and colleges (21.1% of innovators compared to 13.2% of non-innovators); and (c) government, support services and trade bodies (49.5% of innovators compared to 38% of non-innovators). However, Freel (2000) found no evidence that the most innovative firms are more likely to have been involved with joint activity with customers generally (47.5% of innovators had such linkages compared to 43.4% on non-innovators). The study also showed a relatively low number of firms involved in formal collaboration with competitors — only 14.1% of innovators and 9.3% of non- innovators engaged in any form of joint venture with competitors. Chell & Baines (2000) found that "knowledge" business owner-managers in the U.K. were more likely to be active networkers — more that one-half (52%) of the "knowledge" business owner-managers were networkers compared to less than one-quarter (23%) of the "non-knowledge" owners.

In a very innovative piece of research, Shane & Cable (2002) show that direct and indirect ties between entrepreneurs and seed-stage investors influence the financing of new firms. Both direct and indirect ties are positively and strongly related to the probability of investment. Direct ties encourage investment, but are superceded by information from indirect sources. These social ties operate primarily as a mechanism for information transfer between investors and SMEs. Shane & Cable (2002) argue that future research is needed on the effects of social ties on the financing of high technology firms in clusters.

There also is a growing body of marketing research on the importance of managing relationships with customers and suppliers in industrial markets and services (Buttle 1996; Gronroos 1991, 1996; Morgan & Hunt 1994; Sivada & Dwyer 2000). Following this stream of work, Ryans *et al.* (2000) have proposed a strategic planning process which differs from more traditional models in that it introduces a new step in the process — planning and managing critical relationships. This new step occurs after analysis and tentative decisions have been made regarding strategic directions for the firm. They argue that some of these crucial relationships will be with other organizations within the supply chain, while others will be with individuals or organizations outside it. The authors use the concept of a "market web" to capture all the relationships that they believe need to be managed. At the centre of the web is the market chain. The chain consists of the focal company and a number of relationships upstream and downstream from it. Surrounding the market chain are a number of "off-chain" relationships which augment the chain and turn it into a web. The difference between a market web and a cluster is physical propinquity that is found in a cluster, but not in a market web. The second difference between a market web and a cluster is that a cluster includes the presence of networking among non-marketing participants while a market web focuses on marketing participants.

The Ryans *et al.* (2000) marketing planning model was developed on the basis of the author's work with companies in technology-intensive industries, and to our knowledge, no prior empirical testing of the ideas concerning market web linkages in the model has been conducted. Empirical work done by Sivada & Dwyer (2000) can be tied in loosely in that it shows that there is a link between the factors supporting new product development success and alliance success, two areas that on first glance may not appear to be directly related. This research suggests that successful technology firms (well known for the speed at which they introduce new products to the market) may have a skill set which also supports successful new product introductions. This, in turn, can support the development of alliances and relationships necessary for competitive success as prescribed in the Ryans *et al.* (2000) model.

Its interesting to note that this literature suggests that networking is a very important part of the survival strategy for firms during tough times. The traditional databases, however, do not collect data about networking behaviour. The next section of this chapter briefly reviews what studies of these traditional databases have shown that firms can do to survive and prosper during recessionary periods.

Strategies for Success in Tough Economic Times

An article by Marion Stern (2002) summarizes what is known in the strategic management literature about strategies firms follow during a recession. During a recession, there are some costs where the optimum (amount) stays steady or even increases ("good costs") and other costs where the optimum drops dramatically ("bad costs"). "Optimum" relates both to performance through the recession and to the recovery thereafter. "Good costs" in a recession are marketing, expenditures on quality and value, expenditures on product research and development, and expenditures on the introduction of new products. These costs are all associated with business success. "Bad costs" during a recessionary period are expenditures on fixed capital, working capital, manufacturing, as well as general and administrative expenses. Increases in these expenditures during a recession are all associated with lack of success during and following the recession. There were three categories of costs where success or failure depended on the strategic strength of the firm: retaining spare capacity, aggressive pricing (price reductions), and outsourcing. Success in using these strategies would depend on the individual strategic strengths of the firms.

Conclusions

Central to all accounts of cluster formation and development is the notion of linkages and networks among firms. Further, the growing body of literature focusing upon networks and linkages (described above) leaves many questions about the role of networking in SMEs in key sectors including high technology.

Much of the research on regional technology clusters has been undertaken in the United States and Europe (Keeble & Wilkinson 2000; and references therein). By contrast, the literature on the Ottawa technology clusters originated with the work of Guy Steed and his students in the early 1980s (Steed & DeGenova 1983; Steed & Nichol 1985). However, as pointed out earlier in this chapter, although this important technology cluster has continued to develop, it has only recently attracted further attention from academic researchers.

Finally, it is also interesting and important to determine whether technology firms in the Ottawa cluster utilized the strategies outlined in the literature for successfully coping with a recession. Therefore, this chapter now turns toward provision of a contemporary account of the Ottawa technology cluster. Following a brief introduction on the early days in Ottawa, it moves to an examination of the contributions of informal investors to the cluster and the networking and linkage patterns of the firms within the cluster. Finally, approaches used by the firms within the cluster to weather the economic challenges during the past three years are described.

Baseline Profile of the Ottawa Technology Cluster

The Early Days in Ottawa

The Ottawa technology cluster traces its origins to World War II when research in conjunction with the war effort established a cadre of technically competent individuals. This competency enlarged during the 1950s and 1960s with development of satellites, satellite communications, and computer hardware and software. In the late 1960s, the stock of technical competency was augmented by the creation of the Bell-Northern Electric Alliance Research Laboratory known as Bell Northern Microsystems (see also the chapter by Ghent Mallett this volume). At the time, this facility stood alone in a sparsely populated agricultural area outside the western periphery of Ottawa. While this research laboratory subsequently closed, many of its former employees chose to remain in the region. In this context, Vertinsky & Pe'er (2003) have concluded that failures of businesses liberate resources in the community, some of which are immobile, and which therefore form the seeds of future business births. This idea is similar to that of Schumpeter's (1934) "creative destruction." This creative destruction was a factor in the early growth of the cluster.

During the 1970s the first "flagship" companies were formed (Mitel & Nortel), followed, during the 1980s with additional successful firms (Newbridge (then), Cognos, Corel, JDS Fitel (then), among others). Steed & DeGenova (1983) report that in 1981 there were 45 technology-oriented companies established in Ottawa. By 1990, approximately 300 technology-based businesses had been established in Ottawa. This was accompanied by growth in employment by technology-based firms from approximately 8,200 in 1976 (Steed & DeGenova 1983 Table 5) to more than 27,000 by 1990 and, during 2000, to 76,000 jobs (Collins 2000).

An Overview of Ottawa at the Turn of the Millennium

The decade of the 1990s was characterized by the establishment of numerous entrepreneurial ventures, many of which were generated as "affiliates" of some of the larger firms. The "corporate angel" model pioneered by Newbridge Networks and its founder, Terry Matthews, was adopted in other firms. Chart 1 illustrates the growth of technology-based businesses between 1990 and 2000 in Ottawa (Collins 2000).

The latter half of the 1990s was marked both by the growth and proliferation of firms, particularly in the IT sector. In 1995, for example, OCRI (2000) counted 665 firms in the IT sector, 20 of which were public companies. By 2000, OCRI identified more than 1,000 IT firms of which 40 were public companies. While IT firms are the single largest sub sector (Chart 2), they represent about one-third of technology-based businesses (Madill *et al.* 2001).

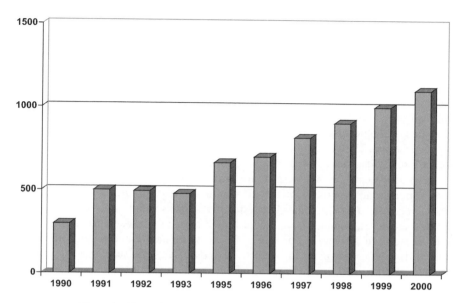

Chart 1: Growth of technology firms, Ottawa 1990–2000.

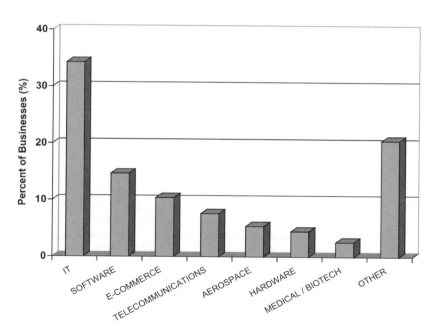

Chart 2: Ottawa cluster sub-sectors.

The result is that the Ottawa region is Canada's fourth largest economic area in which each technology job supports three others (Collins 2000) and where a majority of firms are export-oriented (more than $12 billion in export sales (Collins 2000)). Moreover, the economic development of the Ottawa region presents opportunities for companies across Ontario and in Quebec to supply the cluster with goods and services.

The economic development of the Ottawa region is unique in terms of the role of venture capital (Mason *et al.* 2001). Technology- based clusters in the U.S. such as Silicon Valley, the Bay area, and others developed in close conjunction with large local sources of venture capital. Indeed, the U.S. venture capital sector stands out internationally in terms of size and scope (Reynolds *et al.* 2001) and in terms of its role in cluster development. In Ottawa, however, until the early 1990s the primary (and almost exclusive) source of institutional venture capital was Noranda Enterprise Limited. This venture capital subsidiary of Noranda Inc. made significant equity investments across a variety of advanced technology companies. However, Noranda Enterprise Limited closed in the early 1990s with the result that, as of 1994, there were no private sector institutional venture capital firms located in Ottawa. By 2000, however, the growth of the cluster was such that 14 institutional venture capital firms had a local presence. The growth of venture capital involvement was witnessed by venture capital investments in the Ottawa region of $74 million in 1998, $274 million during 1999, more than $1.2 billion during 2001, and $680 million in 2002. Firms in the Ottawa region have recently been the recipients of approximately one-quarter of the value of venture capital investments made nationally (OCRI 2002; Canadian Venture Capital Association 2001, 2002). Ottawa remains a key focal point for venture capital investment in Canada (see also the chapter by Callahan *et al.* this volume).

Ottawa in 2000: Drilling Deeper into the Cluster

Data collected by means of a survey of the CEOs of both technology firms and non-technology firms in the Ottawa cluster conducted in spring of 2000 provide the baseline data for this chapter. Data collection procedures involved sending questionnaires to the CEOs. Because Katz & Williams (1997) showed that entrepreneurs' weak tie network efforts are less than those of managers, the study controlled for possible differences by studying CEOs of all companies included in the 423 technology-based businesses and to the CEOs of 343 non-technology firms within the Ottawa region. Questionnaires were distributed by fax as part of a personalized mail merge package. The package comprised a fax cover sheet, a personal letter from the research team to the CEO seeking their participation, a one-page description of the research project, a return fax cover sheet and the four-page questionnaire. Follow up faxes were sent to non-respondents after two weeks and these were, in turn, followed up by reminder telephone calls a few days later. From this process, 111 responses were obtained from technology-based firms (26.2% response rate) and 75 responses from supplier (that is, non-technology) businesses (21.9% response rate). Of course, not all respondents answered all questions.

Origins of the businesses   Chart 3 displays the distribution of the age of respondents' firms. The Chart shows that most firms are not "overnight successes," rather a high

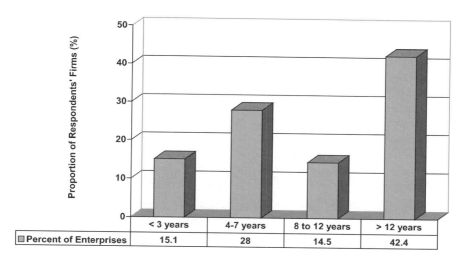

Chart 3: Age distribution of firms.

proportion of firms had been established and had survived for some time. Most firms (88%) were formed in the Ottawa region as independent firms, and the majority (79%) remain independent. Most firms (79%) reported having two or more founders, with a mode of two founders. In 63% of the firms, the founders had worked together before starting their current business. Almost one-half of the founders had previously worked for another small company and one-quarter had worked for a large firm. The backgrounds of the founders were evenly split between technical and business areas.

Sources of knowledge   Chart 4 presents the breakdown of where the founders reported having developed the knowledge they employed to start their firms. Of five key sources of organizational knowledge, almost half of the respondents reported relying on personal R&D outside of previous employment and knowledge gleaned from their previous employer. However, universities, government and other companies were also significant sources. These responses illustrate the importance of the cluster in developing knowledge. In earlier work, it has been found that previous employers are frequently located within the cluster (Cooper *et al.* 2001).

An additional observation relates to the 33% of respondents who reported that the knowledge upon which their company was founded was developed in universities. This percentage is higher than that reported in earlier work because this research utilized a multiple response question, that allowed respondents to identify multiple sources for the knowledge and did not confine respondents to describing exclusively their most recent prior experience (Keeble & Wilkinson 2000). Previous studies have also found university prestige affects technology licensing (Sine *et al.* 2003) but that universities are generally unimportant (Cooper *et al.* 2001). However, the data here shows that universities indeed contribute substantively to innovation and suggests that knowledge from university settings is transferred through employment and personal R&D to business development.

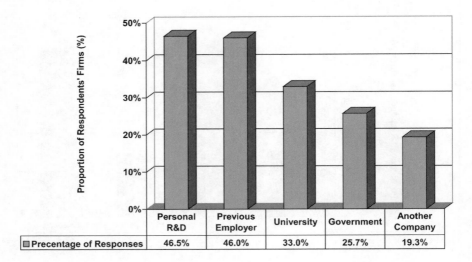

Chart 4: Organizational knowledge sources.

Sources of capital   Table 1 shows that 38 of the 185 respondents to the questionnaire, reported having been financed by institutional venture capital and 42 businesses reported that their firms had received informal investment capital. It is revealing that of the firms that had received institutional venture capital, 63% had been angel-financed. Moreover, of the 42 firms that had been angel-financed 24 (57%) also received venture capital. By comparison, of the 143 firms that had not received angel financing, only 14 (9.8%) obtained venture capital. The link between angel financing and venture capital financing seems clear from these data and provides additional evidence of the importance of angels.

The founders/owners of the 42 businesses that had reported receipt of informal invest-ment were re-contacted by fax or e-mail. They were asked, using open-ended queries, to identify the nature and perceived value of non-financial contributions that angel investors had provided. In all cases, respondents were asked to respond in their own words with no prompting nor with any predetermined categories provided by the researchers. Qualitative responses were received from 33 of these businesses. All responses were transcribed verbatim and coded and scrutinized using QSR NUD*IST, a recently developed tool

Table 1: Breakdown of respondents.

	Had Not Received Venture Capital	**Had Received Venture Capital**	**Total**
Had *not* received informal investment	129 (70%)	14 (8%)	143
Had received informal investment	18 (10%)	24 (12%)	42
Total	147 (80%)	38 (20%)	185

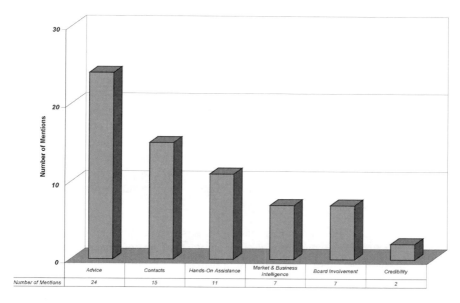

Number of Mentions	Advice	Contacts	Hands-On Assistance	Market & Business Intelligence	Board Involvement	Credibility
	24	15	11	7	7	2

Chart 5: Relative frequency of private investors' non-financial contributions.

for analysis of qualitative data. This step led to the development of a taxonomy of the various types of contributions and measures of the relative frequency with which they were identified. Six themes emerged with the frequencies displayed in Chart 5:

(1) **Advice**, often on financial matters but also including guidance to management on a range of issues. Most respondents note that private investors provide useful and on-going advice with respect to the management of the businesses in which they invest. The types of advice related to:
   - Company financial matters;
   - Choosing professional service providers;
   - Advice on corporate strategy and strategic planning;
   - Managerial and general business advice; and;
   - Marketing.
In the words of the owner-CEOs:

> They [private investors] assisted by providing guidance to management, and . . . they also provided guidance in the development of a corporate governance process and reporting discipline.

> [He] was available for questions and assistance without trying to impose his will on us.

> In addition to making cash available, [the] investor provided assistance preparing our business plan to present to potential investors, provided

legal opinions, helped map strategy when dealing with difficult situations encountered with customers, provided assistance in accessing
government programs, [and] assisted in dealing with banks during
negotiations concerning lines of credit.

(2) **Contacts** with a broad range of individuals who were able to assist in a variety of
ways with the development of the businesses. Private investors were also valued for
the contacts they provided. These contacts included, but were not limited to, purely
financial relationships. To be sure, they included introductions to other investors
and liaisons with other providers of capital however, they also embraced working
relationships with related firms and industry contacts, contacts with potential clients
and customers, and contacts with governments. The following statements illustrate the
variety of contacts provided by angels.

> Both our significant angel investors . . . assisted by providing guidance
> to management, and through their networks of . . . contacts they assisted
> in finding individuals interested in providing additional financing.

> Recommendations for persons to approach to co-invest with the
> identified angel were useful.

> [He] assisted with accountants, lawyers, hosting our website . . . got us
> meetings with his contacts that we would have had to work a lot harder
> to get otherwise.

(3) Hands-on **Involvement**, often at a very basic level; forms of participation include help
with hiring and recruiting, negotiations, provision of "free" business services, etc.
Again, these are best illustrated by means of the words of the respondents.

> [He provided] legal advice, financial negotiations and seeks business
> opportunities . . . Also brought to company rights to exploit several new
> technologies which he uncovered.

> [They provided] office space and office furniture . . .

> [They] provided advice in structuring our PowerPoint business plan.

(4) Involvement with, and on, **Boards of Directors/Advisors** including the identification
of additional members of the Board. Previous studies on informal investor practices
show that a majority of angel investors seek representation on firms' Boards of Directors
and Advisors (Dal Cin *et al.* 1993). However, only seven respondents mentioned such
involvement. Invariably, the presence of angels on the Board of Directors or Advisors
was mentioned in conjunction with some other form of non-financial contribution.
This suggests that Board membership provides private investors with the means to
monitor the needs of the firm and to identify ways in which they can bring their own
"value-added" to the firm. For example:

> Angel sits on the Board of Directors, acts as a reseller of products, provides input for development, marketing, growth opportunities.

> [They] provided introduction to our original part-time CFO, original introductions to VCs, and some customers, introduction to our first executive recruit — VP Marketing, and [they] sat on Board of Directors.

(5) **Market and Business Intelligence**. Private investors provide several forms of market and business intelligence. These include industry information, identification of potential customers, market feedback, product development, and the identification of potential acquisition targets. Examples include, in addition to those identified in previous quotations (above):

> [Non financial contributions included] identification of possible customers, identification of technical partners or competitors . . . payroll benefits, handling employees.

> [Investor provides] close working relationship with key angels — consultancy, re: takeover targets, financing.

(6) **Credibility**. Private investors play an important accreditation role, especially with respect to further financing. As noted previously, the incidence of subsequent financing from institutional venture capital sources is substantially higher for firms that are angel-financed than for firms that have not been financed by private investors.

> My company's ability to brag about a marquis investor opened doors to other investors, and potential strategic allies, and even a CEO.

This accreditation role is not limited to other forms of risk financing, but also relates to banking relationships as well:

> [Private investor(s)] . . . provided bank guarantees for the company line of credit.

Networking in The Ottawa Cluster in 2000

Respondents were asked to rate the frequency of use of linkages with 11 types of individuals and organizations in the Ottawa cluster. They rated usage on 5-point scales ranging from "not used at all" to "used frequently." The value of these linkages was also measured by asking each respondent to rate the value of each linkage on a 5-point scale ranging from "not at all valuable" to "extremely valuable." The wording of the questions employed was as follows:

> Using the following set of 5-point scales, please rate the *usage frequency* of your firm's links with each of the following sectors within the Ottawa region.

Using the following set of 5-point scales, please rate the *value* of your firm's links with each of the following sectors within the Ottawa region.

Table 2 presents these 11 categories of possible linkages along with the means for each scale for technology and non-technology firms.

A scale measuring overall firm linkage and networking was constructed by adding the scores on the frequency of usage of links with the 11 categories of potential linkages. Contrary to expectations based upon previous literature, a *t*-test comparing mean usage (as measured by this summated scale) between technology and non-technology firms showed that technology firms were significantly less linked than the non technology firms in the Ottawa cluster ($t = 3.44$; $p < 0.001$).

Table 2: Usage and value of cluster linkages.

		Technology Firms ($N = 107$)		Non-Technology Firms ($N = 74$)	
		Mean	**Standard Deviation**	**Mean**	**Standard Deviation**
Boards of trade etc.	Usage	1.5	0.86	1.6	0.91
	Value	1.6	0.86	1.6	0.80
Customers	Usage[a]	2.8	1.55	4.0	1.23
	Value[a]	3.5	1.55	4.4	1.16
Economic development organizations	Usage	1.5	0.83	1.7	0.92
	Value	1.7	0.95	1.7	0.89
Firms in industry	Usage[a]	2.2	1.21	2.9	1.26
	Value[a]	2.4	1.27	3.0	1.31
Government research	Usage	1.9	1.16	1.9	1.12
	Value	2.3	1.41	2.1	1.26
Industry research	Usage[a]	1.7	0.94	2.0	1.12
	Value	2.1	1.23	2.2	1.29
Professional organizations	Usage[a]	2.2	1.11	2.6	1.23
	Value	2.2	1.19	2.4	1.19
Service firms	Usage	3.2	1.19	3.1	1.28
	Value	3.4	1.16	3.3	1.22
Subcontractors	Usage[a]	2.8	1.33	3.2	1.37
	Value	3.1	1.41	3.1	1.43
Suppliers	Usage	3.5	1.34	3.7	1.37
	Value	3.5	1.30	3.4	1.28
University research	Usage	1.8	1.06	1.7	0.92
	Value	2.1	1.25	1.9	1.07

[a] Technology and Non-Technology firms differ significantly on these dimensions at a *p*-value < 0.05.

To further explore where the differences between the two types of firms lay, *t*-tests were done comparing technology and non technology firms on each of the 11 specific linkage categories measured in this study (see Table 2). The results reported in Table 2 show that technology based firms had significantly fewer linkages (*p*-value = 0.05) than non-technology firms with: customers, other firms in the industry, firms in the research industry, subcontractors and professional organizations. (The significant differences are identified by the "ᵃ" in the Table).

Table 2 also shows that, regardless of the level of significance, technology based firms, across the board, were less likely to make use of linkages with other organizations. Overall, the mean values reported in Table 2 suggest that technology firms did not use or value highly linkages with a broad range of possible members of the cluster including: Boards of Trade; firms in the industry; government, university and industry research; professional organizations; and economic development offices. The means of usage and value are all significantly below the midpoint (3.0) of these respective scales.

In summary, technology based firms were significantly less linked than were non-technology based firms. In no instance did technology based firms report significantly more linkages with other organizations or individuals in the Ottawa cluster. In no instance did technology firms value their linkages more than non-technology firms in the Ottawa area did.

To further explore the linkage and networking patterns within the Ottawa Cluster, the authors explored the idea that firms' linkages would be stronger with those organizations that had played a role in the development of the knowledge on which the businesses were based. As noted previously, respondents were asked to report sources of knowledge upon which their company was founded. Respondents who reported that their company was founded on knowledge developed in a previous private sector employer were categorized as having developed company source technology in the private sector. Respondents who reported that their company was founded on knowledge developed in a government lab, university or government departments or agencies were classified as having developed company source technology in the public sector. For the purposes of this analysis, respondents who had reported sources of knowledge that spanned both the public and private sectors were excluded. A total of 17 technology firms in the Ottawa technology cluster were built on technology developed in the public sector. The majority of firms (61) had built their firms on technology developed in the private sector. Both groups of firms used and valued customers, service firms, suppliers, and subcontractors. They differed in terms of their relative usage of government research, subcontractors, Boards of Trade, and Economic Development Officers. Firms that had derived their knowledge base from the private sector were less likely to use government research and more likely to use and value links with subcontractors and Boards of Trade.

It was also found that firms that had derived their knowledge base from the private sector differed from those that had a basis in the public sector in terms of usage and value of Economic Development Offices. Private sector firms were significantly more likely to use economic development offices (*t* = 3.34; *p* = 0.001) and more likely to value this usage (*t* = 2.29; *p* = 0.030). However, neither usage nor value received very high scores from either category of firm, with mean usage and value scores of less than 2 on a five-point scale.

Interestingly, the role of networks and linkages continues to be an important theme as ongoing research reveals that one major type of coping mechanism utilized by a considerable proportion of the Ottawa Cluster technology firms is the further development and usage of networks and linkages in surviving the downturn. The chapter now moves to a discussion of how the firms in the cluster have coped with the significant economic challenges occurring as a result of the technology meltdown.

Impacts of the Technology Meltdown

It goes without saying that the period since mid-2000 has been characterized by an economic downturn (the national unemployment rate increased from 6.7% in mid-2000 to 8.0% by December 2001). The primary effect of this downturn was its impact on technology-based firms, particularly on firms in the IT sub sector. According to the CEO of one Ottawa enterprise: ". . . in telecom it has really been a depression, but in tech generally its been a real strong recession." This led the authors to examine what happened to the firms in the Ottawa Technology Cluster since this downturn. In this examination, the authors first studied the survival rates of the firms that were included in the research conducted at the height of the so-called "technology bubble" in mid-2000. Second, the authors investigated what happened to the firms that did not appear to survive, and third, the authors focused this examination on the strategies that were employed by the firms that did survive the recent economic challenges.

Each of the firms that responded to the mid-2000 baseline survey was followed until mid-2003 to address the survival issue. The authors utilized the Ottawa Business Journal Directory as a sampling frame for the 2000 study. The 2003 version of this Directory was also utilized as a way of checking which respondent firms from the mid-2000 study appeared in the mid-2003 Directory. Those respondent firms from 2000 that appeared in the 2003 Directory were classified as survivors. Those that did not appear in the 2003 version of the sampling frame were followed up via telephone and Internet contacts.

A small sub sample of the firms that had agreed to be interviewed further was selected for in-depth case analysis (conducted in 2002) to understand, among other things, firm perceptions of the challenges (and opportunities) faced and strategies for survival.

Comparing Mid-2000 and Mid-2003

Of the 424 technology firms present in the 2000 version of the sampling frame, 230 (54.2%) were also among the 768 technology firms listed in the 2003 version of the Ottawa Business Journal Database. Among supplier firms 209 of the 343 firms (60.9%) were listed in both directories. However, changes in listing do not necessarily convey accurate information about business survival rates. For example, some firms may have changed names, lines of business, or location. To explore the actual continuity of firms, most of those firms whose CEOs had responded to the mid-2000 survey were followed up. The results are listed in Table 3, which presents the current status for those firms. Among respondents that were followed:

Table 3: 2003 Status of respondent firms.

	Technology Firms	Supplier Firms
Firms operating in both 2000 and 2003 with the same name	81 (73.0%)	53 (70.7%)
Firms operating in both 2000 and 2003 but with name change	11 (10.0%)	5 (6.7%)
Firms acquired	4 (3.6%)	0
Inactive firms	3 (2.7%)	1 (1.3%)
Bankrupt firms	2 (1.8%)	0
Firms that moved	1 (0.9%)	1 (1.3%)
No info	1 (0.9%)	1 (1.3%)
Firms that switched database listings (supplier vs technology)	8 (7.2%)	2 (2.7%)
Firms not followed		12 (16.0%)
	111 (100.0%)	75 (100.0%)

- At least 90% of technology firm respondents to the mid-2000 survey were still operating in 2003.
- At least 95% of the supplier respondents that were followed up here were still operating in mid-2003.

Continuity is obviously not the whole story of firm performance. Firms may have survived by downsizing; others may have suffered profitability declines.

Case Studies of Adaptation

To understand better why the survival rate was so high during a period acknowledged to be very challenging to the technology industry, a series of in-depth interviews were conducted with CEO respondents. A copy of the interview protocol is available on request. The focus of the interviews was to try to understand perceptions of the challenges and opportunities faced by the firms and the strategies employed to cope (and even to prosper) in the new economic situation.

Methodology   As part of the original survey distributed to Ottawa businesses in mid-2000, the CEO respondents were asked if they would be willing to participate in further research on this general topic. Of the 185 CEOs who responded to this question, 70% agreed to such interviews. This chapter reports on the results from 12 of these in-depth case interviews. The authors recognize that the small sample size may limit generalizability. Therefore, the data collection effort is being continued even as this chapter is being written. Because of the importance of these results, it is believed that the presentation of these preliminary results is worthwhile.

The purpose of these in depth interviews was to collect detailed qualitative data. Interviews were conducted on the respondents' premises, lasting an average of 1.5 hours and were audio taped with the consent of the respondent. Subsequently, the interviews were transcribed verbatim and, along with salient data on the attributes of the firms, were entered into NVivo 2.0 for coding and analysis.[2] Table 4 summarizes relevant attributes of the firms whose CEOs were interviewed. The Table shows that the participants represent a range of firm ages, a variety of technology sectors, firms that range in size from very small to larger, and firms that serve local, North American and Global markets. The cases while small in number, do cover a wide spectrum of actual business situations.

Challenges faced during the previous two years   The first finding was that for 3 of the 12 firms, their CEOs responded to the query about challenges faced by commenting that their businesses had continued to prosper in spite of, and indeed, because of, the downturn.

> We're not into that same market. So our market place is a bit different than most other sectors. . . . We're a hot item.

> In this economic downturn, we've actually expanded slightly by increasing the staff in anticipation of what's going to happen next year.

> . . . actually we've done very well. We've been obviously somewhat fortunate in the sense that our technology is the future . . . in a lot of ways. Therefore people were investing [and] we've gotten more licensing opportunities with us, . . . so we were somewhat sheltered.

Otherwise, the rest of the firms faced two major groups of challenges: market challenges and financing challenges.

Market challenges were mentioned by 8 of the 12 firms. All of these firms commented on the shrinkage of their respective product markets. The following direct quotations illustrate CEOs' perspectives on the shrinkage of the markets:

> [a very large customer] was telling us to ramp up a year ago May and then at the end of June, a year ago, they said stop.

---

[2] NVivo is the new version of what had been known as NUD*IST, a frequently-employed means of analyzing qualitative data. Qualitative analysis has often been used in economics with the general aim of understanding complex social phenomena. It is also important to recognize that this qualitative approach has the same degree of generalizability as a controlled experiment. The goal is to expand and generalize theories and explanations, not simply to enumerate frequencies (a confirmatory approach or statistical generalization). The presence of alternative hypotheses (handled in quantitative research through randomization) is explicitly examined in qualitative inquiry by judging how well alternative hypotheses fit. The parallel to the analysis of multiple narratives is that of multiple experiments and involves a "replication logic" where there is a "literal replication" among similar CEOs and a "theoretical replication" of different groups of CEOs with differences being interpreted in light of an existing or "working" theory (Yin 1994).

Table 4: Attributes of interviewed firms.

Firm	Age of Firm	Board of Directors	Markets	Legal Status	Sector	Number of Employees	Technology Orientation
1	>10 years	Yes	Global	Limited Company	Manufacturing	11–20	Technology
2	< 3 years	Yes	National	Limited Company	Software development	11–20	Technology
3	>10 years	Yes	Canada & U.S.	Limited Company	Manufacturing	> 20	Supplier
4	>10 years	Yes	Global	Limited Company	Manufacturing	> 20	Technology
5	3–10 years	Yes	Canada & U.S.	Subsidiary	Consultants	11–20	Services
6	>10 years	Yes	National	Limited Company	Consultants	11–20	Services
7	3–10 years	None	Canada & U.S.	Limited Company	Manufacturing	11–20	Technology
8	3–10 years	Yes	Global	Limited Company	Software development	> 20	Technology
9	3–10 years	Yes	Global	Limited Company	Computer Hardware	> 20	Technology
10	>10 years	Yes	National	Limited Company	IT	> 20	Services
11	3–10 years	None	Canada & U.S.	Limited Company	Computer Hardware	11–20	Technology
12	3–10 years	None	Global	Private Firm	IT	1–5	Services

> ... for the last 18 months our backlog has shrunk and shrunk and shrunk and to the point where I've really got to do something about the size of the staff.

> the market shrank ... by about 20% over the past 12 months.

Other market-related challenges included more intense competition ("as a result of the economic downturn ... you have a great many individuals chasing contracts [and] people are prepared to ... go for lower rates") and increased difficulty in closing deals ("its taken longer to actually get closure ... to get the paperwork out the door").

The primary financing challenge (mentioned by 2 CEOs) was accessing venture capital. To be sure, the level of venture capital investment in Ottawa declined during the last two years; however, it still remains disproportionately high in the Canadian context. Therefore, it is not entirely clear that this perceived problem is unique to the last two years. Likewise, the other finance-related challenge mentioned during the interviews, that of managing cash flows, is not necessarily unique:

> I would have to say that cash flow is the most significant one regardless of the economics in our business. . . . The sale of [our product] will vary from a quarter of a million dollars to $3M and the timing of the payment of $3M system will definitely affect your cash flow a lot more than the timing of a $250,000 system. But cash flow is the main aspect of this business that has to be looked at on a constant basis.

Opportunities perceived during the previous two years   The first finding was that only one of the 12 CEOs interviewed responded to the query about opportunities by commenting that he didn't see any. Otherwise, nine of the CEOs identified two types of opportunities associated with the economic downturn: market development opportunities and reduced competition. For example, one CEO stated (in answer to the query about opportunities) "some of our competitors have gone out of business." This was echoed by a second comment that "a common [opportunity] is competitors have gone out of business." Another CEO revealed that:

> for our product line ... we know of a competitor who is having some financial difficulties so obviously ... if they do decide to shut their doors, that would make a major impact on our business.

In terms of market development, geographic expansion was a common theme:

> The opportunity to enter the Asian market. They realize they had a first mover advantage and capitalized on that ... [and] expansion to foreign markets worked well in the face of saturated markets at home.

> There are a couple of companies that we're working with over in Europe [on] the next generation ... systems.

Strategies employed during the previous two years In addition to "being in the right place at the right time," CEOs articulated three specific types of strategies: focusing on market development; re-investing in themselves; and a focus on building relationships. The quotes above help illustrate the focus on market development. The re-investment strategy is exemplified by the following:

> ...one of the reasons why we're the best performing unit ... is that we retooled in this tech recession.

> We redesigned it, implemented new things, ... met with a fair amount of money expenditure. The organization on a whole is still growing. We've added people throughout the world where we needed those services. So I think on the whole, we weathered the storm.

The third strategy was to build and maintain relationships.

> During this downturn we used various contacts to make sure that they [potential clients] are fully aware of us ...

> During the economic downtime, you really have to rely on those relationships to try to strengthen it, to try to carry it through ... and if we didn't have a good relationship with them [customers], a strong relationship, they may not even have purchased what they did this year.

Summary, Discussion and Conclusions

This chapter attempted to paint a picture of the Ottawa Technology Cluster through weaving together a number of its sometimes disparate attributes. To that end, the chapter described the origins of the firms in the cluster, provided a profile of both businesses and founders of these firms, and identified the sources of knowledge and capital that formed the genesis of these firms. It was found that the enterprises that comprise the Ottawa technology cluster are not "overnight successes," that most had been established for a substantial period. Likewise, these firms were not "fly by night" enterprises but are solidly anchored with inputs (knowledge, people, and financial capital) in the local community.

The chapter then showed that informal investors supplied significant non-financial inputs to the technology firms in the cluster in which they invested. These contributions included advice, hands on involvement, sitting on Boards of Directors and Advisors, credibility, contacts, and market and business intelligence. It should be noted that previous literature has shown that venture capitalists are known to provide some of these contributions at times. The implications of this finding for clusters (or potential clusters) that have not attracted significant amounts of venture capital is fairly clear — the development of regionally based informal investment can make significant contributions towards the development of entrepreneurial firms in a region. A significant implication of these findings is that the non-financial contributions from informal investors, along with networks and contacts maintained by these investors, comprises much of the "glue" that holds the fabric of the Ottawa cluster intact. By extension, a well-developed angel community is a powerful force in the development and maintenance of industrial clusters. To the extent that it is possible to encourage angel investment within a region, economic development agencies can adopt and develop policies to nurture the angel community and its interest in firms in a particular region. The Ottawa cluster can serve as an effective model for such situations.

Further, the chapter showed that the Ottawa technology firms are significantly less linked with other individuals and organizations within the cluster than are the supplier firms in the cluster. The technology firms also value these linkages less than the supplier firms did. These findings are contrary to the directions offered by Ryans *et al.* (2000), by Saxenian (1994), and to the conceptual expectations of many. The normative literature argues that technology based firms should have a high number of linkages with outside firms and organizations. For example, Johannisson (1996: 3) reasons that personal networking should be more important in knowledge-based firms where "sense-making and image building make interpersonal skills a generic asset." Alternatively, perhaps technology firms need to be more adept at developing external relationships in order to be yet more successful. The findings that technology based firms were less linked than the non-technology based firms in the cluster merits additional comment. Several possible reasons might explain the finding.

First, engineers and employees with technical backgrounds dominate technology firms, so it is possible that the establishment and maintenance of social ties (especially weak ties) may not be within interests and/or skill sets of this group. Second, the time demands of establishing and maintaining ties may be "too demanding" in technology based companies known for their rapid growth and tremendous pace of technological change. A third potential explanation relates to the role of extra local links and relations. It may be reasonable to expect that technologically specialized firms will be less likely to find qualified peers in the local environment. In other words, specialized technology firms, even when located in a dynamic regional cluster, may be more likely to develop relations with similar firms in other parts of the world than with less similar local firms. This possibility is currently the subject of ongoing research.

It should also be noted that CEO's in technology-based firms did not value relationships with either customers or other firms in the industry as highly as the CEOs of the non-technology firms. It follows that if the firm does not value these relationships as highly, they may not place as much emphasis on the development and maintenance of these linkages. Recent literature in the relationship marketing area has shown that these relationships must be nurtured and supported if they are to be successfully maintained in the long run (Buttle 1996; Morgan & Hunt 1994). The findings reported here, therefore, suggest that the vitality of the Ottawa cluster could be further enhanced through the promotion of additional valued networking and linkages among regional firms.

Lastly, the chapter showed that at least 170 of the 186 (91.4%) firms in the original sample survived the recession. Strategies utilized included market development, re-investment, retooling, and product innovation, and building relationships. It is interesting to compare these strategies to those identified by Stern (2000) for firms in general. Re-investment includes product research and development, expenditures on increasing quality and value, and preparing new products for market introduction. These are all strategies Stern identifies as having been successfully used by all businesses that prospered during a recession. Similarly, market development, because it implies expenditures on marketing, is consistent with the evidence presented by Stern relating to what successful companies do during tough times. Finally, the emphasis on relationship building found in this study is infrequently mentioned in the traditional strategic management literature. However, a significant body of marketing literature (summarized in Buttle 1999) shows the importance to survival of building and maintaining relationships. It is possible that in the PIMS studies that these expenditures may be characterized as marketing expenditures. To the extent this is true, the results in this chapter, are then consistent with the empirical results presented in the strategic management literature.

One of the possibilities raised by these findings is that the importance of relationships as a means for coping with tough times needs further attention in the strategic management literature. Because of the small sample size and qualitative nature of this exploratory research, future large scale study is required to confirm the extent and use of such strategy during recessionary times by other technology firms.

It is striking that the recent "technology depression" has not resulted in greater frequencies of business failure in the Ottawa cluster. Indeed, there is reason to believe that a substantial fraction of firms in the Ottawa cluster may have continued to prosper. Even those that acknowledged the substantial challenges that they faced developed strategies that have enabled them to survive the pressure of market shrinkage.

In summary, the case studies revealed several key findings regarding surviving a technology downturn. First, the key challenges articulated by the CEOs surrounded market development and financing. This finding may not be surprising as it speaks to what is generally understood by an economic recession — customers reduce making orders (or stop altogether) and firms down the line face considerable financial challenges. While perhaps not surprising, a contribution of the study has been to document the reality faced by these firms during the technology depression/recession.

The research also contributes to knowledge development by documenting the strategies used to cope with these challenges. The three key strategies uncovered included market development, reinvesting in the company, and a focus on building and maintaining relationships. The first two of these strategies require financing: market development and reinvestment both demand financial capital. In turn, firms that maintain good relationships with lenders and investors best achieve access to capital.

The strategies uncovered served to underscore the importance of managing relationships in business. This field of theory development and research has gained significant prominence in the academic literature, particularly in the marketing field in recent years (Argote *et al.* 2003; Madill *et al.* 2002; Ryans *et al.* 2000). This research suggests that reliance on relationships might be a key strategy for survival during times of economic trial.

These results prompt speculation as to the future of the cluster. Overall, the picture painted in the chapter of the Ottawa Cluster shows that many firms have successfully employed strategies to cope with economic stresses. It also suggests that the technology firms in the cluster might benefit from increased networking and relationship development within the cluster. Lastly, the chapter has shown the importance of angel investors in building technology firms within the cluster. Overall, the picture bodes well for the continued economic success of the region, in spite of the recent economic shocks.

Acknowledgments

The authors acknowledge financial support from the Social Sciences and Humanities Research Council for this work. The research assistance of Sylvie Menard and Paul Mitchell is also gratefully acknowledged. The editorial suggestions advanced by the editor of this volume have substantially improved this chapter. All errors and omissions are, of course, the responsibility of the authors.

References

Argote, L., McEvily, B., & Reagans, R. (2003). Managing knowledge in organizations: An integrative framework and review of emerging themes. *Management Science, 49*(4), 571–582.

Barney, J. B., Busenitz, L. W., Fiet, J. O., & Mosel, D. (1994). Determinants of a new venture team's receptivity to advice from venture capitalists. In: W. D. Bygrave, S. Birley, N. C. Churchill, E. Gatewood, F. Hoy, R. H. Keeley, & W. E. Wetzel, Jr. (Eds), *Frontiers of entrepreneurship research*. Babson Park, MA: Babson College. Also available at http://www.babson.edu/entrep/fer/papers94/barney.htm.

Bathelt, H. (1991). Employment changes and input-output linkages in key technology industries: A comparative analysis. *Regional Studies, 25*(1), 31–43.

Buttle, F. (Ed.) (1996). *Relationship marketing theory and practice*. London: Sage.

Bygrave, W., & Timmons, J. (1992). *Venture capital at the crossroads*. Cambridge, MA: Harvard Business School Press.

Callahan, J. (1985). A study of the product line development and risk management of small Canadian high technology firms. Working Paper RC-85-04. Ottawa, Ontario, Canada: Carleton University Research Centre for High Technology Management.

Capello, R. (1999). Spatial transfer of knowledge in high technology milieus: Learning vs. collective learning processes. *Regional Studies, 33*(4), 353–365.

Chell, E., & Baines, S. (2000). Networking, entrepreneurship and microbusiness behaviour. *Entrepreneurship and Regional Development, 12*(3), 195–215.

Collins, W. (2000). *Keynote address*. Annual Conference of the Canadian Council for Small Business and Entrepreneurship, Ottawa, Ontario, Canada.

Cooper, A. C. (1973). Technical entrepreneurship: What do we know? *R&D Management, 3*(2), 59–64.

Cooper, A., & Folta, T. (2000). Entrepreneurship and high-technology clusters. In: D. L. Sexton, & H. Landström (Eds), *The Blackwell Handbook of entrepreneurship* (pp. 348–367). Oxford, UK: Blackwell.

Cooper, S. Y. (1998). Entrepreneurship and the location of high technology small firms: Implications for regional development. In: R. P. Oakey, & W. During (Eds), *New technology based firms in the 1990s* (Vol. V, pp. 247–267). London: Paul Chapman.

Cooper, S., Harrison, R., & Mason C. (2001). Entrepreneurial histories and geographies: A reappraisal of the role of the incubator organization. Paper presented at Babson-Kauffman Entrepreneurship Research Conference, June 7–9, Jankoping, Sweden.

Curran, J., Jarvis, R., Blackburn, R. A., & Black, S. (1993). Networks and small firm constructs, methodological strategies and some findings. *International Small Business Journal, 11*(2), 13–25.

Canadian Venture Capital Association (CVCA 2001, 2002). http://www.cvca.ca/statistical_review/index.html.

de Bernardy, M. (1999). Reactive and proactive local territory: Co-operation and community in Grenoble. *Regional Studies, 33*(4), 343–352.

Doyletech Corporation (2002). A family tree of home grown Ottawa-Gatineau high technology companies, http://www.doyletechcorp.com/pubs.htm.

Doutriaux, J. (1984). Evolution of the characteristics of (high-tech) entrepreneurial firms. Paper presented at Babson Entrepreneurship Research Conference, June 7–9, Atlanta, GA.

Florida, R., & Kenney, M. (1988). Venture capital, high technology and regional development. *Regional Studies, 22*(1), 33–48.

Freel, M. (2000). External linkages and product innovation in small manufacturing firms. *Entrepreneurship and Regional Development, 12*(3), 245–266.

George, G., Wood, D. R., Jr., & Khan, R. (2001). Networking strategy of boards: Implications for small and medium-sized enterprises. *Entrepreneurship and Regional Development, 13*(3), 269–285.

Granovetter, M. (1973). The strength of weak ties. *American Journal of Sociology, 78*, 1360–1380.

Granovetter, M. (1985). Economic action and social structure: The problem of embeddedness. *American Journal of Sociology, 91*, 481–510.

Haines, G., Jr., Madill, J., & Riding, A. L. (2002). Value added by informal investors: Findings from a preliminary study (2002). In: Proceedings of the 47th International Council for Small Business World Conference, *Entrepreneurial SME's and strategic relationships: Making the connections* (pp. 1–23). San Juan, Puerto Rico, June 16–19.

Haines, G., Jr., Madill, J., & Riding, A. L. (2003). Informal investment in Canada: Financing small business growth. *Journal of Small Business and Entrepreneurship, 16*(1), 13–40.

ICF Consulting Inc. (2000). *Choosing a future: A new economic vision for Ottawa.* Ottawa, Ontario, Canada: The Ottawa Partnership.

Johannisson, B. (1995a). Entrepreneurial networking in the Scandinavian context: Theoretical and empirical positioning. *Entrepreneurship and Regional Development, 7*(2), 189–192.

Johannisson, B. (1995b). Paradigms and entrepreneurial networks — some methodological challenges. *Entrepreneurship and Regional Development, 7*(3), 215–231.

Johannisson, B. (1998). Personal networks in emerging knowledge-based firms: Spatial and functional patterns. *Entrepreneurship and Regional Development, 10*(4), 297–312.

Johannisson, B. (2000). Networking and entrepreneurial growth. In: D. L. Sexton, & H. Landström (Eds), *The Blackwell Handbook of entrepreneurship* (pp. 368–386.). Oxford, UK: Blackwell.

Katz, J. A., & Williams, P. M. (1997). Gender, self-employment and weak-tie networking through formal organizations. *Entrepreneurship and Regional Development, 9*(3), 183–197.

Keeble, D., & Wilkinson, F. (Eds) (1999a). Special issue: Regional networking, collective learning and innovation in high technology SMES in Europe. *Regional Studies, 33*(4).

Keeble, D., & Wilkinson, F. (1999b). Collective learning and knowledge development in the evolution of regional clusters of high technology SMEs in Europe. *Regional Studies, 33*(4), 295–303.

Keeble, D., & Wilkinson, F. (Eds) (2000). *High technology clusters, networking, and collective learning in Europe.* Aldershot, UK: Ashgate.

Lawson, C. (2000). Collective learning, system competencies and epistemically significant moments. In: D. Keeble, & F. Wilkinson (Eds), *High technology clusters, networking, and collective learning in Europe* (pp. 182–198). Aldershot, UK: Ashgate.

Lawson, C., & Lorenz, E. (1999). Collective learning, tacit knowledge and regional innovative capacity. *Regional Studies, 33*(4), 305–317.

Lindholm Dahlstrand, A. (1999). Technology-based SMES in the Goteborg region: Their origins and interaction with universities and large firms. *Regional Studies, 33*(4), 379–389.

Longhi, C. (1999). Networks, collective learning and technology development in innovative high technology regions: The case of Sophia-Antipolis. *Regional Studies, 33*(4), 333–342.

Madill, J., Feeney, L., Riding, A. L., & Haines, G., Jr. (2002). Determinants of SME owners' satisfaction with their banking relationships: A Canadian study. *International Journal of Bank Marketing*, 20(2 & 3), 86–99.

Madill, J., Haines, G., Jr., & Riding, A. L. (2001). Networks and linkages in regional technology clusters: The case of Ottawa. Paper presented at Babson-Kauffman Entrepreneurship Research Conference, Jankoping, Sweden.

Mason, C., Cooper S., & Harrison R. (2001). Venture capital in high technology clusters: The case of Ottawa. Paper presented at the 9th Annual High Technology Small Firms Conference, 31 May–1 June 2001, Manchester, UK.

Markusen, A., Hall, P., & Glasmeier, A. (1986). *High tech America*. Boston, MA: Allen & Unwin.

McDougal, B. (1986). Digital dreamers. *Small Business* (December 20–24).

Mittelstaedt, M. (1980). Ottawa: The new high-tech haven. *Canadian Business* (June).

Morgan, R. M., & Hunt, S. D. (1994). The commitment-trust theory of relationship marketing. *Journal of Marketing*, 58(1), 20–38.

Oakey, R. P. (1995). *High-technology new firms: Variable barriers to growth*. London, UK: Paul Chapman.

Oakey, R. P., Faulkner, W., Cooper, S. Y., & Walsh, V. (1990). *New Firms in the Biotechnology Industry*. London, UK: Pinter Publishers.

Ottawa Carleton Research Institute (OCRI) (2000, 2002). http://www.ocri.ca.

Pinch, S., & Henry, N. (1999). Paul Krugman's geographical economics, industrial clustering and the British motor sport industry. *Regional Studies*, 33(9), 815–827.

Reynolds, P., Hay, M., Bygrave, W., Camp, M., & Autio, E. (2001). *GEM global entrepreneurship monitor 2000 executive report*. Babson Park, MA: Kauffman Centre for Entrepreneurial Leadership.

Roberts, E. B. (1991). *Entrepreneurs in high technology*. New York: Oxford University Press.

Roy, J. (1999). *Government and governance in high-technology localities: Ottawa-Carleton and Canada's technology triangle*. Unpublished doctoral dissertation, Carleton University, Ottawa, Ontario, Canada.

Ryans, A., More, R., Barclay, D., & Deutscher, T. (2000). *Winning marketing leadership: Strategic market planning for technology-driven businesses*. Toronto, Canada: Wiley.

Saxenian, A. (1994). *Regional advantage: Culture and competition in Silicon Valley and Route 128*. Cambridge, MA: Harvard University Press.

Schumpeter, J. A. (1934). *The theory of economic development*. Cambridge, MA: Harvard University Press.

Shane, S., & Cable, D. (2002). Network ties, reputation, and the financing of new ventures. *Management Science*, 48(3), 364–381.

Sine, W. D., Shane, S., & DiGregorio, D. (2003). The halo effect and technology licensing: The influence of institutional prestige on the licensing of university inventions. *Management Science*, 49(4), 478–496.

Steed, G. P. F. (1987). Policy and high-technology complexes: Ottawa's Silicon Valley North. In: F. E. I. Hamilton (Ed.), *Industrial change in advanced economics* (pp. 261–269). Brekenham, Kent: Croom Held.

Steed, G. P. F., & DeGenova, D. (1983). Ottawa's technology-oriented complex. *Canadian Geographer*, 27(3), 263–278.

Steed, G. P. F., & Nichol, L. J. (1985). *Entrepreneurs, incubators and indigenous regional development: Ottawa's experience*. Unpublished Manuscript.

Stern, M. (2002). Successful strategies for tough times — a strategic imperative backed by evidence from PIMS, www.sau.is/downloads/marionstern.pdf.

Sternberg, R., & Tamasy, C. (1999). Munich as Germany's no. 1 high technology region: Empirical evidence, theoretical explanations and the role of small firm/large firm relationships. *Regional Studies, 33*(4), 367–377.

Sweetman, K. (1982). Ottawa is also our high-tech capital. *Canadian Geographer, 26*(2), 20–31.

Vanhaverbeke, W. (2001). Realizing new regional core competencies: Establishing a customer-oriented SME network. *Entrepreneurship and Regional Development, 13*(2), 97–116.

Van Osnabrugge, M., & Robinson, R. J. (2000). *Angel investing: Matching start-up funds with start-up companies.* San Fransisco: Jossey-Bass.

Vertinsky, I., & Pe'er, A. (2003). *Entrepreneurship research alliance.* Presentation to Entrepreneurship Research Alliance, Halifax, Nova Scotia, Canada.

Yin, R. (1994). *Case study research: design and methods* (2nd Ed.). London, UK: Sage (Applied Social Research Methods Series).

Chapter 6

The National Capital Region's Product Leadership Cluster

Antonio J. Bailetti

Abstract

Clusters of innovative firms are important tools in improving the prosperity of a region. In this chapter, I present a model for the relationship between worldwide product market leadership and the performance of the region where R&D is core to this leadership. This model builds on the corporate strategy, clusters, and systems of innovation literatures. I then identify the product leadership cluster for Canada's National Capital Region, describes its characteristics, and measures its dimensions. This cluster is comprised of 14 firms in which R&D in the region is core to their leadership positions in 16 product markets.

1. Introduction

Clusters of innovative firms drive a region's growth and employment (Roelandt & den Hertog 1999). Policy makers, regional business development officers, and academics have stressed the importance of the relationship between clusters and regional performance (Ghent Mallet this volume; Held 1996; Jacobs & de Man 1998; Porter 1990, 1997, 1998, 2003; Spielkamp & Vopel 1999). Although significant insights have been gained from this effort, researchers have yet to fully develop a theory of clusters. No research to date has explicitly examined the types and dimensions of clusters and how these affect regional performance. I assert that building and maintaining relationships and interdependencies that address the common needs and constraints of the firms in the product leadership cluster can be an important tool to drive the economic performance of a region.

In this chapter, an attempt is made to advance understanding of clusters by explicitly linking product leadership in worldwide markets with the region where the R&D is core to this leadership is undertaken. A cluster type named the *product leadership cluster* is introduced. A product leadership cluster has two salient characteristics. The first

Silicon Valley North: A High-Tech Cluster of Innovation and Entrepreneurship characteristic in this cluster is that each participating firm has one or more products that occupy worldwide leadership positions. The second characteristic is that all participating firms undertake the R&D that is core to their products' leadership positions in the same region.

The objective of this chapter is twofold. The first objective is to develop a model that captures how the product leadership cluster influences regional performance. The second objective is to identify the product leadership cluster for the National Capital Region, describe its characteristics and measure its dimensions. The chapter offers four important contributions:

(a) A theoretical framework, which captures the relationships among worldwide product leadership, the R&D that drives it and regional performance. The framework described in this chapter builds on the competitive aggressiveness, cluster, and systems of innovation literatures. Previous studies offer descriptions of the company and organization types that are part of the cluster and anecdotal evidence of what decisions affect clusters and regional performance (Doyle *et al.* 2000; Ghent Mallett this volume; Heath 1999). Unless the link between cluster dimensions and regional performance is established, it is difficult to assess how cluster related activities could influence a region's performance.

(b) Identification of the methodological issues that arise when identifying a product-based cluster that does not focus on industrial sectors. While the methodological issues that arise when examining sector-based innovation systems are known (Carlsson *et al.* 2002), the methodological issues that arise when working with cluster-based systems are not well understood. This information may guide researchers and regional development officers in making decisions on the issues that matter most when establishing and maintaining an innovation cluster.

(c) Identification of the product leadership cluster for the National Capital Region, its characteristics, and the cluster-related dimensions that may influence regional performance. To the best of my knowledge, this is the first instance where dimensions of a leadership-based cluster such as size, diversity, and predictability have been linked to the economic performance of the National Capital Region.

(d) Further clarification and new ideas are added to the emerging literature on that integrates systems of innovation and clusters. To date, most systems of innovation studies have defined system boundaries along national, regional, technological or sector boundaries (Carlsson *et al.* 2002; Edquist 2003). Only recently, has the link between the literature on clusters and systems of innovation approaches been made (Porter 2003; Spielkamp & Vopel 1999).

This chapter is organized into seven sections. The first section is the introduction. Section 2 provides background material on clusters and firm taxonomies. Section 3 describes a theoretical framework for relating product leadership clusters to regional performance. In Section 4, the methodological issues that arise when identifying a product leadership cluster are discussed. The method used to identify the National Capital Region's leadership cluster is described in Section 5. Section 6 identifies the characteristics of the National Capital Region's product leadership cluster. Finally, Section 7 provides the conclusions of this study as well as the limitations and suggestions for future research.

2. Clusters and Technology Paths

2.1. Cluster Concept

The cluster concept focuses on the linkages and interdependencies between firms, groups and individuals with dissimilar network positions. Most participants in a cluster are not competitors, but share common needs and constraints (Roelandt & den Hertog 1999). The cluster approach differs from the traditional sector approach in important ways (Porter 1997; Roelandt & den Hertog 1999). A sector approach requires representatives of similar firms that compete directly or indirectly in the same product markets to identify and exploit opportunities. For example, a sector approach for addressing export problems may require that Alcatel, Cisco, Lucent Technologies, and Nortel Networks cooperate to arrive at suitable solutions.

A cluster approach requires representatives of firms that operate in different product markets, their customers, suppliers and specialized service providers to identify and exploit synergistic opportunities. A cluster approach for addressing export problems may require that Alcatel, Nordion, Med-Eng, and Smart Technologies, their customers, suppliers, and specialized institutions cooperate to arrive at suitable solutions.

The type of firms that it attracts influences a cluster's behaviour. The next section describes a useful way to classify firms that participate in cluster activity.

2.2. Technological Paths

Firms can be classified into five categories based on the technology path of their principal activity using a Pavitt-like taxonomy.[1] The five categories are:

2.2.1. Science based   These firms use in-house R&D to incorporate advances in science, technology, and standards into their product lines. Their products and technology diversify quickly in a concentric fashion. Science based firms introduce a relatively high number of product innovations. The ratio of innovations purchased to those produced is low; and when innovations are purchased they come from suppliers in sectors other than their own.

2.2.2. Specialized suppliers   These firms use in-house design and operating experience provided by customers to improve the performance of one or more components, software, instruments, materials, or machines. These improvements are subsequently incorporated into modules or turnkey systems. The products and their technology diversify slowly in a concentric fashion. Specialized suppliers use technology to introduce a relatively moderate

---

[1] The taxonomy described in this chapter is based on the taxonomy first proposed by Pavitt (1984) and then modified by Tidd *et al.* (1997). Pavitt-like taxonomies have been used to examine innovative companies in the U.K. (Pavitt *et al.* 1989), Greece (Souitaris 2002), and Italy (de Marchi *et al.* 1996).

number of products. The ratio of innovations purchased to those produced is low; and when innovations are purchased they frequently come from suppliers in sectors other than their own.

2.2.3. Information intensive   These firms use in-house software and technical groups as well as suppliers of system and application software to design and operate complex systems for processing information.

2.2.4. Supplier dependent   These firms use equipment, material and software provided by suppliers, large customers and government research services to complement their non-technical sources of competitive advantage (e.g. marketing, trademarks, aesthetic design). Their products and services slowly diversify in a vertical fashion. The ratio of innovations purchased to those produced is high for supplier-dependent businesses.

2.2.5. Scale intensive   These firms use internal production-, process- and design-engineering groups as well as suppliers of specialized inputs to reduce costs or incorporate new products and services into their large-scale service delivery networks. Their products and services quickly diversify in a vertical fashion.

3. Model for Product Leadership Clusters

The objective of this section is to describe a model that relates the dimensions of the product leadership cluster with regional performance. Figure 1 provides the model for a product leadership cluster. The model describes how important global, regional and company factors influence the product leadership cluster and how this cluster influences regional

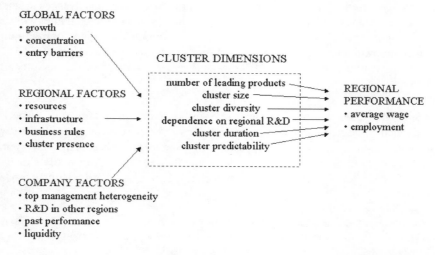

Figure 1: Model for the relationship between a cluster and regional performance.

performance. The focus of this chapter is on the relationship between cluster dimensions and regional performance.

This model expands on the theory and research advanced by the Austrian and hyper competition perspectives of competitive dynamics at the firm level (D'Aveny 1994; Ferrier 2001; Ferrier *et al.* 1999; Lee *et al.* 2000; Smith *et al.* 1992; Young *et al.* 1996). These perspectives suggest that firms that are more competitively aggressive experience better performance. These firms carry out more competitive actions and respond to competitive challenges more quickly (Ferrier 2001). The model shown in Figure 1 extends the findings from the firm level to the local cluster level.

Clusters and regions compete with other clusters and regions in the same way that firms compete with other firms. An important feature of a cluster is its competitive aggressiveness. A cluster's competitive aggressiveness refers to its participants' determination, energy and initiative to perform with the objective to outperform other clusters. I suggest that a cluster's competitive aggressiveness is positively related to regional performance. Competitively aggressive clusters, similar to aggressive firms, should experience better performance. When the product leadership cluster concept is rooted in the region that supports its R&D, the better the cluster performs, the better the region performs.

On the left of Figure 1, the factors expected to constrain and enable the cluster's competitive aggressiveness are identified. Global factors may include industry growth, industry concentration, and barriers to entry. Regional factors may include quality of the resources available to firms (e.g. human, capital, and natural resources, administrative, physical, information, scientific and technical infrastructures), business and investment rules, and cluster presence. Company factors may include the heterogeneity of the top management team, share of total R&D undertaken in other regions, past performance, and liquidity. I propose that the aggressiveness of a product leadership cluster has six dimensions: the number of products that have established worldwide leadership positions, cluster size, cluster diversity, the extent to which firms in the cluster rely on the regional R&D that is core, cluster duration, and predictability of the cluster composition.

On the right side of Figure 1, two measures of regional performance used by Porter (1997) are utilized: average wages and employment. Obviously, other performance measures can be used, however, the key points of this chapter can be made utilizing the two performance measures shown in Figure 1.

The following dimensions of a leadership cluster's competitive aggressiveness influence the relative performance of the region in which the R&D is undertaken.

3.1. Number of Product Markets

The greater the number of product markets in which cluster participants have established leadership positions, the greater the inducements to undertake actions to: (i) start new companies and new business lines; (ii) experiment with new product and process technologies; and (iii) undertake risks with worldwide payoffs. A cluster that includes firms with worldwide successful optical and life sciences products, for example, increases the likelihood of regional investment to exploit new opportunities in biophotonics. The number of product lines, therefore, is positively related to the number of jobs and average pay in the region.

3.2. Cluster Size

The greater the number of firms in a cluster, the greater the inducement to undertake actions to: (i) access specialized inputs and training programs; (ii) rapidly diffuse best practices; and (iii) coordinate transactions across firms. The greater the number of actions that are undertaken in a region, the greater the number of jobs and the average pay in the region. Therefore, cluster size is positively related to the number of jobs and average pay in the region.

3.3. Dependence on Regional R&D

The more cluster participants depend on regional R&D for their product lines successes, the greater the inducement to enhance the quantity and the quality of the resources available in the region. The process of improving the quality and quantity of resources available generates jobs and competitive salaries. The extent of the need for regional R&D, therefore, is positively related to the number of jobs and average pay in the region.

3.4. Cluster Diversity

Prior research suggests that firms that carry out a wide array of competitive actions experience high levels of performance (Ferrier *et al.* 1999; Miller & Chen 1996). I suggest that the greater the variety of cluster participants, the wider the range of action types the cluster will undertake. The wider the range of actions the cluster undertakes, the more opportunities will exist to create jobs at competitive salaries in the region. Cluster diversity is positively related, therefore, to the number of jobs and average pay in the region.

3.5. Cluster Duration

The longer the duration of the cluster, the greater the participants' accumulated experience on how to use the cluster to compete worldwide, which increases decision-making efficiency. The longer the cluster duration, the faster firms can act to identify and exploit opportunities. Cluster duration is, therefore, positively related to the number of jobs and average pay in the region.

3.6. Cluster Predictability

If a cluster never changes, its behavior becomes predictable. Over time, cluster participants work on fine tuning their approaches resulting in more efficient delivery. The cluster acts to support the same companies in similar ways but does not assist non-cluster firms in their efforts to establish product leadership positions. Cluster predictability, therefore, is negatively related to the number of jobs and average pay in the region.

4. Methodological Issues

The objective of this section is to discuss methodological issues with respect to the identification of product leadership clusters. Identifying clusters requires an informed creative process (Porter 1998) and arbitrary decisions by researchers (Carlsson *et al.* 2002). My creative process and decisions were based on two assumptions:

- That important linkages and interdependencies can be established across firms to support their products, which lead worldwide and the regional R&D which is core to these products.
- That these linkages and interdependencies can be important tools to improve regional performance.

Some of the issues identified below may be similar to those that arise when other cluster types are examined. For example, Carlsson *et al.* (2002) identify three methodological issues that stand out as problematic in their research work: level of analysis, cluster population, and performance measurement.

The author of this paper found seven methodological issues to be of interest:

- establishing the starting point to delineate the cluster;
- defining the cluster boundaries;
- identifying the population of the cluster;
- identifying the products that have established leadership positions in their product markets;
- deciding which product category combinations to include in the cluster;
- determining the dependency of a product line on the regional R&D;
- classifying a product based on their company's technological path.

4.1. Starting Point

To identify a cluster, a starting point is needed. Carlsson *et al.* (2002) identify three starting points they have used productively in their studies: a knowledge field (e.g. photonics, bioscience, or physics), a product (e.g. mobile phones, interactive whiteboards, enzymes for industrial applications), and a competence bloc (e.g. a particular function such as fast transportation or security whose needs are satisfied by various complementary products and services). Given the purpose of this study, starting with the product seemed more natural than starting with knowledge fields or product clusters. Thus, the start point for the study was a product. An informed guess is that the results obtained by using technology fields or product clusters would have been very different from those reported in this study.

4.2. Cluster Boundaries

Figure 2 illustrates the key issues pertaining to the boundaries of the product leadership cluster we have studied. This Figure schematically illustrates seven dissimilar products,

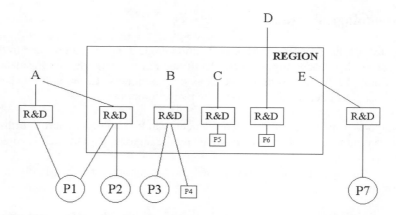

Figure 2: Defining the boundaries of the product leadership cluster.

P1 to P7. The rectangles with an "R&D" inside indicate the locations of the R&D where the products are developed relative to the region. The letters A, B, C, D and E denote companies and they show the locations of the companies' worldwide headquarters relative to the region. Companies A and D have their worldwide headquarters outside of the region. A product inside a large circle (i.e. P1, P2, P3 and P7) indicates that the product has established a worldwide leadership position. A product inside a smaller circle (P4, P5 and P6) indicates that the product has not established a worldwide leadership position. The large rectangle delineates the boundary of the region.

Figure 2 shows that company A develops and sells P1 and P2 and that both products lead in their markets. Only part of the R&D core to P1 is in the region, whereas the entire R&D that is core to P2 is in the region. The product leadership cluster that we intend to identify includes both products P1 and P2. Both have established leadership positions and both rely on R&D located in the region for their market leadership positions. Note that the location of company A's headquarters did not play a role in the decision to include P1 and P2 in the product leadership cluster. Company B sells P3 and P4 and the R&D, which is core to both products, is in the region. Our cluster includes only P3. Product P4 is not included in the cluster because it has not established a worldwide leadership position. Products P5 and P6, sold by companies C and D respectively, are not included in the cluster. These products do not sell worldwide. P7, which is developed and sold by company E, leads worldwide. P7 is not included in the product leadership cluster because the R&D that its core to its leadership position is outside the region. Note that the fact that company E's headquarters is located in the region was not a factor in the decision to exclude P7 from the cluster.

In summary, of the seven products shown in Figure 2, the product leadership cluster only includes P1, P2 and P3. These are the only products that meet the following criteria:

- product has established a leadership position worldwide; and
- the R&D that is core to the product is located in the region.

It is important to note that had I used a different starting point or criteria, the results of the analysis would not have matched those reported above. For example, had I used knowledge field as the starting point and the criteria would have favored the inclusion of products based on the location of company headquarters, the composition of the cluster would have been a different one than the one identified above.

4.3. Identifying Cluster Population

Identifying the population of a cluster is, of course, a key objective for a researcher. Carlsson *et al.* (2002) discuss two issues involved in this exercise. The first is determining whether or not a specific firm belongs to the cluster, and, second establishing whether or not we have found all the firms in the cluster.

In this study, identifying the firms that are part of the cluster is simple. Those firms that develop and sell the products determined to lead worldwide are part of the cluster. In the example illustrated in Figure 2, we determined that P1, P2 and P3 are part of the cluster. Thus, companies A and B that develop and sell these three products are part of the product leadership cluster. In this study I made no attempt to identify the non-firms that are part of this cluster. A non-firm includes organization such as universities, regional development agencies, and specialized government departments. It is assumed that firms would invite non-firms that can add value to join the product leadership cluster.

The second issue is more challenging. To increase the likelihood that we had identified all the companies in the cluster, two approaches were implemented:

- Including the input of 24 individuals with specific expertise and experiences in the process of identifying firms.
- Asking firms that were identified as being part of the cluster from the outset to identify other products and/or firms that could potentially meet the criteria for cluster membership.

4.4. Products that Lead

To define the product leadership cluster, I need to identify products with worldwide leadership positions in their markets. To successfully identify products that lead worldwide, at least three questions require responses:

- What criteria will be used to establish that a product leads worldwide? (e.g. What is meant by a "product has established a worldwide leadership position?")
- What information sources will be admissible to support claims that products have established worldwide leadership positions? (e.g. Responses to questionnaires, opinions from community leaders, customers' assessments, company news releases, non-disclosed company information, government awards, reports from market tracking organizations, studies from academics or consultants.)

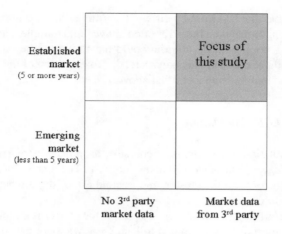

Figure 3: Product categories.

- During how many quarters should evidence of product leadership be collected? (e.g. Is market share data collected for one quarter sufficient to support a claim that a product has established a worldwide leadership position?)

The answers to the three questions are interdependent and it was determined that products could be organized into four categories depending on:

- whether market share data for the product was available from independent 3rd parties such as a market tracking organizations or in studies published by researchers or consultants;
- the number of years the product had been in the market.

Figure 3 illustrates the four categories used to organize products. Each of the four quadrants shown in Figure 3 requires its own definitions of product leadership and guidelines to assure that the product meets these corresponding standards. Moreover, the interval of time required for evidence gathering may also vary across the quadrants.

The top row in Figure 3 includes products in established markets, while the bottom row includes products in emerging markets. The five-year marker was one of those informed, arbitrary decisions to which Porter (1998) refers that was made by the researcher. Products for which no market data was available from 3rd parties are included in the first column. Products for which this data was available are included in the second column. The criteria used to determine product leadership for established and emerging markets are shown below:

4.5. Established Market

A product is a worldwide leader in an established market if there is 3rd party evidence that its worldwide market share has been ranked within the top five or has at least 25% market share in the last three years (2001–2003).

4.6. Emerging Market

A product is a worldwide leader in an emerging market if there is 3rd party evidence that:

(1) The product was bought by at least 5 of the largest incumbent organizations (i.e. customers that buy high volumes of the type of product/service the firm offers),
    or
    the product was bought in large volumes by a new set of customers in a recently created market.
(2) The firm's annual revenue due to the product's sales has grown significantly ($\sim$50%) year after year over a three-year period.
(3) The product started selling within the last five years.

4.6.1. Product categories   The product leadership cluster can de delineated in such a way as to include different combinations of the product categories shown in Figure 3. For example, those firms with products for which 3rd party market reports can be used to support their product leadership positions in both the established and emerging markets can be included in a cluster. This chapter reports the results obtained for one quadrant, located on the upper right corner of Figure 3. This quadrant includes products in large established markets for which market share data was available from market tracking organizations and independent market studies. Different versions of the products had been in the market for at least five years. For this study, it was important to avoid selecting a product as being the market leader based on market share data collected for only one or two quarters. It was decided that, in an established market, evidence collected over a three-year period was required to identify a product as a worldwide leader.

4.6.2. Dependency on regional R&D   A company can depend on the regional R&D in a variety of ways. When identifying a cluster of companies that have interdependence with a particular region, the stronger the region-company interdependence the more significantly the region's performance will be influenced by the performance of the company's products. The link between a company and a region depends on whether:

• the company's headquarters is located in the region;
• the company's products lead worldwide;
• the R&D that is core to the product's market position is located in the region.

Figure 4 illustrates three of the forms the company-region link can take when worldwide leading products are involved. The Xs indicate the location of the company's worldwide headquarters and the P in a circle denotes a product that has established a worldwide leadership position. I suggest that the company's dependency on the region decreases from left to right.

4.6.3. Technological paths   Methodological issues arise when applying a Pavitt-like taxonomy to companies and products. Firms are not limited to simply one of these trajectories and these typologies are not 3-digit level sector dependent. For example, while most large

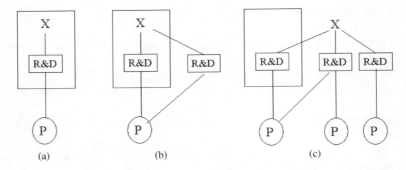

Figure 4: Three potential configurations of the company-region link anchored around worldwide leading products.

telecommunications firms would be classified as science-based, there are also supplier-dominated telecommunications firms. The taxonomy related issue, which is most worri-some, arises when the technological trajectory of a leading product is different from the technological trajectory of the firm's principal activity.

5. Method

5.1. Unit of Analysis

The unit of analysis is a product developed by a company with a presence in the National Capital Region.

5.2. Cluster Boundaries

The cluster boundaries are determined by one attribute associated with the product and two attributes associated with the R&D organization that develops it. The product attribute is that the product has worldwide leadership in an established market. The R&D attributes are that it is core to the development of the product, and that is located in the National Capital Region.

5.3. Time Period

The population in the product leadership cluster is identified as of December 2003.

5.4. Identification of the Cluster Population

A five-step process was used to identify the population of the leadership cluster for established products:

(1) Acquisition of product and company names from community members.
(2) Search for 3rd party market share information.
(3) Identification of the locations of the R&D groups which are core to products' leadership positions.
(4) Acquisition of market information directly from companies.
(5) Acquisition of feedback on different versions of the cluster's population.

5.5. Input from Community Members

Twenty-eight professionals were invited via e-mail to provide names of companies that developed leading products using R&D facilities in the National Capital Region. Each professional was invited to provide up to 10 company names. The 28 professionals were classified into seven community categories based on their source of income: (i) executives in large companies (company with more than 500 employees); (ii) executives in small companies; (iii) federal government employees; (iv) university faculty and technology transfer officers; (v) presidents and managers of professional associations; (vi) service providers and self-employed; and (vii) regional business developers. Fourteen of the 28 professionals were known to the writer and all 28 professionals were deemed to be very familiar with the firms that operate in the National Capital Region.

5.6. Market Share Information

An online search for market share data on the identified companies' products was conducted. The market share data came exclusively from the following sources: market tracking organization whose reports were widely used in industry or market studies prepared by academics, government employees or members of independent research organizations. The leadership performance of these companies' products was then assessed based on the following criteria:

> A product is identified as a worldwide leader in an established market when there is 3rd party evidence that the product's worldwide market share has been ranked within the top five or has at least 25% market share in the last three years (2001–2003).

5.7. Establishing the Location of the R&D that is Core to the Leading Product

The locations of the companies' R&D organizations were obtained from the company websites and/or their annual reports. When it was not clear which R&D locations were core to a product's leadership position, a member of the top management team in the R&D organization located in the National Capital Region was asked to identify the location of the core R&D teams.

5.8. Company Information

Representatives of the identified companies were requested to:

- check the accuracy of the information gathered from market reports and the location of the R&D core to their products' leadership positions;
- provide additional information that could be used to support their products' leadership positions;
- clarify publicly available data.

5.8.1. Obtaining feedback on cluster population   Weekly updates of the cluster population were sent to the professionals who provided company names at the outset. Professionals were asked to:

- examine the cluster population and provide feedback as to the quality and reliability of the sources used to support product leadership positions and the decisions made during the week; and
- provide names of additional companies that may be part of the cluster population.

After four weeks of feedback and ongoing updates, the final population cluster was determined for the National Capital Region based on this information.

6. Product Leadership Cluster

The objective of this section is to identify the participation rate of professionals, the product leadership cluster, and its salient characteristics.

6.1. Participation Rate

Nineteen of the 28 professionals invited to help identify the population of the product leadership cluster for the National Capital Region, actively participated in the process. Table 1 indicates that the overall participation rate was 68% and the participation rate by community category ranged from a low of 25–100%. The professionals who participated in the process provided company and product names, pointed to sources of market share data, facilitated introductions to companies' managers, and provided input on the updated versions of the cluster.

6.2. Product Leadership Cluster

Table 2 identifies the population of the product leadership cluster as of December 15, 2003. This cluster is comprised of 14 firms in which R&D in the National Capital Region is core in 16 established product markets.

Table 1: Rate of participation in the process to identify the National Capital Region's product leadership cluster.

Community Category	Number Invited to Participate	Number of Participants	Participation Rate (%)
Large company executives	4	4	100
Small company executives	4	4	100
Federal government's assistant deputy ministers and director	4	3	75
University faculty and technology transfer officers	4	3	100
Presidents and managers of professional associations	4	2	50
Service providers and consultants	4	2	50
Officers responsible for regional business development	4	1	25
	28	19	68

6.3. Technology Paths and Stock Listings

Table 3 classifies the companies in the product leadership cluster based on the technology path of their principal activity and, and if it is a public company, the stock exchange in which the company's equity is listed. Table 3 also provides the cities where corporate worldwide headquarters are located.

Table 3 indicates that all but one of the companies in the cluster can be classified in the science based and information intensive categories. Companies that fit the supplier dependent and scale intensive categories are not part of the product leadership cluster.

Three of the 14 companies in the cluster are privately held (Mitel Networks, QNX, and Corel). All the 11 public companies trade in U.S. exchanges. Not a single company in the cluster trades exclusively in the Toronto Stock Exchange. Three companies in the cluster (Cisco, Entrust, and RIM) trade in the NASDAQ National Exchange and not in the Toronto Stock Exchange.

6.4. Worldwide Corporate Offices

Table 4 indicates the cities where the worldwide head offices of the firms in the product leadership cluster are located. Seventy one percent of the firms in the cluster maintain their worldwide offices in Ontario, 43% in the National Capital Region, and 28% split between Toronto and Waterloo. Twenty one percent of the cluster population maintains offices in the United States and 7% in Europe.

Table 2: The National Capital Region's product leadership cluster.

Product in Established Market	Company[a]	Product's Worldwide Market Leadership Position[b]
Multi service wide area networks (WAN) equipment	Alcatel	4th by ports with 14.3% market share in 3Q03, 2nd with 17.5% in 2002, and 3rd with 18.3% in 2001 (Dell'Oro 2003a); 2nd by revenue with 25% market share in 2002 (Yankee Group 2003); 4th by sales with 15.5% market share in 3Q03, market share in the 10–23% range since 4Q00 (Synergy Research Group 2003a)
	Cisco	3rd by ports with 14.4% market share in 3Q03, 4th with 15.6% in 2002, and 4th with 14.5% in 2001 (Dell'Oro 2003a); 4th by revenue with 18.1% market share in 2002 (Yankee Group 2003); 3rd by sales with 17.4% in 3Q03, market share in the 14–25% range since 4Q00 (Synergy Research Group 2003a)
	Nortel Networks	1st by ports with 41.8% market share in 3Q03, 40% in 2002, and 32.4% in 2001 (Dell'Oro 2003a: 91); 1st by revenue with 28% market share in 2002 (Yankee Group 2003); 1st by sales with 31.1% market share in 3Q03, market share in the 26–37% range since 4Q00 (Synergy Research Group 2003a)
Carrier routers	Cisco	1st by revenue with 65% in 3Q03 (Moritz 2003); 1st by sales with market share in the 60–80% range since 4Q00 (Duffy 2003; Harvey 2001)
Optical transport equipment[c]	Nortel Networks	1st by revenue with 14.9% market share in 3Q03, 17.9% in 2002 and 18.4% in 2001; 1st by DWDM metro equipment revenue with 28.5% market share in 3Q03, 39.8% in 2002 and 41.8% in 2001; 1st by DWDM long haul revenue with 17.3% market share in 3Q03, 23.2% in 2002 and 21.4% in 2001; 2nd by multi service SONET (Dell'Oro 2003b: 18–35)
Optical components	JDS Uniphase	1st in 2002 and 2nd in 1Q03 (Hawtof 2003a, b); 1st in 2002 (Rigby 2002); 40% market share in 2002 (Red Herring 2002); 1st in Q203 (Bookham Technology 2003)

Table 2: (*Continued*)

Product in Established Market	Company[a]	Product's Worldwide Market Leadership Position[b]
Private branch exchanges less than 400 lines[d]	Mitel Networks*	5th by IP telephony lines shipped worldwide with 9 and 7.5% market share in 2Q02 and 2Q01 (Synergy Research Group 2002); 5th by IP telephony lines shipped in 2Q03 and 1Q03 (Dell'Oro 2003c, d)
Public key infrastructure software	Entrust	1st by revenue with over 38% market share in 2002 (Weiner 2002); 1st by revenue with 38.5% market share in 2001 (Fishbein & Holbrook: 35)
Standalone virtual private networks	Cisco	1st by revenue with 39.3% market share in 2Q03 and 35.7% in 1Q03 (Synergy Research Group 2003b)
Enterprise business intelligence suites and reporting[e]	Cognos*	1st in 2003 (Cognos 2003); 3rd in analytics tools revenues in 2002 (Guglielmo *et al.* 2003); 3rd by dollars spent by customers on solutions based on online analytical processing products with 12.6% market share in 2002 (Pendse 2004); 1st by combined software license and maintenance revenue in 2001 (Supportindustry.com 2002)
Enterprise content management solutions	Open Text	1st by revenue with a market share of 28% (Kessler 2003); world's largest share of enterprise content management business (Content Management 2003)
Desktop graphics	Corel*	2nd with 9% market share in 2003 (Gartner 2003)
Real time operating systems and embedded software development tools	QNX*	5th by shipments of embedded operating systems, bundled products, and related services with 4.7% market share in 2002 (VDC 2003a); 2nd by revenue of embedded software tools for UNIX with 12% market share in 2002 (Gartner Dataquest); 3rd by revenue of real time operating systems, bundled products and related services (VDC 2003b); 4th in real time operating systems with 7% market share in 2001 (Gartner 2002)
Wireless data/voice devices and solutions	Research in Motion (RIM)	4th by converged handheld units shipped with 4.6% market share in 2Q03 (IDC 2003)

Table 2: (*Continued*)

Product in Established Market	Company[a]	Product's Worldwide Market Leadership Position[b]
Time division multiplexing voice/data switching chips	Zarlink Semiconductor*	1st by units shipped with 25% market share in 2003[f] (Confidential market research study prepared for Zarlink Semiconductor 2003)
Cobalt-60	MDS Nordion	1st by revenue with 80% market share (Kupchinsky 2002); 1st by revenue (Ferguson *et al.* 2003: 40)
Medical isotopes	MDS Nordion	1st by revenue with 50–70% market share (House of Commons Debates 2002: 568; Malkoske 2002: 5; Puscas 2002); no significant competition (Chemical and Engineering News 2003)
Pulsatile ventricular assist devices	World Heart*	2nd by revenue in 2003[g] (Confidential market research study prepared for World Heart 2004)

Note: An * indicates that the firm maintains its worldwide corporate office in the National Capital Region.

[a] Each company listed in this table has R&D in the National Capital Region which is core to the product line with which the company has established a worldwide leadership position.

[b] References supporting the products' market positions are shown after the table, they are kept separate from the references used in the text of the chapter.

[c] Total optical transport equipment includes: Dense Wavelength Division Multiplexers (DWDM) long haul terrestrial; DWDM metropolitan; multiservice SONET/SDH; and optical switches.

[d] Includes Internet Protocol PBXs and traditional PBXs.

[e] Includes query and reporting, online analytical processing, data visualization, and event management.

[f] According to rules in the United States, Zarlink must be able to show this research to the Securities and Exchange Commission if so asked. The company does not make this research available to the general public.

[g] The company does not make this research available to the general public.

6.5. Cluster Dimensions

This section provides estimates on the dimensions of the product leadership cluster of the National Capital Region. Thus, the number of product markets is 16 and the cluster population is 14 (see Table 2).

The basic methodological approach used by Wiersema & Bantel (1992) and Ferrier (2001) to develop a composite measure of top management heterogeneity can be used to develop a composite measure of cluster diversity. Two measures of cluster diversity are calculated: technological path and equity market. To calculate technological path diversity, I applied Blau's index of heterogeneity (Blau 1977) to the five different path

Table 3: Firms in the product leadership cluster classified based on their technology path and exchange in which their stocks trade.[a]

	NYSE & TSE	NASDAQ-NM	NASDAQ-NM & TSE	TSE & OTCCB	Private Company	Total	%
Science based	Alcatel (Paris), MDS (Toronto), Nortel Networks (Toronto), Zarlink (Ottawa)	Cisco (San Jose)	JDS Uniphase (San Jose)	Worldheart (Ottawa)	Mitel networks (Ottawa)	8	57
Specialized suppliers					QNX (Ottawa)	1	7
Information intensive		Entrust (Dallas), RIM (Waterloo)	Cognos (Ottawa), Open Text (Waterloo)		Corel (Ottawa)	5	36
Supplier dependent						0	0
Scale intensive						0	0
Total	4	3	3	1	3	14	100
%	30	21	21	7	21	100	

[a] The acronyms used as column headings refer to the exchanges: NYSE = New York Stock Exchange, TSE = Toronto Stock Exchange, NASDAQ = National Association of Securities Dealers Automatic Quotation System, NASDAQ-NM = NASDAQ National Market, OTCCB = Over the Counter Bulletin Board.

Table 4: Location of the worldwide corporate headquarters of the firms in the product leadership cluster.

Location of Worldwide Corporate Headquarters	Number of Firms in the Product Leadership Cluster	% of Cluster Population
Ottawa, Ontario	6 (Cognos, Corel, Mitel Networks, QNX, Zarlink Semiconductor, and Worldheart)	43
Waterloo, Ontario	2 (Open Text, RIM)	14
Toronto, Ontario	2 (MDS, Nortel Networks)	14
San Jose, California	2 (Cisco, JDS Uniphase)	14
Addison, Texas	1 (Entrust)	7
Paris, France	1 (Alcatel Canada)	7
	14	100

categories shown in Table 3: science based, specialized suppliers, information intensive, supplier dependent, and scale intensive. A high score suggests that the cluster is diverse with respect to technological paths. I also applied Blau's index of heterogeneity to the five equity market categories shown in Table 3: NYSE & TSE, NASDAQ-NM, NASDAQ & TSE, TSE & OTCCB and a private company. Once again, a high score suggests that the cluster is diverse with respect to equity markets.

A composite measure of cluster diversity was obtained by adding the two standardized diversity measures described above. The cluster's technological path diversity index is 0.3 and the equity market index is 0.8. The composite measure is 0.6. This suggests that the diversity in equity markets is greater than the diversity of technological paths. The percentage of firms with worldwide corporate offices in the National Capital is used as a proxy around the need for regional R&D. Table 3 indicates that this percentage is 43%.

It was not possible to measure the cluster's duration for lack of data. The market data to indicating in which quarter a product became a world leader was not available to us. Given that the criteria used to identify products required three years evidence, it can be concluded that the average duration of the product's leadership position was greater than 3 years. The 1993–2003 cluster predictability based on product markets could not be measured due to lack of data. It was not possible to identify the products that led in 1993. Data difficulties can be overcome in the future by continuously and consistently tracking the products that lead worldwide. Cluster predictability based on the companies that existed in 1993 is 0.8.

7. Conclusions and Suggestions for Future Research

In a global economy, companies are increasingly using local knowledge, relationships and motivation to compete (Porter 1998). Research on the relationship between an innovative company cluster and regional performance is relatively new. A theoretical framework that focuses on the interdependence between a cluster's dimensions and regional performance does not exist.

In this chapter, I proposed a model for the interdependence between six dimensions of a particular type of cluster and two measures of regional performance. Firms are identified as being part of a product leadership cluster based on the leadership position of one or more of their products and their dependency on a region in which the R&D is core. The most difficult analytical methodological issues arising from various studies of innovation systems have only recently become known. The studies used to report these difficulties are all sector based, not cluster based. This chapter identified the seven methodological problems, which arose when identifying product leadership clusters and their characteristics. The product leadership cluster for the National Capital Region is identified and its characteristics described. So far, this cluster is comprised of 14 firms in which regional R&D is core in 16 product markets.

The limitations of this study are typical of those studies undertaken in emerging research areas where there is a lack of theoretical framework and easily accessible data. While methodological issues abound, guidelines on how to effectively overcome these issues are not widely understood.

Several areas of study for future research seem promising. Research in corporate strategy has flourished particularly on methods for aggressive competition. Yet, these methods have not been used to examine the relationship between clusters and regional development. If Porter is correct, and I believe he is, companies will increasingly rely on regions to compete against their distant rivals (Porter 1998). It seems natural to apply what has been learned from the literature on competitive aggressiveness at the firm level to the cluster level. Further study and applications of the framework developed by Ferrier (2001) seem particularly promising.

A second area of potential research would be to compare the cluster-region relationships proposed in this chapter across different regions known to host large clusters of innovative companies. A third area of potential research would be to measure the relationship between the antecedents and the consequences of clusters comprised of innovative companies. While narratives about the structures of these clusters are always interesting, perhaps the time has come for an increased emphasis on measurement.

Acknowledgments

I wish to express my appreciation to Peter Leach for many helpful ideas and comments and to the 19 professionals who assisted in the identification of the product leadership cluster for the National Capital Region. I would also like to thank Anne Marie Bourgeois for her editorial assistance.

References

Blau, P. M. (1977). *Inequality and heterogeneity*. New York: Free Press.
Bookham Technology (2003). *Thinking optical solutions*. http://www.newfocus.com/company/USInvestorPresentationOct03.pdf. Accessed on 28 February 2004.

Carlsson, B., Jacobsson, S., Holmén, M., & Ricckne, A. (2002). Innovation systems: Analytical and methodological issues. *Research Policy*, *31*, 233–245.

Cognos (2003). META Group gives Cognos top marks for market presence and performance, April 3. http://www.cognos.com/news/releases/2003/0403.html. Accessed on 28 February 2004.

D'Aveny, R. (1994). *Hypercompetition: Managing the dynamics of strategic maneuvering*. New York: Free Press.

Dell'Oro (2003a). Routers report 3Q03. *Dell'Oro group*, November. Redwood City, CA: Dell'Oro Group.

Dell'Oro (2003b). Optical transport report 3Q03. *Dell'Oro group*, November. Redwood City, CA: Dell'Oro Group.

Dell'Oro (2003c). Shipments of enterprise VoIP lines exceed 1 million in 1Q03. *Dell'Oro group*, July 16. http://www.delloro.com/PRESS/PressReleases/2003/IPTelephony071603.shtml. Accessed on 28 February 2004.

Dell'Oro (2003d). Enterprise VoIP line shipments rise 23% in 3Q03. *Dell'Oro group*, November 18. http://www.delloro.com/PRESS/PressReleases/2003/IPTelephony111803.shtml. Accessed on 28 February 2004.

Doyle, D., McDougall, G. M., & Doyle, J. (2000). *A vision of high-technology activity in Eastern Ontario during the period from 2000 to 2030*. Ottawa, Ont., Canada: Doyletech Corporation.

Duffy, J. (2003). Cisco's loss is Juniper's gain. *NetworkWorldFusion*, February 18. http://www.nwfusion.com/edge/news/2003/0218mktshare.html. Accessed on 28 February 2004.

Editorial (2003). Open Text buys Ixos. *Content Management*, October 29. http://www.cmfocus.com/xq/asp/sid.0/articleid.ED7A6D92-8177-4119-BD4E-DAD0F4A67D14/qx/display.htm. Accessed on 28 February 2004.

Edquist, C. (2003). *The internet and mobile telecommunications systems of innovation*. Cheltenham, UK: Edward Elgar.

Ferguson, C. D., Tahseen, K., & Perera, J. (2003). Commercial radioactive sources: Surveying the security risks. *Monterey Institute of International Studies, Center for Nonproliferation Studies*, Occasional Paper #11. http://cns.miis.edu/pubs/opapers/op11/op11.pdf. Accessed on 28 February 2004.

Ferrier, W. J. (2001). Navigating the competitive landscape: The drivers and consequences of competitive aggressiveness. *Academy of Management Journal*, *44*, 858–877.

Ferrier, W. J., Smith, K. G., & Grimm, C. (1999). The role of competitive action in market share erosion and industry dethronement: A study of industry leaders and challengers. *Academy of Management Journal*, *42*, 372–388.

Gartner (2002). Embedded software development tools and real time operating systems: The challenges ahead. *Gartner, Inc*. Stamford, CT: Gartner.

Gartner (2003). 2002 Worldwide embedded software tools market share. *Gartner Dataquest*. Stamford, CT: Gartner.

Government of Canada (2002). Comments made by Mrs. Cheryl Gallant. *House of Commons Debates* (Vol. 138), Number 009, 2nd Session, 37th Parliament, October 10. http://www.parl.gc.ca/PDF/37/2/parlbus/chambus/house/debates/Han009-E.PDF. Accessed on 28 February 2004.

Guglielmo, C., Myron, D., Picarille, L., & Schnieder, M. (2003). The 2003 market leaders (Part 2): Which vendors are leading the industry? *CRM Magazine*, September. http://www.destinationcrm.com/articles/default.asp?ArticleID=3431. Accessed on 28 February 2004.

Harvey, P. (2001). Router numbers support Cisco. *Light Reading*, August 21. http://www.lightreading.com/document.asp?doc_id=7586. Accessed on 28 February 2004.

Hawtof, B. (2003a). No safe haven found in 2002 global OC market. *RHK Annual Market Share Report, Optical Components*, March. http://www.rhk.com/rhk/research/research_detail.jsp?sku=33010. Accessed on 28 February 2004.

Hawtof, B. (2003b). RHK global OC decline slows; Agilent slides into first. *RHK Market Update Report, Optical Components*, June. http://www.rhk.com/rhk/research/research_detail.jsp? sku=33011. Accessed on 28, February 2004.

Heath, R. (1999). The Ottawa high-tech cluster: Policy or luck? In: T. J. A. Roelandt, & P. den Hertog (Eds), *Boosting innovation: The cluster approach* (pp. 175–191). Paris, France: Organization for Economic Cooperation and Development.

Held, J. R. (1996). Clusters as an economic development tool: Beyond the pitfalls. *Economic Development Quarterly, 10*, 249–261.

IDC (2003). Second quarter 2003 worldwide handset shipments increased more than 19% year over year. *IDC Press Release*, August 1. http://www.idc.com/getdoc.jhtml;jsessionid= QE5RAHJVKU0L4CTFA4FCFGAKMUDYWIWD?containerId=pr2003_07_31_151031. Accessed on 28 February 2004.

Jacobs, D., & de Man, A. P. (1998). Clusters, industrial policy and firm strategy. *Technology Analysis and Strategic Management, 8*, 425–437.

Kessler, S. (2003). A good story for open text. *Business Week Online*, October 7. http://www. businessweek.com/investor/content/oct2003/pi2003107_3307_pi008.htm. Accessed on 28 February 2004.

Kupchinsky, R. (2002, June 20). Dirty bombs and cobalt pencils. *Crime and Corruption Watch, 2*(24). http://www.rferl.org/corruptionwatch/2002/06/24-200602.asp. Accessed on 28 February 2004.

Lee, H., Smith, K. G., Grimm, C., & Schombirg, A. (2000). Timing, order and durability of new product advantages with imitation. *Strategic Management Journal, 21*, 23–30.

Malkoske, G. R. (2002). Medical isotopes: Maintaining an essential source of global supply. Speech to the Canadian Nuclear Associations' Nuclear Industry Winter Seminar, Ottawa, February 19. http://www.cna.ca/english/Speeches-Releases/presentations/Grant%20Malkoske. pdf. Accessed on 28 February 2004.

de Marchi, M., Napolitano, G., & Taccini, P. (1996). Testing a model of technological trajectories. *Research Policy, 25*, 13–23.

McCoy, M. (2003). Protein drugs linked to radioisotopes emerge as a promising therapeutic class. *Chemical and Engineering News* (October 20th), 16–17. http://pubs.acs.org/cen/NCW/print/ 8142bus2.html. Accessed on 28 February 2004.

Moritz, S. (2003). Cisco router sales surge. *TheStreet.com*, November 13. http://www.thestreet. com/pf/tech/scottmoritz/10126476.html. Accessed on 28 February 2004.

Pavitt, K. (1984). Sectoral patterns of technical change: Towards a taxonomy and a theory. *Research Policy, 13*, 343–373.

Pavitt, K., Robson, M., & Townsend, J. (1989). Technological accumulation, diversification, and organization in UK companies 1945–1983. *Management Science, 35*, 81–99.

Pendse, N. (2004). Market share analysis: More important than ever, but harder to measure. *OLAP Report*, March 2. http://www.olapreport.com/Market.htm#background. Accessed on 28 February 2004.

Porter, M. (1990). *Competitive advantage of nations*. New York: Free Press.

Porter, M. (1997). Knowledge-based clusters and national competitive advantage. Presentation to *Technopolis 97*, September 12. Ottawa, Canada.

Porter, M. (1998). Clusters and the new economics of competition. *Harvard Business Review* (November–December), 77–90.

Porter, M. (2003). Clusters and regional competitiveness: Recent learnings. Presentation to *International Conference on Technology Clusters*, November 7. Montreal, Canada.

Puscas, D. (2002). Special Report MDS Inc. *Polaris Institute Corporate Profiles*, April. http://www. polarisinstitute.org/corp_profiles/public_service_gats/corp_profile_ps_mds.html#Anchor-57691. Accessed on 28 February 2004.

Red Herring (2002). A glimmering light. *Red Herring*, October 21. http://www.redherring. com/Article.aspx?f=Articles/Archive/investor/2002/10/jds-uniphase102102.xml&hed=A% 20glimmering%20light. Accessed on 28 February 2004.

Rigby, P. (2002). Components to rebound in 2003? *Light Reading*, December 10. http://www. lightreading.com/document.asp?doc_id=25537&site=lightreading. Accessed on 28 February 2004.

Roelandt, T. J. A., & den Hertog, P. (1999). Cluster analysis and cluster-based policy making in OECD countries. In: T. J. A. Roelandt, & P. den Hertog (Eds), *Boosting innovation: The cluster approach* (pp. 9–22). Paris, France: Organization for Economic Cooperation and Development.

Smith, K. G., Grimm, C., & Gannon, M. (1992). *Dynamics of competitive strategy*. Newbury Park, CA: Sage.

Souitaris, V. (2002). Technological trajectories as moderators of firm-level determinants of innovation. *Research Policy, 31*, 877–898.

Spielkamp, A., & Vopel, K. (1999). Mapping innovative clusters in national innovation systems. In: T. J. A. Roelandt, & P. den Hertog (Eds), *Boosting innovation: The cluster approach* (pp. 91–123). Paris, France: Organization for Economic Cooperation and Development.

Supportindustry.com (2002). Interest in business intelligence tools remains strong. *Weekly e.Newsletter*, June 25. http://www.supportindustry.com/newsletter/062502.htm. Accessed on 28 February 2004.

Synergy Research Group (2002). Enterprise IP telephony's rapid success continues to threaten the future of traditional PBXs. *Synergy Research Group*, August 19. http://www.synergyresearchgroup. com/8-19-02.html. Accessed on 28 February 2004.

Synergy Research Group (2003a). *3rd Quarter 2003 multi service WAN equipment*, November 26. Phoenix, AZ: Synergy Research Group.

Synergy Research Group (2003b). In post 9/11, network security investment remains unphased by IT spending cuts. *Synergy Research Group*, November 22. http://www.srgresearch.com/store/press/11-22-02.html?SID=1&. Accessed on 28 February 2004.

Tidd, J., Bessant, J., & Pavitt, K. (1997). *Managing innovation: Integrating technological, market and organizational change*. New York: Wiley.

VDC (2003a). Winds of change: VDC finds embedded OS market share shifts. *VDC*, March 17. http://www.vdc-corp.com/embedded/press/03/pr03-23.html. Accessed on 28 February 2004.

VDC (2003b). The embedded software strategic market intelligence program 2002/2003. *VDC*, *Volume II A: Embedded/Real-Time Operating Systems and Toolkits*, 36. http://www.vdc-corp.com/embedded/reports/03/br03-10.html. Accessed on 28 February 2004.

Weiner, N. (2002). Public key infrastructure (PKI) market trends. *Faulkner Information Services*, June. http://ccrma-www.stanford.edu/~jhw/bioauth/andre/PKImkttrendJun02.pdf. Accessed on 28 February 2004.

Young, G., Smith, K., & Grimm, C. (1996). Austrian and industrial organization perspectives on firm level competitive activity and performance. *Organization Science, 7*, 243–254.

Chapter 7

How Technology-Intensive Clusters are Organized in the Ottawa Region

Alan O'Sullivan

Abstract

The collective nature of organizational action in technology-intensive clusters is discussed. Three organizational roles are identified that enable collective action horizontally (cluster legitimation) and vertically (system integration and module supply). The extent to which cluster organizing is actively occurring along both horizontal and vertical dimensions in the Ottawa area is examined.

Introduction

A cluster is a concentration of organizations engaged in the transformation of similar and highly specialized bases of knowledge and skills into products. As an economic phenomenon, clustering is attributable to the pursuit of a kind of knowledge-based locational advantage: geographical proximity facilitating inter-firm learning about opportunities and how to exploit them. Proximity makes opportunities more visible. By providing a general work context rich in informational cues that prompt interactions between individuals, as well as prompting individual creativity and activity, clustering makes more available the valuable inputs necessary to exploit these opportunities flexibly and rapidly, ultimately enhancing innovation productivity.

At least three specific kinds of knowledge-based locational advantages can be associated with clustering (Porter 1990, 1998). Firstly, proximity can make individuals more likely to develop close informal relationships in the form of personal relationships and community ties that foster inter-company trust and facilitate the flow of information that is closely related to the highly specialized bases of knowledge and skills that firms use to create their products. A second form of locational advantage is more logistical: proximity facilitates the coordination of activities across company boundaries such as to optimize collective productivity. A third form of locational advantage is rooted less in cooperation or sharing than in rivalry: proximity enhances the knowledge of other local firms' costs, projects, etc., and this knowledge can have significant motivational effects as firms strive to benchmark against each other.

However, while proximity might put these advantages within reach, making the most of them will require organized action of some kind — these advantages are not just "in the air." This chapter considers clustering as an organized process — that is, a cluster not just as a static entity but as a dynamic process of organizing — and identifies three organizing roles that need to be performed in order to enable firms to avail themselves of these locational advantages.

I first draw on the literature on inter-firm networks to conceptually position the notion of cluster. This discussion can be thought of as specifying in a general sense the social architecture of clustering. Next I identify the first of the three distinct cluster-organizing roles, and examine this role with respect to the Ottawa region. This first role is cluster-legitimation. It has both internal and external aspects: inter-firm interactions and cooperation must be promoted as a valid and necessary thing to do (internal legitimation), and the location must be sold to the broader world as a place with industry-specific knowledge-based attractions (external legitimation). Various kinds of agents could perform this role: a government body, a trade association, or even a single large "anchor" firm, but I emphasize what I call a "cluster administrative organization."[1]

I then draw on the literature on product architecture to focus on how cluster relations relate to the actual investments that firms make, and identify two more cluster-organizing roles. These second and third roles are complementary and are performed by firms actually generating together technology and new products: these are the roles of system integrator and module supplier. While these second and third roles could be performed within a single firm, their being performed by different firms such that the roles are at once independent and integrated is more conducive to clustering. Again, I examine these roles with respect to the Ottawa region.

The chapter closes with suggestions for further research.

Clusters and Networks

It has become widely accepted that for organizations to meet their objectives and prosper depends on the nature of their relationships with other organizations. Reliance by firms on inter-firm relationships to meet their performance objectives has grown considerably in recent years as firms seek to reduce research and development costs and risks, increase production efficiencies, and gain access to new markets and competencies (Doz & Hamel 1998; Hagedoorn 1995). Over about the last two decades, an increasingly important part of research interest in these inter-firm relationships has focused on multi-firm networks.

Multi-firm networks can be organized in two fundamental ways, essentially differing in their proportions of vertically organized and distributed (or, horizontal) relations. One way is for all exchanges, communications, and interactions to be anchored around some

---

[1] The term is adapted from the Human & Provan (2000) study of networks.

central dominant firm. Such a network is essentially an accumulation of dyads focused on the dominant firm — for example, a multi-firm network composed of suppliers to a single central buyer where relations among the suppliers themselves are not encouraged.

Alternatively, a multi-firm network could be organized in a more decentralized way, such that exchanges, communications, and interactions within the network are multilateral. That is, the network is relatively decentralized and interactions are much less standardized — it is not dominated by some central organization.

Although dyads are the building blocks of both kinds of network, the formation and maintenance of the multilateral kind of networks is more complex: member firms have relationships not only with each other, but with the same third parties as well, and these relationships are heterogeneous both in terms of one relationship compared to another and in terms of the content of any given relationship. More precisely, ties are multiplex (that is, inter-firm ties will simultaneously be of a variety of kinds such as business, information, or friendship) dense (the number of interactions, or links in the network, expressed as a proportion of the total possible links among network members, is relatively high), and relatively informal and subject to change (Human & Provan 2000). Operationally, this network form involves implicit and open-ended contracts, which means that social mechanisms that promote shared understanding and that develop norms for behaviour will be critical to the network's functioning effectively. Inter-firm interactions are facilitated by these social mechanisms, but these interactions in turn create and re-create the network structure. Thus, social embeddedness — defined as the social-psychological and associated informational correlates of firms' (or individuals') relations with each other — is necessary to govern a functioning network.[2]

Knowledge-intensive networks are likely to be high in task complexity and also subject to rapidly changing contexts: both characteristics encourage inter-firm relations in order to maximize access to necessary capabilities and maintain necessary flexibility (Powell 1990; Powell *et al.* 1996). Social embeddedness reduces coordination costs and helps safeguard exchanges between firms by reducing behavioural uncertainty, thereby making multilateral relations feasible.

There are four major social mechanisms that allow a multilateral network to function (Jones *et al.* 1997). Firstly, any network (not just multilateral) must have identifiable boundaries to be recognized as an organized form. This implies *restricted access* to the exchanges that define the network (to maintain a certain level of embeddedness, networks must not get too large). Restricting access helps reduce coordination costs by reducing variance in expectations and attitudes, and to the extent that it makes membership more stable will also help in the development of shared ways of communicating and interacting.

These effects are further enhanced by the development of a *macro-culture* composed of broadly shared and tacit behavioural norms, socialization processes that generate convergent expectations, and a shared language for expressing complex information. Establishing such a macroculture can take many years and will also likely require an energetic third party (say, a coordinating entity) to institutionalize it.

---

[2] Social embeddedness has two aspects: the degree to which exchange parties consider each other's needs and goals, and the degree to which the network as a whole succeeds in controlling attitudes and behaviours; these are called relational and structural embeddedness, respectively (Granovetter 1985, 1992).

Two other defining features of a multilateral network are *collective sanctions* (to encourage certain behaviours and discourage others) and *reputation* (which conveys valuable information about a firm). Both characteristics help reduce monitoring costs and are significant to making exchanges less open to abuse.

Clusters can be thought of as multilateral networks: cluster-oriented research has always emphasized the multiplicity of relationships that firms typically avail themselves of within the geographic region of interest, and has also emphasized the informal and dynamic nature of these relations (Piore & Sabel 1984; Porter 1990, 1998). Apart from the emphasis on geography, distinctive features of cluster-oriented research include an emphasis on unusual levels of innovation productivity and inter-firm relations of an especially varied and dynamic nature. That is, "cluster" denotes not just a decentralized, multi-firm network that is more than the sum of its dyads, and not even just relationships within an industry value chain but also relationships with organizational actors outside the industry value chain, such as relationships across value chains and relationships with local authorities and non-profits such as universities.

Clusters, like networks, are crucially defined by interaction: unless firms are engaging with other local firms — attending common social and business events, buying and selling, partnering in various ventures, all of which form embedded ties among firms in the cluster — not much information will be flowing between them, and the cluster won't exist in a very meaningful way.

Legitimacy, and Cluster Emergence and Evolution

However, for a (technology-intensive) cluster to function meaningfully as a network needs to be explained as a cluster would seem to inherently lack or possess only weakly the social mechanisms by which any multilateral network functions. That is, because membership of a cluster is defined by geographical location, access by any firm is really only restricted by the extent to which any firm faces (fairly passive) constraints on locating in the cluster. Secondly, the extent to which a macroculture is present in a cluster will be a function of the frequency and intensity with which the firms in the cluster interact with each other. Left to themselves, firms might, over many years, eventually develop such interactions. But in fast-paced, technology-intensive industries, they may well have failed before they have arrived at that point.

Thirdly, the possibility of collective sanctions in a cluster is questionable, as determining and applying such sanctions presumes a stability and intensity of coordination that is quite beyond what is normally identified with a cluster. Finally, for reputation to operate as a social mechanism depends on the speed and accuracy with which reputational information can be disseminated — something that again relies on membership stability and degree of interaction. Also, from a cluster perspective, reputation as a social mechanism is further devalued because of its limited ability to influence interactions with start-ups (though this might be mitigated by the individual reputations of those sponsoring the start-up).

To make clustering more effective, therefore, requires direct action to strengthen one or more of these social mechanisms and make a cluster more like a functioning multilateral network. This will enhance the flow of specialized information between firms that makes clusters a valued economic phenomenon. The key to achieving this is to recognize the objective to be one of legitimizing the cluster, and the inter-firm knowledge-sharing activity that a true cluster supposes. Acquiring legitimacy is crucial to the success of any organization or organizational structure: legitimacy significantly determines whether an organizational structure can satisfy its resource needs (DiMaggio & Powell 1983; Meyer & Rowan 1977). This legitimating activity needs to achieve a generalized perception that the actions, activities, and structure of a cluster are desirable and appropriate (Human & Provan 2000; Suchman 1995).

If the cluster is not seen as legitimate internally, firms won't gear their actions to local interaction; if it's not seen as legitimate externally, the local firms will be unable to leverage location to motivate relationships with firms elsewhere, for securing venture capital or influencing government initiatives, etc. Legitimization of a cluster need not require all firms in the cluster to interact directly with one another, but it does imply that there is a sense of collective destiny by which member firms see themselves as part of the cluster and are committed to having it prosper.

Where does legitimation start? The idea of a cluster — that firms who might think of themselves as wholly independent or even as competitors need to collaborate (or, that they have " pre-competitive" relations) — itself is by now widely accepted. Therefore, legitimation begins with establishing the position of a particular regional agglomeration of firms presenting itself as a cluster. A powerful central firm might be thought capable of generating both kinds of legitimacy for a region in which it has significant operations but, as discussed above, its very dominance militates against dense, decentralized network ties. Such ties are characteristic of multilateral networks and have been associated with cluster resiliency and vitality. For example, Saxenian (1994) identifies these characteristics with Silicon Valley for the last three decades. Her discussion of the contrasting fortunes of Silicon Valley and the relatively sparse cluster centred on Digital Equipment Corporation in the Boston area suggests that multilateral rather than central-buyer dominated clustering is crucial to the economic vitality of a cluster.

On the other hand, a small- to medium-sized firm cannot, by virtue of resource constraints, undertake the task of organizing the cluster on its own. At the same time, such relatively small and resource-poor firms are likely to benefit disproportionately from having the cluster organized.

A third option is some sort of cluster administrative organization (CAO). Such an entity would be sponsored by cluster members but be formally independent of any of them. A significant strategy for achieving legitimacy is organizational isomorphism: mimicking the form of existing organizational structures. Thus, for a CAO to be credible it would need to have a clear mission statement, defined governance structure (named directors, various committees, etc.), a sustainable resource base, a staff (perhaps paid and full-time), and so on. Likely crucial to the success of the CAO role will be addressing the question of legitimacy in the eyes of *which* stakeholders. Stakeholders will be internal (i.e. firms in the cluster) and external (organizational actors in the region but not in the cluster itself, and organizational actors outside the region but for whom cluster activity is relevant).

An internal stakeholder emphasis is consistent with focusing on getting member firms to interact and knowledge flowing between, and filling positions in the CAO with individuals with a background in the cluster. A corollary would be that financing would rely on the firms themselves rather than from external sources such as government grants, and would be applied to interaction-oriented uses (e.g. seminars and workshops) as part of a long-term effort to build trust and commitment among members.

An external-legitimacy orientation, on the other hand, would see the primary task as selling the image of the cluster. Actions consistent with this would be encouraging a membership base beyond cluster firms, seeking external funding earlier rather than later, and using a relatively high proportion of resources for marketing or promoting the cluster.

Human & Provan (2000), in their study of the contrasting fortunes of two (wood-products) multilateral networks, have labelled these legitimacy-building strategies respectively as "inside-out" and "outside-in." The latter is a strategy of building cluster strength through external success, perhaps in the belief that internal legitimacy will follow from such success. Human and Provan found evidence that internal legitimacy should be concentrated on first as otherwise internal divisions can develop such as to make developing embedded ties increasingly difficult. Once internal ties have been embedded, it will then be necessary to become more externally-oriented, in order to sustain the network over the long term. Evidence for the success of this dualistic approach to strategy — different strategic orientations separated in time — has also been found at the level of individual firms, for example, Burgelman's (2002) study of Intel, and of work groups (Gersick 1988).

Application to the Ottawa Area

I now apply the preceding discussion to an examination of CAOs in the Ottawa area. To do so, I focus just on technology-intensive clusters identified by others (e.g. Ottawa 20/20): telecommunications, microelectronics, photonics, wireless, software, life sciences.[3] Table 1 gives an overview of various CAOs in the Ottawa area (no CAOs were identified for telecommunications and microelectronics), and supports several observations about CAOs in the Ottawa area.

The first thing to note from the table is the distinction between CAOs and what might be called "super-CAOs" (see columns 1 and 4). Super-CAOs are CAO-type entities that seek to be relevant to several clusters, and the table identifies two of these in the Ottawa area: OCRI — the Ottawa Centre for Research and Innovation — and OMN — the Ottawa Manufacturers' Network. The fundamental organizing principle of these super-CAOs seems to be to motivate interactions primarily in terms of a specific value-adding activity, rather than in terms of a specific cluster. Of the two super-CAOs, OCRI seems to have a much more prominent role in the region. The rest of Table 1 describes CAOs for the software (Software Process Improvement Network (SPIN), and Ottawa Software Cluster), photonics (Ottawa Photonics Cluster), wireless (Ottawa Wireless Cluster), and life-sciences (Ottawa Life Sciences Council) clusters. These are the principal organizing entities for technology-intensive clusters in the Ottawa area. Other entities that influence cluster

---

[3] I am distinguishing between wireless and the broader telecommunications cluster as wireless has a distinct (and relatively new) CAO.

Table 1: Cluster administrative organizations (CAOs) for technology-intensive clusters in the Ottawa area.

Name	Year Founded	Purpose	Target Audience	Typical Activities and Frequency	Number of Corporate Members	Resources
OCRI	1983	Ottawa's lead economic agency for fostering the advancement of the region's globally competitive knowledge-based economy		Monthly registration for OCRI's suite of events exceeds 1,300	400+ (about 200 technology firms; informal OCRI estimate)	Annual corporate membership fees: sliding scale based on company revenues, and ranging from $500 to $10,000; Individual membership fees: $300 Event fees; government funding; private/public project funding Staff of 58
45th circuit (OCRI)	2000	Increasing understanding and competence in a wide range of legal issues of particular importance to technology firms	In-house counsel, technology specialists in private practices, public sector counsel, as well as a spectrum of other company officials with a need or interest in emerging legal issues	Monthly speaker events. Speakers are legal professionals & are invited from the Ottawa area elsewhere in and N America		
Zone 5 (OCRI)	1997	Professional development for technology- marketing community; providing a highly focused networking environment; informal coaching of small and medium sized companies	Companies marketing technology hardware products, software, and services, from start-ups to the largest internationally active firms			
IT in health care (OCRI)			Health care providers, policymakers, IT entrepreneurs, technology developers, and students	Occasional seminars IT infrastructure development efforts and their costs/ benefits; technology adoption experiences; and new public initiatives to support IT in health care		
TEB: Technology Executive Breakfast (OCRI)	1993	Top-level networking	Senior executives and management in technology-related enterprises, with a focus on emerging companies	Monthly		
TechTalk Ottawa technology research workshops (Joint OCRI/CITO: see n.8 in text)	1999	Facilitate the flow of research information between high-technology companies and universities and colleges		Bi-monthly technology-research workshops		
Innotalk applied innovation seminars (Joint OCRI/CITO)		Help companies find effective answers to process, systems and technology issues		Seminars featuring expert speakers from industry and academia		

Table 1: (*Continued*)

Name	Year Founded	Purpose	Target Audience	Typical Activities and Frequency	Number of Corporate Members	Resources
SPIN: Software Process Improvement Network OCRI has partnered with the Ottawa SPIN since it's inception	1996	Promote process improvement, increased process maturity and high quality software-based products	Those developing, managing or procuring software-based products or systems, especially software professionals engaged in software process improvement.	Six main events each season (averaging 100 people from over 50 different companies)		No membership fee, modest event fee, corporate sponsorship
Ottawa Software Cluster	2000; refounded 2002	Networking, coaching, partnering	Software founders, owners, and executives	Irregular	50 (informal estimate)	Corporate sponsorship; event fees
Ottawa Wireless Cluster	2002	Networking, industry advocacy, manage media image, business development services to members	Wireless executives, entrepreneurs, engineers, marketers, and professionals	Monthly seminars September through to June); investor and partnering meetings	60	Corporate sponsorship
Ottawa Photonics Cluster	2000	Provide leadership in the Ottawa photonics sector		No regular local events listed	81	Annual memberships range from Individual 50, corporate 150, premium 1000 (includes a rotating banner on the OPC home page)
Ottawa Manufacturers' Network	1991	Networking; promote knowledge of issues in technology selection, supply chain management, logistics, test and packaging, and quality and reliability. 5 special interest groups (SIGs) to provide a more focused collaboration and networking forum	Ottawa area manufacturing companies from all sectors of industry and other relevant government and educational entities.	Monthly lunches/seminars. Featured speakers, panel discussions, training sessions, and tutorials	44	Annual corporate membership fees: sliding scale based on number of employees, and ranging from $300 to $4,000 Individual: $75. Event fees; 2 part-time employees
Ottawa Life Sciences Council	1994	Facilitate and promote investment in companies and technologies; transfer technologies to the private sector; expand new and existing companies through investment, business development, strategic partnering, and national and international marketing; creation of research parks. Biotechnology Incubation Centre is an OLSC spin-off; the OLSC is also currently contemplating a pilot-scale production facility	All those with an interest in the life-sciences sector	Frequent seminars and workshops, and annual conference series ("BioNorth")	60	$107 (individual) to $1605 (institutions/hospitals); corporate sponsorship; event fees. 8 full-time employees

Sources: CAO websites viewed during October/November 2003 (http://www.ocri.ca; http://www.ottawasoftwarecluster.ca; http://www.ottawawirelesscluster.com; http://www.ottawaphotonics.com; http://www.olsc.ca; http://www.omnet.ca).

organizing have been excluded because they are too general, too specific, or too informal in their remit or form.[4]

The table also indicates that cluster-organizing activity is a mostly recent phenomenon in the Ottawa area (see column 2): up to 1994 (when the OLSC was founded) OCRI and the OMN were the only CAO-type entities in existence, and 45th Circuit (an OCRI sub-unit), OSC, OWC, and OPC all date from only 2000 or later. Furthermore, the telecommunications and microelectronics clusters have no dedicated CAOs, nor sub-units within CAOs (with the possible exception of an OMN sub-unit focused on semiconductors acting as a CAO-type entity for at least part of the microelectronics cluster). It seems fair to conclude that clusters in the Ottawa area, at least until very recently, have been under-organized, and that there is still much untested potential for cluster organizations to realize.

Columns 5, 6, and 7 (respectively, typical activities and frequency, member firms/number of firms in cluster, and resources) give some indication of vitality of the various CAOs and super CAOs. OCRI, discussed in more detail below, seems to be very active and very well resourced, and the OLSC looks to be similarly vital though a fairly distant second to OCRI. The OWC seems to be doing a lot with modest resources; SPIN,[5] with only 6 regular events a year is moderately active but must get by with even fewer resources — an assessment that would probably apply equally to the OSC — and the OPC seems close to being dormant.[6] Finally, the OMN is active but only moderately resourced; it is also struggling to address a perceived legitimacy deficit (see below).

The remainder of this section concentrates on just the two super-CAOs: OCRI and the OMN. The justification for this is the pervasive influence of OCRI and the availability of recent data on the OMN. Concentrating on these two super-CAOs also permits a measure of comparison between like entities that forms the basis for some focused inferences about CAO-type entities in general as well as in the Ottawa area.

Super-CAOs

OCRI   OCRI is a twenty-years old organization that describes itself as "Ottawa's lead economic agency for fostering the advancement of the region's globally competitive knowledge-based economy" (http://www.ocri.ca), and seeks to foster links not just among firms, but also between industry, government, and educational institutions. OCRI is easily

---

[4] Examples, respectively, are The Ottawa Partnership (a group of private and public leaders founded in 1999 to ensure the co-ordination and alignment of activities of Ottawa's economic agencies), the Ottawa Software Engineers Group (a group initiated by Macadamian Software Inc.), and a loosely-organized, unnamed network among semiconductor professionals. Note that I have included both SPIN and the Ottawa Software Cluster because of their distinct focii (respectively, technical and top-level software personnel).

[5] SPINs are all over the world, with each started locally but linked through mutual contact and the SEI (Carnegie-Mellon University's Software Engineering Institute).

[6] At time of writing, the next listed event on the OPC website (http://www.ottawaphotonics.com) is Photonics North (September 2004) — a Canadian Photonics Consortium event — with local liaison provided by OCRI, not OPC. Also, the OPC website shows no evidence of "premium membership" rotating banners. Both facts suggest poor internal legitimacy. Indeed, personal communication with OCRI affirms that this CAO is currently being reconstituted.

the most expensive CAO-type entity to join in the Ottawa area, and has by far the largest membership and complement of staff (see Table 1).

OCRI involves itself in a wide range of industries, and has membership categories that include general business services such as accounting and printing, as well as categories for firms in the various technology-intensive clusters. OCRI also involves itself in a wide range of economic issues — the latter are expressed broadly in terms of "Developing and enriching Ottawa's talent" and "Marketing Ottawa to attract talent, investment and business" (http://www.ocri.ca), and extend, for example, to such community-based initiatives as promoting literacy.[7]

This suggests that OCRI pays significant attention to an external-legitimacy oriented strategy. In OCRI's case this apparent strategy is reinforced by (and, indeed, reinforces) a significant reliance on external funding (OCRI receives substantial funding from local government and additional funding from provincial and federal levels), and the breadth of the initiatives it involves itself with. This emphasis on external legitimacy is not surprising for a CAO (or, super-CAO) that has been around for as long as OCRI.

Equally, though, OCRI's usefulness and continued survival also depend on its having built substantial internal legitimacy. While OCRI appeals to a wide range of local firms, including those outside the technology-intensive clusters, Table 1 indicates that in a great deal of what it does OCRI emphasizes promoting multilateralism among local technology firms, both among the firms themselves and between the firms and local higher education institutions and with government. Various OCRI sub-units exist to animate the interactions that foster such linkages. For example, "45th circuit" and "Zone5" are both very active, activity (rather than cluster) oriented sub-units: the former addresses the corporate-legal needs of firms, while the latter addresses technology-marketing needs. The "TEB" and "Innotalk" seminar series, and the "TechTalk" series of workshops similarly strive to cut across clusters in their appeal; the latter two are run jointly with CITO, a further indication of OCRI's own embeddedness.[8] Indeed, very few of OCRI's organizing energies seem to address cluster-specific needs — those that come closest perhaps being IT in Healthcare (life sciences cluster) and SPIN (software cluster), and of these two only the latter is really a distinct (and semi-autonomous) organizational unit.

However, OCRI provides varyingly significant levels of assistance to all of the cluster-specific CAOs: it provides a physical home to each of the OSC, OPC, OWC, and OMN, while also providing assistance with venture-capital raising, entrepreneurial training, and some other services to all of these CAOs plus the OLSC.

OMN   The Ottawa Manufacturers' Network is, at 12 years since founding, somewhat younger that OCRI. It focuses on building local excellence in manufacturing, and an interest in this is the defining attribute for membership. The OMN also has various special interest

---

[7] "LectureOttawa" is an initiative matching local businesses and public institutions with French language schools, and offering employees from participating businesses the opportunity to read one-on-one with children in JK, SK and Grade One classes (OCRI press release, Nov. 4, 2003).

[8] CITO denotes Communications and Information Technology Ontario. This is an Ontario Centre of Excellence for communications and information technologies that tries to connect academic and industry innovators in the development and commercialization of new technologies.

groups (SIGs), one of which — the Semiconductor SIG — targets many of the firms in the local microelectronics cluster. However, most if not all of 40-plus Ottawa semiconductor firms are fabless (that is, have no fabrication plants and so have limited direct involvement in manufacturing).

The OMN has few assets; it relies on financial resources drawn mostly from membership fees, and for human resources has a volunteer advisory board and two part-time employees. Alternative sources of funding include sponsorship funds and event fees. Both are relatively modest. Financially, the OMN is likely no worse off, and may indeed be even better off, than other Ottawa CAOs (most of whom have no membership fees), apart from OCRI and the OLSC.

A recent study of OMN membership was conducted under the auspices of the OMN by a team of University of Ottawa MBA students (Bhanot *et al.* 2003). The OMN advisory board commissioned the study because of various concerns the board had with how the OMN was performing as an organizing entity. These concerns included a perceived lack of awareness of the OMN, a membership base that is not growing, the belief that the networking opportunities presented by OMN events were underutilized, and that the OMN was not properly facilitating knowledge sharing. Clearly, these concerns indicate a sense of both internal and external legitimacy deficits at the OMN.

The MBA research team conducted an electronic survey of the OMN membership in early fall 2003. Unfortunately, the response rate of 10% was poor, especially for a survey with the backing of the OMN itself. Nonetheless, the study gives some insight into the achievements and challenges the OMN, and perhaps other local CAOs, are facing, and at the very least can form a basis for further research on CAOs in the Ottawa area.

Like OCRI, the OMN offers both corporate and individual memberships, of which it has 44 and 64, respectively. Given that there are just over one thousand technology-intensive firms alone in the Ottawa area (OCRI data), this seems a very modest level of membership, and is indicative of low external legitimacy. There are two probable explanations for this low membership figure: that the issues the OMN seeks to address are not perceived as especially significant (lack of external legitimacy causes poor membership take-up), and/or the OMN is addressing legitimate issues but does so ineffectively (lack of internal legitimacy causes membership attrition).

With regard to the former possibility, manufacturing is indeed an under-performed activity in the Ottawa area: there is a disproportionate emphasis on research and development activity for products that are then manufactured outside the region Ottawa 20/20).[9] Consistent with this general character of economic activity in the Ottawa region, 53% of respondents in the survey viewed R&D as their core activity, greater than fabrication and assembly combined (though respondents chose more than one core activity). Also, 60% of respondents were employees of firms employing fewer than 100 people, while only 12% were working for firms employing more than 1,000. However, this compares with approximately 91% of Ottawa's technology-intensive firms (OCRI data) employing fewer than 100 people. While the OMN does not explicitly target only technology-intensive

---

[9] The economy of the region also, of course, relies heavily on services (professional services and tourism are two recognized clusters).

firms,[10] this does point to a disproportionate reliance on larger firms. This could well be an artifact of small firms' tending not to engage in (relatively fixed-asset intensive) manufacturing activity.

However, it is well recognized that a deep understanding of manufacturing issues during any development process will be significant to innovation productivity (Hauser & Clausing 1988). Something considerably more than 4.5% or so of local firms might reasonably be expected to be conscious of the significance of manufacturing issues to their work, and to be attracted to the right kind of CAO that addresses such issues in interesting ways.

Consistent with the earlier conceptual discussion, respondents affirmed "networking" and "knowledge-sharing" (70 and 59%, respectively) to be the main reasons for joining ("improved capabilities" was next at about 34%). Likewise, Table 1 indicates that these are central activities for other CAO-type entities. On a variety of measures — access to useful information, networking, value for money, overall enjoyment of OMN events — the OMN consistently scored an average of between 5 and 6 on a 7-point scale. Also, 65% of respondents' corporate memberships were of greater than 2 years' duration (for individuals the figure was 53%).[11]

Views on the special interest groups (SIGs) were solicited in addition to those on the OMN as a whole. Of the six SIGs, "lean manufacturing" was the highest rated (averaging 5.53 on a 7-point scale, and higher than any satisfaction rating on any dimension for the OMN overall), and "semiconductors" was the lowest (at an average of 4.34 — lower than any satisfaction rating on any dimension for the OMN overall). The latter may perhaps be influenced by the fabless nature of all forty or so Ottawa semi-conductor firms.

As this survey examined just one (super) CAO, and attracted only a modest response rate, any conclusions must be made with caution. Nonetheless, the study does at the least permit some interesting observations, both with respect to the OMN itself and to CAOs in general.

With respect to the OMN itself, the very modest take-up of corporate memberships in general, the relative reliance on larger firms for these, and the relative reliance on firms outside the technology-intensive clusters, are all suggestive of a lack of external legitimacy both in the region in general and in the technology-intensive clusters in particular. This observation is reinforced by the fact of the OMN's never having engaged in much true "marketing," having to date relied on word of mouth and a few trade publications to drum up interest. However, satisfaction levels seem quite positive suggesting good internal legitimacy (with the possible exception of the semiconductor SIG).

Thus, recalling a point made in the conceptual discussion earlier, the OMN seems to have correctly emphasized internal legitimacy in its formative years but to have waited too long to address external legitimacy. It is probable that while the resulting deficit in external legitimacy can be remedied to some extent, the delay has meant that technology-intensive cluster needs have been under-served. This point is further supported by the semiconductor SIG — the only SIG clearly focused on a distinct technology-intensive cluster — attracting

---

[10] Questions on industry affiliation revealed that less than half (43%) of the respondents worked in any of the technology-intensive clusters (however, telecommunications, at 19%, was the most common affiliation among all respondents).

[11] Individual memberships, though more numerous, are financially insignificant (see Table 1) and are dominated by consultants looking for business.

the poorest satisfaction levels of all six SIGs. It could also mean that OCRI or more focused CAOs (such as the OLSC or OWC) have expanded or emerged to fill a gap left by the OMN.

The study also supports several observations with respect to CAOs in general. Firstly, it is important for CAOs to be attentive to the need to shift emphasis between addressing internal and external legitimacy, and to set explicit objectives for this.

Secondly, the relative performance of CAO vs. super-CAO is elucidated to some extent by the SIG findings. The very focused SIGs can be viewed as akin to CAOs. The highest rated SIG is closest to the OMN manufacturing orientation, and the lowest rated is focused on firms who don't do manufacturing. Also, none of the OCRI sub-units is cluster specific (consistent with OCRI as a whole), except SPIN — a quasi OCRI sub-unit — and it seems among the less active of its sub-units. This suggests that the needs of a given cluster are best served by a dedicated and independent CAO.

Such distinctiveness may be a higher-return (but also higher-risk) evolutionary path for CAOs. This speculation is further supported by returning to Table 1 and referring to the details on (cluster-specific) CAOs. There are four of these, besides SPIN: OSC (software), OPC (photonics), OWC (wireless), and OLSC (life sciences). Of these the latter two are cluster-specific and independent, and seem very robust: wireless is the youngest of all four and seems especially active — it is targeting a recently-emerged and booming cluster — and the OLSC is the best-resourced. On the other hand, the OPC seems almost dormant, no doubt due to the presently troubled state of its target cluster, and the three year-old OSC has already had to be re-formed.

Thirdly, the two preceding observations, and the conclusions about the OMN specifically, may be related to speculate that super-CAOs' true value relative to CAOs must reside in a superior ability to manage the contrary impulses of building internal and external legitimacy, and more specifically to build external legitimacy. OCRI seems strong on both counts: its age and resources evidence strong external legitimacy, and internal legitimacy seems to be well addressed through various sub-units (see Table 1). Because such internal differentiation is costly (e.g. sub-unit event costs), it is probable that a super-CAO needs to address external legitimacy concerns sooner than would be the case for a CAO. This is because sub-units of a super CAO seem to do best adopting an activity-based (or, cross-cluster) rather than cluster-specific focus, and this focus necessarily limits the density of ties among its target audience. An external legitimacy focus therefore promises to better generate the resources necessary to support the diverse sub-unit missions, and is therefore the higher-return evolutionary path.

Product Architecture Roles

Because a cluster is organized, interactions and exchanges are significantly non-random; but neither are interactions and exchanges so organized — or, determined — that they are uniform. Rather, interactions and exchanges are patterned, and this patterning reflects a division of labour with respect to the product output of the cluster. The previous section discussed a cluster as an organized entity, focusing on horizontal relations among firms. This section addresses cluster organizing in terms of two product-architecture based roles:

the relation between OEMs (who perform the role of "system integrators" for a product architecture) and firms from whom they source various technologies (who perform the role of "module suppliers" for a product architecture).

The architecture of a product describes which parts of the product do what: how the internal structure of a product is organized such as to implement product functionality. A product architecture defines how a part fits within a subsystem, and how that subsystem fits within the overall product, but in order to do the latter it is also necessary to define how the subsystems interact with each other. Many product architectures, and probably all technology-intensive products, are composed of components organized into subsystems, with these subsystems organized into the "product system" or architecture.

Any system, including product systems, organizes components in hierarchies of subsystems. This hierarchical structure means that the system has an aggregate functioning that emerges from the functioning of its subsystems, the functioning of which in turn emerges from their respective components (Alexander 1964; Holland & Miller 1991; Simon 1969).

Multiple interactions are a consequence of this systemic characteristic. Though inter-actions between individual components are often simple and direct, multiple interactions and feedback between components within subsystems, between components across subsystems, and between subsystems at various hierarchical levels create a complicated network of relationships (Simon 1969). That is, interactions within the system do not merely follow hierarchically-ordered pathways: a complex product's aggregate functioning is dynamic in that it emerges from multilateral interactions between its subsystems. Thus, malfunctioning in a component can lead to failure in several subsystems (through a series of interactive failures across subsystems), leading to failure in the system.

This network of interactions leads to non-decomposability as a third system character-istic. An entity is non-decomposable if it cannot be separated into its components without seriously degrading its capabilities or performance: "When a set of subsystems is richly joined, each variable is as much affected by variables in other subsystems as by those in its own. When this occurs, the division of the whole into subsystems ceases to have any natural basis" (Ashby 1960: 213, quoted in Singh 1997).

If we apply these ideas to a cluster, we can view the cluster as a system, and firms within it as subsystems. Even more broadly, a cluster can itself be viewed as a subsystem of an economic region. Fundamentally though, to speak of a cluster as a system requires specification of the organizing forces behind the system and the nature of relationships within it, that is, explaining the local forces that impart not just a coherent and distinctive architecture to what would otherwise be atomistic firms, but that also impart an evolutionary impulse that maintains coherence and distinctiveness of the cluster.

The previous section addressed cluster organizing through the discussion of cluster administrative organizations. But the nature of relationships within a cluster are only loosely accounted for by any relationship a firm has with, or through the agency of, a CAO. This is because any given firm's relationship with a CAO is a fairly simple dyad (and hierarchical in the sense that the CAO, even though it has no formal power over the firm, operates at a more systemic level). And while it is true that a CAO provides an arena whereby firms can interact with each other, the previous section discussed these in only the very general terms of "networking" or "learning."

Whatever the embeddedness of inter-firm transactions — that is, whatever the inter-firm social and informational correlates of firms' relations — the innovation productivity of a cluster depends on how such relations relate to actual investments. This is especially so when the subject of interest is a cluster in a technology-intensive industry, given the premium on fast-paced technological innovation in such industries. Because a firm's innovation investment is significantly accounted for by the product-architecture role the firm plays, the investments that firms make in executing these roles make more available the valuable inputs and learning necessary to exploit opportunities flexibly and rapidly, and the visibility of such investments is precisely what animates the concentrated activity that defines a cluster. Thus, examining cluster dynamics in terms of product architecture roles in a cluster is a way of connecting inter-firm interactions — competitive and cooperative — to the very patterns of investment that give coherence, distinctiveness, and vitality to a cluster, and ultimately drive its evolution.

Product Architecture, and Cluster Emergence and Evolution

In the early development of an industry, products are integral in architecture, that is, the boundaries between components of the product, and the interactions across these boundaries, are not well defined (Christensen 2000). Effective markets at the interfaces between research, materials, components, product design and manufacturing are impeded because it is difficult to determine how a part or subsystem that might be procured from a given firm will interact with other elements of the product system. Innovation in an integral period is dependent on high levels of adaptive coordination across different specialisms and subsystems. Because such intensive coordination is typically too challenging for several firms to achieve together, it will need to occur in-house. That is, doing it all in a single firm is beneficial where de facto industry standards do not exist. A cluster — or, perhaps, proto-cluster — may form at this stage but would be mostly composed of firms trying to develop most or all of the product in-house.

But a desire for innovation productivity motivates a reduction in coordination needs by developing and adopting common technical standards to govern component and subsystem interactions. The growing maturity of knowledge about the underlying technologies makes this possible. These common technical standards impose a structure on the complexity and variety of product-development problems that firms deal with, and are crucial in enabling components or subsystems developed by independent firms to connect and interact without performance disadvantages. As this becomes a general phenomenon in the industry, the industry becomes modularly organized. For example, until 2003, SMS (short message service) usage in North America was plagued by a lack of interoperability across the networks of competing carriers. By now agreeing to interoperability carriers have in effect adopted a common set of industry standards to which the population of technology providers can now direct their resources, rather than fragmenting these across a range of mostly incompatible technologies as had been the case up to recently. This makes technology-market linking less differentiated and more standardized, and thus also less integral.

Product modularity denotes breaking down the interactivity of a product in order to facilitate autonomous development of subsystems, typically by independent firms with specialized cost- or knowledge-based capabilities. Relative to vertically-integrated development, it allows a much more efficient organization of informational and material inputs and outputs between firms. This adds value in several ways: by increasing the range and variety of core products, by increasing the range and variety of technologies complementary to these products, and at the same time making this variety available relatively rapidly and economically. Modularity is therefore a powerful solution to managing complexity while simultaneously increasing variety (Baldwin & Clark 2000; Ulrich 1995). Those organizations — and, I might add, clusters — that can incorporate it into their design processes in a progressive and superior fashion are likely to achieve a greater success in introducing new products (Baldwin & Clark 2000), and superior long-term competitive advantage. However, successful modularity crucially depends on clear, communicable standards to specify performance of each subsystem and interactions between subsystems (and the independent firms developing and producing them).

Industry standards by themselves will likely be insufficient to program integration into a specific multi-firm design effort such that independently designed subsystems will effortlessly come together to form a well-functioning final product system. Standards originated by and specific to a lead firm will significantly supplement the role of industry standards in facilitating modularity between a group of collaborating firms. The standards or "design rules" (Baldwin & Clark 2000) specify which aspect of value creation or functionality is assigned to which subsystem, what is required in each team's output and for the product offering as a whole, technical specifications, core templates, database protocols, and in particular specifications of the interface characteristics of the work of the different specialism or subsystem teams (anticipating how changes in one component could affect changes in another).

Thus, in a modular environment a firm competes either as an architect/system integrator, that is, setting the standards that govern firm and product-subsystem interactions, or as a module-designer/supplier who conforms to the standards set by others (Baldwin & Clark 2000).

A *system integrator* specifies the standards by which a product is assembled, and then sources or itself originates subsystems that conform to these standards. The most powerful kind of system integrator originates these standards for a whole industry, for example, Intel significantly originates (and controls) product standards for microprocessors. However, in many industries the standards by which goods are assembled are commonly shared and non-proprietary. Whether the system integrator originates the standards or not, the system integrator that sources subsystems from external suppliers plays a valuable and powerful role in organizing the efforts of independent firms in developing a product and bringing it to market.

The *module supplier* is a role that depends on system integrators sourcing development and production externally. The simplest kind of inter-firm exchange is for the supply of a fairly standardized service or component. However, the module-supplier role presumes some effort at subsystem integration work by the supplier, that is, the supplier integrates various components to deliver a functioning subsystem. The more complex this work is, and assuming overall integration (of all subsystems into the final product) is not highly standardized (making the final-assembly task almost trivial from a technical-knowledge perspective), the more module-supplier and system-integrator will need to work closely together. Indeed, it is probable that significant benefits would also accrue from having module suppliers work closely with each other, that is, to form more a multilateral than buyer-centred network. However, achieving this undoubtedly requires sophisticated managerial talent.

Modular forms possess survival benefits over integral forms. Systems evolve through the accretion of interrelated modules or components within a hierarchy. To the extent that these systems are nearly decomposable — i.e. interactions between individual modules are relatively insignificant when compared to interactions within them — they are stable. In an evolutionary selection environment, such stability is rewarded with system survival (Simon 1969).

Vertically integrated organizations can retard cluster development because vertically integrated firms are relatively resource intensive and inwardly oriented in their relationships and therefore effectively internalize the functions of a cluster. From the perspective of a vertically integrated organization, the well-established attractions of inter-firm exchanges include the spreading of development risk, access to a wider pool of capabilities, and efficiency gains (due to a market basis for the pricing of work; both capability access and efficiency gains are also attributable to inter-firm specialization). Even if a firm wishes to decline such exchanges, knowledge leakage from the firm will enable the rise of competitors at the system and/or subsystem level.

The tendency for modularity to increase as an industry ages suggests that a system-integrator firm may, in the early stages of modularity, be an important seed-bed for spin-offs and start-ups of firms focused on particular product modules. More generally, integration is essentially the organization of diversity, and a firm performing high-value adding integration work — at either the system or subsystem levels — is likely to be an especially significant organizing and evolutionary influence for a local cluster as such work likely presents many diverse and knowledge-intensive opportunities for contributions by other firms.

Product modularity, then, is *inevitably* associated with an increase in inter-firm exchanges. This has varying implications for cluster development. It could be that the need for interactive learning migrates away from the product system to the subsystem level. This could manifest itself in three distinct paths of cluster evolution: it could lead to new clusters, each anchored on a specific subsystem; it could lead to the strengthening of an existing cluster through subsystem suppliers assuming ever greater responsibilities (and becoming increasingly horizontal in their interactions); or it could lead to the emergence of a new cluster around one or a few re-configured system-integrator operations. Alternatives 1 and 3 are evident in the PC industry (Silicon Valley, and Dell's Austin, Texas operations, respectively); alternative 2 is evident in the auto industry.

However, the intimacy levels between system integrator and module supplier (or between module supplier and sub-subsystem suppliers) are likely to be inverse U-shaped: initially increasing as work is outsourced, but eventually decreasing as interfaces between subsystems, and their final integration, becomes highly standardized. Thus, beyond some point, the more modular product architecture becomes it would follow that the locational advantages of clusters anchored on a system integrator diminish. This is because the need for learning about subsystem interactivity falls away with ever-clearer specification of interfaces and performance requirements, and therefore there is a diminished attraction for subsystem suppliers to locate close to product assemblers, as well as to suppliers of other subsystems. It may be, though, that clustering persists for historical reasons: having once co-located the various players in the product architecture remain co-located, with sunk costs — which could include the costs of having formed CAOs — likely to be an especially significant factor. However, historical reasons in themselves are likely to be an insufficient basis for long-term cluster prosperity.

Finally, modularity is not an end state — eventually a new integral architecture, offering superior performance, is likely to emerge. The cycle from integral to modular and back to integral seems to vary widely across industries (Christensen 2000; Fine 1998). For example, the computer industry presently seems to be becoming increasingly integral, a trend that is being significantly driven by the expansion of both Microsoft and Intel (both of whom have historically been module suppliers) into segments vertically related to their core businesses.

A general conclusion to this discussion would therefore be that cluster evolution is significantly driven by the evolution of product architectures. Consequently, a cluster will prosper to the extent that it can recycle financial and human capital rapidly and efficiently, and configure it vertically or horizontally, consistent with such cyclical variations (Fine 1998: 229–230). Such abilities likely require considerable levels of redundancy in a cluster: many independent firms playing one or other of the architectural roles. This recalls Saxenian's (1994) observations, noted earlier, on the contrasting fortunes of the computer-industry cluster centred on DEC in the Boston area and the relatively distributed one in Silicon Valley.

Application to the Ottawa Area

Technology-intensive industry in the Ottawa area is heavily concentrated in the broad telecommunications industry — 3 of the 6 clusters are telecommunications based, and a fourth, microelectronics, is also significantly telecommunications oriented. The telecommunications industry continues to undergo a broad cycle of change similar to that which has occurred in the computing industry over the last twenty years or so — becoming much more modularly organized. For example, telecommunications consumers now build their own supply chains through the choices they make in buying Internet, cell, long distance, and local loop services and products.

Table 2 details the distribution of Ottawa firms across the various technology-intensive clusters in terms of employment size. The table allows several observations about the various clusters, observations that build on the discussion around the significance of product architecture roles to cluster organizing.

Firstly, firms with fewer than 10 employees account for between 1/3 and 1/2 of all firms in every cluster, firms of between 10 and 99 employees similarly account for between 1/3 and 1/2 of all firms in every cluster, and firms of more than 100 employees account for only between 9 and 15% of any cluster. On the other hand, larger firms, i.e. the top 4 firms in each cluster, account for a disproportionate amount of employment: ranging from a low of 14.2% in software to highs of 59.4% and 60.2% in wireless and photonics, respectively (though these figures must be treated with some caution: see notes to tables). And, as Table 3 indicates, several firms have a considerable presence in more than one cluster.

As for the other two clusters — The life sciences and software clusters have, respectively, the highest and second highest proportion of very small (< 10 employees) firms. Conversely,

Table 2: Distribution of firms, by employee size and by cluster.

Number of Employees	<10	11–99	>99	Total Firms	Local Employees (Adjusted)[a]	% Cluster Employed in 4 Largest Firms (Adjusted)[b]
All technology intensive	457 (44.2%)	484 (46.9%)	92 (8.9%)	1033		
Telecommunications	90 (37.2%)	127 (52.5%)	25 (10.3%)	242	12204	29.2% (A, N, G, M)
Microelectronics	59 (38.1%)	76 (49%)	20 (12.9%)	155	8162	38.37% (A, N, J, I)
Photonics	27 (39.7%)	31 (45.6%)	10 (14.7%)	68	4699	60.2% (A, N, J, C)
Wireless[c]				62	4900	59.4% (A, N, M, S)
Software	243 (49.1%)	226 (45.7%)	26 (5.2%)	495[d]	22628	14.2%
Life sciences	38 (52%)	24 (32.9%)	11 (15.1%)	73	3647	36.2%

Source: OCRI data. This table is based mostly on OCRI data (current for mid-2003). Wireless data was obtained from the Ottawa Citizen (October 7, 2003). Some firms are active in more than one cluster and were counted for each cluster they are active in, but adjusting employment numbers to avoid double counting (see Note a).

[a] The figures reported in the table were compiled as part of a simultaneous OCRI survey of all technology clusters. Determining the appropriate cluster(s) for a firm and its employment levels (and distribution across different clusters) is more or less impossible to do precisely. For any firm with a presence in more than one cluster, the OCRI data included total local employment in the employment counts for each cluster. This considerably overstates the employment levels in each of the relevant clusters. The figures reported here attempt to adjust the OCRI count for cluster employment levels (*but not for the number of firms*) by dividing total employment of the largest "multi-cluster firms" (see Table 3) proportionately across each of the relevant clusters. For example, the OCRI data includes the local Nortel employment of 6,000 in each of telecommunications, microelectronics, and photonics (the OCRI data does not recognize wireless as a distinct cluster). I calculated the Nortel contribution to employment in each of these clusters as 6000/4 = 1500. This adjusted calculation is both incomplete (it adjusts for only the 10 largest firms in each cluster) and crude. However, it clearly better reflects actual employment levels in cluster technologies and may in fact be not far from a good approximation: the Ottawa Citizen of Nov 6, 2003 reported, for example, Nortel's optical networks division — its photonics employment — as being 1700 (as opposed to the 1500 reported here as an adjusted figure).

[b] The "four largest" was chosen as the basis for calculation because this is the standard number of firms on which calculations of industry concentration are made (Porter 1980). A: Alcatel (500), N: Nortel (1500), G: General Dynamics Canada (815), J: JDSU (430), I: IBM (700), M: Mitel (750), C: Cisco (400), S: Siemens (160). For software, the firms counted as largest are Cognos (1300), Anjura (950), Corel (540), and Zamax (526). For life sciences, the companies counted as largest are I-Stat Canada (520), MDS Nordion (400 — another 400 are assigned by my calculations to Microelectronics), Gamma Dynacare (250), and DEW Engineering and Development Ltd. (150 — another 150 are assigned by my calculations to Software).

[c] Breakdown unavailable. Total employment for the wireless cluster was calculated by adding my calculations for Alcatel (500) and Nortel (1500) to the 2900 reported for all other companies in a recent supplement on the sector in the Ottawa Citizen (October 7, 2003).

[d] "Software Directory" (August, 2003) produced by Ottawa Global Marketing (OGM), a program of OCRI's, estimates that in the greater Ottawa area there are only about 250 companies with software development as a core commercial activity, and these companies employ more than 30,000 people. However, these figures are problematic as they include companies not normally thought of as software companies — for example, Nortel Networks, which is the largest private sector employer of software engineers in Ottawa.

Table 3: Firms among the top 10 (by employee numbers) in two or more clusters.

Telecommunications	Microelectronics	Photonics	Wireless	Software	Life Sciences
Nortel	Nortel	Nortel	Nortel		
Alcatel	Alcatel	Alcatel	Alcatel		
Mitel			Mitel		
	JDSU	JDSU			
	MDS				MDS
Breconridge	Breconridge				
				DEW	DEW
Telesat Canada	Telesat Canada				
Innovance Networks		Innovance Net-works			
	QNX		QNX		QNX

Source: OCRI data.

software has the smallest proportion of larger firms (> 99 employees), and Table 2 disguises the fact that the larger life sciences firms are, in fact, relatively small — all life sciences firms have considerably fewer than 1,000 employees, and only 10 have 100 or more employees (OCRI data). The software cluster is regarded as fairly mature and as having peaked in Ottawa, whereas the life sciences cluster is an emerging cluster, though lacking scale in Ottawa (Ottawa 20/20). Both clusters, though especially software, have important technological relations with the other clusters. For example, the software cluster includes a number of firms engaged in developing software for Internet applications; and there is an emerging cluster in biophotonics (for which the OLSC is performing a sort of pre-CAO role).

The relative concentration of a cluster is an indicator that much of the opportunities made visible by clustering are related to the product architectures being pursued by the dominant firms. Such opportunities could be pursued in terms of module supply to these big firms (generating a dominant central buyer network), or supplying directly to the user an end-product that is in fact a module in a wider system of use defined by, say, a Nortel product architecture in wireless and photonics. The pursuit of such opportunities could be spun out from these larger firms — for example, in its former incarnation as Newbridge Networks, the Ottawa unit of Alcatel, had an "affiliates program" that made this a central part of its technology strategy (see the chapter by Callahan *et al.* this volume).

In each of these scenarios, the cluster is effectively being organized in a vertical dimension by the product-architecture investments of the larger established firms driving the investments made by other local firms. But the figures tell us little about the precise nature of the vertical relations between the established firms and the rest of the cluster, and nothing at all about horizontal relations.

On the other hand, the earlier discussion on integrality being an abiding feature early on in a technology's development would imply opportunities in the newer clusters that are only remotely connected to the product architectures of large established local firms, with other smaller and newer firms pursuing new integral architectures. It may well be that the commanding presence of the large established firms in wireless and photonics is a transient phenomenon (much as it was with IBM in the PC industry). Integrality seems especially probable in the life sciences cluster given the novelty, technological distinctiveness, and local absence of truly large firms in this cluster. Determining whether this might really be so would require a much closer examination of trends in these industries, of the strategies that firms are pursuing, and the fit between the two.

However, a research project currently being pursued by another team of MBA students at the University of Ottawa is attempting to address some of these points through examining how one of the large established firms operating in more than one of the clusters is attempting to implement a supplier-management program. The firm is seeking to access external technological capability rather than acquire a firm possessing the desired capability (or technology). The implication is that this firm (and other peer organizations) are moving to a more relationship-oriented approach to their external relations and consequently playing a more direct role in organizing the clusters on an on-going basis. This requires new internal processes for these firms, and the need by supplier firms to adapt to such processes likely changes the dynamics of a cluster to the extent that cluster firms are also suppliers.

Conclusions

The locational advantages identified with clustering are accessed and created by inter-firm interactions. These interactions have horizontal and vertical dimensions, and this chapter has presented a descriptive review of how clusters in technology-intensive industries in the Ottawa area are organized in terms of these dimensions. In doing so I have presumed for these clusters high learning needs, owing to changing product demand, and high co-ordination needs, owing to integrating diverse specialist contributions to complex product systems.

This examination of cluster organizing has merit to the extent that it advances understanding about how cluster interactions can be structured such as to produce high-performance organizations. However, this chapter is more indicative than conclusive in this regard, and suggests many issues that merit further investigation.

Firstly, with regard to the Ottawa area, the evidence points to there being more scope for CAO activity than is currently being realized. To validate this presumption, however, would require measures for more clearly evaluating performance of new or existing CAOs. Provan & Milward (2001) observe that evaluating the effectiveness of network-type organizations is difficult and has been neglected. However, their work suggests several categories for evaluation: firm-level and cluster financial and technological performance, CAO legitimacy (such as the ebb and flow of membership levels), CAO resource acquisition, and the cost and range of the services provided by the CAO. But, to illustrate the difficulties of CAO-performance evaluation, what if member firms adopt a funding-minimization view (and resource levels suggest that this is probable for at least some of the Ottawa CAOs) — say, in an effort to control for agency problems? Then these last two measures will be made quite hollow. Equally, CAOs themselves, faced with the need to satisfy diverse stakeholders, may feel constrained to keep problems to a minimum by keeping costs, and therefore services, to a minimum.

With respect to the vertical organization of the Ottawa clusters, the data produced here suggests that this dimension is indeed significant. As already noted, Saxenian's (1994) work argues for the superiority of horizontal organizing in maintaining cluster vitality. Given that the total number of Ottawa technology firms is only about 4% of the number of Silicon Valley firms (OCRI data), it may be inevitable that there will be a necessarily greater reliance on larger firms, and therefore vertical organizing. In any case, more research, much of it at the firm-level, will be necessary to present a clear picture of the extent and quality of vertical organizing in the Ottawa clusters.

The discussion assumed that CAOs will be of most benefit to smaller firms because of the resource constraints they face. This assumption needs to be validated. To the extent that larger firms can benefit from CAOs, it may be that they need to develop more formal means for capturing such benefits, relative to smaller firms. For example, in larger firms how employees actively exposed to cluster interactions plug into the *intra*-organizational network, plus their formal decision-making power, likely influences whether and how the firm can benefit from CAO mediated interactions. Furthermore, what might be the additional significance to cluster organizing, if any, of these large firms having a presence in more than one cluster? One presumption could be that such a presence promotes inter-cluster collaboration. It should also be noted that the discussion of dominant local firms in this chapter assumed that their role is that of system integrator and that system integration influences cluster organizing only when the system integrator is located within the cluster. This assumption also needs to be tested.

Are the cluster-organizing influences of a CAO and dominant firm exclusive or complementary? If they are exclusive, it means that firms learn either from their peers or large customers, but not both to any significant extent. The fact that there are CAOs in photonics, wireless, and life sciences, but not in the older clusters of telecommunications and microelectronics, could imply that the type of interaction that firms find worthwhile (horizontal or vertical) changes over time, and with it the character of cluster dynamics. For example, CAOs might be especially significant to cluster development early in an industry's emergence. However, the three tables together make clear that industry age is not a reliable indicator of CAO vitality — as a comparison of the respective CAOs for photonics and wireless makes clear (furthermore, the Human & Provan (2000) study referenced earlier examined the emergence of two CAO-like entities in the (very mature) U.S. wood-products industry). The tables also indicate that the presence of a dominant firm alone cannot explain the absence or presence of a CAO and/or a low or high level of active clustering. For example, Nortel has a significant presence in each of telecommunications, microelectronics, photonics, and wireless, yet only wireless has an active CAO.

With regard to CAO/dominant-firm complementarity, it would seem plausible to suggest that a CAO could, for example, play a valuable role specifically geared to animating module-supplier to module-suppler interactions. This could be especially so when such firms are seeking to serve system integrators located outside the cluster. An additional aspect of complementarity could be time based: for example, a CAO could be focused on developing internal legitimacy while a large local firm is putting the cluster on the map, that is, developing external legitimacy, or could come into being partly as a result of such prior efforts by a large local firm.

Finally, returning to the issue of CAO performance, an expanded scope to this issue is surely worthwhile. One focus for such research should be the interactive influence of founding conditions such as backgrounds of founding individuals, board representation, and industry conditions on CAO- legitimacy building (On the basis of anecdotal and other evidence not reproduced here, these all seem to have been significant factors in the success of the OWC relative to the OPC). Further research that investigated the strengths of super-CAOs relative to cluster-specific CAOs and whether and how to develop relationships between both kinds of entity, the nature and usefulness of CAO links to industry- (or national-) level entities, and comparisons between CAOs in the same industry (but different geographical regions) would also help pin-point roles appropriate to CAO-type entities such that they, and by implication the clusters they serve, prosper.

Acknowledgments

I wish to express my appreciation to Jérôme Doutriaux of the University of Ottawa and Mike Justinich formerly of OCRI, both of whom helped with data.

References

Alexander, C. (1964). *Notes on the synthesis of form*. Cambridge, MA: Harvard University Press.

Ashby, W. R. (1960). *Design for a brain*. New York: Wiley.

Bhanot, R., Coger, J., & Simpson, N. (2003). *A marketing and communications plan for the Ottawa manufacturers' network*. MBA project, University of Ottawa.

Burgelman, R. A. (2002). Strategy as vector and the inertia of co-evolutionary lock-in. *Administrative Science Quarterly, 47*, 325–357.

Christensen, C. (2000). *Innovation and the general manager*. New York: McGraw-Hill/Irwin.

DiMaggio, R. J., & Powell, W. W. (1983). The iron cage revisited: Institutional isomorphism and collective rationality in organizational fields. *American Sociological Review, 48*, 147–167.

Doz, Y., & Hamel, G. (1998). *Alliance advantage: The art of creating value through partnering*. Boston, MA: Harvard Business School Press.

Fine, C. H. (1998). *Clockspeed: Winning industry control in the age of temporary advantage*. Reading, MA: Perseus Books.

Gersick, C. (1988). Time and transition in work teams: Toward a new model of growth. *Academy of Management Journal, 31*, 9–42.

Granovetter, M. (1985). Economic action: The problem of embeddedness. *American Journal of Sociology, 91*, 481–510.

Granovetter, M. (1992). Problems of explanation in economic sociology. In: N. Nohria, & R. G. Eccles (Eds), *Networks and organizations: Structure, form, and action* (pp. 25–56). Boston: Harvard Business School Press.

Hagedoorn, J. (1995). Note on international market leaders and networks of strategic technology partnering. *Strategic Management Journal, 16*, 241–251.

Hauser, J., & Clausing, D. (1988). The house of quality. *Harvard Business Review* (May–June), 63–74.

Holland, J. H., & Miller, J. H. (1991). Artificial adaptive agents in economic theory. *American Economic Review, 81*, 365–370.

Human, S. E., & Provan, K. G. (2000). Legitimacy building in the evolution of small firm multilateral networks: A comparative study of success and demise. *Administrative Science Quarterly, 45*, 327–368.

Jones, C., Hesterly, W., & Borgatti, S. (1997). A general theory of network governance: Exchange conditions and social mechanisms. *Academy of Management Review*, *22*, 911–945.

Meyer, J. W., & Rowan, B. (1977). Institutionalized organizations: Formal structure as myth and ceremony. *American Journal of Sociology*, *83*, 340–363.

Ottawa Citizen (2003, Thursday, October 7). Semi-annual high-tech supplement.

Ottawa 20/20 — Economic Strategy. Ottawa, Ontario, Canada: City of Ottawa Business Development Branch, Services Department. April 2003.

Piore, M. J., & Sabel, C. F. (1984). *The second industrial divide: Possibilities for prosperity*. New York: Basic Books.

Porter, M. (1980). *Competitive strategy: Techniques for analyzing your business and competitors*. New York: Free Press.

Porter, M. (1990). *The competitive advantage of nations*. New York: Free Press.

Porter, M. (1998). Clusters and the new economics of competition. *Harvard Business Review* (November–December), 77–90.

Powell, W. W. (1990). Neither market nor hierarchy: Network forms of organization. In: B. M. Staw, & L. L. Cummings (Eds), *Research in organizational behavior* (Vol. 12, pp. 295–336). Greenwich, CT: JAI Press.

Powell, W. W., Koput, K. W., & Smith-Doerr, L. (1996). Inter-organizational collaboration and the locus of innovation: Networks of learning in biotechnology. *Administrative Science Quarterly*, *41*, 116–145.

Provan, K. G., & Milward, H. B. (2001). Do networks really work? A framework for evaluating public-sector organizational networks. *Public Administration Review*, *61*, 414–423.

Saxenian, A. (1994). *Regional advantage: Culture and competition in Silicon Valley and Route 128*. Cambridge, MA: Harvard University Press.

Simon, H. A. (1969). *The sciences of the artificial*. Cambridge, MA: MIT Press.

Singh, K. (1997). The impact of technological complexity and inter-firm cooperation on business survival. *Academy of Management Journal*, *40*, 339–368.

Suchman, D. (1995). Managing legitimacy: Strategic and institutional approaches. *Academy of Management Review*, *20*, 571–610.

Ulrich, K. (1995). The role of product architecture in the manufacturing firm. *Research Policy*, *24*, 419–441.

Websites of CAOs viewed during October/November 2003: www.ocri.ca; www.ottawasoftwarecluster.ca; www.ottawaphotonics.com; www.ottawawirelesscluster.com; www.olsc.ca; www.omnet.ca.

Chapter 8

The Role of Venture Capital in Building Technology Companies in the Ottawa Region

John Callahan and Ken Charbonneau

Abstract

This chapter reviews the role of venture capital in building technology companies in the Ottawa region. We find four distinct periods of venture capital activity in the region: before 1990, between 1990 and 1997, between 1997 and 2001, and between 2001 and 2004. These periods are relatively distinct in terms of the investors present in the market, the companies seeking capital, the investment climate, and the contribution made by venture capital to business development of the Ottawa region. The key question that this chapter tries to address is: has venture capital helped technology companies create value in the region? We propose that the answer is not a straightforward yes or no.

Introduction

The objective of this chapter is to describe the role that venture capital has played in the development of technology companies in the Ottawa region. We ground our description in four periods of time: before 1990, between 1990 and 1997, between 1997 and 2001, and between 2001 and 2004. We find these periods to be relatively distinct in terms of the investors present in the market, the companies seeking capital, the investment climate, and the contribution made by venture capital to business development.

The role of venture capital in the creation of value remains a controversial one in the research literature. Ideally, a venture capital investor can bring many things to an entrepreneurial venture — capital first of all, of course. Venture capital can accelerate the development of a venture and allow it to hit market opportunities in a timely way. Venture capitalists may also bring a wealth of operating and company governance experience. They may bring connections with customers, suppliers, partners, and potential executive hires. It is the experience of entrepreneurial companies in general, however, that venture capital can

Silicon Valley North: A High-Tech Cluster of Innovation and Entrepreneurship
ISBN: 0-08-044457-1

have serious negatives. We argue that there have been instances in which venture capital involvement has not been beneficial on balance for companies in the region.

There are many natural sources of conflict between venture capitalists and entrepreneurs. As equity investors, venture capitalists want the companies in which they invest to be successful. There are many versions of "success," however, in any situation as complex as building a new company. For the founding team of entrepreneurs, successful innovation can be the creation of a company of which they can be proud, that provides a good living, and may provide real equity value at some time in the future. This process might take 10, 15, even 20 years and still be successful. Entrepreneurs are normally not diversified — their entire fortunes will be tied up in their companies. On the other hand, a venture capitalist will have a reasonably diversified portfolio of a dozen or more investments. Moreover, for the venture capitalist success is very specific and clear cut. A VC invests only with the prospect of realizing real equity value through a liquidity event like acquisition or an initial public offering — generally within a period of 5 to 7 years (Lerner 1994).

Venture capital investment in the region goes back at least 30 years, but significant VC investment in the region is relatively new. Most of the venture capital invested in the region has been invested within the last five years. The role of venture capital in the growth of industry clusters like that of Ottawa, have been addressed by others. Kenney & Florida (2000) and Banato & Fong (2000) address the role of venture capital in the Bay Area south of San Francisco. Mallett (2002) and Mason et al. (2002) have written about Ottawa. It is a good time for a fresh look at the role of venture capital in the Ottawa region, however, because we have just passed through a full cycle of boom and bust. Much has changed over the last couple of years.

The key question that this chapter tries to address is: to what extent has venture capital helped technology companies create value in the Ottawa region? The chapter is organized as follows. We first present four small case studies that illustrate venture capital investment in the region, for better and for worse. In the following section, we describe the financing of startup companies and the role that venture capital plays in this financing. We then review the question as to whether or not, in general, venture capital creates value. The following section forms the core of the chapter. In it we review the four periods of venture capital involvement in the Ottawa region. We then conclude by addressing the basic question of the chapter: has venture capital helped technology companies create value in the region? We propose that the answer is not a straightforward yes or no.

Four Case Studies

We first present four small case studies of VC investing in the Ottawa region: two definite failures, and two much more successful investments. VC firms heavily invested in Zenastra and Trillium and the companies went out of business soon after. Tundra is a successful public company that was VC backed. Catena, a more recent company very heavily supported by VC money, had the potential to become a significant, successful public company when it was acquired by Ciena in 2004. We present these case studies to illustrate the role of venture capital investment in the region.

Zenastra (1999–2001)

Zenastra started up in February 1999 as Nu-Wave Photonics (Bagnall 2000a). In 1997 an Iranian immigrant, Hamid Hatami-Hanza brought the technical idea that formed the basis for the company to Peter Brownhill, a former Bell Canada executive. Brownhill, impressed with the potential of the idea contacted Patrick Shea, a former Bell colleague in 1998. Shea had successful start-up experience and was at the time investing as an angel in the region. Shea contributed seed money to keep the idea moving forward. In 1999, with promising lab results Shea facilitated $4 million in financing — $1 million from friends and $3 million from three venture capital funds: Ventures West Management Inc., VenGrowth Investment Fund Inc. and Bank of Montreal Capital Corp (also BDC and Eastern Technology Seed Investment Fund). Nu-Wave was officially launched in February 2000.

The company attracted a number of high quality executive and technical personnel, many from local optical networking giants Nortel and JDS. By April 2000 they had 40 engineers employed.

On May 19 2000, the company announced what to that date was the largest venture capital deal in the history of Ottawa — $40 million U.S. The lead underwriter for the deal was Yorkton Securities with HSBC Securities (Canada) acting as co-underwriters. The full investor list was never released but the placement was syndicated to a number of Canadian and U.S. institutional and private clients, and included BDC Venture Capital Division, VenGrowth Investment Fund, BMO Technology Investment Program, Ventures West, Triax Growth Fund, Jefferson Partners and Lawrence & Company. The company had intended to raise significantly less than it did but the underwriters found the level of investor interest to be very high and urged Nu-Wave to consider a much bigger deal.

Announced at the same time as the VC placement was the appointment of Peter Scovell as President and CEO. Scovell was the former head of Nortel's Optoelectronics Group. His appointment was effective on June 5. Another notable appointment in June of that year was that of Ken Hill as chief scientific officer. Hill was an "optical legend."

By the start of 2001, the market for optical telecommunications products had softened considerably — as had investor enthusiasm. That spring Zenastra was looking for new financing. In March of that year Scovell was still talking, however, of taking staffing levels from 200 to 350 by the end of the year. The company also maintained that its plans for a new $40 million manufacturing plant in Kanata were still firm (Enman 2001). The plans for this new plant were finally shelved publicly in August of 2001. At the end of that month, the company was still struggling to find new financing and cut staff by 160 — 64% of its workforce.

By October of 2001, Zenastra was out of business. It later resurfaced as Broadwave Photonics Inc. in February 2002. Syracuse, N. Y.-based Broadnet Technologies Inc. and China's Shenzhen Laserwave Optoelectronics Co. Ltd. struck a deal with Zenastra's bankruptcy trustee in late December of 2001 to acquire the majority of its capital assets, leases and intellectual property. Start to finish the company lasted three years. From its official launch to going out of business was two years. It spent over $40 million U.S. in its final 18 months.

Trillium (2000–2002)

Trillium Photonics was spun out from a technology incubator program at the National Research Council (NRC) in the spring of 2000. Two research scientists from NRC's photonics systems group of the Institute for National Measurement Standards founded the company: Piotr Myslinki who served as the company's initial president and CEO, and Simon Boothroyd who became its CTO. Mylinksi and Boothroyd licensed the technology on which the company was based from the NRC. This licensing was facilitated by a policy change by NRC from a few years earlier to foster more commercialization of technologies developed in its labs.

Trillium planned to develop and sell optical amplifiers that could operate in dynamic rather than static networks. Their target customers were integrated manufacturers like Nortel who produced systems for the core of the developing optical Internet market.

The company received an initial VC investment of $6.5 million (U.S.) from the very prominent Silicon Valley venture capital firm of Mohr Davidow in August 2000 while still housed in the NRC incubator facilities (Guly 2001). At the time, the firm had about a dozen employees and planned to have its first product out the door by the end of 2001. The investment was Mohr Davidow's first in the Ottawa region. At the time, the firm had plans to invest a total of $100 million (U.S.) in the region.

Mylinski anticipated the hiring of an experienced CEO right from the start. In July of 2001 the company brought in Brian Jervis to be president and CEO. Jervis resigned from the CEO role at Kestrel Solutions to take the position; Kestrel folded its four-month-old Ottawa operation when he did so. Kestrel had been expanding in Ottawa during the spring of 2001 as other companies like Nortel, Sedona Networks (a local start-up that went out of business in 2001) and Cisco were laying-off engineers and support staff. Jervis was a Nortel veteran. Subsequent to Nortel he had served as Executive Vice President of the Switching Products Group for Newbridge Networks, a position from which he was fired in late 1999 (Bagnall 2002).

In January 2002, Trillium received a second round of VC financing — this time for $29 million (U.S.). The VCs on this round were Spectrum Equity, JK&B Capital and Mohr Davidow. Nine months later in October 2002, Trillium ceased operations and a significant amount of the second VC round was returned to investors.

Tundra (1995–Present)

Tundra was formed from Newbridge Microsystems, a division of Newbridge Networks Corporation. It began operation as an independent company in December 1995 and was one of the first Newbridge spin-offs — known as affiliates.[1] Tundra designs, develops, markets and sells semiconductor chips that perform bus-bridging functions in embedded computer systems. It does not manufacture the chips that it sells. The company went public early in 1999.

---

[1] The Newbridge affiliate program is described below.

Table 1: Principal shareholders in Tundra just prior to IPO.

Shareholder	Percentage of Share Ownership
Newbridge networks	37.1
VenGrowth	17.8
Adam Chowaniec	2.8
James Roche	4.0
All other directors and senior officers	6.1

Note: Created from data in the Tundra IPO Prospectus of January 26, 1999.

The current president of Tundra, Jim Roche, was a founding member of Newbridge Networks in 1986 and along with Adam Chowaniec led Tundra out of Newbridge. Tundra benefited from continuous and strong management schooled in entrepreneurship within Newbridge by Terry Matthews, the most successful entrepreneur the Ottawa region has seen.

VenGrowth invested $6.9M in Tundra between 1995 and 1999. Table 1 contains a list of the investor's in Tundra just prior to its IPO. The 17.8% share of ownership held by VenGrowth was diluted during the offering to 13.1% — this share represented a market value of $16.6M for VenGrowth.

Capital Alliance Ventures Inc., a local VC firm, was one of the original investors in Tundra, investing $144,617 in 1995. In its last fiscal year before going public (ended April 30 1998), Tundra had revenues of $20.1M and net earnings of $473K. In the fiscal year ended April 30 2003, its revenues were $34.0M and it lost $32.0K. In spite of incurring losses during the downturn in the chip market in 2001 and 2002, Tundra is once again profitable and remains a very strong competitor in its market.

Catena (1998–2004)

Catena Networks was founded in 1998 by five ex-Nortel employees and managers. It builds integrated broadband access systems that enable service providers to deploy voice, data and video services and to migrate to packet-based networks. Its value proposition to service providers is anchored on reduced cost through leverage of their currently installed equipment — an attractive one for carriers hard pressed to make a profit in the current industry environment.

Catena was a "major venture capital play." It secured U.S. $192M in venture financing from some of the high-tech industry's most influential investors:

- Attractor Investment Management.
- BCE Capital.
- Berkeley International Capital.
- Bessemer Venture Partners.
- Goldman Sachs Group, Inc.
- J. & W. Seligman & Co.

- JPMorgan Partners.
- Lighthouse Capital Partners.
- Menlo Ventures.
- Morgenthaler Ventures.
- Munder Capital Management.
- Silicon Valley BancVentures.
- Stanford University.
- WestAM.
- Worldview Technology Partners.

This is the largest amount of VC capital raised to date by an Ottawa company. Many of the other regional startups recently well financed by venture capital went under over the last few years,[2] so Catena represented an important test of the ability of venture capital to create value.

This value was realized in February 2004 when Catena was acquired by Ciena, a U.S. telecommunications equipment maker, for $645M in shares. Catena had proven unique in its ability to increase sales to carriers during the telecommunications downturn, posting ten consecutive quarters of increasing sales.

Venture Capital and the Financing of Startup Companies

Venture capital firms raise money from investors and then make high-risk investments in new businesses, with the expectation of high-returns. When raising money, a VC firm will set up a separate fund often with a specific investment policy and a stated subscription limit. It raises money up to this limit and then invests. The investors become limited partners in the fund that is run by the VC firm as a general partner. As limited partners, the investors (typically wealthy individuals,[3] corporate investors and pension funds) play no role in managing the fund. Although VCs often invest their own money in their funds, for the most part VCs invest other people's money.

VC firms open, fund, invest and subsequently terminate different funds, some appealing to retail investors and others to institutional investors, on a regular basis. Termination usually takes place after around ten years. This horizon is based on the fact that it takes a VC-backed company between five and seven years to reach a liquidity event — acquisition, dissolution or initial public offering (IPO) of shares to the public. Add two or three years to invest funds raised and you arrive at the normal ten-year time period. The termination date of a fund is generally specified up front — a typical example would be ten years with the option for the VC firm to extend for a couple of years in case the fund investments do not reach liquidity on schedule. In some cases, venture capitalists may exercise control rights to force bankruptcy of an under performing investee company. This may allow the VC fund

---

[2] See Table 9.

[3] There are labour sponsored funds that cater exclusively to individuals and are accessible to those who are not necessarily wealthy. They raised significant amounts of venture capital in Canada during the 1990s.

to recoup some investment through ownership of preferred shares that are paid out before common shares.

Limited partners pay VCs management fees generally between 1 and 3% of the their investment. Once a fund is terminated, the limited partners get their money back first. Then the VC firm as general partner receives "carried interest" of around 20% of the capital gains realized by the fund over its lifetime. The limited partners receive the rest. It is only at fund termination that the limited partners realize liquidity on their investment.

Venture capital firms tend to specialize both geographically and by area of business. VC investing requires specialized knowledge and contact with prospective companies. It also takes a lot of time. It can take 9 or 10 months or more between initial contact and actual investment in a company.[4] As a result, VC firms do not handle the volume of invested funds regularly handled by fund managers of more liquid established stocks. The fees charged to investors by VCs are correspondingly higher.

The investor returns on a venture capital fund are typically generated by a small fraction of their investments. One study of venture capital portfolios reported that about 7% of investments accounted for more than 60% of the profits, while fully one-third resulted in a partial or total loss (Bhidé 2000: 145). It is actually a minority of startup companies that require VC funding. The vast majority of entrepreneurial start-ups are sole proprietorships in the service industry with limited opportunity for growth (Bhidé 2000: 13).

For those start-up companies that do have business models requiring significant up-front expenditures on product/service development and business infrastructure creation, the normal sequence of financing is shown in Figure 1.

The Stages of New Venture Financing

(i) Seed financing   Seed financing, usually in the tens of thousands of dollars range, takes a startup from idea to opportunity and the development of a real business plan. Individuals are important investors at this stage. The company founders are the first to invest — actual dollars and even more commonly sweat equity, i.e. they flesh out their opportunity in the form of a business plan and, perhaps, a product prototype for no cash compensation. This type of initial investment can extend to employees as well. If the founders are intent on raising venture capital, they will definitely have to go to "family and friends" to raise equity capital in this early stage. The ability to go to friends and family and convince them to invest is regarded as a sign of commitment by the founding entrepreneurs to a real, quality opportunity.

Angel investors also provide seed financing. Angel investors are individuals who invest their own money. In the Ottawa region, there are three kinds of angels. There are those who see being an angel as a career. They act much like VCs. They may form a group with a fund and have management fees. They often try to co-invest with VCs. A second type is the passive angel investor with a high net worth who has made his or her money

---

[4] During the fevered investment environment of the late 1990s, this interval shrank. It has since lengthened again significantly.

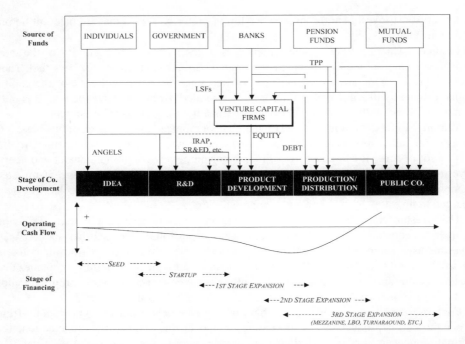

Figure 1: The role of venture capital in the financing of startup companies. *Note:* Reprinted with permission from Doyle (2003). The federal government's Technology Partnerships Program (TPP), Industrial Assistance Research Program (IRAP), and Scientific Research and Experimental Development (SR&ED), as well as Labour sponsored funds (LSVs) are described in the chapter.

in non-technology types of business. They may own a chain of successful restaurants, for example. They play the stock market, invest in property and in VC funds, but also invest directly in startups. The third type is the retired serial entrepreneur who knows technology-based business. They invest not only for the returns but to give something back to the community.

Angels generally keep a low profile in their communities, not wanting to be pestered by start-ups looking for money, but preferring to find investment opportunities through their personal business networks. In the Ottawa region, angels invest in the $50K to $150K range. The level of angel financing tends to be higher in the States — usually between $100K and $500K. Because angels often have deep knowledge of an industry and of the entrepreneurs that drive them, they bring credibility and contacts with their investments (see also the chapter by Madill *et al.* this volume).

(ii) Startup financing Individuals, particularly angels, remain important sources of financing in the startup phase when the company undertakes R&D, prepares product prototypes and initiates contact with potential customers. At this stage, however, government and venture capital firms also become important.

The federal government has a variety of programs to help startup companies. The Industrial Assistance Research Program (IRAP) of the National Research Council Canada (NRC) and Technology Partnerships Canada (TPC) support innovative small and medium enterprises by investing in projects in the pre-commercialization stage. The Scientific Research and Experimental Development (SR&ED) Program is a federal tax incentive program designed to encourage Canadian businesses to conduct research and development (R&D). The SR&ED Program is the largest single source of federal government support for research and development. The Technology Partnerships Program (TPP) supports partnerships between postsecondary institutions and small and medium-sized Canadian companies to a maximum of $150,000 annually, with the industrial partners providing the balance in cash and in kind. Activities aimed at demonstrating the technical and economic feasibility of an invention or discovery are eligible for funding.

Venture capital firms start to become important at this stage particularly if the "burn rate"[5] of the company increases and they need the amount of financing that VCs can provide — generally over a million dollars.[6] VC investments are very commonly *syndicated* — there will be a lead VC that organizes a group of VC firms to invest in a start-up. They are also commonly *staged*, so that multiple rounds of venture capital investment may be required to take an early-stage firm to liquidity. Each funding round is negotiated at the current valuation of the firm, and often dilutes the ownership of existing investors.

Like angels, VCs supply many other things to a new venture in addition to financing. They often bring a deep knowledge of technologies and markets, and as a result can add significant value in terms of business model and marketing strategy. VCs can have large networks of contacts — with other investors, customers, potential partners, and managers. These contacts can be of great value to a new venture. Investment in a start-up by a prestigious VC also brings credibility in both the financial and product markets.

(iii) First stage expansion   As companies enter product development their cash "burn rate" can increase significantly. It is when this happens that VC funding is critical. Government also plays a role here, as do individual investors but are of less importance than VCs. The first or Series A venture capital often occurs at this stage.

(iv) Second stage expansion   Second and third round VC financing (series B and C rounds) occur during this stage. Companies may also use the TPP program during this stage. Banks may get involved at this stage, especially if the company is generating cash flow from customer sales.

(v) Third stage expansion   As a startup grows and proves its business model, investment risk can decrease. At this point the need for capital can increase substantially to finance growth, market expansion and other related activities. Under these circumstances, a start-up can look to institutional investors called "merchant banks" for financing. Investments at

---

[5] A startup company's burn rate is the rate at which it spends money.
[6] Note that individuals can invest in venture capital funds via labour sponsored funds described below. They are labeled LSFs in Figure 1.

this stage are called late stage venture capital or mezzanine financing. Merchant banks have large amounts of funds available to them, and the lower risk and likely shorter horizon until liquidity of late stage venture financing can be attractive to them. They generally invest in the form of debt, sometimes convertible to equity. As debt investors, one of their principal concerns is that the company has the cash flow to service the debt.

The Venture Capital Investment Process

Venture capital firms are interested in learning early about potential investments, and use their personal networks to locate such opportunities. In rare instances, a venture capitalist may become involved in the development of a new venture before it is ready for investments of the size and type appropriate for VCs. More commonly, however, the deals seek out the VC, who often maintains a high profile in their investment community — spending significant amounts of time at business events and conferences. The timing of VC financial entry into an opportunity can depend greatly on the supply of and demand for good opportunities by VCs. During the bubble years of 1998 through 2000, very early entry — before real sales — was the norm. Since the bubble burst in 2001, many VCs have been investing more conservatively and later in the opportunity development cycle.

VCs refer to "deal flow" to describe the flow of investment opportunities that they see. Deal flow is the lifeblood of a VC firm. Because they normally see so many business plans, they have tough filters to control their workload. Of the business plans that they see, they finance only a very small percentage (Nesheim 2000). Just reading a business plan can take hours, and VCs can receive hundreds per month. Some VCs do not accept any unsolicited business plans. They do take seriously business plans brought to them by personal contacts and individuals that they know and trust (Shane & Stuart 2002). This is one of the reasons that angel investment can be so important for a new venture intent on raising venture capital. A well-connected angel can personally introduce the founding entrepreneurs and their business opportunity to potential VC investors (Fenn & Liang 1998).

VCs screen deals initially based on such factors as investment stage, investment size, industry sector and geography. If a deal gets through this screening, the first questions asked of the entrepreneurs driving an opportunity are of the form, "So what? Who cares? Why you?"[7] In other words: What is the core of the opportunity and why is it important? Who are the customers and what pain is the start-up going to solve for them? And, what competitive advantage does the start-up bring to the table that will ensure that they can make money with the opportunity? Subsequent discussions elaborate on these themes. VenGrowth, a VC firm active in the region, uses the following decision criteria in evaluating opportunities: people, market, customer traction, competition, product idea, technology and timing. Other VC firms may have somewhat different criteria, but the core elements — experienced managers,[8] proprietary products, minimum investment thresholds, and extensive due diligence — are fairly uniform across VC firms (Bhidé 2000: 152).

---

[7] These questions have actually been copyrighted by an Ottawa consulting company, Reid-Eddison.

[8] There is a saying in the venture capital community that "the three most important things about a deal are people, people and people." A variation on this is that "the five most important things about a deal are people, people,

Venture capitalists look to a liquidity event like divestiture (i.e. acquisition by another company) or an initial public offering (IPO) to cash out. As a result, a venture capital backed company must plan and work towards such a liquidity event from the start if they wish to raise venture capital.

If a VC is still interested in investing after reviewing the company's business plan and talking with the principles, the VC will issue a term sheet to the company. This term sheet outlines what the VC sees as the basis for a financing deal. If the company accepts the term sheet, then *due diligence* by the VC begins in earnest on the company, the entrepreneurial team, and the opportunity. During this period of due diligence, the company is normally restricted from "shopping the deal around" to other investors for a specified period of time — in a sense, acceptance of the term sheet gives the VC an option to invest. This due diligence period can last several months, and is always a period of high stress and high cost in terms of management attention for the company.

Valuation of a startup, required as part of any deal, is a complex task (Timmons 2001). Quantitative models are used — multiples of sales, discounted multiples of future earnings, comparison with previous and concurrent deals, previous valuations at angel seed rounds — but many of the factors are qualitative. Qualitative factors focus on the match between what is required to be successful and the strength of the core management team, and of future market and technology trends.

Structuring the deal is the last stage before closing the investment. A good deal structure is one in which the goals of the VCs and of the entrepreneurs are aligned to the greatest extent possible. Important considerations include the equity share allocated to each party, the investment instruments used, the staging of disbursements to the company, the allocation of proceeds upon a liquidity event and control over significant company decisions.

The investment instruments used in VC deals have changed over the last few years. In the past, it was usual for VCs to purchase common shares of the companies in which they invested. They became investors on the same level as the founding entrepreneurs, family and friends, and angels. In the last few years, VCs have taken to insisting on convertible preferred shares and the senior liquidation rights that come with them (Kaplan & Stromberg 2000). These shares generally have minimum return features of two to three times the original sums invested. This means that when a liquidity event occurs, the VCs get paid before the common shareholders at a minimum payout that is a multiple of their initial investment. In addition, the VCs often participate in proceeds that exceed the minimum payout, parri passu with the common shareholders. In combination, the preference payout and participation in excess proceeds is often referred as "double dipping." These terms are very tough.

When a deal has been signed, the start-up firm gets a cheque for the initial "tranche" of the VC funds to be invested. It is rare for the full deal amount to be paid in one lump sum.[9] As part of the contract, the start-up must meet defined milestones to get successive tranches of the deal. These milestones take a variety of forms such as product development events, hiring key personnel, and meeting sales targets.

---

people, market and product." Good people will find good opportunities, and more importantly, be able to execute on them.

[9] This was not the case during the Internet and dot.com "bubble" when VCs commonly paid out the full amounts of an investment stage in one cheque.

VCs are very active investors. Commonly, they participate as active members of the board; recruiting management and key technical personnel; developing business strategies; monitoring the company's performance; and facilitating subsequent financing rounds (Kaplan & Stromberg 2001). VC firms have even been known to function much like the chief financial officers of their client companies if these companies do not yet have adequate internal financial controls and competencies. This is usually short lived, however, and a VC will actively aid in recruiting such competencies for a company. VC-financed firms are more likely and faster to professionalize by adopting stock option plans and hiring external business executives, such as a vice-president of sales, or an external CEO (Hellman & Puri 2002). As stated earlier, VCs will only invest in an opportunity if there is a good likelihood of some liquidity event within their five to seven year investment-horizon.

The Rise of the Bay Area Model

Although venture capitalists invest risk equity in new ventures, it has long been common-place for VCs to demand securities senior to common equity when they invest. These senior securities are either convertible debentures or preferred shares. In contrast, individuals such as founders buy straight, common shares and angel investors usually invest in convertible debentures or common shares when they invest in a company.

The use of senior securities, most often preferred shares, was complicated by the adoption of the "Bay Area model" of VC investing. In the Bay Area south of San Francisco, VCs have for a long time demanded not just preferred shares but also pre-determined liquidation preferences for these shares based on the initial investment — liquidation preferences, for example, of 2 or 3 times. This model came to the Ottawa region with the influence and the influx of American VCs during the "bubble" between 1997 and 2001.

Consider the following small example that illustrates the issues inherent in the use of shares with liquidation preferences for early, individual, straight equity investors. Say a company starts with $2M in straight equity. Sometime later, it considers a VC round of financing. A VC values the company before investing (i.e. pre-money) at $3M. The VC invests $9M so that the company has a value after the VC investment (i.e. post-money) of $12M. The VC has a 3-times liquidity preference on the preferred shares that were received in exchange for the $9M investment. This means that upon the occurrence of a liquidity event (IPO, acquisition or liquidation), the VC gets the first $27M in proceeds before any of the other investors get anything. If the firm goes IPO for $25M, which might otherwise sound like a good deal for the founders, the founders and other initial individual investors would get nothing.

The situation is even worse because VCs sometimes also demand a "double dip." Consider the previous example. If the VC had a "double dip" clause in his deal and the firm did go IPO for $50M, the VC would receive $27M plus 75% (he would own 9/12 of the company) of the remaining $23M.

This situation can get very complicated with successive rounds of VC financing when different preference levels are established for successive issues of preferred shares, each with their own liquidation preferences. It can be really disastrous for straight equity investors in the case of a down round — when valuations of the company for a second round are below that of a preceding round. This became very common during the aftermath of the "bubble" — after 2001.

It is frequently the case, however, that a deal cannot be executed without the approval of the common shareholders. In such a case, when by contract a VC would get everything and to not sell the company would mean that it would go under so that no one would get anything, the VC might end up carving off a portion of the proceeds of the deal (10–15%, for example) for the common shareholders to get the deal done.

Venture Capital and the Creation of Value

Callahan & Muegge (2003) review the surprising controversy in the research literature as to how successful VCs actually are at fostering innovation. This section summarizes the salient findings of this review. There are three popular arguments. The first is that VCs free innovative firms from capital constraints and add genuine value that helps them become successful. A more neutral stance is that VCs identify the best new ventures, and are the intermediary gatekeepers for funding. The most negative position is that VCs back only conventional ideas. Unconventional innovative ventures are screened out as too risky, and never receive funding. The research to date is inconclusive.

What is clear, however, is that VC-backed firms are more successful than non-VC backed firms, both before and after IPO. Venture-backed firms bring product to market faster (Hellman & Puri 2002), "professionalize" earlier by introducing stock option plans and hiring external business managers (Hellman & Puri 2000), time IPOs more effectively to the market (Lerner 1994), and have higher valuations at least five years after IPO (Gompers & Brav 1997). Venture-backed IPOs pay lower fees and are less under priced (Megginson & Weiss 1991).

Causation, however, is more difficult to establish. Do venture capitalists add value that makes it more likely for their portfolio firms to succeed, or are they simply good at picking winners? Research suggests that VCs do have some impact on their portfolio firms (Hsu 2000; Kortum & Lerner 2000). Other studies imply that there are limitations to the value added by VC influence. Ruhnka et al. (1992) investigated the strategies employed by 80 venture capital firms to deal with the "living dead" investments in their portfolios — ventures that were self-sustaining but failed to achieve levels of growth or profitability necessary for attractive exits such as IPO or acquisition. Venture managers were able to achieve a successful turnaround or exit in 55.9% of living dead situations, regardless of the age of the VC firms, their size, or the relative availability of investor personnel for monitoring investees. From the invariance of this result, the authors argue that the causal factors were outside VC control.

Bhidé (2000: 141–142) argues that:

> VC-backed entrepreneurs face extensive scrutiny of their plans and ongoing monitoring of their performance by their capital providers. These distinctive initial conditions lead them to pursue opportunities with greater investment and less uncertainty, rely more on anticipation and planning and less on improvisation and adaptation, use different strategies for securing resources, and face different requirements for success.

Table 2: Differences between bootstrap and big money startups.

	Bootstrap	**Big Money**
Money	Earn it	Other people's
Initial focus	Customers	Exit
Product	Incremental	Highly engineered
Markets	Niche	$1B
Org. structure	Fluid	Rigid
Time horizon	Near term	Long term
Media profile	Low	High
Personal sacrifice	High	Low

This would suggest that the venture capital process may actually screen out the most significant innovations in favor of minor variations of what has come before. Other research suggests that venture capitalists frequently engage in "herding" — making investments that are very similar to those of other firms.

During the Internet and dot-com "bubble" of the late 1990s and early 2000, many startup ventures received large disbursements of very early venture capital funding. Since the collapse of the bubble, anecdotes have emerged describing the destructive effects of such large amounts of early money. The business model of a startup venture is like an untested hypothesis — the real test is making a profit from paying customers. Availability of early money can hide problems in a business by delaying such a test. Some very early stage startups redefined success in terms of financing — achieving the first (or the next) venture capital investment round. Bootstrapping, the creation of a business without significant outside financing, is again becoming popular because of the relatively limited supply of venture capital money — and it may not be a bad development.

The differences between bootstrapped and "big money" startups are summarized in Table 2. Bootstrapping forces focus on cash flow and the immediate needs of customers in niche addressable markets. Freed of cash flow constraints, big money startups can try for highly engineered product "home runs" with a view of striking it rich and cashing out. Big money allows for significant compensation packages, so the personal sacrifice of principals can be very low. When one reads about big money startups, the news all too often centers on their financing progress rather than success with real customers.

In summary, venture capital would appear to at least help bring innovation to market. However, the selection process may not always identify and fund the most significant innovations, and especially in times of abundant supply, there may be disadvantages to "big money."

Four Eras

We now describe the role of venture capital in building companies in the Ottawa region using the four eras shown in Figure 2.

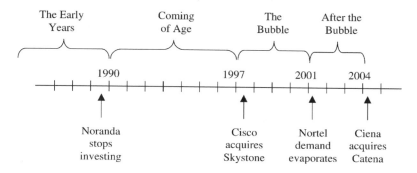

Figure 2: Four eras.

The Early Years (Before 1990)

The only local venture capital operation in the early years was Noranda Enterprises. Companies looking for venture capital investment either dealt with Noranda or put on a suit and tie and went to Toronto. Noranda Enterprises started out within the treasury department of Maclaren Power and Paper Company. Owned by an Anglophone family, headquartered in Montreal and very profitable, the company looked to venture investments in the early 1970s as a means of diversification particularly given the rising separatist threat in Quebec at the time. Doug Cameron headed their venture capital operations and became well known in the Ottawa business scene.

In 1979 Noranda Inc., a very large integrated mining and metals company acquired Maclaren. Maclaren continued to operate very independently, and their venture capital operation continued under the direction of Cameron. In 1983, the venture capital operation was set up as a separate unit named Noranda Enterprises headed by Cameron. Rick Charlebois who had joined Maclaren in 1980 also went with Noranda Enterprises. Noranda Enterprises remained the only local venture capital operation through the 1980s. Their first venture investment was in 1973 in Lumonics, an Ottawa company, specializing in the application of industrial lasers. The second was with Mitel in 1975. Other local investments included DY 4, Cognos, Kasten Chase, Simware, Norpak and Cadence. Noranda stopped investing around 1989 and shut down in 1993.

The overall role of venture capital in the region during this era can be illustrated through the experiences of the region's early *anchor companies*. The identification of these 12 *anchor companies*, as being particularly important for the development of the region, was confirmed in interviews with prominent, local venture capitalists. The companies include Nortel Networks and its former R&D subsidiary Bell-Northern Research, Mitel, Newbridge, Corel, JDS, Cognos, CDC, Leigh Instruments, DY-4, Gandalf, Systemhouse and Lumonics (Pappone 2000).

Nortel has had the largest presence in Ottawa for many years. An integrated telecommunications equipment supplier, it started out as Northern Telecom. Until 1996 it had an R&D subsidiary named Bell-Northern Research (BNR) that was jointly owned by Northern Telecom and Bell Canada. BNR ceased to exist as a separate subsidiary and was integrated piecewise into the operating divisions of Northern Telecom during a corporate reorganization in which Bell Canada divested itself of Northern Telecom and Northern Telecom changed its name to Nortel. The name was changed again to Nortel Networks when Nortel acquired Bay Networks in 1998.

In the early years, Northern Telecom and its principal Ottawa presence, BNR, were supported by captive sales to the Canadian Bell system of telecom carriers (BCTel, Alberta Tel, NorthwestTel, SaskTel, Manitoba Tel, Bell Canada, QuebecTel, NBTel, MT&T, IslandTel and NewTel). As a large, well-established public company, it received no venture capital investment while establishing itself in the Ottawa region.

Mitel Networks was a very different story. It was started in 1972 by two entrepreneurs from Great Britain, Michael Cowpland and Terry Mathews, who left Nortel in the wake of the failure of its subsidiary, Microsystems International. An appealing story is that Cowpland and Matthews were going to import and sell a "mulch-as-it-mows," environmentally friendly lawn mower and that Mitel was a contraction of Mike and Terry Lawnmower (see the chapter by Ghent Mallet this volume). The lawnmowers got stuck in transit and did not arrive until the fall. Mitel's first actual product was a tone receiver (an electronic device used to translate musical tones in touch tone phones into electronic signals for telephone systems — based on Cowpland's Ph.D. thesis at Carleton University). Mitel focused on customer premises telecommunications equipment — PBXs and key systems. A U.S. regulatory decision in 1976 determined that businesses could own their own telecommunications equipment. Mitel was successful very quickly.

Mitel used venture capital to get started. Mitel's first round of financing was by the founders, Mathews and Cowpland, and some local angel investors. The second round of $100K came from Helix Investments of Toronto headed by Ben Webster. A third round of about $200K came from Maclaren. Subsequently, Mitel completed an IPO on the Toronto and Montreal Stock exchanges in 1979 and then got listed on the New York Stock Exchange in 1981. British Telecom acquired Mitel in 1986, and Mathews and Cowpland went on to found Newbridge and Corel, respectively. Neither of these new companies used venture capital. Both were financed by their founders from the proceeds of the sale of Mitel.[10]

Newbridge started up in the spring of 1986. Sod turning for its new headquarters took place on April 1 1987. Mathews used $14 million of his own money to start Newbridge. Some other individuals invested but there was no VC money used. During its early years, however, Newbridge also received $15.8 million in grants and repayable loans from Industry Canada, a department of the Canadian federal government. Newbridge subsequently repaid these funds, and became a public company in July 1989.

Cowpland started Corel in the same way — with his own funds. Corel started in 1985 before the BT acquisition of Mitel became final. Cowpland came close to taking Corel public based on a business plan focused on desktop publishing. The plan was to purchase laser printer engines and computers and tie them together with proprietary software for

---

[10] In 1998, Mitel acquired the Plessey semi-conductor division of GE Co. PLC of Britain for $225M (U.S.). In February 2000, Terry Matthews bought the Mitel name and communications systems division from Mitel. Mitel subsequently renamed itself Zarlink Semiconductor.

desktop publishing. This IPO effort was withdrawn at the last minute. When CorelDRAW became a big software hit, Corel did complete its IPO in November 1989.[11]

Cognos, a world leading company in business intelligence software, was founded in 1969 as a consulting company with the name Quasar Systems focused largely on federal government contracts. In the early 1980s they made the difficult transition to become a product company. Its first product was Powerhouse, a 4th generation platform/language for building corporate IT solutions that Cognos still sells. As product revenues ramped up it sold its consulting division. In 1982, Maclaren invested about $2 million in Cognos just before Maclaren set up as Noranda Enterprises. Cognos went public in August of 1986. At the time of the public offering, Michael Potter (the CEO) owned 44% of the company; Noranda Enterprises Ltd. owned 26%; and 400 individuals — mostly employees —owned the balance (Chrom 1986). Doug Cameron of Noranda remained a prominent member of the Cognos Board for many years afterwards.

SHL Systemhouse was founded in 1974 by Rod Bryden, John Kelly and Jack Davies. Kelly and Davies provided funding and "sweat equity"; Bryden provided the other half of the financing (Ottawa Business Journal 2000). Bryden personally put up $50,000 plus $200,000 from a holding company owned by himself and a partner. Between the founding of the company in 1974 and initial public issue of shares in 1980 (CBC 2003), a VC company named Charterhouse — a U.K. based VC headed in Canada by John Hardy — invested a small amount in Systemhouse.

Des Cunningham and Colin Patterson founded Gandalf on their credit cards. Gandalf was a classic example of how to patiently grow a real business and then go public when critical mass was reached. No VC capital was used. The business was bootstrapped using retained earnings and bank borrowings. The company went public in 1981 in a cross border IPO that was a first for an Ottawa founded company. Gandalf dealt with a large U.S. VC later after its merger with Infotron in 1991. The VC was helpful but by that time the ailing Gandalf was a workout problem that eventually failed. In July 1996, Gandalf sought protection from its creditors and sold its most valuable assets to Mitel.

Computing Devices of Canada (CDC) was an Ottawa original, founded in 1948 by two Polish immigrants, George Glinski & Joe Norton (Smillie 2003). It got its start manufacturing a position and homing indicator that kept track of an aircraft's position and indicated the return route to its base. A large contract for the Kicksorter, a digital pulse counter designed at the Chalk River Laboratories of Atomic Energy of Canada Limited (AECL), had a significant influence on the company's growth. A large number of these devices were purchased by AECL from 1957 until 1963 when they were replaced by an early version of the DEC PDP minicomputer. CDC was founded before the development of organized venture capital. Investment capital for the company came from Peter Mahoney who had successful movie projection and electronics businesses. CDC was sold to Control Data Corporation in 1966 and then was acquired by General Dynamics from Control Data in 1998.

Four engineers — the "dynamic foursome" — founded DY 4 in 1979. The company started out as a manufacturer of microcomputers — its Dynasty line of eight bit CPM machines. It pioneered the use of local area networks and early in the 1980s had the

---

[11] Corel was acquired by Vector Capital in the spring of 2003.

largest installed base of LANs in the Canadian computer industry. However, in 1981 IBM entered the PC market with 16 bit DOS based machines which quickly established market dominance and became a de-facto industry standard. DY 4's computers were not compatible with the IBM standard and sales dropped off rapidly. Just prior to the decline in sales for their microcomputers, DY 4 was involved in the development of a speech synthesizer and in a naval project for the Department of National Defence. These contracts required expertise in the development of board level electronic systems using the VME design standard. DY 4 was venture funded by CBC Pension funds in 1981 1983 and 1989 and by Noranda Enterprises in 1983 and 1989.[12] Noranda was particularly important to DY 4 when the company suffered a difficult crisis and almost went out of business. The company went public in 1993. Noranda Enterprises and the CBC Pension Fund owned about 50% of DY 4 when it went public (Lacasse 1993). DY 4 was acquired by C-MAC in 2000.[13]

Leigh Instruments was founded in 1961 by John Shepherd, Chester Mott, Maurice Price and Dick Steacie who left CDC together. It got its start by licensing an NRC crash position indicator. The company was acquired by U.K.-based Plessey Company PLC in 1988 for $100M. By 1991, it was bankrupt. One of the founders, John Shephard, was married to a Findlay. The Findlay's from Carleton Place were early investors. Maclaren came in later but not as a start up investor.

JDS was founded in 1981 by four Bell-Northern Research employees, Jozef Straus, Philip Garel-Jones, Gary Duck, and Bill Sinclair. Straus joined the company full time five years after its founding (Hill 2001a, b). The company started out designing and manufacturing passive optical components and later branched out to active components. The company grew organically in its early years based on the technological competencies and market knowledge the founders developed while at BNR. The original name of the company was JDS Optical. The name changed to JDS Fitel as part of a partnership deal with the giant Japanese industrial wiring and cable company, Furukawa Electric. JDS had been distributing Furukawa products in North America for some time. Furukawa put up $9M in return for half of JDS, half the seats on the board of directors and a full-time liaison person on staff. It was a "hand shake deal." The deal allowed JDS to ramp up operations as demand increased.

JDS had approached several investors in Ottawa and across North America. "They would ask how much business we were doing. We would say $9M," says Straus. "They would ask to see our business plan to get to $50M. We would say that we don't know how to do a business plan and all we want to do now is to get to $12M. They would say, 'Well, thank you very much but it is obvious you don't have vision' " (Hill 2001c).

In March 1996 JDS Fitel completed one of the largest initial public offerings (on the TSE) in Canada's history with a $93.7M offering. After a number of acquisitions and a merger of equals in 1999 with Uniphase Corporation of California, JDS Uniphase Corporation became a globally dominant supplier in optical components and subsystems. The company has since suffered through the telecom meltdown of 2001 and 2002 but remains a significant force in its markets (Figure 3).

---

[12] Venture capital firm SB Capital Corp. of Toronto was also a shareholder.
[13] C-MAC itself was acquired by Selectron in 2002.

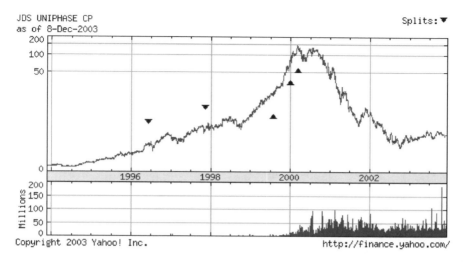

Figure 3: The Share Price History of JDS Uniphase. *Note:* Reprinted with permission of Yahoo! Inc. © 2004 by Yahoo! Inc. YAHOO! and the YAHOO! logo are trademarks of Yahoo! Inc.

Al Buchanan, Gordon Mauchel and Alan Crawford left Leigh Instruments in 1981 to found Lumonics. They licensed laser technology developed in the Defence Research Establishment. Buchanan left the top spot at the company at the end of 1984 to run his own consulting business. In 1985, Lumonics completed a private placement with Canadian and U.K. institutional and private investors that netted $23.8 million. Lumonics issued 1.4 million common shares at $17.50 a piece with Noranda Enterprise Ltd. — already the company's largest shareholder — grabbing 200,000 of the new shares (Barr 1985). In 1987, Noranda Enterprises made open market purchases of between $2.5 and 2.75M in Lumonics shares, bringing Noranda back up to the 30% ownership level it had held for about 14 years (Provencher 1987). Lumonics was acquired in May 1989 by the Japanese conglomerate, Sumitomo Heavy Industries Ltd. Sumitomo purchased more than 95% of outstanding Lumonics shares, including the 31% stake held by Noranda Enterprises Ltd. Lumonics went public in 1995. The company merged in 1998 with General Scanning Inc. of Watertown, Massachusetts, to form GSI Lumonics. Little of the Lumonics operation is now left in Ottawa.

Table 3 summarizes the venture capital involvement in the region's 12 "anchor companies."

Coming of Age (1990–1997)

The Ottawa region came of age between 1990 and 1997. The number of tech workers in the region doubled between 1990 and 1996 — to 700 companies and about 41,000 workers (Pappone 2000). During this period, significant development centred on Terry Matthews

Table 3: Summary of venture capital involvement in the region's anchor companies.

Company	Lifespan as an Independent Company in Ottawa	Use of Venture Capital
CDC	1948–1966 (acquired by control data corp.)	None
Cognos	1969–present (started as Quasar, changed name to Cognos in 1982)	Yes (Noranda Enterprises Ltd. owned 26% when Cognos went public)
Corel	1985–present	None
DY 4	1979–2000 (acquired by C-MAC for $250M, itself acquired by Selectron in 2002)	Yes (Noranda resources and the CBC pension fund owned about 50% of DY 4 when it went public in 1993)
Gandalf Technologies	1970–1996 (bankrupt)	None
JDS	1981–present (merged in 1999 with Uniphase)	None
Leigh Instruments	1961–1991 (acquired by U.K.-based Plessey Company PLC in 1988 for $100M, bankrupt in 1991)	None (Maclaren was a late stage investor)
Lumonics	1970–present (acquired by Sumitomo in 1989, merged with General Scanning in 1998 to become GSI Lumonics, little left now in Ottawa)	Yes (Noranda Enterprises was an important early investor)
Mitel	1972–present (acquired by British Telecom in 1985 for $322M, name and some assets later re-purchased by Terry Matthews in 2001)	$100K from Helix, $200K from Maclaren
Newbridge	1986–2000 (acquired by Alcatel for $7.1B)	None
Nortel/BNR	1959–present (Northern Electric Research and Development Laboratories established in Ottawa in 1959)	None
SHL Systemhouse	1974–1995 (acquired by MCI for $1B)	Very little

and Newbridge, its affiliate program and the U.K.-based venture capital firm, Celtic House, he founded.

The Newbridge affiliates program was a very successful corporate venturing program. It started in 1993 as Newbridge embarked on a high growth phase. The program was designed to provide an entrepreneurial outlet for Newbridge's best people and to provide a way to make money from technologies that Newbridge had developed but would not pursue internally. The formula was that Newbridge provided an incubator environment (space, IT, Legal, HR, finance), including strategic direction and access to lead customers. Typically Matthews (directly or through Celtic House) provided seed funding for the first 12 to 18 months of development. At the time the companies were founded it was normal for Matthews to own 33%, Newbridge 33% and the founders 33%. A 15 to 20% stock option pool was also maintained for granting to employees so that there was a high degree of employee ownership in the companies. Once the companies had a product developed and some initial customers (at least trials completed), they typically raised additional capital. Newbridge normally maintained a stake of 25–40% (depending on degree of strategic importance) as other investors came on board. The Board of Directors usually included Matthews as Chairman, a senior Newbridge executive, the company CEO, and two independent directors. Matthews also set up Severn Bridge Investments to allow Newbridge employees to invest in these companies. Twenty-four Newbridge affiliate companies were set up in this way. Some prominent examples are shown in Table 4. Approximately $1B was added to Newbridge's net income through the affiliates program. Severn Bridge Investments made a cash-on-cash IRR in excess of 80% for Newbridge employees.

Because of the success of the Newbridge affiliates, and the role that Terry Matthews played as lead investor, venture capital firms were eager to invest. Venture capital investments in some of the affiliates (for which data was available) are also listed in Table 4.

Matthews started Celtic House, his own venture capital firm, in 1994 with his own $25M (Fellers 2001). He also invested the $75M that he realized from his investment in Skystone when it was acquired by Cisco in 1997. Moreover, Matthews reinvested all his Celtic House earnings. Between 1994 and March 2001, Celtic House invested in 40 companies, 6 now public and 10 acquired. By March 2001, a second Celtic House fund was half way through investing $250M. Generally the firm invests in the early stages of a company, looking for a 20–25% equity stake. Because of Matthews' experiences as an entrepreneur, the firm has not advocated downside protection agreements, such as ratchets and anti-dilution clauses. It invests in products — no services, portals or application service providers (ASP), and typically avoids consumer products. The firm has invested in companies focusing on Internet infrastructure, telecommunications, wireless technologies and data storage.

The 1990–1997 era was marked by a number of IPOs of local companies. Extraordinarily, ten local companies went public in 1993 alone. Table 5 lists these companies together with VC involvement in them. It is evident from the table that VC financing was not a critical determinant in most of these companies. Of the ten, only DY 4 had significant VC funding. This may be symptomatic of the fact that between 1989 (when Noranda Enterprises stopped investing) and 1994 (when Celtic House and Capital Alliance Ventures started up and the Business Development Bank of Canada set up an Ottawa operation) there were no locally headquartered VC firms in Ottawa. It may also be symptomatic of

Table 4: Prominent newbridge affiliate companies and their liquidity events.

Affiliate	Some VC Investments as of 1998	Liquidity Event
Abatis Systems		2000, acquired by Redback Networks, US$700 million in Redback shares
Cambrian Systems	VenGrowthat — least $25M	1998, acquired by Nortel, US$300 million in cash
Castleton		Merged into West End Systems
CrossKeys Systems	Capital Alliance and others - $10.8M	1997, IPO
FastLane Technologies		2000, acquired by Quest Software, $100 million in Quest shares
PixStream	VenGrowth	2000, acquired by Cisco, $369 million in Cisco shares
Televitesse		Merged in Telexis (now March Networks)
TimeStep Corporation	Altamira, Celtic House — $6,000,000	1999, re-acquired by Newbridge, $100 million
Tundra Semiconductor	BDC; Capital Alliance; VenGrowth — $3.4M	1999, IPO
Vienna Systems	None	1998, acquired by Nokia, $130 million cash
West End Systems	Capital Alliance, VenGrowth, others — $20M	Bankrupt

Note: Adapted with permission from Haw (2003). The middle column was created by the authors with data from Bagnall (1998).

how unattractive VC funds can be. The founder of one of the companies in Table 5 said his company "avoided venture capital like the plague" (O'Brien 2003).

It was during this period that changes in legislation facilitated the development of funds that raised venture capital from ordinary, retail investors. Labour Sponsored Investment Funds (LSIFs) are corporations sponsored by labour organizations[14] designed to invest in small and mid-size Canadian businesses subject to the following criterion:

- Less than 500 employees.
- Less than $50 million in assets at the time of investment.
- Maximum $15 million investment.

---

[14] Some of these sponsorships are referred to as "rent-a-union" associations by critics.

Table 5: VC involvement in local companies that went public in 1993.

Affiliate	VC Involvement
AIT	None
Calian	None — A service company with many government contracts, it bootstrapped with $100K in angel financing.
Canadian Bank Note	None — CBN had been in business for a long time at the time of their IPO.
DY 4	Noranda resources and the CBC pension fund owned about 50% of DY 4 when it went public.
Fulcrum	None — The sole owner at IPO was Datamat Ingregneria dei Sistemi S.p. A., of Rome, Italy.
Jetform	None — Jetform was employee owned at IPO.
Microstar	None
Mosaid	Very little — BG Acorn owned 10% of Mosaid at IPO (Standard Microsystems Corp. had made a strategic investment and also owned 10% at IPO.)
Plaintree	Yes — corporate VC funding Had early investment BCE Ventures Corp.[a] Also capital from Gandalf and later from Delaney & Walters of Sherritt.
Seprotech	None

[a] BCE Ventures was founded in 1988 with $84M pool created by fusing the venture capital operations of BCE Inc. and Northern Telecom Ltd and with an investment strategy weighted toward communications and information technology.

Based on the idea that venture capital supports technologies important to Canada's long-term economic well being, the federal and provincial governments offer tax credits to Canadians who invest in LSIFs. The Federal Government offers a 15% tax credit on a maximum LSIF investment of $5,000 each year. Most provincial governments across the country offer an additional 15% tax credit on eligible LSIF investments, creating a total federal and provincial tax credit of 30%. The Ontario Government offers a 20% tax credit on research oriented investment funds (ROIF) LSIFs, generating a total of 35% in tax credits. If investors redeem their LSIF investment within 8 years, the tax credits are clawed back by the governments.

An LSIF is also a Labour Sponsored Venture Capital (LSVC) Corporation, however the opposite is not the case. In order for an LSVC to offer Ontario tax credits or refunds to investors, it must also be a LSIF. These types of retail, tax related venture capital funds now account for a significant percentage of all venture capital raised in Canada and figure prominently in the Ottawa region. VenGrowth has several such funds. Working Ventures, a national VC firm based on such funds, was active in the late 1990s in the region.

Capital Alliance Ventures Inc. (CAVI) is a local LSVC founded in 1994 by Denzil Doyle and Rick Charlebois. Doyle was a pioneer manager in the region. He worked for CDC and started a successful Canadian operation for Digital Equipment Corporation in the 1960s.

Table 6: 1996 Investments by VC firms active in the region (the figures are not limited to local investments).

VC Firm	Invested in 1996	Number of Investments	Smallest/Largest Investment
Working Ventures	$21.7M	15	$500K/$5.4M
Capital Alliance Ventures	$16.3M	12	$475K/$2.0M
Celtic House International	$20–25M	8	
Business Development Bank	$7.4M	7	$500K/$1.8M
VenGrowth	$22.3M	4	$2M/$12.5M

Note: Created from data from Bagnall (1998).

Charlebois worked with Doug Cameron at Noranda Enterprises. CAVI raised significant amounts of capital and invested in a number of local firms. Because LSIFs and LSVCs are eligible as tax-deductible retirement savings, most funds are raised in January and February. CAVI raised $5M in 1995, $25M in 1996 and $10M in 1997 (Doyle 2003; McIntosh 1997).

Table 6 describes the investment activity in 1996 of VC firms active in the Ottawa region. Note that the figures are not limited to investment in regional companies.

The Bubble (1997–2001)

The acquisition of Skystone by Cisco in June 1997 for $89M (U.S.) in Cisco shares and cash[15] marked the start of the "bubble economy" in the Ottawa region. The company had been in business for only a couple of years. It was developing optical networking chips. The acquisition made its founder Antoine Paquin a household name in the region. If so much could be made in so little time, the "game had changed."

The VCs who had invested in the company and shared a big payday were Celtic House — which in 1997 had invested $4.5-million U.S. in Skystone for a 19% stake in the company (Bagnall 2000b) — and a prominent Boston firm, Furneaux & Company run by David Furneaux. Furneaux & Company later changed its name to Kodiak Venture Capital. Furneaux was from the United States, and looked very smart on the Skystone deal, so the sale of Skystone was important for another reason — it marked for the business community the start of significant U.S. VC involvement in the region.

Kodiak invested in 12 local companies including Extreme Packet Devices and Philsar Semiconductor. In March 2001, Dave Furneaux, Kodiak's managing general partner, said the firm would soon close a second fund worth between $275 and $300M (U.S.), and that it seemed likely a large portion of it would work its way north. "Ottawa is where it's happening, and we're committed to this area," said Furneaux (Ottawa Business Journal

[15] Skystone was Cisco's first acquisition in Ottawa, and formed the foundation from which Cisco expanded to approximately 400 employees in the region.

Table 7: VC investing in the Ottawa region.

	1998	**1999**	**2000**	**2001**	**2002**	**2003**
Amount of VC investment in the Ottawa region[a]	74	274	1,261	922	735	249
Number of VC Deals in the Ottawa region	41	51	75	54	51	21
Average deal size[a]	1.8	5.3	16.8	17.1	14.4	11.9
Amount of VC Investment in Canada[a]	NA	2071	4931	3372	2575	1486
% of $ for Ottawa	NA	13.2	25.5	27.3	28.5	16.7

Note: Created using data supplied by the Entrepreneurship Centre, Ottawa Center for Research and Innovation.
[a] $M (Cdn).

2001). As mentioned above, the investment by the American VC firm, Mohr Davidow, of $6.5M in Trillium Photonics in 2000 was regarded by the VC firm as the first of $100M it would invest in the region.

During this period, more than 20 Ottawa-area technology firms — including Extreme Packet Devices ($600 million), Innovative Fibres ($260 million) and Cadabra Design ($190 million) — were sold to multinationals for huge valuations. Paquin, for example, sank part of his Skystone winnings into Philsar Semiconductor, a wireless chipmaker he sold to Conexant in early 2000 for roughly $280 million.

Table 7 shows the amounts of venture capital investment in the Ottawa region since 1997. Remarkable is the steep rise in investments between 1998 and 2000. By 2000, over a quarter of every dollar of VC investment in Canada was invested in the region. Also remarkable is the equally dramatic increase in the average size of the deals, from an average of $1.8M (Cdn) in 1998 up to $17.1M (Cdn) in 2001. Deal size and number of deals decreased subsequent to 2001.

The dramatic increase in the number of large deals done during this period is even more apparent in Table 8. In the table only deals of $30 million (Cdn) or more are listed. There were no such deals in 1998 and 12 in 2000.

This period marked the establishment of two local VC firms: Skypoint Capital founded by Leo Lax[16] and Andy Katz in 1998, and Venture Coaches founded by Claude Haw in 2000. Lax and Haw had been managers at Newbridge and heavily involved with the affiliates program. Katz had been with a local accounting firm, Deloitte & Touche, and had handled the Newbridge account from the early years. In 2001, VenGrowth, which is headquartered in Toronto, opened an Ottawa office with the appointment of Pat DiPietro and Mark Janoska as partners. The environment in which VCs were investing is tellingly described by the following recent quote from a local VC (Katz 2003).

---

[16] Lax was also an investor in Skystone.

Table 8: VC deals in the Ottawa region: $30M (Cdn) and over.

Year	Company	Size of Deal ($M Cdn)
1998	None	
1999	Eftia OSS Solutions Inc.	45.00
	Catena Networks Inc.	43.95
2000	Bridgewater Systems Corp	30.00
	Sedona Networks	31.90
	SiGe Microsystems	34.00
	webPLAN	50.00
	Cogency	30.00
	Eftia OSS Solutions Inc.	44.70
	Peleton Photonic	31.00
	Ubiquity Software Corp	63.00
	Catena	90.00
	Innovance Networks	115.00
	MetroPhotonics Inc	62.50
	Zucotto Wireless Inc.	53.60
2001	Zucotto Wireless Inc.	52.40
	Watchfire	37.40
	Tropic Networks	92.00
	Eftia OSS Solutions	30.90
	SiberCore Technologies Inc.	30.00
	Quake Technologies Inc.	46.43
	Ceyba	142.00
	Optovation	32.01
2002	Trillium Photonics Inc.	46.30
	Catena	120.23
	Innovance	88.00
	SiGe Microsystems Inc.	65.00
2003	Tropic Networks	30.30
	BreconRidge Manufacturing Solutions	37.50

Note: Created using data supplied by the Entrepreneurship Centre, Ottawa Center for Research and Innovation. The companies are listed in the temporal order of their VC deals.

If you look back to the 1999–2000 timeframe, VC's protected deals. When we were investigating a seed investment, we would always use code words in place of the company's real name. Right now there is a company in Montreal called Virtual Conexions, which we intend to invest in shortly. Back then, not only would I not say their name out loud, I wouldn't have shown it to you. I wouldn't show it to anyone outside of Skypoint. We would have a code word because the mere existence of an opportunity that Skypoint was looking at might have lead to a competitor trying to scoop the deal. They would think nothing of that. They would say: 'You don't need Skypoint, here's our term sheet.'

VCs had to act quickly or investment opportunities would disappear to the competition. As a result of this pressure, VCs also shortened due diligence periods. VCs were also driving companies very hard during this period to grow quickly. Consider the following quote from the lead founder of a local startup during this era (Dodge 2002):

> We were under a lot of pressure to grow fast and do high-profile public relations. One of our competitors had already gone public on much less revenue, and our California-based VC wanted to see us follow suit quickly. My public relations expenses and airline bills were astronomical. At the same time, we were trying to run a business. The bubble was pushing our burn-rate. Once you get on that ride, you can't get off. You couldn't ask if it makes sense for a company that's only a year old to go public. Those conversations went nowhere.

After the Bubble (2001–2004)

For Ottawa, the first sign that the bubble would end is marked by the collapse of demand for Nortel products in early 2001. At the end of 2000, Nortel had a global workforce of 95,000 employees, with 16,000 based in Ottawa. In 2001, Nortel announced four separate restructuring plans to reduce the workforce and control spending. By 2002, Nortel had streamlined operations to a workforce of approximately 37,000, including 6,000 positions in Ottawa (Nortel Networks Corporation 2003). They laid off 10,000 employees in the region.

The end of this period, and real signs of resurgence in technology business in the region was marked by the acquisition of Catena Networks by Ciena in February 2004.

The differences in VC investing before and after the bubble burst are illustrated by comparing two companies, Espial and Serence. Espial was founded in 1997 by three friends in their 20s, Allan Wille, Jaison Dolvane and Kumanan Yogaratnam. Espial was developing embedded software products to allow customers to surf the Web on their televisions through set-top boxes. The company obtained significant angel funding in 1998, and $12M in funding in the third quarter of 2000 from the American VC firm Greylock and from Invisible Hand, a private investment fund and incubator out of New York. A second round of VC funding totaling $16.5M was provided by VenGrowth, Greylock, Sussex Capital and Invisible Hand. VenGrowth led this round with a $12M investment.

In 2001, after the bubble burst, a trio of former Espial employees including Wille started another company, Serence, focusing on a software platform for providing real time desktop information awareness and notifications. Older and more experienced from the Espial venture, the founders of Serence never did find equity financing.

There have been a number of striking failures in the post bubble era of startups financed with huge amounts of VC money. Table 9 lists some of the most prominent.

Table 9: Prominent VC funded failures since 2001.

Company	Year Failed	VC Investments ($ Cdn)	Totals ($ Cdn)
Sedona	2001	$9.5M (1999), $31.9M (2000)	$41.4M
Zenastra	2001	$3M (1999), $58.8 (2000)	$61.8M
Trillium Photonics	2002	$9.6M (2000), $46.3M (2002)	$55.9M
Ceyba	2003	$22.2 (2000), $142.0M (2001)	$164.2M
Innovance	2003	$115.0M (2000), $88.0M (2002)	$203.0M
Optovation	2003	$32.0 (2001), $3.0M (2002)	$35.0M
Zucotto Wireless	2003	$2.5M, $3.5M, $53.6M (2000), $52.4M (2001)	$112.0M
Total for the seven companies			$673.3M

Note: Created using data supplied by the Entrepreneurship Centre, Ottawa Center for Research and Innovation.

The data in Table 9 do not include two other well-known VC funded failures that had a significant presence in Ottawa, Silicon Access Networks and Accelight, because these companies operated in the States as well and were funded there by American VCs. Both went bankrupt in 2003. Silicon Access Networks received $124M (U.S.) in VC funding, and Accelight about $85M (U.S.). These figures are not included in the $3.3B (Cdn) in VC funding raised in the region between 1998 and 2002.

Just these seven companies listed in Table 9 made a large dent in this $3.3B. Many more VC backed companies in the region have gone out of business or are having great difficulty staying in business.

During this period, angel investors have been squashed in many down rounds. They have been hurt by lower valuations and the liquidity preferences demanded by VCs since 1997 as explained above. As a result, angels stopped investing during this period. Most have left the scene permanently and the fragile angel networks that had been built up over the preceding 20 years have been significantly weakened. This has affected deal flow to the VCs. This has impelled some of the VCs to move upstream and establish angel kinds of operations.

There was also a new local VC firm founded during this period. StartingStartups began its life as an incubator, helping very new companies. In early 2002, the firm started to raise its first labour-sponsored fund in an attempt to become a venture capital firm for seed and early-stage companies in the Ottawa and Kitchener-Waterloo areas. Its incubator, which had hatched five companies, was shut down and the firm changed its name to Axis Capital. It currently has seven portfolio companies managed in two separate funds.

Venture capitalists have suffered through the last two or three years along with local technology companies. Because labour sponsored funds (LSIFs and LSVCs) target retail investors, their operations are heavily regulated and their funds are valued on a regular basis. Valuations of their non-marketable stakes in private companies are recorded at cost and re-valued if different values are established by subsequent investment rounds or in the case of a more mature company, valuation on the basis of sustained earnings, cash flow or sales.

Table 10: Recent returns[a] for labour sponsored funds active in the Ottawa region (as of October 30, 2003).

Funds	One Year Return	Two Year Return	Three Year Return	Eight Year Return
Axis Series I	22.27	–	–	–
Axis Series II	–	–	–	–
Working Ventures Opportunity	−10.56	−12.19	–	–
Capital Alliance Ventures	−4.83	−18.10	−17.27	1.12
VenGrowth I (capped December 1999)	−4.55	−9.74	−16.97	3.32
VenGrowth II	−8.02	−6.36	−4.76	–
Average for all such funds	−1.08	−9.21	−11.58	1.03

Note: Created using data supplied by MoneySense.ca, http://www.moneysense.ca/.
[a] Periods over 1 year are compound annualized returns.

Table 10 presents returns over the last few years for labour sponsored funds active in the region. Notice first how seriously these VCs have suffered since 2000. Both Capital Alliance Ventures and VenGrowth I raised money in the 1990s and invested during the bubble. Over the last three years, each has lost about 17% per year for their investors. Contrast this performance with that of Axis Capital's Series 1 fund that raised money more recently and recorded a 22% gain in the last year, a year during which the stock markets in general have been on a bull run. Timing has been very important.

It is because of these recent returns that there has been consolidation in the VC industry. This consolidation is likely to continue for some time. Locally, CAMI, the firm set up by Doyle and Charlebois to manage CAVI, merged with Technology Investments Management Corporation (TIMCO) of London, Ont. in January 2003 — the merged firms operate under the TIMCO name. Even more recently, Venture Coaches merged with Skypoint — the merged firm operates under the Skypoint name.

Has Venture Capital Created Value in the Region?

So, has venture capital created value in the region? We would like to summarize answers to this question using a dialogue format — a possible dialogue between Mr. Positive and Mr. Negative:

> Mr. Positive:
> First I would like to say that venture capital played a large role in the early years of the region — particularly Doug Cameron of Noranda Enterprises. Noranda invested in Cognos very early, for example, and Cameron remained a Director on their Board for many years. Now Cognos is Canada's preeminent software company with sales of over $500M (U.S.) per year, and a dominant position in their market.

Mr. Negative:

I will give you the Cognos example — a great one. But overall, venture capital was not that important in the development of the region in the early years. Much more important were the National Research Council, the Defense Research Establishment, and the presence of Bell-Northern Research and its forerunners. And it was really entrepreneurs who built the region's tech industry. Remarkably, many of them were immigrants. In fact, Noranda shut down in the late 1980s. Cognos was a real successful investment for Noranda, as were Mitel, DY4 and perhaps Lumonics, but they had lots of failures as well. The four VC successes that I just mentioned were significant but certainly not the whole story in the early years. Besides, the amounts of money invested by VCs during this period were very small by today's standards.

Mr. Positive:

Well what about the VC operation started by Terry Matthews in the 1990s — Celtic House? It made a lot of money.

Mr. Negative:

Terry made a lot of money for himself and for other investors in Newbridge and in the affiliates program. But that was early. Celtic House made a lot of money through investments related to the Newbridge affiliates program. But these companies were heavily supported by Newbridge, so the Celtic House success is not representative of the VC industry.

Mr. Positive:

How about the $3.3B that VCs brought into the region over the last 5 years — that has had a tremendous impact.

Mr. Negative:

Yes, I live here, so for sure it has benefited the region — that is a lot of money. But it has had some negative effects as well. For entrepreneurs, getting VC money itself came to signify success. It was the start, however, of their problems. Money from customers is the key, and if a lot of VC money kept a company from testing its business model with real customers, then the VC money was a bargain with the devil. Even a big initial valuation did not mean much for the founders of a company. When they went for a next round and the company's valuation was down, they would get squashed by the liquidity preferences, ratchet clauses, etc. that the VCs would demand. In a situation like this, and you have to admit that it was fairly common here, the founders and employees might have stock options but they would never be in the money.

Mr. Positive:

But there was a tremendous infrastructure built during the period of intense VC activity — 1999, 2000 and 2001. Accountants, lawyers, business advisors — the number of people who knew how to do deals, write contracts, etc. increased a lot. The region has a lot of this kind of expertise now. It is much easier to do deals.

Mr. Negative:

Yes, that's a good point. Let just hope, though, that business picks up soon. If not, a lot of this expertise is going to be lost. And what about the angel networks that built up over years here. There were a lot of private investors in Ottawa, many of whom had made money in tech business and wanted to give back to the community. That network has been seriously crippled. It will be interesting to see how the VCs adapt to this. Can they do some of the really early stage angel financing themselves? I doubt it.

Mr. Positive:

That is a problem. But there have been some really promising VC developments locally: CAVI, Venture Coaches, Skypoint Capital, Axis Capital, permanent offices for VenGrowth and BDC. A lot of the banks have VC operations now.

Mr. Negative:

Well, CAVI is now managed by TIMCO out London, Ont., and Venture Coaches has just merged with Skypoint. VCs everywhere are hurting because of the downturn in the economy in 2001 and 2002, given the amounts of money that they invested during this period and just before. Ottawa VCs are in the same boat. There will be more failures and consolidations. The word is that everyone is suing everyone else in town — there is a lot less money on the table than everyone hoped for. And as for banking based VCs, even the VC community doesn't give them good marks. Companies need investors who understand how to run a business. When a crisis occurs in a business, VC reps on the board need to know what to do. Just cutting spending is not a solution most of the time. That can do real damage to a company struggling to survive. And what's more, over the past few months almost all of the banks have announced the closure of their VC arms.

Mr. Positive:

But the Ottawa region is on the world map now. American VCs know about the wealth of technical talent here, and they will be back.

Mr. Negative:

That's true to an extent. But they sure are gone now. They look after some of their old investments, but there is no new U.S. money in town now. Lets hope that they have long memories for the good times, and come back when things turn up.

So, has venture capital created value in the region? The answer is not a straightforward yes or no. In interviews with local VCs we asked the following question: How would you rate the contribution of venture capital to the building of technology-based companies in the Ottawa region? We leave you with the opinions of three local VCs themselves when asked the question. The first is pointedly critical of VCs without operating experience (Doyle 2003):

Venture capitalists sometimes have an inflated view of the value they bring to an investee company; unless they have had hands-on operating experience in a small company, they have a difficult time understanding the needs of the entrepreneur;

the second highlights the role of entrepreneurs over that of VCs (Charlebois 2003):

> First and foremost you need the entrepreneurs. You can have all the venture capital in the world but if you don't have a Terry Matthews to help set the stage and show what can be achieved you don't have anything . . . I would rank the entrepreneurs substantially ahead of the venture capital . . . I think you have to be very careful the way you apply venture capital. Is it important? Absolutely, but I would always rank the entrepreneurs way ahead of the venture capitalist;

and the third emphasizes the positive role VC investments have played in the community (Haw 2003):

> I think that the impact of high levels of venture investment in Ottawa has been phenomenal. Even for the companies that blew through a lot of money in a short period of time, it still creates jobs and attracts talent to the region. Three billion dollars were invested between 2000 and 2003. Three billion dollars has incredible spin-off effects. The accounting firms, law firms, banks, etc. have more people and more expertise because of that three billion. We're able to attract people back to Ottawa. Even some of the local disasters that raised an incredible pool of capital and did some really silly things, like allocating $40 million to a manufacturing plant when the industry was going the opposite direction, produced experienced and battle-scarred people. They learn and say, "Gees, I don't want to do that again. We made a couple of mistakes there." Even the disasters produce some good results for the community.

There are real opportunities for further research on the core question of this chapter. A first step would be the expansion of Table 5 to investigate the role that venture capital played in all of the IPOs in the region between, say 1990 and the present. Such a study could include acquisitions as well.

In *The Innovator's Dilemma*, Christensen (1997) distinguishes between disruptive and sustaining innovations. Disruptive innovations target markets that are potentially very large but are hard to specify with precision early in development. Sustaining innovations target well defined markets with well established customer benefit criteria. In his new book, *The Innovator's Solution*, Christensen uses the distinction between disruptive and sustaining innovation to argue that companies developing disruptive products and services should "be patient for growth, not for profit" (Christensen & Raynor 2003: 258). Some research questions based on this idea are: With what frequency do Ottawa startups attempt disruptive innovation? Do VCs in the region treat disruptive and sustaining opportunities differently? Are these VCs patient for growth but not for profit when providing financial support for disruptive innovations? Are the contributions of VCs to the development of disruptive innovations different from their contributions to the development of sustaining innovations?

There is also fundamental work to be done on measuring the contributions of VCs to their investee companies. This issue is related to issues involved in manager contributions to shareholder value in companies. Considerable progress has been made in this area (see, for example, Rappaport 1997).

Another set of research issues arise from the differences and similarities among VCs: independent VC firms and bank-based VCs; Canadian and American VCs; VCs that generate retail labour sponsored funds and VCs that generate financing in more conventional ways from corporate investors and pension funds. Do bank-based VCs operate differently than independent VC firms? Do they add more or less value to their investee companies? Have the contributions of American VCs that operate in Canada been different than Canadian VCs?

There is some urgency for researching these questions. The business history of the region is not being captured in a systematic way. Many of the founders and managers of the early companies who have first hand knowledge on these questions have already died, or retired and moved away.

References

Bagnall, J. (1998). Venture financing soars: Up 131%, but new deals are becoming increasingly scarce. *The Ottawa Citizen* (May 27), G.8.

Bagnall, J. (2000a). Firm sets venture capital record: Startup lands $50M, largest placement in region's history. *Ottawa Citizen* (April 3), A1.

Bagnall, J. (2000b). The deal that changed the rules . . . and transformed Ottawa. *The Ottawa Citizen* (September 25).

Bagnall, J. (2002). Soul-searching and hard feelings: (Part 1): Inside Story: How Alcatel acquired Newbridge Networks. *The Ottawa Citizen* (May 30), E.2.

Banato, D. P., & Fong, K. A. (2000). The Valley of Deals: How venture capital helped shape the region. In: C. M. Lee, W. F. Miller, M. G. Hancock, & H. S. Rowen (Eds), *The Silicon Valley edge: A habitat for innovation and entrepreneurship* (pp. 295–313). Palo Alto: Stanford University Press.

Barr, G. (1985). Lumonics to acquire U.S. laser firm. *The Ottawa Citizen* (Sep 17), D.1.

Bhidé, A. V. (2000). *The origins and evolution of new businesses.* New York: Oxford University Press.

Callahan, J., & Muegge, S. (2003). Venture capital's role in innovation: Issues, research, and stakeholder interests. In: L. V. Shavinina (Ed.), *The international handbook on innovation* (pp. 641–663). Oxford, UK: Elsevier.

CBC (2003). Rod Bryden: Dealmaker. http://www.ottawa.cbc.ca/ottawanews/bryden/chronology.html, accessed December 11 2003.

Charlebois, R. (2003). Personal communication. June 16.

Christensen, C. M. (1997). *The innovator's dilemma: When new technologies cause great firms to fail.* Boston, MA: Harvard Business School Press.

Christensen, C. M., & Raynor, M. E. (2003). *The innovator's solution: Creating and sustaining successful growth.* Boston, MA: Harvard Business School Press.

Chrom, S. (1986). Cognos Inc. set to go public. *The Ottawa Citizen* (June 28), E7.

Dodge, J. (2002). Personal communication. November 15.

Doyle, D. (2003). Personal communication. May 7.

Enman, C. (2001). Downturn? What downturn? How three companies are coping. *Ottawa Citizen* (March 26), D8.

Fellers, C. R. (2001). Celtic House Intl. crosses the border. *Venture Capital Journal* (March 1). http://www.findarticles.com/cf_dls/m0ZAL/2001_March_1/70974965/p1/article.jhtml.

Fenn, G. W., & Liang, N. (1998). New resources and new ideas: Private equity for small businesses. *Journal of Banking and Finance*, 22(6–8), 1077–1084.

Gompers, P. A., & Brav, A. (1997). Myth or reality? The long-run underperformance of initial public offerings: Evidence from venture- and non-venture-capital-backed companies. *Journal of Finance* (December), 1791–1821.

Guly, C. (2001). Trillium photonics gets set to flower: Amplifier speeds net traffic. *The Ottawa Citizen* (Mar 7), E2.

Haw, C. (2003). Personal communication. June 20.

Hellman, T., & Puri, M. (2000). The interaction between product market and financial strategy: The role of venture capital. *Review of Financial Studies* (Winter), 959–984.

Hellman, T., & Puri, M. (2002, February). Venture capital and the professionalization of start-up firms: Empirical evidence. *The Journal of Finance*, 57(1), 169–197.

Hill, B. (2001a). Kestrel closes up shop. *The Ottawa Citizen* (July 7), D.2.

Hill, B. (2001b). The Four Cooks' series: Growing pains. *The Ottawa Citizen* (July 16), B.2.

Hill, B. (2001c). JDS in the beginning series: Growing pains. *The Ottawa Citizen* (July 16), B.1. FRO.

Hsu, D. (2000). *Do venture capitalists affect the commercialization strategies at start-ups?* MIT Industrial Performance Center working paper, June. http://globalization.mit.edu/globalization 00–006.pdf.

Kaplan, S., & Stromberg, P. (2000). *Financial contracting theory meets the real world: An empirical analysis of venture capital contracts*. University of Chicago Graduate School of Business, Working Paper.

Kaplan, S., & Stromberg, P. (2001). Venture capitalists as principles: Contracting, screening, and monitoring. *American Economic Review*, 91(2), 426–430.

Katz, A. (2003). Personal communication. June 18.

Kenney, M., & Florida, R. (2000). Venture capital in Silicon Valley: Fueling new firm formation. In: M. Kenney (Ed.), *Understanding Silicon Valley: The anatomy of an entrepreneurial region* (pp 98–123). Palo Alto: Stanford University Press.

Kortum, S., & Lerner, L. (2000). Assessing the contribution of venture capital to innovation. *Rand Journal of Economics*, 31, 674–692.

Lacasse, D. (1993). Growing pains: Dy 4 Systems of Bells Corners makes big splash with investors on first day of going public. *The Ottawa Citizen* (Apr 20), F1.

Lerner, J. (1994). The syndication of venture capital investments. *Financial Management*, 23, 16–27.

Mallett, J. G. (2002, October). *Silicon Valley North: The formation of the Ottawa innovation cluster*. Information Technology Association of Canada.

Mason, C., Cooper, S., & Harrison, R. (2002). Venture capital and high technology clusters: The case of Ottawa. In: R. Oakey, W. During, & S. Kauser (Eds), *New technology-based firms in the new millennium* (Vol. II, pp 261–278). Oxford, UK: Pergamon Press.

McIntosh, A. (1997). Milkyway stake hinders Ventures fund: Ottawa-based labour investment fund languishes behind pack. *The Ottawa Citizen* (August 26), C3.

Megginson, W., & Weiss, K. (1991). Venture capital certification in initial public offerings. *Journal of Finance*, 46, 879–903.

Nesheim, J. L. (2000). *High tech start up*. New York: Free Press.

Nortel Networks Corporation (2003). Annual and Quarterly Reports 1993–2003.

O'Brien, L. (2003). Personal communication. December 11.

Ottawa Business Journal (2000). Rod Bryden: Ottawa's consummate risk-taker. September 17.

Ottawa Business Journal (2001). Kodiak assures IPO market will rebound. March 6.

Pappone, J. (2000). Timeline Series: Boomtown. *The Ottawa Citizen* (September 24), C4.

Provencher, N. (1987). Noranda adds to stake in Lumonics. *The Ottawa Citizen* (November 24), B2.

Rappaport, A. (1997). *Creating shareholder value: A guide for managers and investors*. New York: Free Press.

Ruhnka, J. C., Feldman, H. D., & Dean, T. J. (1992). The living dead phenomenon in venture capital investments. *Journal of Business Venturing, 7*(2), 137–155.

Shane, S., & Stuart, T. (2002). Organizational endowments and the performance of university start-ups. *Management Science, 48*(1), 154–170.

Smillie, K. (2003). Computing devices I, from the computer and me: A retrospective look at some computers and languages. http://www.cs.ualberta.ca/~smillie/ComputerAndMe/ComputerAndMe.html.

Timmons, J. A. (2001). *New venture creation*. New York: McGraw-Hill.

Chapter 9

The Role of Universities in Developing Canadian Silicon Valley

Robert E. Armit

Abstract

Ottawa as Silicon Valley North is a splendid case history in the development of an advanced technology economy. Its two research universities, the University of Ottawa and Carleton University, have each been involved in the growth and change in the region. Part of this is associated with the performance of the universities as traditional institutions doing their work in education, research and community service in a responsible and respectable manner. Part of this may be attributed to the two universities "joining in" as Ottawa took on all of the traits of a regional economic cluster supporting its economic development. Part of the involvement is demonstrated in the efforts of the two universities supporting technology transfer in their jurisdictions. Silicon Valley North is a story of industry, government and universities growing and changing in tandem and developing a successful regional economy in Ottawa.

Introduction: Research Universities and the Economy

A university plays a significant part in the development of the immediate economy in which the university is set. Further, a university can affect economies in many other regions especially through their graduates and university research. As important and simple as this may sound, the models to understand the impact of the universities in the economy are limited and partial in their scope. A kind of shockwave was created in 1997 when Bank Boston published the report entitled "MIT: The Impact of Innovation." An opening remark is telling. "This study is the first effort to measure the national job creation impact of a single research university . . ." (1997: 2). What they found is that MIT has a huge impact on economies throughout the USA and around the globe. "If the companies founded by MIT graduates and faculty formed an independent nation, the revenues produced by the companies would make the nation the 24th largest economy in the world" (1997: 2).

Silicon Valley North: A High-Tech Cluster of Innovation and Entrepreneurship
ISBN: 0-08-044457-1

Not all research universities can have this magnitude of impact like MIT. Looking at the research university in the economy wherever it may be located is a good exercise. The late Dr. Gordin Kaplan, previously on faculty at both the University of Ottawa and University of Alberta, asked the question in this way: If you had to choose between having Stanford University or General Motors in your economy, which one would you select? Responses fall on both sides and the question causes excellent dialogue (Kaplan 1984).

Ottawa, Silicon Valley North and the Purpose of this Chapter

In Canada, considerable attention is given to the growth of the economic region of Ottawa, often referred to as Silicon Valley North. From a modest group of engineering-based enterprise following World War II, Silicon Valley North has developed into a vibrant band of enterprises and persons. Like MIT, this is an impressive story in scientific research, advanced technology and entrepreneurship. It is a different story than MIT itself or than MIT in the region of Boston for that matter. Ottawa has two research universities that have played a role in developing Canadian Silicon Valley. These universities are the University of Ottawa and Carleton University. This chapter looks at the nature of their role in the development of Silicon Valley North.

Ottawa is by any definition a successful economy (Heath 1999). Historically, the city revolved around the resource sector, largely lumbering, and served as a transportation hub on the Ottawa River, the Gatineau River, the Rideau River and the Rideau Canal. The Ottawa River linked the area to the St. Lawrence and Montreal while the Rideau River and Canal linked Ottawa with Kingston and Lake Ontario. In 1857, Ottawa was named Canada's capital city and government employment has been important ever since. More recently, the advanced technology sector has grown in the post World War II period to parallel government

Exhibit 1: SVN firms and employment in selected years.

Year	Number of Firms	Employment
1960	20	2,600
1965	35	3,800
1970	140	9,400
1975	200	18,000
1980	300	22,000
1985	350	25,000
1990	300	28,000
1995	665	35,000
2000	1,350	74,000
2002	1,430	70,000
2003	1,500	65,000

Source: For 1960–1985: Doyle, D. (1991). For 1990, 1995, 2000, and 2002: Doyletech Corporation (2003). For 2003: OCRI website at http://www.ocri.ca.

employment and has led to the description of the region as Silicon Valley North. In 2003, the region had more than 1,500 advanced technology companies employing some 65,000 individuals (see Exhibit 1 and specifically OCRI www site http://www.ocri.ca). This is up from 300 firms employing 22,000 people in 1980 and 20 firms employing 2,600 people in 1960 (Doyle 1991). Government employment stood at approximately 75,000 persons in the region in the year 2000 period. This was down from previous levels since the number of federal employees in Ottawa fell in the mid- and late 1990s as a result of government employment and budget cutbacks. In contrast, advanced technology employment moved up with the technology explosion in 1998–1999 to peak in the year 2000 and then leveled out and fell back somewhat in the period following the technology downturn beginning in March 2000. The fact is that government policies and economic conditions have an impact on employment. Ottawa's 2001 Census population is 774,072 persons.

Introducing the University of Ottawa and Carleton University

Ottawa's two major universities, the University of Ottawa and Carleton University, are generally regarded as middle-sized universities in the country and they are quite different. The University of Ottawa was established by the Oblate Fathers as the College of Bytown in 1848 (see University of Ottawa website at http://www.uottawa.ca). The institution moved from Lower Town close to the Ottawa River to its present more southerly but still close to downtown location in Sandy Hill in 1856. In 1861, the College, like the city "Ottawa" in which it is located, was renamed and, five years later, elevated to university status by royal charter. The University of Ottawa has been conferring undergraduate degrees since 1872, master's degrees since 1875 and PhDs since 1888.

Originally a liberal arts college, the University of Ottawa nonetheless began teaching pure and applied sciences in both French and English well before the turn of the century. Following a major reorganization in 1965, the University joined the ranks of Ontario's provincially funded institutions. Its nine faculties — Administration, Arts, Education, Engineering, Health, Sciences, Law, Medicine, and Social Sciences — offer a full range of undergraduate and professional programs. The School of Graduate Studies and Research administers an equally broad array of graduate programs leading to masters and doctoral degrees in most of the disciplines taught at the University. In 2001, the University of Ottawa had 19,274 full-time students, 962 faculty members and sponsored research of $150,848,000 (see Exhibit 2).

Carleton University on the Rideau Canal was founded in 1942 with "the good fortune to be located in Ottawa, Canada's national capital, which is one of the most beautiful cities in North America, with outstanding cultural and recreational facilities" (see Carleton University website at www.carleton.ca). The smaller university of the two, Carleton has four teaching faculties: Arts and Social Sciences, Engineering and Design, Public Affairs and Management, and Science. All offer master's and doctoral programs, many of national, some of international prominence. The university is located down the Rideau Canal from downtown Ottawa and the University of Ottawa but with a central location. In 2001, Carleton University had 14,076 full-time students, 652 faculty members and sponsored research of $46,214,000 (see Exhibit 2).

Exhibit 2: Enrollment, faculty and sponsored research at the University of Ottawa and Carleton University 2001.

Data for 2001	University of Ottawa	Carleton University
(1) Full time undergraduates	16,763	12,357
Full-time graduate students	2,511	1,719
Full-time enrollment	19,274	14,076
(2) Faculty	962	652
(3) Sponsored research	$150,848,000	$46,214,000

Source: Enrollment and faculty counts: Association of Universities and Colleges of Canada website at http://www.aucc.ca Sponsored research: The Impact Group (2002).

Traditional Roles of Universities and the Silicon Valley North Context

Traditionally, universities perform three roles in the economy and broader society (see Exhibit 3). Specifically the three roles are education of highly qualified people, objective research and community service. In this sense, the university provides its immediate community and the economy and society with people for jobs, ideas on the human condition and how things are accomplished and activities that build a better community.

These roles have been associated with universities since the birth of the modern university and are generally accepted throughout the world. Changes have occurred and continue to occur in the manner in which the roles are interpreted in different time periods

Exhibit 3: Traditional roles of a university and some trends.

Traditional Roles of a University	Current Trends and SVN Impact
(1) Education	SVN is knowledge based development which requires more university graduates in line with business strategies to grow
(2) Research	Companies in SVN seek leading edge knowledge and association with the brain trust of the community which enhances industry-university relations and collaborative activity
(3) Service	The community service function of faculty grows as society seeks knowledge and scholarly opinions of its experts and as economic development is affected by university activities in education and research

and societal settings. This predictably is the case in our contemporary setting. In Canada, universities have emerged as strong institutions in all provinces. There has been remarkable growth across the university system. This occurred first in the mid-1960s with the baby boom generation entering the system. The North American economy moved in recent decades to include a greater proportion of knowledge-based industries, the types associated with Silicon Valley North. Appropriately, universities have stepped up activities in their three roles. The University of Ottawa and Carleton University have done this effectively. For example, there are clearer relationships between the supply and demand conditions in highly qualified occupations (for example software engineers), research is more closely associated with industry and users external to the university, and community service often includes an element of economic development as part of the service role of the university. There is an interesting context for this work.

Compared to major cities in the country, Ottawa has the highest proportion of university educated and degree holding persons in its population. The actual 2001 Census ratio was 34.7% of the population aged 25–64 years of age (see OCRI website at http://www.ocri.ca). It is reasonable to associate this cohort with the government and advanced technology sectors of the economy and with the professional services side of the service sector. A good proportion of these persons comprise the professional and managerial side of Silicon Valley North. Ottawa relates to university education.

Ottawa is a research-intensive economy. The research is distributed among industry, government and universities. The largest research performer is Nortel, a leading global player in telecommunications. Even through the recent three-year downturn in the telecommunications industry from 2001 through 2003, Nortel has maintained a large (albeit reduced) research staff in Ottawa with a world product mandate. A significant number of other companies in advanced technology perform research in Ottawa. Government research represents the second level of research effort in the region based on expenditures. Government research is centered in the National Research Council and research performing federal departments like environment, agriculture, energy, health, forestry and the department of industry through the Communications Research Center. The third players in this line-up are the two research universities. The University of Ottawa is the larger of the two with a larger faculty count and with the medical-related research. Carleton University has substantive sponsored research in engineering and science. There are two features of Silicon Valley North to appreciate in this structure. First, unlike many or most Canadian cities with research universities, the research in Ottawa is undertaken on a larger scale in industry and in government than it is in the two universities. Second, Ottawa is among the leaders in research undertaken on a proportional basis compared to other Canadian regions. This is a good location for a research university.

Ottawa is a community-oriented city. Industry, government and universities and colleges all contribute to the common weal. When called upon for expert opinion, the two universities are responsive and giving. This is valuable in the nation's capital city where the press in particular has need for comment on world events in real time by seasoned professionals. As markets and opportunities increasingly turn global, the resident expertise in the university system gains greater value and a larger audience. Here, the connection with economic development gains salience.

Economic Clusters and How a Region Like Ottawa Grows

When the period of Silicon Valley North is defined from 1947 through the 1960s into the 1990s and now into the new millennium, the economy of Ottawa reflects well two clear distinctive patterns in economic development and the position of universities in each pattern (see Exhibit 4). The first model may be called the "traditional" model of how a region grows. Here the center point is a manufacturing plant. In Ottawa, this would be a lumber mill, a paper plant or a high technology operation like Nortel Networks, Mitel, Alcatel (cf. Newbridge), Gandalf, Computing Devices, Corel, Cognos, JDS Uniphase, Altera, and their like. The manufacturing sector is the base industry of the economy. New jobs in manufacturing bring new growth to the region. CN Rail published a report in the 1960s on "What Increased Manufacturing Employment Means to Community Growth." This was a highly used document in economic development circles at the time and for good reason. The empirical data showed for example that 100 new manufacturing jobs worked right through the community: 123 more school children, 113 more households, $356,000 more retail sales each year, 479 more people, 4 more retail establishments, 136 more motor vehicle registrations and 49 more workers employed other than manufacturing.

This traditional model continues to have support. Reports on the economy contain lists of manufacturers, employment levels, revenues and related information such as intended new investment. Economic multipliers are often raised in discussions around manufacturing. The multiplier points to the impact of the manufacturing activity in the economy as a whole as work is undertaken. The CN Rail report provides a broad brush on one multiplier. It could be expanded to include activities of companies supplying the manufacturer, growth of services and infrastructure like hospitals, and can vary anywhere from less than 1 times base activity to 6 of 7 times by way of example. In this model, the university is seen in its traditional way as an educational institution with students, faculty and research. There is separation among industry, government and universities.

Circa 2000, attention turns to a new model that is called "economic clusters." It is captured in work of The Impact Group out of Toronto.[1] Ottawa is used as an example of an economic cluster and with good reason. While the region shows the positioning and benefits of the traditional model well, it is reflective through the course of time in creating something new and important. And the two universities have played a big role in bringing this about. Here are details and a comparison.

An economic cluster relates to a region and some complement of goods and services and to the manner in which industry, government and universities join together to make the cluster an economic success. Ottawa has developed a cluster in telecommunications and computer software, and the players that make the cluster happen are found in industry, government at all levels and universities and colleges. From the work of Roger Voyer of The Impact Group (ibid), eight characteristics of economic clusters are discerned. In presenting these eight characteristics at a national conference in 2003, related contributors at the conference identified three additional characteristics (see Exhibit 4). From this, there

---

[1] The Impact Group (2003).

Exhibit 4: SVN as a cluster and the contrasts between 2000 and 1966 in the Way Economic Development is approached and how universities connect.

Circa 2000 Meaning in the "Clustering Approach" to Economic Development	Circa 1966 Traditional Economic Development and "How a Region Grows"
(1) Local leaders address needs with groups forming across industry, university and government with industry leading and universities in the mainstream. OCRI in SVN is a model.	(1) Economic development needs are assigned to government economic development departments.
(2) Regions grow from within and carry a belief in local strengths and assets including university strengths.	(2) To grow, regions seek to attract new people and companies largely independent of universities.
(3) Champions are important and the cluster works with network power and teams involving industry, university and government.	(3) Organizational and bureaucratic positional power prevail.
(4) Funding of businesses is complex and relatively new sources of funding include venture capital, tax credits and strategic alliances.	(4) Traditional funding prevails through banks, grants and historical sources like families and friends.
(5) Information networks are prominent including the WWW, intranets, teams and just-in-time information flow and acquisition.	(5) People are book wise and rely on internalized knowledge, specialists and bureaucracy to work.
(6) Education, training and research move to the forefront in the new economy and universities work closely with industry and government in real time.	(6) Universities are at arms length from industry and government.
(7) The staying power in a cluster relates to the region and to people: career changers and new ventures are prominent.	(7) Staying power is industry or organization specific and people move when jobs are shut down.
(8) Entrepreneurs come from industry, university and government and are increasingly important in development.	(8) Entrepreneurs come from industry and major attention falls on large organizations and mega projects.

Exhibit 4: *(Continued)*

Circa 2000 Meaning in the "Clustering Approach" to Economic Development	Circa 1966 Traditional Economic Development and "How a Region Grows"
(9) Inter-regional comparisons are structured and information from benchmarking is used by the regions in visioning exercises and setting goals.	(9) Regional economic comparisons are seen as a matter of history.
(10) Clusters connect people from industry, university and government and connections build synergy and information.	(10) Silos predominate in the way sectors operate.
(11) In a cluster, the media are players in attention drawing and problem solving.	(11) The traditional media are observers, critics and record keepers.

Source: The first eight characteristics of clusters in column 1 are based on analysis by Voyer, R. (2003). Ron Freedman, also of The Impact Group, added media to the list. The remaining two came anonymously from an expert from Montreal. Examples in the "Clustering Approach" reflect my experience in economic analysis and in technology transfer that has involved activities in university, government and industry over 20 years. The "How a Region Grows" in column 2 represents my observations based on the experiences in economic development in western Canada in 1966. See CN Rail (1966).

are then eleven characteristics of clusters that give clusters a different sense of purpose and direction than what might be the case from the traditional model of economic development. These clusters and the Ottawa situation in particular did not start with a master plan. Rather the characteristics have been interpreted from the successful actions of teams of people working successfully in Ottawa and places like Ottawa around the world to do things effectively. Roger Voyer from The Impact Group is one analyst who made his mark in capturing this work with his eight characteristic clusters model. Others add and modify to the specific characteristics as occurred at the Ottawa meeting. Here is an introduction to the eight plus three or eleven characteristics of clusters and what they mean in the context of universities and Silicon Valley North. Voyer's original eight are the first eight on the list:

(1) A cluster has leaders locally or regionally addressing a need. These leaders come from industry, government and universities. In the traditional way of doing things, many needs were assigned to a specific sector. Economic development was done essentially by an arm of government. Now these needs are addressed by the teams drawn from all sectors. While members may come from industry, government or the university, they take off their sector hats when they enter problem-solving sessions and serve the common good. Ottawa saw the merits in collaboration in the early 1980s and

formed the Ottawa Carleton Research Institute, now Ottawa Center for Research and Innovation. Known as OCRI, the organization draws from all three sectors of industry, government and education in a significant way. Both the University of Ottawa and Carleton University supported OCRI financially and strategically from its inception. Much of what occurs in Ottawa and Silicon Valley North is now defined in terms of economic clusters.

(2) A cluster believes in support of local strengths and assets. Historically, regions sought to develop by attracting new assets, people, companies, and investments from outside the region in a significant way. Now, regions as clusters largely grow from within and attract external resources because of this internal development. Graduates of the University of Ottawa and Carleton University have job opportunities in Ottawa as a result of the Silicon Valley North phenomenon. Companies in Ottawa consider universities like Queen's University in Kingston and McGill University in Montreal to be part of the Ottawa labour market. This is important since both Queen's and McGill have large student bodies and outstanding faculty. The two universities are within a two-hour drive of Ottawa.

(3) A cluster supports the roles of its champions and acknowledges its leaders and players. Networks have emerged over the recent period as a response to the needs for rapid information and to the overlapping mandates of industry, government and education. Traditional bureaucracy and organizational power have been tempered with more efforts in networks. Leaders can emerge from anywhere in the network. New companies can be formed anywhere in the network from all sectors. Universities are doing more collaboration in real time and are active as never before with industry and government. Faculty from the University of Ottawa and Carleton University sit on boards and are forming their own companies. Faculty is increasingly active outside the university precinct and industry is increasingly found on campuses. Clusters are active exchanges. These are different times than twenty or forty years ago.

(4) A cluster supports various forms of business financing. Indeed, financing of enterprise and research are becoming highly complex. Traditional industry funding has been in banking and equity markets. Today, funding is found through traditional sources and tax credits, grants, venture capital, and strategic alliances. Research funding in university has never been as significant as it is now. Sponsored research is big business. Part of this is attributed to the growth of the knowledge economy and the enhanced position of the university in mainline developments. Granting sources from government in particular are prominent. Contracting and endorsements with firms such as those in Silicon Valley North are important. Sponsored research is watched carefully as a measure of the activity of the university. Both the University of Ottawa and Carleton University have formed offices of sponsored research and industry-university liaison. This activity serves to prompt new activity on campus and encourage cluster development.

(5) A cluster has information networks that are highly developed. Never has information been more important, nor has the technology in support of information exchange ever been better. These are the times of the World Wide Web, the Internet, the intranets, and teams. While still valuable, the idea for people being book wise is not as prominent as it has been. Information networks are fast and sophisticated. Faculty is connected

to research and education projects around the globe and around the corner. The University of Ottawa and Carleton University are among the leaders in information system development. It is clearly an area in which they contribute to Silicon Valley North and an area from which they benefit in their work.

(6) A cluster places a premium on education, training and research. Highly qualified people are a key element of knowledge-based enterprise. Whereas in traditional settings and traditional industry, universities are at arm's length from industry and government, today universities are working closely with industry and government often in real time. In Ottawa, this connection is encouraged through OCRI. Both universities are active with the economic clusters.

(7) A cluster has staying power. Traditionally a community and economy moved with its major companies. When a company was on the ebb, declines were experienced across the board. When a company was on the flow, many enjoyed the growth. Clusters have staying power through the commitment of people in the cluster to the region, to effective career changing strategies, to new ventures replacing declining enterprise and to redefinition and rejuvenation of the cluster in tune with product-market demands and the skills of the people in the region.

(8) A cluster has entrepreneurs and entrepreneurial drive. Entrepreneurs are people who set up their own businesses and work towards success in their enterprises. Entrepreneurial drive represents the motivation and imagination behind entrepreneurs and people who think and act like entrepreneurs even though they may be located elsewhere in the economy. Traditionally, entrepreneurs come from industry, and while they have always been important, professional management has drawn an equal amount of attention in career planning. In 2000, entrepreneurs have reached a new crescendo in significance as innovation has increased in importance and entrepreneurs have an advantage in introducing new products and new markets. Further, in the new economy entrepreneurs come from any one of industry, government and universities. Both the University of Ottawa and Carleton University have academic programs in entrepreneurship, they encourage faculty and students to consider setting up a company as a career choice and they support spin-off companies. This is a period of academic and scientific entrepreneurship.

(9) A cluster is alert to benchmarking its achievements against other regions. In casebook business planning, goals are set and measurements are made to see how the region as an organization is doing. For example, one measure of innovation is the number of patents issued to persons in a specific region. In the past interregional comparisons are seen largely as a matter of history. The comparisons were interesting but they did not drive plans. In clusters today, benchmarking among regions is standard practice and benchmarks are used in visioning exercises and goal setting. This can include the sponsored research levels achieved by professors, major awards received from principal granting agencies, contract research associates and industry relations indicators. The information heightens the role of competition and comparative information in testing directions and evaluating results. The University of Ottawa and Carleton University monitor their technology transfer and research activity against other universities on an ongoing basis. This is an important contributor to the regional database. For a region as a whole, Montreal has prepared an excellent set of performance indicators that are

produced under the title Montreal International "Performance Indicators 2002 — Great Montreal Area."

(10) A cluster is committed to inter-sector relationships. Industry, government and educational organizations see the value in connecting with other sectors and building synergy with them. This is quite a change from the traditional relationships where silos tended to form and dominate activities. For example, industrial research has been done essentially by industry in the past. Now, the cross sector boundaries are broken down and industry problems are often addressed in university research settings. The contrast is dramatic and significant for organizations like the University of Ottawa and Carleton University, dedicated as they are to Silicon Valley North.

(11) A cluster reinforces communication and openness and work with the media. One of the significant changes in the last twenty years is the nourishment of the media as a player in community development and performer in community problem-solving. In the traditional model, the media was essentially an observer, critic and record keeper. The action roles that are current are popular. Often the media turns to the University of Ottawa and Carleton University for involvement in projects in which the media are active.

In summary, as clusters have formed among industry, government and educational institutions, the University of Ottawa and Carleton University have each become more active in aspects of the economy and growth and change of Silicon Valley North. This relationship is not exclusive. Many companies in Ottawa such as Nortel & Alcatel have global perspectives and deal with universities in other regions. Many graduates from Ottawa universities go elsewhere to work. Research moves internationally. This is good in the system and there has never been a question of quality of graduates from the regional universities. The University of Ottawa and Carleton University are solid educational institutions. The research that they conduct and work with other organizations in Silicon Valley North strengthen the universities in terms of education and research contributions.

Research and Technology Transfer in Research Universities

Research universities like the University of Ottawa and Carleton University support major research programs in their campuses. In disciplines like business, medicine and science and engineering by way of example, problems for examination can be connected to the activities of the Silicon Valley North and to industrial problems. Support for research can be garnered from industry and government within the economic cluster and region. There are several ways in which research at the university is attached to industry and government. This work falls under the banner of technology transfer and industry-university relations.

For a university like the University of Ottawa or Carleton University, technology transfer represents the movement of new ideas, products and processes out of the institutional research framework into the broader community including industry and government. One vector for technology transfer is Silicon Valley North. Here, the geographical proximity makes the relationships appealing for both the universities and the industry and government. The associations are not exclusive and various vectors for technology transfer tend to form

Exhibit 5: University related vehicles of technology transfer.

(1)	Publications in journals and books, the patent literature and reports
(2)	Consulting engagements
(3)	Conferences, seminars and workshops
(4)	Institutes, centers and groups
(5)	Affiliate programs
(6)	Research consortia and research chairs
(7)	Patents and licenses, copyright and trademarks
(8)	Contract engagements
(9)	Facility and equipment arrangements
(10)	Research and science parks and new business incubators
(11)	Spin-off company formation
(12)	Joint ventures
(13)	Guest company arrangements
(14)	Personnel exchanges
(15)	Students, undergraduates, graduates and part-time
(16)	Continuing education programs

Source: Armit, R. (1998).

in the global environment. The universities in Ottawa are active throughout the world with their research and industry and government in Silicon Valley North similarly relate to research universities elsewhere to work with them. Still, the clusters within Ottawa serve the players well. The following discussion shows how universities transfer technology (see Exhibit 5).

First and foremost, research faculty publishes their research results. This publication of results can be undertaken in the scientific literature or in the patent literature or both. Copies of publications are widely circulated to people and organizations interested in new findings in specific fields. In the case of breakthrough technology with commercial potential, the patenting option has certain appeal. The patent literature reaches an audience that can vary from the audience drawn to the scientific literature and to cumulative research development. Both the University of Ottawa and Carleton University have patent programs and associated licensing programs. This is a significant component of technology transfer.

Research professors consult to industry and government. This is important for both the professors and for the client groups. Professors have breadth of knowledge and abilities to communicate. As current knowledge gains greater relevance in industry and government on a day-to-day basis, the availability of university faculty in the immediate region has an advantage to industry and government. A good way to access this knowledge is through consulting agreements. Both the University of Ottawa and Carleton University permit faculty to consult within specific guidelines in terms of time.

There are scientific conferences, seminars and workshops that bring together people who are involved in a field of research and application. Faculty of the University of Ottawa and Carleton University are active in these types of events locally and internationally as organizers and as presenters.

Exhibit 6: SITE as an example of a SVN-University of Ottawa Institute success.

The University of Ottawa has responded to demands for highly qualified persons in information technology in SVN with the formation of SITE, the School of Information Technology and Engineering. Within the Faculty of Engineering, SITE offers leading-edge information technology and research with close ties to the industry. Vice presidents of companies such as IBM, Nortel and eighteen others have worked closely with professors to develop the curriculum and ensure that teaching is relevant to real problems and situations faced by the industry. The new degree offered by SITE in Software Engineering is the first program of its kind in Canada with an emphasis on telecommunications and business administration and was created in response to a need expressed by local industry.

U of O Professor Receives CITO Funding to Test E-commerce Systems

Ottawa, May 26 2003. Prof. Robert Probert of the School of Information Technology and Engineering (SITE), has received $292,000 in funding from Communications and Information Technology Ontario (CITO) for his research in testing e-commerce systems.

Probert expects his research to improve the quality, cost and time-to-market of e-commerce products. A multimedia component of the research project may also improve accessibility of e-commerce to consumers who are visually impaired or not familiar with computers. E-commerce has become critical for many businesses, and Probert's industry partner IBM is matching the CITO funding award.

Probert is Coordinator of the Nortel Networks Advanced Software Engineering Research and Training (ASERT) Laboratory at the University of Ottawa and was the founding director of SITE in 1997.

CITO is an Ontario Centre of Excellence whose mission is to support academic research and build partnerships with the private sector to help bring new technology from research labs to Ontario companies.

Source: OCRI website at http://www.ocri.ca.
   University of Ottawa website at http://www.ttbe.uottawa.ca.

New forms of activity at the industry-university interface have become prominent in the past decade. Within universities, there has been growth of institutes, centers and groups. Often funding support for research is made in the name of the institute, center or group. Organizations from outside the university can become involved. These are prevalent in medicine (for example, heart research) and science and engineering (for example, environmental research). Two prominent institutes are described in Exhibits 6 and 7. The first is SITE or the School of Information Technology and Engineering at the University of Ottawa. The second is the Microelectronics Fabrication Laboratory at Carleton University.

External organizations may join an affiliate program at the university to support activities in a specific field and gain quick access to results of research. Research chairs at universities can be seen as research consortia in support of excellence in research. OCRI has supported a number of research chairs at the University of Ottawa and Carleton University by putting

Exhibit 7: The Microelectronics Fabrication Laboratory as a SVN-Carleton University facility.

The Microelectronics Fabrication Laboratory is a flexible facility for manufacturing silicon integrated circuits and devices in support of research on process technology, device physics and modeling, innovative circuit techniques, photonics, biomedical devices, and microelectromechanical systems (MEMS). The facility was opened in 1993 as part of the new Minto Center for Advanced Studies in Engineering, and is the result of over 25 years of experimental research in semiconductor devices at Carleton.

Source: OCRI website at http://www.ocri.ca.

together funding programs from different sources. Other research chairs are established by the university or universities involved working with industry, government, and donor groups among others.

Research affiliate programs are consortia where industry and government pay a fee to join a group at a university or associated with a university to undertake research work in specific fields. Research affiliate programs are built into provincial centers of excellence in fields like manufacturing and materials and information technology. Both the University of Ottawa and Carleton University are active in these centers of excellence and the head office of the center in information technology (CITO) is located in Silicon Valley North (see Exhibit 6).

Exhibit 8: The Ottawa Life Sciences Technology Park and University of Ottawa.

The Ottawa Life Sciences Technology Park

The Ottawa Life Sciences Technology Park (OLSTP) is a 22-acre research and development park for the life sciences sector. The park is located in the heart of one of Canada's largest concentrations of clinical, medical and life sciences research and technology organizations. The Ottawa area offers close proximity to Canada's regulators and a large pool of talented researchers, managers and development staff. The first building in the park was a multitenant building equipped with wet laboratories for medical technology companies. Other structures have followed. Recent developments in incubation of new enterprise are impressive in the Ottawa Biotechnology Incubation Centre (OBIC). OBIC has facilities on and off the Park. The Ottawa Life Sciences Council (OLSC) is located in the Park.

The OLSTP works with the motto *Where Technology, People and Opportunities Meet*. The site is located in the Alta Vista area of Ottawa adjacent to the Ottawa Health Sciences Centre (OHSC). The OHSC is the designated centre of tertiary care for Ottawa and the surrounding region. The Park is within walking distance of seven area institutions: the Ottawa Hospital (General Campus), the Children's Hospital of Eastern Ontario, the Perley Hospital, the Rehabilitation Centre, the Children's Treatment Centre, and the University of Ottawa's faculties of medicine and health sciences. The University of Ottawa was the driving force behind the formation of the OLSTP.

Source: Based on http://www.olsc.ca/buzz/researchparks.php and related information.

Research consortia are formed to undertake work in specific problems such as applications in telecommunications, environmental research and their like. Contract research generally is available as a way for external organizations with a specific problem to engage university faculty to solve the problem. Contracts are a step beyond faculty consulting engagements and are organization-to-organization arrangements. Some may involve faculty or special equipment arrangements. A clear advantage of clusters like Silicon Valley North is that the argument for special equipment in the university reaches beyond one sector of users. The connections in Ottawa favor these arrangements. Students gain exposure to leading edge technology and carry this knowledge into their jobs.

University related research parks such as Discovery Parks in British Columbia or the Edmonton Research Park in Alberta and technology business incubators such as InNovaCorp in Halifax in Nova Scotia have grown popular in the period since 1980 in many regions of North America. In Silicon Valley North, the University of Ottawa was the leader in forming the Ottawa Life Sciences Technology Park and its associated incubation program (see Exhibit 8). Carleton University built the Carleton Technology and Training Center on its campus. Both contribute to the business dimensions of technology in Ottawa and to campus activities. Spin-off companies are part of the technology transfer possibilities in universities. This form of transfer is available to faculty and to students. Carleton University has established a Foundry Program for incubation of technology and new enterprise (see Exhibit 9).

Often in a spin-off situation, there is a connection to the university in technology ownership and a license is written as part of the transfer agreement. At the University of Ottawa,

Exhibit 9: Carleton University Foundry Program.

The Carleton University Foundry Program is a novel initiative to inspire university researchers including faculty, staff and students to take their research in a commercial direction and to support them in forming core technical teams. The Foundry is a 3-phase program consisting of, at its core, a pre-seed fund (Carleton Technology Advancement Fund) that will spur additional technological breakthroughs by Carleton researchers, a front-end, pre-commercialization support service and a back-end, post-project, commercialization advisory service.

What makes the Foundry Program truly effective is its dependence on numerous external business and technical advisors, seasoned entrepreneurs and angel investors. These individuals provide valuable feedback and advice to increase the success of new technology ventures initiated by the Foundry Program.

As an example of the program applied to proof of concept, a young company called Okulus Networks is developing technology to track the real-time location of items and persons accurately using 802.11 Wireless Network. This technology will address the logistical problem within a high-volume dynamic environment where items or personnel require tracking. Founded by Carleton graduate student Vincent Ng and Dragoslav Culum, Okulus Networks received a Foundry award to pursue the development of an advanced prototype of their technology.

Source: http://www.carleton.ca/foundry/about/index.html.

ownership of patents taken out by research faculty falls with the university. At Carleton University, ownership is shared jointly between the faculty member(s) and the university. In contract research, the terms of the contract prevail in terms of patent ownership. A key point is that there is room for technology entrepreneurs to emerge at the University of

Exhibit 10: Ægera Therapeutics Inc. includes Apoptogen Inc., a SVN-University of Ottawa spin-off company success.

Ægera Therapeutics Inc. was founded in May 2000 through the merger of Apoptogen Inc. and Exogen Neurosciences. Prior to the merger, Apoptogen and Exogen Neurosciences were two private, drug discovery companies at early stages of corporate development.

Apoptogen Inc. was created in December 1995 around discoveries of a novel family of apoptotic control genes known collectively as Inhibitors of Apoptosis Proteins (IAPs). Multiple patent applications on the IAPs form the intellectual property basis of the company. Apoptosis is centrally involved in several clinical disorders such as stroke, brain injury, glaucoma and cancer. Apoptogen intends to use its novel technology to develop therapeutics that can modulate the apoptotic process. Apoptogen's scientific founders, Drs. Robert Korneluk and Alex MacKenzie have earned worldwide recognition for their pioneering work in the fields of medical genetics analysis of neuromuscular disorders. In particular, they possess unique expertise on the genetics and biochemical regulation of apoptosis. Drs. Korneluk and MacKenzie hold appointments at the University of Ottawa.

The combination of the companies effectively situates Ægera in a globally competitive position in the field of neuronal signal transduction and apoptosis. The technologies of the two companies translate into extensive in-depth knowledge of the life, death and growth pathways in the central nervous system. In particular, Ægera understands and has patents on the specific molecular targets against which a therapeutic must intervene in order to preserve neuronal life. The scientific founders of Ægera are:

- Dr. Philip Barker, Associate Professor of Neurology, Neurosurgery, Anatomy and Cell Biology, Montreal Neurological Institute, McGill University and the Centre for Neuronal Survival.
- Dr. David Kaplan, Professor of Neurology and Neurosurgery, Montreal Neurological Institute, McGill University.
- Dr. Robert Korneluk, Professor of Paediatrics, Faculty of Medicine, University of Ottawa, and Director, Medical Genetics Laboratory Research Institute, Children's Hospital of Eastern Ontario.
- Dr. Alex MacKenzie, Associate Professor of Paediatrics, Faculty of Medicine, University of Ottawa; Acting Director, Children's Hospital of Eastern Ontario (CHEO) Research Institute, and attending physician CHEO.
- Dr. Freda Miller, Professor of Neurology and Neurosurgery, Montreal Neurological Institute, McGill University.

Source: University of Ottawa technology transfer web site http://www.ttbe.uottawa.ca/transf/ industry/201.html.

Ottawa and at Carleton University. One example is Aegera Therapeutics, which is tied to the University of Ottawa (see Exhibit 10). This impressive spin-off is connected to world leading research conducted by scholars in Ottawa with worldwide impact. Cadabre Design was established by a professor from Carleton University and ultimately sold to interests in the USA including firms from Silicon Valley itself (see Exhibit 11). The institutions will support faculty and students efforts to get going with their enterprises.

Other arrangements are possible. For example, a company may come onto the campus to work in a specific engagement. This is termed a guest company arrangement. Joint ventures are more common than in the past. Here a project is defined and undertaken among parties. Personnel engagements may be struck. This can involve faculty, students or research staff from industry. There are examples of students working on site in companies in Silicon Valley North as part of their graduate student research. This is one side of cooperative education programs. Continuing education programs may be developed to embrace technology transfer between the university and students enrolled in the courses. Students as they graduate and accept work are a major way that knowledge from the university moves out into the community and economy.

Exhibit 11: Cadabra design as a SVN-Carleton University spin-off company success.

Dr. Martin Lefebvre launched a company in 1994 to commercially exploit specific electronic automation design algorithms that had been described in his PhD thesis at Carleton University and further developed when he joined faculty. Lefebvre worked through an agreement with Carleton University and provided a royalty to the university for a specified period of time in the event that net revenues were realized. Lefebvre was active with various funding agencies in his research including centers of excellence in microelectronics. A SVN angel investor took interest in the research and product potential and assisted in the early stages of the company.

In December 1996, a SVN labour sponsored venture fund Capital Alliance Ventures Inc. (CAVI), invested in Cadabre. The initial company product was already on the market and for the year ended August 1996 generated revenues of $2.1 million and net income of $671,000. CAVI's initial investment of $2.0 million was in the form of preferred shares. CAVI chair Denzil Doyle joined Cadabre's board of directors. In April 1999, the company raised an additional US$6.0 million from a group of California venture capital firms. Then in October 2000, the company was taken over by Numerical Technologies Inc. of San Jose in the heart of Silicon Valley.

CAVI through its original investment realized a substantial profit when the transfers were put in place and share sales realized. The Ottawa operations of Cadabre were a research and development center for some time. Carleton University received a royalty on product sales for a number of years in accordance with the agreement. This is a success story with all stakeholders receiving benefit. It also brought together skills from different fields of activity in Silicon Valley North and in this case Silicon Valley itself.

Source: Capital Alliance Ventures Inc. and notes of Robert Armit.

Technology transfer can occur at an early stage of the research process or at any of the subsequent stages of the research. Technology transfer bridges the university research with external users and unlocks the commercial possibilities for research. Many examples of technology transfer involve more than one specific form of technology transfer. For example, contract research, patenting and publication are all wound together in a technology transfer agreement. Timing and the way the schedule of activities work is important to the project and its commercial potential. The future would seem to hold increased activity in technology transfer and industry-university relationships. Canada's universities are pledging to increase commercialization work as part of a national innovation agenda. Silicon Valley North is clearly involved. The one key point in universities like the University of Ottawa and Carleton University is that the integrity of university research must be maintained in this new environment of technology commercialization. The base of the university remains excellence in education, research and service.

Perspective on the Role of Universities in Developing Canadian Silicon Valley

Ottawa as Silicon Valley North is a splendid case history in the development of an advanced technology economy. Its two research universities, the University of Ottawa and Carleton University, have each been involved in the growth and change in the region. Part of this is associated with the performance of the universities as traditional institutions doing their work in education, research and community service in a responsible and respectable manner. Part of this may be attributed to the two universities "joining in" as Ottawa took on all of the traits of a regional economic cluster supporting its economic development. Part of the involvement is demonstrated in the efforts of the two universities supporting technology transfer in their jurisdictions.

Universities affect their immediate economy in many ways. Some are highly visible like employment, payroll and local purchasing. Everyone in the region knows the day fall classes begin as students are seen and felt in the economy. Some ways universities affect the area are subtle and indirect. Support for international students, for example, can pay huge benefits in the immediate term and in the long term. A significant purchase by the university of a product from a new company is a major contribution to the company. There are good stories to tell about the University of Ottawa and Carleton University in each of these areas and in the development of the Canadian Silicon Valley in Ottawa. This is a different story than the one struck by BankBoston on MIT, set as it is around enterprise driven by MIT graduates. Rather Silicon Valley North is a story of industry, government and universities growing and changing in tandem and developing a successful regional economy in Ottawa.

References

Armit, R. (1998). Improving the institutional framework and the system of information, education and training for experts. In: A. T. Balaban, E. N. Carabateas, & F. T. Tanasescu (Eds), *Science and technology management* (pp. 82–90). Amsterdam, Netherlands: NATO, IOS Press.

Association of Universities and Colleges of Canada. http://www.aucc.ca.

Bank Boston (1997, March). *MIT: The impact of innovation.* Boston, MA: Bank Boston.

Carleton University. http://www.carleton.ca.

CN Rail (1966). *What increased manufacturing employment means to community growth.* Montreal, Quebec, Canada: CN Rail.

Doyle, D. (1991). From white pine to red tape to blue chips: How technology based industries can provide continued prosperity for the Ottawa-Carleton region. Cited in Heath, R. (1999). The Ottawa high-tech cluster: Policy or luck? In: T. J. A. Roelandt, & P. den Hertog (Eds), *Boosting innovation: The cluster approach* (pp. 175–191). Paris, France: Organization for Economic Cooperation and Development.

Doyletech Corporation (2003). *The family tree of Ottawa-Gatineau high technology companies 2002.* Ottawa, Ontario, Canada: Doyletech Corporation. Cited with permission.

Heath, R. (1999). The Ottawa high-tech cluster: Policy or luck? In: T. J. A. Roelandt, & P. den Hertog (Eds), *Boosting innovation: The cluster approach* (pp. 175–191). Paris, France: Organization for Economic Cooperation and Development.

Kaplan, G. (1984). *Convocation address of vice-president Gordin Kaplan.* Edmonton, Alberta, Canada: Notes of Robert Armit.

Montreal International "Performance indicators 2002 — Great Montreal area" www.montrealinternational.com.

Ottawa Center for Research and Innovation (OCRI) http://www.ocri.ca.

The Impact Group (2002). *Canada's University innovation leaders.* November 5. National newspaper supplement prepared for distribution in Canada by Research Infosource Inc. and the Impact Group.

The Impact Group (2003). *Technology clusters-by accident or design.* Presentation at the Research Money Conference, February 19. Ottawa, Ontario, Canada.

University of Ottawa http://www.uottawa.ca.

Voyer, R. (2003). Clustering: A contact sport. Paper presented at Research Money Conference, February 19. Ottawa, Ontario, Canada.

Chapter 10

The River Runs Through It:
The Case for Collaborative Governance
in the National Capital Region

Gilles Paquet, Jeffrey Roy and Chris Wilson

Abstract

Canada's National Capital Region (NCR) presents a unique example of a border region. Separated by the Ottawa River, Ottawa, in the province of Ontario, and Gatineau, located in the province of Québec, comprise an area of over one million people. Labour markets and worker mobility, linguistic and cultural identities, and many aspects of quality of life are interwoven within the region. Yet, the governance of this entity remains inadequate for the challenges ahead, including a growing technology focus. This chapter examines both the current context and future prospects for reform.

Introduction

Canada's National Capital Region (NCR) presents a unique example of a border region — albeit one within a national polity. Separated by the Ottawa River, Ottawa, in the province of Ontario, and Gatineau, located in the province of Québec, together comprise a metropolitan area of over one million people (roughly three quarters of this population on the Ontario side).

Ottawa is both typical and unique: typically engaged in attempts to create the conditions for local success in a globalizing economy, as with all cities; and unique in being the nation's capital with a corresponding trans-border dimension extending across the Ottawa river to include Gatineau, Québec. Already, Ottawa promotes itself internationally as a region of more than one million people (making use of the inter-provincial capital region),[1] and

---

[1] Such references can be found in a variety of promotional literatures and local area profiles, including online information found at the City's economic development agency — the Ottawa Centre for Research and Innovation (www.ocri.ca).

worker mobility, linguistic and cultural identities, and many aspects of quality of life are interwoven with the trans-border composition of the region.

This chapter begins with a consideration of the role of city-regions in a globalizing world, and then examines the current contours of this region in terms of both the separateness and shared aspects of socio-economic and political development in the NCR. We then provide a forward-looking prescription for how governance might evolve in a positive manner — the basic tenant of which is a strengthened focus on interdependencies and collaboration in order to improve the holistic prospects for the region as a whole.

City-Regions in the 21st Century

Globalization and the rapid development and diffusion of information and communication technologies are said to be changing the importance of national borders (Eger 1997). As cities and regions[2] emerge as central organizing units of governance and economic development in the 21st century, the patterns of clustering and innovation become interwoven with localizing governance conditions and the inter-related actions of public, private and civic actors (Paquet 1997).

While much has been made of local governance systems possessing the greatest adaptive capacities in such a turbulent environment, realities are more varied and complex (Paquet & Roy 1995). Many such entities remain shackled or over-shadowed by weak fiscal capacities, historically fragmented identifies, and a variety of both vertical and horizontal coordinating difficulties — governance difficulties — that exert great influence on local action and regional prospects (Organization for Economic Cooperation and Development 2002).

This chapter examines the critical issue of whether local governance adequately reflects both the current and expected degrees of integration within the Ottawa — Gatineau radius: we define local governance as the collective capacity of all stakeholder to coordinate resources and actions in an effective and efficient manner. We also consider the implications of this examination for a city-region's ability to prosper in an increasingly knowledge-based economy.

Local Governance and Collective Action

In a knowledge-based socio-economy driven by technological change and innovation, new challenges are emerging. Two sets of forces have tended to bring forth the present explosion of interest in localizing systems of innovation and governance: the new importance of city-regions as a result of globalization on the one hand, and the spatial determinants of learning and adaptation on the other (Caves & Walshok 1999).

Naisbitt (1994) and Courchene (1995) characterize such shifts as the emergence of a "global paradox" with a simultaneous focus on globalization and localization.

---

[2] For purposes of this chapter, we assume that the terms "city" and "region" may be used interchangeably, as well as adjoined as a "city-region," taken to mean a primarily urban centre, or set of centres defined collectively on the basis of a common, sub-national territory.

Scott (1994) identifies the key determinants of regional competitiveness as the establishment of a "network system" (Cohen & Rogers 1995). What matters in this network system are relationships nourished through a collaborative culture that are, in turn, embedded and re-enforced by proximity. Such positive forms of network-based adaptation and decision-making underpin shared learning — or social learning. Social learning refers to "the process of interaction through which individuals and organizations learn from each other and consequently adapt, innovate, develop new arrangements, conventions and rules" and collective intelligence "refers to the creative and discriminative capacities of a group, organization or community" (Coe *et al.* 2001). Through social learning capabilities, collective intelligence can be enhanced over time.

City-regions are often put forth as uniquely able to achieve the critical mass required to attract and support high degrees of specialization — specialized labour, knowledge, business services, while making use of shared externalities generated from within a concentration of financial, human and intellectual resource flows. Through these special qualities, city-regions contribute in a unique and significant way to an enterprise's flexibility, responsiveness and innovation (TD Bank 2002). The conceptual dynamics of good governance and collective learning build on these relational synergies. It is within such a context that much has been made of the concept of social capital — networks of civic engagement — as an indicator of cultures of trust that translate into greater collaborative capacities (Fukuyama 1995). Yet, the degree to which city-regions or local systems of governance are able to foster collaborative ties and deepen civic-based mechanisms to nurture such collaboration is a complex issue (Storper 1997).

In North America, California's Silicon Valley (situated between San Jose and San Francisco) is often put forth as a reference point indicative of the differing perspectives on the importance and existence of civic engagement. Thus, whereas Saxenian (1994) lauds the region's ability to foster collaborative ties in the marketplace, much evidence points to a lack of social cohesion (i.e. a growing polarization of wealth and opportunity) between various segments of the region as defined by both ethnic and economic lines (Joint Venture: Silicon Valley Network 2003). While some optimists such as Henton *et al.* (1997) point to civic entrepreneurs — community-building leaders and essentially creators of social capital — as a remedy on display on Silicon Valley and elsewhere, there is little direct evidence that such movements are reversing the socio-economic patterns of polarization and fragmentation.

Barnett (1997) has synthesized the problem area in the form of three main governance challenges that are particularly relevant for federalist regimes such as Canada and the United States: (1) what size, level and structure of government is best suited to perform an enabling role in economic development processes today; (2) how can government facilitate activity by the private and voluntary sectors in order to bring about pluralistic, network and participative governance; and (3) how can higher-level governments facilitate the work of lower-level government in the discharge of their duties?

The analysis of these three challenges in a Canadian context reveals a serious mismatch between what is required and what is available (Vander Ploeg 2002; Wong 2002). Canada's governments would appear to be omnipresent, overpowering, ill coordinated, non-cooperative and most certainly not bent on giving subsidiarity much of a role in the philosophy of governance. Local government in particular most certainly lacks the policy tools and jurisdictional authority to effectively play their stewarding role in the new governance (Roy 1998).

Yet it is at the local level that new forms of multi-stakeholder dynamics are taking shape, often driven by non-state actors and new partnership-based arrangements. Such arrangements depend on, and are shaped by the altering nature of borders and boundaries in determining what precisely defines a city-region in this new century.

Borders and Boundaries in Flux

This interface of local governance and economic development creates a new division of roles and responsibilities amongst local, national and trans-national stakeholders and processes. A regional entity such as Silicon Valley carries a brand that transcends local boundaries, much as it is a reference point for many regions around the world. For example, it is used as a point of comparison throughout much of Europe (invoking simultaneous claims of what to replicate and what to avoid). Thus, in the late 1990s Stockholm was dubbed Europe's Wireless Valley.

As well, Copenhagen and Malmö, dubbed the Human Capital of Europe, face a mutual quest to foster new clusters of technology and research-intensive activities — struggling to balance the economic and entrepreneurial dynamism, typified by Silicon Valley, while maintaining a more Northern European focus on social cohesion (Hudson 1995). These examples of Øresund in Europe (the trans-border region joining Copenhagen in Denmark with Malmö in Sweden with a recently constructed fixed link bridge[3]) and Silicon Valley in California point to issues of both borders and boundaries that shape local governance everywhere, and how they are very much in flux as cities and regions attempt to determine how best to align themselves locally in order to compete effectively in a globalizing economy.

Border regions present special governance challenges that in many ways are not all that unique to such cross-border entities. Silicon Valley is once again a useful case in point — where this entity is well known as a city-region in economic, and more arguably social terms. Yet, at the same time, the region is politically fragmented across just over 20 municipal units without any over-riding political body responsible for its collective development.[4]

Political identities are contentious and often contested, and they may or may not easily align with emerging economic and social identities that collectively define a city-regional entity. Indeed, it is within such a context that Canada's National Capital Region presents a unique example of a border region — albeit one within a national polity. Separated by the

---

[3] The Øresund region is the biggest and most densely populated big-city area in Scandinavia with approx. 3,5 million people over a 20.859 km² area, which gave a population density of 168 per/km² in 2000. On the Danish side of the Øresund region, the population density is double that of the Swedish side. Of a total Danish population of 5,3 million people, 45% live in the Øresund region (corresponding to 2/3 of the total population of the region), whereas 12% of Sweden's population live in the Øresund region (corresponding to 1,1 million of Sweden's total population of 8,9 million people).

[4] Joint Venture: Silicon Valley Network is perhaps the closest example of a regional governance authority, bringing together representation from the public, private and civic sectors on a region-wide basis. Yet, these ties, as important as they have been to local initiative, are largely voluntary and without direct democratic legitimacy.

Ottawa River, Ottawa, in the province of Ontario, and Gatineau, located in the province of Québec, together comprise a metropolitan area of over one million people (roughly three quarters of this population on the Ontario side).

Ottawa/Gatineau

The Ottawa-Gatineau region (formerly known predominantly as Ottawa-Hull, Hull and Alymer now parts of the enlarged city of Gatineau) exists in reference to its common boundaries as Canada's Capital Region. However, the patterns of economic, political and social integration are more complex and varied.

The notion of a cross-border region applies here in a limited sense. Unlike national boundaries with formal separations of sovereignty, freedom and commerce, the inter-provincial boundary, symbolized by the Ottawa River is rather porous. People and merchandise can freely cross via any one of five bridges linking the two major cities (Ottawa & Gatineau), each one a gateway into their respective provincial entities (Ontario & Québec). Notwithstanding the fact that no physical barrier prevents movements between provinces, the border does exist in many ways, particularly given the political separateness of Ottawa and Gatineau within their distinct provincial jurisdictions (see also the chapter by Materazzi this volume).

The region has witnessed, and continues to be shaped by significant socio-economic change. One might suggest that although the official status of the National Capital Region remains relevant and in tact today, the essence of the label is perhaps shifting. Whereas yesterday's image is a national place of political power, today's vision is also one of a technopolis of innovation and entrepreneurship.

Recent events have crystallized the importance of transitional challenges. For example, the federal government's 1994 Program Review, a review process of all federal programs and spending for the Government of Canada, served as a notable turning point for both sides of the river as it led to the announcement of job losses estimated at nearly 45,000 across the federal public service.

Consequently, for the National Capital Region, a downsized federal government would no longer serve as the exclusive engine of prosperity to the extent that it once did. Technology thus became the primary focus, and the most recent volatility in high-technology industries has underscored the uniquely fortunate private — public balance of economic activity and employment that underpins the area.

Historical Context and Political Setting[5]

In 1857, Queen Victoria decided that Ottawa would become the capital of Canada, in part for its geographical remoteness, neutrality from other candidate cities, and nexus of Upper

---

[5] Except where noted (separately references), all figures and data reported in this chapter originate from publicly available Statistics Canada census documents from 1996 to 2001 in the form of Community profiles (Statistics Canada 2001), available online, Government of Canada: http://www12statcan.ca.

Canada and Lower Canada. This selection underpinned the first socio-economic expansion, developing rapidly around the federal government presence.

Today, the Ottawa-Gatineau region extends over 5300 square kilometres. The total population is 1,063,664. On the Québec side of the river, there is a total of 257,568 residents, or 24% of the Ottawa-Gatineau region. This is a 4.2% increase since the 1996 Census. Eighty-eight percent of these people are living in the newly amalgamated city of Gatineau. The rest is rural. The territory has a size of over 2000 square kilometres (38% of the whole region), which equals to a population density of 126 per km^2 (the density is 681 per km^2 when only considering the City of Gatineau).

On the Ontario side of the river, there are 806,096 residents, a 7.2% increase from the 1996 Census. On that total, 96% are living in the newly amalgamated city of Ottawa. The territory covers a total of close to 3300 square kilometres (62% of the whole region), which equals to a population density of 246 per square kilometres (the density is 279 per km^2 when considering only the City of Ottawa). For the whole region, 51% of the population have English as first language, 32% have French, and close to 17% have another first language. Close to 45% of the population is bilingual (both French and English), which is the second highest rate of bilingualism in the country after Montreal.

The Québec side of the river is predominantly Francophone with 79% of residents having French as first language and 13% having English. The Ontario side of the river is predominantly Anglophone with 64% of the population having English as their first language and 17% having French. Ottawa is culturally more diverse than Gatineau and less homogeneous.

There are three, somewhat overlapping levels of governments with jurisdiction over the Capital territory. Locally, the two key and recently enlarged municipalities are Ottawa on the Ontario side and Gatineau in Québec. Each municipality has specific powers and is taking care of specific dossiers over the territory, but at the same time their power and roles are all intermingled with their respective provinces who not only regulate municipal affairs but also serve as the primary delivery agents of health care, education, and many aspects of economic development.

The nature of the relationship between municipalities and provinces is similar on both sides of the river, featuring large degrees of influence by provincial authorities on local governments. For example, when the Ontario government began devolving power and responsibilities to local authorities and amalgamating local governments in key urban centres, after a short time lag the province of Québec began similar shifts.

Today, local — provincial relations remain dynamic, influenced in each province by recent elections and the arrival of new (Liberal) governments. The situation is fluid and uncertain, with both provinces facing fiscal deficits, although the threat of fiscal offloading seems more pronounced in Québec, where aggressive tax and spending cuts are expected — the very same conditions of Ontario during the late 1990s. Further compounding the uncertainty is the Québec government's refusal to completely shut the door on the possibility of de-amalgamating the recently former and enlarged cities (notably Montreal, Québec City, and Gatineau).

In addition, to these levels, Canada's National Capital Region has a regional planning authority — the National Capital Commission — in charge of planning, developing and using the federal government's properties in the region as a source of pride and unity for Canadians. It is a Crown Corporation of the Government of Canada and with significant land holdings in Ottawa and Gatineau it has given rise to a long and complex history of both cooperative and conflictual relations with local governments in the area.

The 1992 initiative, *Partners for the Future — A Strategic Vision for Ottawa-Carleton*, acknowledges the inter-provincial border as a barrier to better governance and economic development. The study, led by the Regional Municipality of Ottawa-Carleton (RMOC — having now since amalgamated into the new and current City of Ottawa) envisioned the creation of a regional partnership that would join together local authorities on both sides of the river with representatives from all levels of government, the private sector, education and the community (Regional Municipality of Ottawa-Carleton 2002: 4). As will be discussed below, the report may now be regarded as having been ahead of its time, particularly when local governments had not yet amalgamated in both Ottawa and Gatineau (making cross-border attempts at collaboration more complex and less likely).

Economic Infrastructure and Human Capital

Historically, business and government activities have mainly been situated in the central core of Ottawa but the expansion of high-technology has mainly contributed to the growth of Ottawa's west end (formerly the separate communities of Nepean and Kanata). The Québec side of the river has also experienced sprawl beyond the former core of Hull, with suburban growth in rapidly expanding, outer segments of Gatineau. The result is increased pressure on transportation infrastructure.

This infrastructure in Ottawa is well developed with a recently expanded highway link between the City and the major provincial road artery connecting Montreal and Toronto (Highway 401), an international airport, and trains connecting the region with the whole continent. But in recent years, some problems have emerged from fast growth of businesses and residential areas (especially attributed to the high-tech boom). Important issues regarding transportation in Ottawa-Gatineau are related to the inter-provincial border.[6]

There have been growing calls in recent years for a new bridge over the Ottawa River, which would help such problems. There has even been discussion for constructing two bridges at both ends of the region that would be linked to a peripheral highway around the whole region. But it seems impossible to come to an agreement in terms of where that bridge should be and who should pay for it, as fiscal and political tensions across local, provincial and federal levels have overshadowed a still-elusive consensus locally as to precisely what is required.

In terms of economic opportunity, amongst major urban centres in Canada, Ottawa-Gatineau is becoming more diversified due to the rise in prominence of technology as a complementing engine of employment and opportunity. There are now hundreds of companies engaged in sectors such as telecommunications, photonics, microelectronics, software and life sciences. The story of Ottawa's technological roots is a distinctive blend

---

[6] One of the main routes for trucks linking Québec and Ontario goes through the heart of Ottawa. These trucks contribute to enhanced traffic congestion, noise, etc. And overnight truck activity in the downtown core of Ottawa has resulted in many complaints in recent years. There are important traffic congestions for some 40,000 people crossing the river every weekday from Québec to Ontario for work, school, or other activities.

of private ingenuity and public subsidy (see also the chapters by Ghent Mallett, and by Madill *et al.* this volume) that carries forward to this day, with a strong base of public sector research and technology institutions serving as a magnet for entrepreneurs and companies alike.

Such a public — private mix has often been transformed into a backdrop for somewhat idealized, local portrayals and such a dynamic also partly underpinned the 1990s emergence of Ottawa as "Silicon Valley North" with over 80,000 employees in technology-based companies by 1999. This level of employment has, of course, more recently declined due to the global pullback of technology sectors, with forecasts mixed as to how quickly a recovery can be expected. The federal government now employs roughly 80,000 people in the region, with a considerably demographic refurbishment of the managerial ranks across the federal public service expected to translate into considerable hiring nationally — and particularly locally in the NCR (Moritz & Roy 2000).

Moreover, the rising prominence of technology within the public sector, denoted by e-government and government online strategies, is a relatively recent convergence of private and public interests that will likely continue to spur the local technology sector — particularly in the consulting and service oriented segments where the federal government alone spends several billions of dollars annually on technology-related purchases and consulting services (a national figure, albeit highly concentrated in the NCR where a high portion of technology managers are based, including the Department of Defence, the government-wide Chief Information Officer's Branch, and the headquarters of the Royal Canadian Mounted Police, Canada Customs and Revenue Agency and Canada Post, to name but a few).

The boom of the high-tech sector is only taking place on the Ottawa side of the river, mainly in the Western part of the city. So far, Gatineau has been less successful in attracting these types of industries, as much of the expansion of technology-based clusters occurred through the 1990s on the Ontario side of this region. Such a dynamic provides testament to the importance of proximity in reenforcing the clustering of firms within specific territories (despite, in the case of Québec, more generous research and development incentives, an approach now under review by the new provincial government of Québec led by Liberal Premier Jean Charest).

In terms of the knowledge and education infrastructure the region is endowed with a significant base of teaching and research facilities across a range of both private and public institutions. On the Québec side of the river there are two technical colleges (one French and one English) and one university — the latter offering courses primarily in French, but also English and Spanish. In Ottawa, there are three universities (Carleton University — English, Ottawa University — French and English, St-Paul University — French and English) and 2 colleges (1 French and 1 English; see also the chapter by Armit this volume).

Indeed, despite higher tuition and training costs some 5,000 students travel daily from Québec to Ontario within the NCR. In terms of education attainment, the population on the Ontario side of the river is more educated, with 76.8% of the population over 15 years having a high school diploma and 27.2% having a university degree (the Ontario portion of the Capital region has the highest percentage of the population with a university degree in Canada). On the Québec side of the river, 67.3% of the population over 15 years have completed high school while 18.5% have a university degree (well above national and provincial levels).

Intra-Regional Disparities

The intermingling of work and living patterns results in thousands of people crossing the river — border each day. According to a 1995 study by the provincial government of Québec, on any given week day nearly 40,000 people left their home on the Gatineau side of the river to go work in Ottawa during peak morning commuting hours: inversely, over 14,000 people travelled from Ottawa to work on the Gatineau side of the river, figures that remain relevant benchmarks today, given the rise and subsequent contraction of technology-based industries in the late 1990s (Ministère des transports du Québec 1995).

Although labour mobility is significant from one province to the other inside the region, it is noteworthy that many types of diplomas or certain qualifications are not easily transferable from one province to another. Education is under the responsibility of provinces and therefore, diplomas obtained in certain provinces are not necessarily valid in terms of recognition and professional accreditation across all other provinces. It is the case for Québec and Ontario, for example, that primary and secondary level teachers require additional qualifications in order to be employed in the neighbouring province.

The provincial border also restricts construction workers, a long time dispute that has once again become a topic in renewed discussions by the new governments in place in both provinces. Recently, the Government of Ontario passed retaliatory legislation meaning construction workers from Québec would not be able to work in Ontario. The move significantly affected over 4,000 workers, most of which are from the Ottawa-Gatineau region, and the issue became a major irritant between Ontario and Québec.

Household income is significantly higher in Ottawa than in Gatineau. In 1999, the average household income was \$59,325 in Ottawa and \$46,878 in Gatineau. The average monthly unemployment rate for the whole region was 7.5% from January to March 2002, slightly lower than the national rate of 7.7%. It has risen significantly over the last year, steadily increasing from 5% in March 2001. This is due to important job reductions in the high-tech sector. For the same period, the unemployment rate for Ottawa was 7.4% while it was 8.9% for Gatineau. The unemployment rate is historically higher in Gatineau than in Ottawa.

An objective comparison of cost of living across Ottawa and Gatineau is difficult since it rests on many variables and choices that ultimately shape a particular lifestyle and the manner by which any given lifestyle is best suited to one side of the border region or the other. For example, Ontario's housing is significantly more expensive than on the Québec side of the river.[7] But income taxes in Ontario are significantly lower most levels of revenues. For families with children, day care is very expensive in Ontario compared to Québec where it is subsidized by the government (at a fixed cost of \$5 a day). As such, cost of living on one side or the other side of the river depends on a number of variables, including working arrangements and commuting, number of dependents and housing (Canadian Municipal Housing Corporation 2002). Moreover, language is another important factor for choosing where to live for area residents.

---

[7] In March 2002, the average sale price of a house on the Ontario side of the river was \$199,424, an 18% increase compared to March 2001: rent is also significantly more expensive in Ontario where a 2-bedroom apartment for example will cost approximately 60% more in Ottawa than in Gatineau (www.ottawa.com).

Another factor of comparison is quality of life. On the Ottawa side of the river, there are more people, smaller properties, and less green spaces for example, but for many people, proximity is an important locational factor. For people more interested in green spaces or more rugged terrain, and for whom proximity is not a factor, the Québec side may be preferred. For certain types of living arrangements it may become advantageous to work in one province and live in the other. This is especially true for Québec residents working in Ontario. They pay less rent in Québec and less for day care, while benefiting from a larger pool of jobs in Ontario, often with higher salaries than might be available in the province of Québec. Such differentials are some of the main reasons why thousands of people cross the river to work in Ottawa each morning.

In sum, there are important disparities in terms of costs, quality of life, linguistic and cultural identities, albeit co-existing with economic and political interdependencies. Will future economic and technological prospects bring the area closer to realizing stronger intra-regional ties across the river? The case for deeper and more holistic governance grows stronger when once considers the common challenges that lie ahead.

Challenges Ahead — Interdependence versus Independence

One common challenge facing many city-regions, though particularly those with multi-level governance jurisdictions overlapping one another, is the notable distinction and growing inter-relationship between economic interdependence and political independence.

With respect to economic interdependence, there appear to be signs of a growing degree of recognition that all components of the National Capital Region must assert themselves collectively — as parts of a more unified city-region (Paquet 2001). Yet, Ottawa — Gatineau presents a different form of economic convergence given the decline in relative terms of inter-provincial vs. international trade of a more north — south variety. Thus, the economic integration of Ottawa — Gatineau is more inward driven, tied largely to a common economic focus of Ottawa and Gatineau on three broadly-defined areas of growth: public sector infrastructure and operations of a newly-expanding federal government, an expanding base of emerging clusters of high-technology industries, and an inter-connected tourism base reflected by the shared role of serving as Canada's Capital.

A deeper level of cross-provincial labour market integration and a common presence of the federal government on both sides of the Ottawa River tend to reenforce the political space of the National Capital Region. Recent political amalgamations on both sides of the river create new possibilities for bilateral relations between two cities (in place of some 15 municipal units). The federal government's significant land holdings and their maintenance by the National Capital Commission (NCC) have led to growing recognition of the need for some form of tri-partite mechanism to guide to fostering of a truly regional system of governance (explored more fully below).

A formation of such a mechanism, and its eventual evolution will take time. The roots of such governance, however, make a good deal of sense and are likely to be nurtured by a more favourable political climate nationally with a new federal government in 2004 (led by a new Prime Minister Paul Martin) more open to new approaches to support the emergence of stronger cities across the country. Moreover, due to its own political agenda, featuring a greater place for cities, and a yearning for a greater national unity, this new federal government is likely to be particularly receptive to closer ties across the provincial border, re-enforcing the predominantly federalist culture of western Québec (it should be noted that Ottawa and Gatineau are similarly situated on the periphery of their provinces and neither carry provincial capital status).

Nonetheless, an important limitation on political integration is the significant degree of provincial jurisdiction over municipal affairs and many key areas of economic and social development (including health, education, and, to some degree, the environment). Irrespective of the partisan nature of the governments in power, Toronto and Québec City (the provincial Capitals respectively of Ontario and Québec) represent important gravitational points for Ottawa and Gatineau respectively, a link that remains a significant variable in local development processes, both economic and politically.

Locally, with respect to future ties across the Ottawa River any progress begins from the common and joining premise of two cities within a common and uniquely multi-level governance environment. As the National Capital Region, unique federal attributes of the Capital are one factor — the beautification of federal lands and the cultural endowments and celebrations that come with Capital City status. Yet, economic impacts also matter: as the federal government, once again expanding and hiring, provides a common base of employment security for both sides of the river.

Politically, there is also the basis of similar values — though whether there is growing convergence in this sense is a more contested proposition. Western Québec has always been among the most federalist locales in Québec, sharing this placement to some extent with parts of Montreal. Accordingly, Ottawa is part of the most bilingual portions of the province of Ontario, tying together the National Capital Region in a setting of linguistic duality that is preserved by the constitution and enforced by hiring and promotional practices of the Government of Canada.

At the same time, Ottawa's population growth, fuelled as of late by high technology industries has made the urban areas on the Ontario side somewhat more cosmopolitan and diluted the proportions of French-speaking peoples accordingly. Whether the City of Ottawa should function as a bilingual institution has been a contentious issue for the newly amalgamated municipality, and so while the politics remain complex and often fractured geographically and linguistically, there is still an underlying attachment to the traditional vision of Canada as a bi-cultural nation. This vision is guarded forcefully by the federal government and its local apparatus (the NCC), as well as the locally based headquarters of Heritage Canada and a variety of "national" cultural institutions and bodies (such as the Museums of Civilization, Science and Technology and Natural Sciences, the National Arts Centre and the National Gallery).

Within such a setting, it is perhaps the economics of the region's development that will alter the meaning and place of the border and drive Ottawa — Gatineau toward closer ties than have traditionally been the case. In particular, the emergence of a strengthening knowledge-based economy has stimulated more growth for the region as a whole, creating a new set of challenges, opportunities and frictions — considered below.

In terms of challenges, in competing with locales around the world the Ottawa region is itself a new identity used for international marketing in reference to a unified socio-economy of over one million people (a figure inclusive of both the Ontario and Québec sides of the National Capital Region). The bilingual workforce of the area is deemed an asset in this regard, as the extended area shows early signs of viewing itself as a city-region competing in a global environment in an increasingly intensive manner.

Yet, the economic evolution creates new tensions — as proportionally more investment and development by the private sector occurs in Ottawa, leaving Gatineau struggling to compete (aided, to some degree, by strong provincial government incentives for companies to cross the border into Québec). The expansion of development risks becoming increasingly uneven, one example being the fact that housing and real estate markets of Gatineau are fuelled by the Ottawa-based growth (creating chronic shortages in the rental market on both locales).

As a result, there are growing infrastructure requirements for the National Capital Region that reflect its holistic needs — even while planning in many areas such as social services, education, health care and housing continues to be managed within distinct and quite separate political systems. What discussions have taken place to date in terms of issues such as infrastructure expansion, for example, have by and large taken place in a divisive manner across a multitude of local, provincial and federal processes. Concerted dialogue has been in short supply.

This mix of identity and infrastructure is a dynamic one that could be negated by two possible shifts — one national and one local. Nationally, any change in the government, particularly toward one more open to decentralization and federal downsizing could alter the investment prospects of resources in the National Capital Region. Locally, even presuming political continuity, there is no strong tradition of concerted and collaborative governance between the federal government and local municipalities.

It is within such a context that the post-amalgamation scenario of a troika of key players (the two Cities of Ottawa and Gatineau and the federal NCC) must be examined. The nature of federal action and how it asserts itself will be an important variable, as will be the ongoing power struggles between local, provincial and federal actors. What will also be determinant is the extent to which collaboration for the city-region as a whole is fully viewed and appreciated as an essential aspect of future development.

A Focus on Technology

How does the rising prominence of technology-based industry shape the prospects for city-regional governance to emerge, and to what extent is the emergence of this form of governance necessary for Ottawa and Gatineau to remain globally competitive locales for a knowledge-based economy?

In terms of the former, it is important that technology, and its usage as a platform for innovation, entrepreneurship and wealth-creation serves as a common platform on which the foundations of a city-region can be constructed more forcefully, across the river than has been the case in the past. As has been noted, regional marketing has already encompassed the broader area as the basis of a global identity, and many aspects of tourism have moved in a similar fashion (such as the promotion of many local area attractions — museums, sports franchises and the Casino to name but a few, as accessible points of interest for populations and visitors from both sides of the river).

It would appear unlikely, particularly in the short term, that technology companies and their leaders will become engaged participants and proponents for the emergence of city-regional governance. The technology industry is struggling, a mere shadow of itself some five years ago, and so survival is the order of the day.

Moreover, much of the short and medium term planning horizons of companies involving public sector authorities exist within existing structures, on either side of the river in their respective municipal setting. Issues such as local taxes, development fees and evolving provincial priorities and spending plans are enough to occupy the attentions of most firms. Nonetheless, there are some reasons to expect that over time the attentions of the technology industry will shift increasingly to city-regional dimensions of governance, and there is certainly a case to be made that such a shift should occur.

Firstly, the overall quality of life, increasingly viewed as a shared externality for all firms in the National Capital Region seeking to both recruit and retain highly skilled workers, is rooted within many cross-border aspects of living in Ottawa (or Gatineau). Federal lands and parks and a variety of recreational activities are key attributes of a positive lifestyle in the otherwise bleak Canadian winters, and a strong basis for preserving and enhancing a holistic picture of life in the National Capital Region.

Secondly, the growing centrality of human capital and the necessity of any successful city-region to be a magnet for both Canadians and (new and potential) immigrants is well recognized. The bi-cultural aspect of the National Capital Region is an asset in this regard, and one that needs to be nourished into a stronger and more effective multi-cultural setting for the strengthening of ethnic communities through their networks of social capital and economic activity.

Immigration, however, remains controlled by the federal government, albeit with a separate agreement for select provinces, notably Québec. As in the United States, where the technology industry has been an important voice on updating immigration policies to underpin the expansion of technology industries, often within select locales (Wong 2002), companies can be, and must be important stakeholders in shaping this debate in the future — and in particular, in localizing this discussion from the perspective of the changing demographic profile and evolving socio-economic needs of the National Capital Region.

These evolutions — quality of life and ethnic diversity — will collectively define the workforce of tomorrow, the central platform for economic success and a critical prerequisite to any level of sustained success that Ottawa and Gatineau may have in achieving meaningful status as a Silicon Valley North. Their prospects are stronger collectively as opposed to separately in this regard — yet, what is lacking to build on these collective prospects are more concerted and integrative governance mechanisms. New and expanded measures are required for building city-regional governance.

Building City-Regional Governance

In Ottawa/Gatineau, the challenge for more collaborative action is becoming more localized and dependent on the ability of political leaders in each municipality to forge common ground on their complementary need for expanded infrastructure. Nonetheless, in a similar fashion, forging supportive ties to both provincial and federal governments will be crucial to securing the financial resources to proceed. What is unique about the National Capital Region in Canada is that the federal presence in this particular urban centre will always be proportionally more influential than elsewhere in the country.

Yet changes are in order. In the Ottawa Citizen, the local, daily newspaper, one finds reference to a study by Laurence Aurbach (Ottawa Citizen 2001) that celebrates the bossy style of the NCC and the merit of autocracy (and the use of the power of eminent domain) by the NCC as an important contributor to the success of Ottawa as a vibrant and liveable city. There is no doubt that the NCC has done much to help steward the growth of Ottawa in liveable ways. However, it cannot expect to continue to play its role in the future as it did in the past. In private, public and civic organizations, hierarchical and autocratic styles of leadership have been replaced by more collaborative and participative approaches. Consequently, the challenge for the NCC of the future is that it will have to become less a boss and more a broker — facilitating action via dialogue and collaboration.

The complexity of the tasks faced by capital cities in general and by Ottawa in particular (because of its being nested at the border of two provinces) means that it would be unwise to expect that one source of authority would be able to perform the governing task alone. The governance of capital cities is akin to a game without a master (where power is dispersed across actors and authorities, and rules and responses must be negotiated, maintained and adapted). The baroque (i.e. irregular, unusual, somewhat complex) arrangement that is required will also have to be different in the future from what it has been in the past — in order to overcome the local divisions in favour of a more outward-looking vision built on inward cooperation (Paquet 2002).

This new form of leadership is no less transformative than the earlier style, but it requires different skills and a new mindset. The special challenges must therefore be kept in mind as one is trying to find ways to improve the governance of capital cities like Ottawa.

> The NCR is a city-region. And in a globalized economy, city-regions are becoming more important economically as nation-state capitals are becoming relatively less important politically.

This paradoxical set of forces (that have given to Ottawa more importance on the world stage while lessening its role within Canada) means that no simple formula can be used to define the governance of capital cities. It depends a lot on the vernaculars — the characteristics of the localities. A composite city like Ottawa gains world prominence through its high-tech sector while it loses influence through the erosion of the nation state that has lost power outward to transnational agencies, downward to regions, and sideways to multinationals. There is no way to govern this composite creature except through distributed governance.

> The NCR must strive for a distributed and shared governance regime and recognition of the plurality of communities and stakeholders contributing to Ottawa's growth.

The many roles of Ottawa on the international, federal, provincial and local scenes, and the variety of socio-economic forces (private, public, civic) at work within the area call for a governance regime that can accommodate these different roles and forces. This has to be a multi-layered governance that requires a degree of complexity commensurate with the degree of complexity of the system to be governed. Consequently, what is regarded by some as an unduly complex governance regime, encompassing two separate municipal systems and a National Capital Commission, may turn out to be exactly the sort of complexity likely to provide competitive advantage, provided coordination and collaboration lead to all parties contributing positively both individually and collectively.

> The NCR needs collaborative governance and leadership.

The need for a distributed governance regime comes with a price tag: the necessity to collaborate. This has been particularly difficult in the past with the multiplicity of towns over the territory of the national capital region. But collaboration can easily be facilitated in the new world where a Troika is possible (coordination of the NCC, the City of Ottawa, and the City of Gatineau). Collaborative governance is transforming the traditional structure of accountabilities and calls for new forms of collaborative leadership.

> The NCR may require some de-capitalization while retaining capital functions.

The present schizophrenia of capital cities in terms of their dual purposes of housing institutions with both national and local purposes, and the strong sentiment that the national/international roles are taking precedence over the local engagement has led to some questioning of the cost/benefit ratio of the burden of being a capital. What might be required for a Troika to work? A number of plausible points come to mind:

- The recognition of the equal power of the three partners.
- Real power being devolved by provinces to the city-regions.
- A real territorial coordination authority granted to the NCC.
- A change in the composition of the board of the NCC to include more locals.
- The recognition that partnerships and alliances are necessary.
- A sense of the region as a counterweight to provincial and federal weights.
- Some citizen education in order to strengthen collective recognition as to both the challenges and choices that lie ahead.
- Transparent and collective reporting on the state of the region.
- A true consultation philosophy and a true spirit of cooperation.

None of this will evolve overnight. What is required is the development of a climate of trust and cooperation. Recognition and expanded dialogues are precursors to addressing complexity and finding common ground (Yankelovich 1999). Such ingredients are essential in building a more robust and collective system of governance to guide the future development of the region as a whole and maximize the prospects for sustained success. Although there may be much to gather and learn from experiences elsewhere, the heart of what is required must be tailor-made both for and within the unique parameters of the NCR.

Unfortunately, caution is the order of the day — and it appears that progress will be, at best, incremental. Politically, despite the success of the Ottawa 2020 exercise (an Ottawa-based public consultation and visioning exercise, led by the City and held in 2001, designed to think big and look ahead), and its valuing of this city-regional perspective, precise action on the sorts of directions listed above has not yet taken hold.

Conclusion

The socio-economic, political and technological fortunes of Ottawa and Gatineau are becoming increasingly intertwined within their common rubric of the National Capital Region. Nonetheless, this chapter has revealed that despite such interdependency, recognition has not yet been translated into concrete action. Although it makes strategic sense to conceive of the NCR as a city-region, unified and competitive with other such entities in Canada and elsewhere, a lack of governance mechanisms across the major political actors, coupled with an unevenly concentrated set of technology industries on the Ontario side within which many companies continue to struggle through recent market volatility are barriers to more meaningful regional perspectives and strategies. As a result, while local populations are mobile and intertwined in many aspects of daily life a common identity has yet to take hold.

Some observers may not be enthralled with the NCR as a brand, since it has historically denoted the political flavour of the region more than one shaped by innovation and entrepreneurship. Yet, whatever the brand chosen and adopted, Capital cities are quite often sources of both public research and private ingenuity and this balance must be embraced and built upon rather than discarded. If Ottawa and Gatineau are to emerge collectively as a Silicon Valley North (one of many given the numerous aspirants to such a title) than it should be on terms most unique and relevant for their region.

As Canada evolves into an increasingly knowledge-driven and urbanized country, its city-regions will be at the core of development, as reflected by the growing movement within these entities for more autonomy, recognition and resources (Paquet & Roy 2004). To be effective in this league, stakeholders within Ottawa and Gatineau must do more — together, to recognize the growing interdependencies of their labour markets, knowledge and research infrastructures and quality of life and act concertedly to strengthen them.

References

Barnett, R. (1997). Subsidiarity, enabling government and local governance. In: H. R. Hobson, & F. St-Hilaire (Eds), *Urban governance and finance: A question of who does what* (pp. 62–79). Montreal, Quebec, Canada: Institute of Research on Public Policy.

Canadian Municipal Housing Corporation (2002). *Research highlights — December 2002 (Socio-economic series 115)*. Ottawa, Ontario, Canada: Government of Canada.

Caves, R. W., & Walshok, M. G. (1999). Adopting innovations in information technology: The California municipal experience. *The International Journal of Urban Policy and Planning, 16*(1), 3–12.

Coe, A., Paquet, G., & Roy, J. (2001). E-governance and smart communities: A social learning challenge. *Social Science Computer Review, 19*(1), 80–93.

Cohen, J., & Rogers, J. (Eds) (1995). *Associations and democracy, real utopias project V.1.* New York: Verso.

Courchene, T. J. (1995). Glocalization: The regional/national interface. *Canadian Journal of Regional Science, 18*(1), 1–20.

Eger, J. (1997). Cyberspace and cyberplace: Building smart communities of tomorrow. *San Diego Union-Tribune* (October 26), 17.

Fukuyama, F. (1995). *Trust: The social virtues and the creation of prosperity.* New York: Free Press.

Henton, D., Melville, J., & Walesh, K. (1997). *Grassroots leaders for a new economy.* San Francisco: Jossey-Bass.

Hudson, C. (1995). *Does the local context matter? The extent of local government involvement in economic development in Sweden and Britain.* Boulder, CO: Westview Press.

Joint Venture: Silicon Valley Network (2003). *Regional index of Silicon Valley.* San Jose: www.jointventure.org.

Ministère des transports du Québec (1995). *Enquête origine-destination 1995 — region de l'Outaouais.* Montreal, Québec, Canada: Ministère des transports du Québec.

Moritz, R., & Roy, J. (2000). Federal IT workforce: Demography, community renewal, and leadership. *Canadian Government Executive, 4*(6), 12–15.

Naisbitt, J. (1994). *Global paradox.* New York: William Morrow and Company.

Organization for Economic Cooperation and Development (2002) *Territorial review of Canada.* Paris, France: Territorial Reviews and Governance Division.

Ottawa Citizen (2001). 18 June.

Paquet, G. (1997). States, communities and markets: The distributed governance scenario. In: T. J. Courchene (Ed.), *The nation-state in a global information era: Policy challenges. The Bell Canada Papers in economics and public policy* (pp. 25–46). Kingston, Ontario, Canada: John Deutsch Institute for the Study of Economic Policy.

Paquet, G. (2002). *Ottawa 20/20 and Baroque Governance — A report on the smart growth summit of June 2001.* Ottawa, Ontario, Canada: Centre on Governance, University of Ottawa.

Paquet, G., & Roy, J. (1995). Prosperity through networks: The bottom-up strategy that might have been. In: S. Philips (Ed.), *How Ottawa spends 1995–96* (pp. 137–158). Ottawa, Ontario, Canada: Carleton University Press.

Paquet, G., & Roy, J. (2004). Smarter cities in Canada. *Optimum Online, 33*(1), forthcoming.

Regional Municipality of Ottawa-Carleton (2002). *Partners for the future — A strategic vision for Ottawa-Carleton.* Ottawa, Ontario, Canada: Regional Municipality of Ottawa-Carleton.

Roy, J. (1998). Canada's technology triangle. In: J. de la Mothe, & G. Paquet (Eds), *Local and regional systems of innovation* (pp. 239–256). London, UK: Kluwer Academic Publishers.

Saxenian, A. (1994). *Regional advantage: Culture and competition in Silicon Valley and route 128.* Cambridge, MA: Harvard University Press.

Scott, A. J. (1994). *Technopolis.* Los Angeles: University of California Press.

Statistics Canada (2001). Community profiles. Ottawa: http://www12.statscan.ca.

Storper, M. (1997). *The regional world: Territorial development in a global economy.* New York: Guilford Press.

TD Bank (2002). *Final report from the TD forum on Canada's standard of living.* (Co-sponsored study with Conference Board of Canada from which the final report is available online at: http://www.td.com/economics/standard/final_report.pdf.)

Vander Ploeg, C. G. (2002). *Big city revenue sources: A Canada-U.S. comparison of tax tools and revenue levers.* Calgary, Alberta, Canada: Canada West Foundation.

Wong, D. (2002). *Cities at the crossroads: Addressing intergovernmental structures for Western Canada's cities.* Calgary, Alberta, Canada: Canada West Foundation.

Yankelovich, D. (1999). *The magic of dialogue — Transforming conflict into cooperation.* New York: Simon and Schuster.

Chapter 11

Technological Development in Gatineau, the Quebec Sector of Silicon Valley North

Franco Materazzi

Abstract

While a large proportion of the high tech industry is located in Ottawa, Gatineau, in the province of Quebec, has also experienced substantial development in this field. The city enjoys the benefits stemming from the proximity of 33 federal research centers in Ottawa and the presence of a pool of leading specialists. Also, on the plus side are the number of Ottawa-based entrepreneurs who have chosen to take advantage of the very favorable tax treatment offered in Quebec for R&D activities and the fairly ready availability of venture capital in Quebec for start-ups.

Introduction: Economic Integration of the National Capital Region

Ottawa became the capital of Canada in 1857. In 1969, to give expression to the bilingual and bicultural nature of the country, the Canadian government of the day established a broad series of policies, among them extension of the National Capital Region to take in an area in the province of Quebec that includes the recently created City of Gatineau[1] on the north side of the Ottawa River, across from the City of Ottawa. Gatineau is also the major urban center (75% of the population) of a wider administrative region called the Outaouais, comprising large rural areas.

This political decision led to the construction of federal government offices in what is now the City of Gatineau as well as the development of major road infrastructures, sewage treatment facilities and drinking water filtration plants which facilitated the development of the region and contributed to a closer integration of its economy with that of Ottawa.

In addition to an increased federal presence, a greater interpenetration has occurred in the expanding housing markets, recreation and tourist activities, as well as the economic sectors, particularly the high tech sector which has been the spearhead of Ottawa's economic development.

---

[1] Product of the amalgamation in 2000 of 5 cities — Aylmer, Buckingham, Gatineau, Hull and Masson-Angers.

Silicon Valley North: A High-Tech Cluster of Innovation and Entrepreneurship
© 2004 Published by Elsevier Ltd.
ISBN: 0-08-044457-1

Gatineau's integration into the overall technological development of Ottawa and the National Capital Region is reflected in two ways:

- By the strong presence of Gatineau residents working in Ottawa's high tech companies and in the 33 federal research centers located in Ottawa (the proportion runs between 10 and 25%, depending on the company or research center);
- By the fact that more than 75% of the technology enterprises in Gatineau were started by Ottawa-based entrepreneurs or by Gatineau residents who had previously worked in Ottawa companies or institutions.

Providing an overview of R&D activity in the Outaouais region is a little more complex than for other regions of Quebec. This was the hard lesson learned by the Conseil de la science et de la technologie du Québec (Quebec's Science and Technology Council). According to its *2001 Situation Report: The Regional Dimensions of Innovation in Québec* (Conseil de la Science et de la Technologie du Québec 2001), the Outaouais is among the Quebec regions that theoretically would be expected to have poor potential for technological development, since the amount of university, government and private sector research carried out in the region is low. Yet the technology sector here is burgeoning. For stakeholders in the region, the explanation for this paradox is quite simple: Gatineau has a highly skilled technology-sector labor force working in the federal research laboratories and in private companies in Ottawa.

In fact, the Outaouais ranks high among Quebec's 17 regions (on a per capita basis) for many technological occupations (Statistics Canada 2001):

• Management of natural sciences and engineering	3rd place
• Scientists	2nd place
• Engineers	6th place
• Computer scientists	1st place
• All occupations	3rd place

Technological development in Gatineau also benefits from the proximity of the federal research centers and the universities in Ottawa, where research positions are often held by residents of Gatineau. Finally, there is the impact created by Ottawa-based entrepreneurs who for various reasons have decided to establish operations in Quebec and who can count on hiring experts living on the Ontario side of the Ottawa River.

The following sections outline the history of Gatineau's technological development and profile the companies and research centers in the city, establishing links wherever possible between growth in this region and the development that has taken place in Ottawa.

Historical Background[2]

The first technological development initiative in the Outaouais can be traced back to 1982. That year, the Société d'aménagement de l'Outaouais (SAO, the Outaouais Development

---

[2] Information excerpted from Materazzi (2003).

Agency), in cooperation with the Quebec Ministry of Industry and Commerce as well as stakeholders in the area, set up a committee to promote high technology, recommending an increased presence of federal research centers on the Quebec side of the National Capital Region, and the development of a Quebec technology cluster in the National Capital. The work of this committee led to the launching of a number of projects by both industry and the research centers, which will be discussed later. This early activity in the region occurred in parallel with the creation of a new Ministry of Science and Technology in Quebec. The Ministry was subsequently approached to fund a number of projects.

In June 1985, an assessment of scientific and technological activity in the Outaouais region carried out by the Conseil de la science et de la technologie du Québec (Quebec's Science and Technology Council) estimated annual R&D expenditures in electronics and computer science in the region at $2.9 million. Today, based on a study done in early 2002 (Materazzi 2002), I can peg R&D spending in these sectors at more than $30 million a year.

In the early 1980s, there were 5 technology companies located in Gatineau compared to nearly 200 on the Ottawa side. By far the largest company in Gatineau was Northern Telecom, with more than 1,200 employees working on developing prototypes for digital transmission and hybrid circuits. The plant shut down in the late 1980s. The other major company in the area was Gandalf, which manufactured communications systems and had more than 300 employees but did no R&D. In the mid-1980s, it too ceased operations.

Starting in 1983, other companies made their appearance in Gatineau, changing and diversifying the technological landscape. Some became very influential. In 1985, for example, two companies, ACDS (geomatics) and CML Technologies, both experienced strong growth and each had R&D projects worth $2 million. Crawley R&D (digital animation of films) had the largest project of its type in Canada (with a value of $6.5 million and a staff of 55 employees), but after a year of operations and various financial difficulties, the company shut down this venture. The start-up of ACDS incidentally was the result of a transfer to entrepreneurs in Ottawa and Gatineau of computer-assisted design (CAD) technology developed by Public Works Canada.

Next it was Adga's turn to launch a major project to develop performance support systems using cutting edge multi-media technologies. The value of this multi-year R&D project was more than $5 million. The project was initially managed by André Maisonneuve, who had been a senior executive with ACDS. Another company active at the time was G&A Imaging (secure documents with digital images), which in 1987 initiated major R&D projects worth several million dollars. G&A Imaging (now Imageware) was able to round out its team with a number of top programmers picked up from ACDS, including Simon Grégoire who in 1998 became one of the founders of Hemera, now another major player in Gatineau. Hemera may in turn generate spin-offs in the future.

There was a lull in the creation of major new technology ventures until the mid-1990s, when a number of new companies came on the scene, including some that located in the Centre de développement des technologies de l'information (Center for Information Technology Development). In addition to the attractive R&D tax credits available in Quebec, the Center provided tax credits for pre-marketing activities. Some 20 companies took advantage of the pre-marketing tax credit program before it was abolished in 2003. Those companies will however continue to benefit from this tax break for the balance of the 10-year contract they originally signed. The Technology Business Development

Center, an incubation center without walls located in Gatineau, was and still remains greatly instrumental in the emergence of many new firms.

The Situation in 2003 and Future Directions of the Industry

In Gatineau today, there are over 40 high-technology companies, most with more than 5 employees. The majority has their premises either in the Center for Information Technology Development or in the Gatineau Technoparc. These companies can be grouped by sector, although some have interests that extend beyond a single category, and could easily be listed under several sectors:

Telecommunications: 8
Databases and geomatics: 5
Equipment and microelectronics: 5
Management software: 6
Internet and multi-media: 11
Computer services: 5
Security-related software: 3

From this list it is evident that the technology companies in Gatineau are active in the same areas of information technology as Ottawa companies, but that some sectors such as microelectronics are less well represented than in Ottawa. For instance, the absence of the life sciences sector is also evident. Furthermore, no sector has a significant critical mass. Thus, for example, companies that have been listed together under the heading of Internet and multi-media offer very different applications, including training, e-commerce, Website development, Internet service, and so on.

If one scans the list to identify common enabling technologies, you will find that digital imaging is used in several sectors (geomatics, security, and the Internet and multi-media sectors). The following companies, while scattered across a number of sectors, all work closely with digital imaging technologies (data capture, compression, processing, storage, and transmission): PCI Geomatics, Intergraph Canada, CubeWerx, Imageware, Synercard, Training Innovations, Hemera, SourceWorks, Callisto, CIRI Lab, I3 and possibly a few others as well.

Based on a 2002 study (Materazzi 2002), the following observations can be made about the development of this industry over the last 10 years:

- There has been a large increase in hiring at CML Technologies and its spin-offs (SolaCom Technologies and Versatel).
- A number of computer integration service companies have started up or have expanded, creating nearly 200 new jobs (Influatec, FSG Consultants, CIA, Stay Technologies, and i4design).
- Several new companies have entered the market, and are actively hiring employees (Tomoye, MultiCorpora, and ObjectWorld).
- At the same time, however, Innovative Fiber (Alcatel) closed its operations in Gatineau, resulting in the loss of several hundred jobs, and Multidev was taken over by an Ottawa company.

A large proportion of the 40 companies established operations in the region recently; just 13 of them were in existence before 1995 and only 4 date back to before 1990. The start-up of these companies can be attributed to a number of factors. One is the growing presence of venture capital groups in the region since the early 1990s. In fact, among 29 enterprises studied, half were financed by venture capital groups, primarily the Fonds regional de solidarité Outaouais (a labor-sponsored fund), the Société de Diversification Économique de l'Outaouais (SDEO, or Outaouais Economic Diversification Corporation), Cap-Gest-Dev, the Caisse de dépôt et de placement du Québec (Quebec's government-run pension fund manager), and Innovatech. The majority of these companies have received several rounds of financing and are looking for still more capital. Most have backing from at least 2 investment institutions, and a few have 3 or 4 backers.

The government programs, such as Canada Economic Development for Quebec Region and Investissement-Québec, especially the loan guarantees to banks, are extremely useful. Caisse Desjardins and the Banque Nationale are the banks of choice for these companies. The Technology Business Development Center has also incubated a good number of these start-up companies.

To sum-up, over the last 10 years, the growth of the technology sector in Gatineau has clearly been encouraged by the total package of government financing programs and by the ready availability of venture capital in Quebec. In the last few years, however, although there have been only a few closures, there have been major cutbacks in employment by the larger players (except CML and related spin-offs). Many companies continue to face a pressing need for capital, while the sources of financing are weaker and more selective. A certain rationalization can therefore be expected in the coming years, as can a slight reduction in the number of start-ups.

Research Centers

Paralleling the growth of new companies, numerous development projects were undertaken by the research centers over the years, concentrated in the areas of software, computer-aided design, geomatics, remote sensing, computer-assisted translation, and computer-aided learning. These projects were began in Gatineau in the early 1980s as a result of the awareness of the potential offered by the high technology sector spread among the SAO and a group of other regional stakeholders including the Quebec Ministry of Industry and Commerce, the Office de la planification et du développement du Québec (the former Quebec Social and Economic Development Planning Agency), the Conseil régional de développement de l'Outaouais (CRDO, the Outaouais Regional Development Council), the Université du Québec à Hull (UQAH), now Université du Québec en Outaouais (UQO), and the Collège de l'Outaouais.

Impetus for these projects came from the "technological orientation" of the Quebec government, which had created a Ministry of Science and Technology and had held regional socio-economic summits to which submissions could be made for project funding. The following are examples of projects that had an important impact on the Outaouais region and the City of Gatineau. They also illustrate the networking that developed between the companies and the research centers, as well as among the individuals involved in the field.

Centre d'excellence en télédétection (Center of Excellence in Remote Sensing) (from 1983 to 1989)

Also known by the name Qualimage, this Center was initially piloted (1983) by a company called Technologie des ordinateurs de l'Outaouais (TOO; Computer Technologies of Outaouais) and was later supported by the City of Gatineau and the SAO. The stimulus for it can be traced to the potential relocation to Gatineau of the Canada Centre for Remote Sensing (CCRS) and the strong possibility that businesses associated with CCRS would then be attracted to the Aéroparc in Gatineau. The project as such never came to fruition. However, after laying the groundwork over a period of several years, in the late 1980s the region saw the establishment in Cantley (near Gatineau) of a receiving station for the remote sensing satellite Radarsat.

Centre de logiciel de l'Outaouais (Outaouais Software Center) (from 1985 to 1989)

The Outaouais Software Center was set up by a group of organizations, comprising the SAO; a consortium of companies that included ACDS, CML Technologies, MOI Informatique and Crawley R&D; UQAH; and the Collège de l'Outaouais. The Center's business plan featured two main areas for development, computer-assisted translation and computer graphics. The Center focused on computer-assisted translation, despite its inherent promise, to concentrate on computer graphics. This paved the way for formation of the International Computer Graphics Research Center, a description of which follows.

Centre de recherche international en infographie (CIRI, the International Computer Graphics Research Center or ICGRC) (from 1989 to 1998)

ICGRC grew out of the Outaouais Software Center, and specialized in computer graphics, particularly spatial reference information systems (geomatics). It was founded by a group of companies including ACDS, C3I, Oracle and ADGA. Over the years, it received funding from CRDO and the Communauté urbaine de l'Outaouais (CUO, the Outaouais Urban Community) as well as from Hiérapolis. One of its mandates was to work with l'Agence de traitement de l'information numérique de l'Outaouais (l'ATINO, the Outaouais Digital Data Processing Corporation) on the development of an integrated multi-sector, multi-criteria decision-making system for regional management of the Outaouais.

In addition to this work, ICGRC was directly or indirectly involved between 1995 and 1998 in the management of major research projects in partnership with other local businesses (CubeWerx and NDI Datawarehouse). For example, one of these, known as the MERCATOR project, involved the Canadian Coast Guard and other federal government departments and aimed to develop electronic navigation charts.

Since 1998, the partners have gone in different directions. CubeWerx, for its part, joined forces with other partners to form the International Interoperability Institute (I3), a description of which follows. And in 1999, Ron Carrière, president of ICGRC/CIRI and former president of ACDS, set up Coredge, a new company specializing in knowledge management. In 2002, this company reclaimed the name CIRI and today is known as CIRI Lab.

Centre de développement d'Oracle (Oracle R&D Center) — NDI — CubeWerx (from 1983 to the present)

Oracle Corporation's world-class R&D center in Gatineau was dedicated to the development of a system of multi-dimensional (space and time) databases, which was a world first at the time. The Center operated for nearly 5 years, until the early 1990s. The product developed there was subsequently integrated into Oracle's standard products sold around the world.

After the closure, Oracle's workforce was absorbed by NDI Datawarehouse, a company specializing in the production of electronic marine charts. Eventually, NDI Datawarehouse was bought out in part by the former employees of Oracle who were working together at NDI. The result was the birth of CubeWerx, a company whose mission is developing "middleware" to allow the interconnection of proprietary data bases and GIS softwares. CubeWerx has become a world leader in this field.

Institut international d'interopérabilité (I3 or the International Interoperability Institute) (from 2000 to 2003)

The goal of I3 was to develop standards for interoperation between various proprietary geographic information systems, to act as coordinator of interoperability projects and to provide the necessary training. The Institute was set up by a group of 10 companies in Gatineau, including CubeWerx, PCI Geomatics and Holonics Data Management. The federal government departments of National Defence and Natural Resources Canada were also involved.

The Institute operated between 2000 and 2003 with funding provided by its members and by Canada Economic Development. However, it was unable to achieve a sustainable level of self-funding to continue its operations under the existing structure. As a result of the implementation of projects under the federal Geo-Connections program, there was an increase in the number of interoperability projects, but the Institute was unable to take advantage of these opportunities because of various jurisdictional issues and it closed. However, companies that had been involved in I3 such as CubeWerx, Holonics and PCI are still very active in these areas.

Hiérapolis (from 1994 to 1998)

The Hiérapolis project followed on the heels of the trail-blazing OCRINet in Ottawa, the first urban broadband network connectivity project in Canada. Its mission was to establish a similar network in Gatineau, the first regional information highway in Quebec. Once established, the broadband network linked scores of institutions in Gatineau, spurring the development of software tools and content by businesses in the region.

Hiérapolis was piloted by the CUO (and its 5 cities) in cooperation with Digital Equipment Canada (DEC), Vidéotron, a multi-media research center at the Canadian Museum of Civilization, and various companies from inside and outside the region.

Nearly $15 million was invested in the infrastructure and the development of applications and content. Financing was provided by Quebec's Fonds d'autoroute de l'information (Information Highway Fund of Quebec), the CUO, the CRDO, the Federal Office for Regional Development — Quebec (FORD-Q), and participating companies. The pilot project ended in 1998. Since then, there has been a wide-scale commercial introduction of broadband networks and services by the telecommunication companies.

Centre de recherche en technologies langagieres (Language Technologies Research Center (from 2003 to 2005)

Plans to create the Language Technologies Research Center, at a cost of some $15 million, were announced in 2003. Implementation is already underway and will continue during the next 2 years with the construction of a building on the UQO campus. The new Research Center is the result of a partnership between the National Research Council of Canada, the Translation Bureau of Canada, UQO and the Association de l'industrie linguistique/Language Industry Association (AILIA) of Canada. Its purpose is to develop leading-edge technologies in the areas of computer-assisted translation and text localization. The Center will also offer space for incubation projects to foster start-ups.

Creation of the new Language Technologies Research Center marks for the first time that many federal research organizations have been involved in establishing a research center of this magnitude in Gatineau. This is the culmination of a long process in which there have been some successful projects and others that were failures. The process is an ongoing one, and other projects are under discussion with the federal government, which could improve the balance of the technological infrastructure between the two sides of the Ottawa River.

Of course, various federal departments and agencies have been involved with Gatineau companies in other projects related, for example, to geomatics and remote sensing. And this is very important for accelerating high tech development in the Quebec part of Silicon Valley North, because the federal government is a major producer of scientific research, as well as an eager client for new technologies.

Conclusion

Therefore, Gatineau companies are experiencing growth in the same fields that have given Ottawa its strength (e.g. telecommunication software) and they are integrated with the clusters in Ottawa. In addition, a mini-cluster in digital imaging is emerging in Gatineau and there is potential for another cluster in linguistics technology, as the result of an investment of nearly $15 million to be made by the National Research Council (NRC) of Canada in partnership with the Université du Québec en Outaouais (UQO).

With most cluster-type development models, success is clearly often due to the presence of universities with science and engineering programs and associated research laboratories. At present, the regional university, UQO, located in Gatineau, has three programs: two in computer science and one in computer engineering, including telecommunications applications. UQO plans to launch a biology curriculum within a few years.

The involvement of UQO professors in strategic developmental research projects is increasing every year. For example, an optoelectronics laboratory is up and running at UQO, as is a cyber-psychology laboratory. The new Language Technologies Research Center is expected to open soon. Advanced research is also being done in the areas of telecommunication software and robotics.

UQO, however, is by far the smallest amongst the universities in the National Capital Region, and the government of Quebec will have to invest substantial amounts to encourage the development of new study programs in science and engineering capable of accelerating the long-term technological development of the region. Further joint initiatives between UQO and the federal research centers to establish new laboratories will also stimulate technological development through pooling of researchers and professors, as well as sharing of infrastructure and supporting equipment.

Acknowledgments

I am grateful to Diana Trafford for her assistance in translating my chapter from French into English. The Université du Québec en Outaouais financial support for her work is also gratefully acknowledged.

References

Conseil de la Science et de la Technologie du Québec (2001). *2001 situation report: The regional dimensions of innovation in Québec*, English summary, March. Available at http://www.cst. gouv.qc.ca.

Materazzi, F. (2002). *Portrait technologique de l'outaouais* [Technological Portrait of the Outaoauis, May, in French only). Gatineau, Que., Canada: F. M. Consult.

Materazzi, F. (2003). *Bref historique des activités de R&D privées et publiques dans l'outaouais 1980–2003* [Brief History of Private and Public R&D Activities in the Outaouais 1980–2003, in French only]. Gatineau, Que., Canada: F. M. Consult.

Statistics Canada (2001). *Census 2001*. Ottawa, Ont., Canada: Statistics Canada.

Chapter 12

Developing Knowledge Workers in Silicon Valley North: It Is Not Just About Training

Lorraine Dyke, Linda Duxbury and Natalie Lam

Abstract

Effective career development practices can contribute to employee recruitment, reten-tion and productivity. Using data from interviews with 110 key personnel and surveys completed by 1509 knowledge workers in Silicon Valley North, this chapter explores the need for employee development, what employees want from their careers, key employee development strategies, tailoring the development approach and developing managers who develop people. A variety of initiatives are recommended which go beyond simply providing training. Key strategies include fostering a sense of accom-plishment, providing stimulating work, developing breadth and supporting learning. The specific development needs of employees with different career orientations are also explored.

Introduction

Silicon Valley North is a highly stressful competitive environment. The information tech-nology industry is in constant flux. Challenges include the new global business environment of stronger competition, downsizing, customers requiring new levels of quality, and reduced product cycle times (Donnelly *et al.* 1993). These challenges are made more complex by the fact that the industry has experienced both rapid expansion and rapid contraction in recent years.

The instability in the industry poses significant challenges for managers. As information technology providers scramble to keep up with these changes, they are also wrestling with people issues that add another layer of complexity to the problem (Cross 1999). While many people view high-tech companies as "docking stations for techies who follow their own drummers," the reality is that these organizations are mired in the same management, people and organizational problems that affect any company or institution (Cross 1999: 50).

The challenges these organizations face include selecting, developing and retaining a workforce that can meet constantly changing requirements while sustaining the company's market or its culture.

This chapter examines a critical aspect of talent management: developing knowledge workers in this turbulent environment. Developing employees benefits both employees and the organization. Developing employees enhances employee job satisfaction and organizational commitment resulting in a reduction of turnover. It also helps to ensure that employees have the skills to face new challenges that arise from the rapid pace of change.

The high tech industry is characterized by cycles of boom and bust. The information and communication technologies industry was slower than other industries to recover from the recession of the early 1990s (Vaillancourt 2003). Then from 1996 to 2000, employment in this sector grew four times faster than in the economy as a whole (49% compared to 11%; Bowlby & Langlois 2002). In 2001, a downturn hit the computer and telecommunications sector causing employment in this sector to fall by 10% in one year (Bowlby 2003) while the rest of the economy grew slightly (a net gain of 0.7%; Bowlby & Langlois 2002). Employment in the sector appeared to stabilize starting in 2002 but turmoil and restructuring continued (Bowlby 2003). Year to year comparisons hide significant shifts in employment patterns. Employment has fluctuated up and down significantly since the 2001 peak (Software Human Resources Council 2003; Wolfson 2003). Restructuring has resulted in a continuing decline in high tech employment for the lowest skilled workers while employment for higher skilled workers (technical employees, managers and professionals) has stabilized and for some groups improved since 2002 (Bowlby 2003).

Fluctuating employment levels pose significant challenges for high tech managers trying to supply the right talent at the right time. Canadian employers have had to compete openly for recruits (Gower 1998). A survey of employers in the computer systems design industry during the 2000 boom found a vacancy rate of 12% with over one third of vacancies having been unfilled for 4 months or more (O'Grady 2002). Ottawa-Gatineau has the highest concentration of information technology specialists in Canada (Habtu 2003). In Silicon Valley North, high tech employment fluctuated from a high of 68,500 in March 2001 to a low of 47,400 in July 2002. By the beginning of 2003, employment in Silicon Valley North had rebounded to 58,700 but within 10 months, it had fallen again to 48,000 (Labour Force Survey 2003). In-depth analysis of recent labour force data show that high tech firms have been laying off thousands of manufacturing and clerical staff while recruiting large numbers of engineers, engineering technicians, computer programmers and systems analysts (Bowlby 2003). This recent recruiting of knowledge workers is taking place at a time when many have grown skeptical about the career potential of the industry.

Finding qualified, well-trained IT personnel is a huge challenge for many tech companies; keeping them is often an even greater one (Gionfriddo & Dhingra 1999). The high tech sector has experienced high turnover in recent years, estimated by some to be as common in this sector as "flipping on a computer" (Hein 1998). In quantifiable terms, members of the industry have estimated the attrition rate to be as high as 40% (Hein 1998). As competitive pressures continue, high technology companies will need to devote considerable effort to recruiting the right mix of staff and retaining key staff.

Research would suggest that organizations who are interested in recruiting, retaining and motivating knowledge workers need to pay attention to their career development and career

management practices. To make career development programs and initiatives more meaningful to knowledge workers in Silicon Valley North, we first need to have a comprehensive
understanding of their career goals and aspirations and their career management strategies.
We need to know what development strategies work and which do not. We need to know if
different groups of employees have different needs and career aspirations. Unfortunately
human resource practitioners and organizations who are interested in addressing this issue
will find little relevant empirical data on these issues to guide their decision making. The
research summarized in this chapter provides a significant step forward in this direction.

The data in this chapter come from a major study, conducted in the fall of 1999, on the
career development of knowledge workers in Silicon Valley North.[1] This research was done
in association with 7 of the 10 largest high tech companies based in the National Capital Region of Canada (i.e. Ottawa, Kanata, Nepean). The objectives of this study were to identify:

- the career goals and aspirations of knowledge workers in Silicon Valley North;
- the strategies employees in this sector use to develop their careers;
- what these employees perceive that their organization has done to help or hinder their
  career development;
- changes that would make it easier for knowledge workers in Silicon Valley North to meet
  their career development goals; and
- the consequences of inaction in this area (especially with respect to intent to turnover).

A study on career development in the high tech sector is highly relevant as there is little
empirical data on career development practices in this critical sector of the economy. The
empirical data presented in this chapter should be of value to all stakeholders in the career
development of knowledge workers in the high tech sector: managers, employees, and
human resource practitioners.

Overview of the Research

The data reported in this chapter comes from two sources:

- Semi-structured telephone interviews, which were conducted with 110 knowledge
  workers who had been identified by the seven participating high tech companies as "key
  personnel."
- A random sample of 1,509 knowledge workers from Silicon Valley North (representing 6
  high tech companies) who were surveyed regarding career aspirations, career strategies,
  work attitudes and behaviours, and work history.

This chapter uses the data from these studies to paint a "broad brush" picture of how
technology companies can develop their knowledge workers. Readers who are interested
in examining the data in greater depth should consult Duxbury *et al.* (2000).

---

[1] Those interested in the full report are referred to Duxbury, Dyke & Lam (2000).

Interview Methodology

A semi-structured interview was developed to explore the issues outlined above. Career development is a complex process with many variables playing a potential role. Interviews provide the opportunity to gather in-depth and detailed information about complex subjects by making it possible for the researchers to seek clarification on a particular response and probe with additional questions. Such flexibility ensures that complex information is not lost. This format was also chosen not to limit analyses to categories that were defined a priori.

After completion of the first 20 interviews, audiotapes were reviewed and a coding scheme was developed using content analysis which is the measurement of the semantic content (the what) of the information. The coding scheme consisted of categories of responses for each question which could be rated as present or absent for each participant. The preliminary coding scheme was then applied to 30 different interviews by a coder. In ambiguous cases the coder recorded the responses verbatim and discussed them with one of the principal investigators. Ambiguities were resolved by clarification of decision rules. The remainder of the tapes were then coded. Coders were monitored through regular meetings, spot-checking of tapes and availability to consult on coding questions.

A short (four-page) survey was designed to collect demographic information (age, gender, marital status, education etc.) and career histories (job type, jobs since graduation, promotions, time in work etc.) from interview participants. This survey was sent to participants prior to their interview. To ensure participant confidentiality, identification numbers were used to link survey responses to the interviews.

Survey Methodology

The questionnaire was developed using measures employed in previous research wherever possible. These were supplemented and refined following pretesting. In selecting measures for inclusion in the questionnaire, we tried to limit the questionnaire length while also exploring fully each of the study's objectives. The result was a 14-page questionnaire including sections on work background, career aspirations, work environment, work attitudes and behaviours, work and personal life, and demographics.

The sample was drawn in a manner similar to that used to select participants for the interview study. Six of the 10 largest high tech organizations in the National Capital Region participated in the survey. Each organization sent questionnaires to all of their knowledge workers. This sampling procedure resulted in a sample of 4100. A total of 1509 questionnaires were returned resulting in an overall response rate of 37%. The number of companies participating and the high response rate overall provide some confidence in generalizing the results to Silicon Valley North as a whole.

The Interview Sample

Not surprisingly, given how this sample was selected, almost two-thirds of the employees who participated in the interviews (63% of the total sample) supervised the work of others (i.e. held a management position). The 32% who were not managers all held professional positions (e.g. systems analysts, programmers, marketers, systems designers, project managers). Almost all of the respondents (97%) had a post-secondary education with 64% holding at least one university degree.

The "key" personnel who participated in the interviews had, on average, 14 years of work experience. They had typically worked for 3 different employers. They had been employed by their current organization for an average of 6.6 years and in their current position for 2 years.

Three quarters of the sample were male. The majority were in their 30's (52% were 30–39, 31% were over 40, and 18% were under 30). A large majority (79%) of interviewees were married. In addition, 51% had children and 15% had elder care responsibilities.

The Survey Sample

A majority of survey respondents (58%) reported working in the area of product development, engineering or programming. The next largest group of respondents (13%) worked in technical support or customer support. Thirty-one percent of those surveyed managed the work of others. The respondents were a highly educated group with 97% having had some post-secondary education; most (66%), a university degree.

Survey respondents had an average of 12 years of full-time work experience with 75% of that occurring within the high tech sector. On average they had worked for 4 different employers and had been with their current organization for 5.5 years. Respondents had spent an average of 2 years in their current position.

The survey sample was also predominantly male (67%). The average age of respondents was 36. Most employees in the sample had some family responsibilities: 73% were married, 50% had children, and 15% reported some elder care responsibilities.

The demographics (age and gender) of both the survey sample and the interview sample mirror data on the information technology labour force as a whole (Habtu 2003). One key difference is that the samples reported on here are more highly educated than the information technology labour force as a whole (Habtu 2003). This difference reflects the explicit focus of this research on knowledge workers.

The Need for Employee Development

Most writers on career development now recommend that responsibility for employee career development be shared between employer and employee. While two-thirds of the high tech employees who participated in this research espoused this view, only one-quarter believed it actually happens. Most respondents (59%) said that within their organization the responsibility for their career development rests with the employee.

The data suggest that most high tech companies cannot be considered best practice with respect to career development. Only a third of survey respondents felt that their organization supported their career development. In the interviews, only one in seven "key" employees felt that their department supported their career development; 25% felt that their department did *nothing* to support them with respect to the achievement of their career aspirations and goals. Similar attitudes were expressed with respect to the organization overall. Only one in four "key" employees felt that their organization supported their career development; 20% felt that their organization did *nothing* to support them with respect to the achievement of their career aspirations and goals. This lack of career support was a significant source of frustration for one in six "key" personnel. One in four "key" employees said the fact that their company did not offer any career development programs (either formally or informally) had made career development harder for them. When asked what piece of advice they would offer their company with respect to the issue of career development, one-third of the "key" employees asked their company to establish good career development initiatives.

While the evidence would suggest that many high tech companies do not take on shared responsibility for the career development of their knowledge workers, other data indicates that this is not due to a lack of interest or demand on the part of the employees. Rather, the data indicate that many high tech employees have given considerable thought to what they want to achieve and are quite proactive in developing their careers. The majority of the survey respondents have career goals and have engaged in career planning.

The interview data would suggest that employees have responded to this lack of organizational support by taking personal control of their career development and doing it on their own (i.e. sidelining the organization). The down side of this approach from the organization's point of view is that it is associated with diminished employee loyalty and commitment and with higher turnover. As shown in Table 1, supervisory career support and organizational career support are more highly correlated than salary with satisfaction with career, job satisfaction, organizational commitment, thoughts of leaving the organization and intent to turnover.

These data would suggest that many Silicon Valley North companies need to implement more effective career development programs. For some high tech employers this may require developing new initiatives, for others it may require that existing programs be formalized or redesigned to better meet the needs of employees. The interview and survey data give us some idea of what types of programs need to be developed and/or improved in Silicon Valley North companies. The remainder of this chapter examines what high tech employees want in their careers, key employee development strategies, tailoring the development approach and developing managers who develop people.

Table 1: Career support, salary and attitudes.

Attitudes	Supervisory Support	Organizational Support	Salary
Satisfaction with career	0.401***	0.341***	0.162***
Job satisfaction	0.486***	0.441***	n.s.
Organizational commitment	0.379***	0.412***	−0.053*
Have thought about leaving	−0.248***	−0.271***	0.120***
Intent to turnover	−0.432***	−0.397***	n.s.

What High Tech Employees Want in Their Careers

In order to provide appropriate support to employee career development it is important to understand employees' goals. One study of career management practices found that where there was a match between individual and organizational career plans, employees were over 3 times more likely to be satisfied and over 5 times less likely to look for work elsewhere (Granrose & Portwood 1987). Since turnover is costly, understanding employees' career goals has financial as well as organizational benefits. To gain an understanding of what high tech employees want from their careers, the interviews and surveys explored how knowledge workers in Silicon Valley North define success, what achievements they value, what their career goals are and what developmental opportunities they seek.

The Meaning of Success in the High Tech Sector

Media reports have often focused on the substantial salaries of high tech workers giving the impression that money is a key measure of success in this sector. But "career success" means different things to different people. This diversity of values was as evident in the high tech sector as elsewhere.

In the interviews, key high tech personnel were asked how they define career success. Just over half of the sample (54%) defined career success as satisfaction (e.g. being happy in the job). Almost half of the sample (45%) defined career success in terms of recognition (i.e. extrinsic rewards — money, "fame," and recognition). The third most important theme, learning, was chosen by a significantly smaller proportion (26%) of the sample.

In the survey, high tech employees were given a forced choice between two definitions of success. Specifically the survey asked respondents to indicate on a 4-point scale (with no midpoint) whether their personal definition of career success focuses on "financial rewards and influence" or "personal satisfaction and respect." The results indicated that:

- personal satisfaction and respect was more important to 68% of respondents; and
- financial rewards and influence were the primary focus of 32% of respondents.

The Achievements That Technology Workers Value

To further assess high tech workers' definitions of success, survey respondents were asked to indicate how important 15 different achievements were to their personal definitions of success. The achievements most important to employees' personal definitions of success (chosen by at least 80% of respondents) were:

- doing work that is enjoyable (important to 97%);
- a personal sense of accomplishment (94%);
- being able to learn and develop new skills (92%);
- a salary that provides a comfortable lifestyle (90%); and
- balance between work and non-work life (83%).

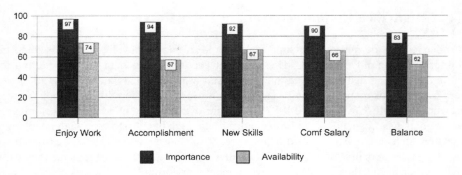

Figure 1: Importance and availability of achievements. *Note:* Reprinted with permission from Carswell Press.

Respondents were also asked to indicate whether or not these 15 achievements were available to them in their work. On average, there was a gap of 16% between the percentage of respondents indicating that an achievement was important to them and the percentage reporting that it was available to them. As portrayed in Figure 1, these gaps were even greater for the 5 achievements identified as most important. The gaps for these 5 achievements averaged 26% with the largest gap related to the achievement of a personal sense of accomplishment (a gap of 37%). Since a personal sense of accomplishment was number two on employees' ranking of important achievements, this is an issue which high tech companies need to address if they hope to better meet employees' needs.

High Tech Employees' Career Goals

Key personnel who were interviewed for this research were also asked about their career goals over the medium-term. Respondents had the following career aspirations over the next five years:

* 33% indicated that they saw themselves in some form of management position;
* 25% described their goal in terms of progress (succession up the ranks, some job that builds on this one, a clear step up, more responsibility);
* 20% described their goals in intrinsic terms (a job I enjoy, that yields satisfaction, enhances my skills, lets me learn, have influence, make a contribution);
* 19% said they aspired to be in some other area of interest (e.g. more technical, more product related, another department of interest);
* 13% mentioned some specific position or job title that they aspired to;
* 10% said that in five years they expected to own their own company; and
* 7% saw themselves in senior management.

Only 5% of respondents mentioned leaving the high tech field suggesting that "key" Silicon Valley North personnel see themselves as remaining in this sector in the medium term. No one in this group mentioned that they expected to move to the U.S. in the next five years.

The Most Desired Career Opportunities

In addition to examining high tech workers' medium-term career goals, the survey also explored what career opportunities they aspired to over the short-term. Respondents were asked how likely it was that they would take advantage of 13 different career opportunities if they were offered to them. The work opportunities, which employees wanted most, were:

- a challenging new assignment (sought by 84%);
- a special work opportunity (74%);
- advancement (72%);
- intensive training funded by their employer (71%);
- an opportunity to be mentored (59%); and
- greater opportunity to interact with senior management (55%).

Their interest in these career-enhancing experiences far outpaced their interest in reducing their work involvement through leaves of absence (20%) or a reduced work week (27%).

To determine whether or not these Silicon Valley North employees were in fact receiving these opportunities, survey respondents were also asked whether they had experienced any of these career-enhancing opportunities. These developmental experiences are the experiences that help employees to grow in knowledge and skills, thus making them more valuable employees and expanding their career options. Respondents were asked whether they had experienced eight possible developmental opportunities over the preceding two years. Table 2 shows the percentage of respondents interested in each of these opportunities followed by the percentage who had experienced them over the past two years and the gap between the two percentages.

Table 2: Opportunities desired and experienced.

Opportunities Desired and Experienced	Desired (%)	Experienced (%)	Gap (%)
A new assignment that challenges me	84	52	32
A special work opportunity	74	32	42
Advancement to a higher position	72	37	35
An opportunity for intensive training funded by my employer	71	19	52
Opportunity to be mentored by a more senior employee	59	15	44
Greater opportunity to interact with senior management	55	23	32
The opportunity to help younger employees develop professionally	47	40	7
A parallel assignment	46	33	13

Note: Reprinted with permission from Carswell Press.

As Table 2 shows, only one developmental opportunity had been experienced by a majority of respondents — a challenging assignment (52%). The next most common experiences were the opportunity to help younger employees develop professionally (40%), and advancement (37%). The opportunities that had been experienced by the fewest respondents were being mentored (15%) and intensive training funded by their employer (19%). There are particularly large gaps between the number of employees desiring vs. experiencing: intensive training (52% gap), mentoring (44% gap), special work opportunities (42% gap), and advancement (35% gap).

Key Employee Development Strategies

The achievements and opportunities that study participants aspire to point to important ways for high tech organizations to better develop their employees. By tailoring their employee development strategies to employees' values and goals, organizations can make more efficient use of development resources and enhance employee satisfaction and commitment. Four key strategies are discussed below: fostering a sense of accomplishment, providing stimulating work, developing breadth and supporting learning.

Fostering a Sense of Accomplishment

The survey data indicate that while obtaining a sense of accomplishment from one's work is of key importance to knowledge workers in Silicon Valley North (94% said this was important), for many this need is not being met (37% of the sample). "Key" employees also place a high value on a sense of accomplishment with half of the respondents in this group saying that they would consider themselves to be successful in their career if others recognized that they did their job well.

Based on these data, it would appear that high tech companies need to do a better job of providing opportunities for employees to experience a personal sense of accomplishment from their work. Recognition from one's immediate manager is key to experiencing a personal sense of accomplishment. To facilitate this, managers should be given training on how to give and receive feedback. Organizations should make employees more aware of existing recognition and awards programs. They should also find new ways to provide recognition for work accomplishments. Finally, companies in this sector should review salaries, especially within the non-management ranks since concerns about salary are often about recognition.

Providing Stimulating Work

Many Silicon Valley North workers appear to be "adrenaline junkies" in that they thrive on constant challenge and the fast pace of change within the sector. A significant proportion of the people who are attracted to jobs in high technology thrive on change. One third of the "key" respondents found the fast pace of the high tech sector to be rewarding (it's exciting, it's a "rush"); 20% said that the diversity and variety of work in the sector ("lots of opportunities here"; "love the complexity") was, for them, the most rewarding aspect of working in the high tech sector. For this group, working in an exciting, fast moving, ever-changing work environment is stimulating and challenging.

Not all high tech employees find the fast pace of change rewarding but a majority do value being challenged. Over 80% of survey respondents said that they wanted a challenging assignment. Unfortunately, just over half felt that they had been given such an assignment (a gap of 32%). This large gap is reflected in respondents' intent to turnover. Seventy-six percent of employees in the sample had thought about leaving their organization. The two main reasons were to earn a higher salary and to engage in more interesting work. Almost two-thirds (63%) of the survey respondents who said they had considered leaving their current organization attributed this decision to the lack of stimulating and challenging work in their present organization.

In the interviews, approximately one third of "key" employees said that they were contemplating leaving their current organization because their present job was not challenging enough and did not offer any opportunities for growth. This group indicated that they would reconsider and stay with their current company if the right project came along — something that interested and challenged them.

To provide challenge to employees, managers need to understand the skills and aspirations of individual subordinates. Managers should regularly discuss employee assignments and aspirations with each subordinate. Requiring managers to conduct semi-annual development reviews with their staff is one way to formalize this process. Many managers will require training to effectively execute these responsibilities.

Empowering knowledge workers and involving them in the decision-making process can make work both more challenging and meaningful. Assignments can be made more challenging for employees by giving employees as much autonomy as possible. The opportunity to interact with those above them in the organization (e.g. sit in on meetings, or a task force) can expand employees' experience. High potential employees can be offered the opportunity to act as a group or team leader to stretch their abilities. Stretch assignments, which require employees to develop new skills, are particularly welcome to many Silicon Valley North workers.

The interview data indicate that some of the things that make a work environment stimulating are the fast pace, the diversity and variety of work, and being in a "growth" department (as opposed to working in a department which is in a steady-state or shrinking). This suggests that Silicon Valley North employers rotate employees between assignments. This increases variety and challenge. In addition, rotating employees between growth departments, and smaller, more specialized departments will provide more employees with the opportunity to experience the "high" of working in a growth area.

Developing Breadth

Both the interview and survey data indicate that "breadth" of knowledge and experience seems to be one of the most important determinants of career advancement and career success in Silicon Valley North. Breadth, as defined by participants in this study includes more job-related experience in the high tech sector, more lateral moves both within the organization and between organizations to increase experience, movement to a different department, working in a number of different departments or companies, broadening one's expertise, formal training programs and learning on the job. Employees with a wide variety of job-related experience in the information technology area are more likely than those with relatively little relevant job experience to be considered "key personnel" by their organization. Managers in both samples, had more job-related experience in the high tech sector, and had made more lateral moves, both within their organization and between organizations. Thus both sets of data suggest a strong link between breadth and career success in the high tech sector.

Not surprisingly, given the above data, many individuals in this sector equate career development and career success with the acquisition of breadth. "Key" employees, for example, advised colleagues who were interested in either career development or advancement to "increase their breadth of knowledge and skills." Forty percent of the employees in this group had themselves employed such a strategy. The importance of breadth to career development is further illustrated by the survey finding that managers, departments and the organization were considered supportive of employees' careers if they helped employees acquire breadth. In addition, one in five "key" employees felt that their organization supported career development by facilitating the acquisition of breadth.

Unfortunately, while increasing one's "breadth" and knowledge seems to be critical to career development in this sector (and a key career development strategy used by high tech employees), the majority of the employees in both samples felt that they were not receiving help in this regard. Even the "key" employees who participated in the interview study felt that they were not getting the kinds of opportunities they needed to increase their breadth; only one-third of "key" employees felt their supervisors were helping them acquire the breadth they needed to advance; only 15% felt either their department or their organization was helping them to broaden their experience.

These data suggest that career development programs in the high tech sector should be designed to increase and showcase employees' breadth. Our recommendations with respect to breadth are based on the suggestions given by employees in the interviews. First and foremost, high technology companies need to develop a compensation system, which recognizes and rewards breadth as well as depth. While in-depth knowledge of technologies is important, many opportunities for technology and employee development can be facilitated through cross-fertilization. The high tech sector has a need for both in-depth knowledge and breadth amongst its knowledge workers. Recruitment, development strategies and compensation should reflect that need. To increase employees' breadth, high tech organizations should provide opportunities and support (i.e. give time and funding) for the following types of career development activities:

- educational leave;
- technical and managerial training;
- lateral movement within the organization (i.e. permit and encourage movement between jobs and departments);
- cross functional/cross department contacts (i.e. committees, tasks forces, social events);
- on-the job learning; and
- mentoring.

The data would suggest that mobility is one way that high tech employees acquire breath and job experience. Both the interview data (years in current organization, lateral moves) and the survey data (percent making a lateral move) indicate that employees (especially managers and "key" employees) in the high tech sector are very mobile. Mobility within this sector takes many forms: between companies and within the company; within a function and between functions (note that the movement between functions appears to occur more frequently than movement between companies). Why do high tech employees make lateral moves? The data suggest that the decision to change jobs or companies is part of a career development strategy and is undertaken with the objective of gaining breadth (i.e. enhancing skills, exposure) which is, in turn, seen as increasing the likelihood that one will be promoted. The data also suggests that this type of strategy does indeed seem to work: managers in both samples were more likely than non-managers to have made lateral moves; virtually all those in the "key" employee sample had made lateral moves and those who were promoted in the last 5 years were more likely than those who had not been promoted to have made a lateral move within a function.

Given the importance of mobility within the sector, high tech companies who wish to retain key employees need to design programs, which facilitate movement *within* their organization. Consequently, we would recommend that high tech companies make it easier for employees to make lateral moves by identifying some of the most likely lateral moves both within and between departments. Employers need to identify viable cross-functional career paths and make the information on these career paths easily accessible to employees. Organizations can also facilitate movement between departments and functions by giving employees cross-training and making them aware of what types of tasks and functions are being done within the organization. In conjunction, employers should establish an accountability framework so that employees, who want to move within the organization, are not prevented from doing so by managers who do not want to lose valuable human resources. These strategies should help to validate lateral moves. Given the reality of flatter organizations, the high tech sector needs to help employees see that up is not the only way to go. Lateral moves should also help to satisfy employees' needs for new challenges and learning opportunities.

Supporting Learning

Within the high tech sector, educational attainment appears to be positively associated with the acquisition of breadth, career development and advancement. Almost half of the "key" employees interviewed said their career development strategy was to increase the amount of formal education they had by joining a specific program such as a high tech MBA, a management program, or an advanced technical degree. One third of "key" employees linked education and training to career development. Within this group, one-third advocated independent learning (people within this group saw keeping on top of the technology to be critically important), one third advocated training, and one third felt that degrees counted and that employees who were interested in advancement should increase the amount of formal education they had. Just over a quarter of the "key" employees defined career success as being related to learning.

The data also show a strong link between organizational support of education and training and the belief that the organization supports career development. For example, one third of "key" respondents felt that their organization supported career development by supporting education and training. Although there appears to be a consensus within both data sets that education is key to career development within this sector, the data also shows that many organizations are not providing the desired support in this area. For example, one in ten "key" respondents said that their organization made it harder for employees to develop their career by not supporting training or education (e.g. no time off, no tuition support). While almost three quarters of survey respondents desired intensive training funded by their employer, only 19% had actually received such an opportunity (a gap of 52% between what was desired and what was experienced). The opportunity for continuous training and education is critical in a sector where the absence of such learning often leads to obsolescence. Unfortunately, the data would suggest that such opportunities are simply not available in many of the high tech organizations which participated in this study.

We recommend that Silicon Valley North organizations establish supportive policies around education, training and learning. By this we mean:

- employees should be given time off for education and training;
- employees should be given funding for education and training (e.g. tuition reimbursement, money to attend conferences); and
- employees who successfully complete additional education or training should receive some sort of recognition upon completion.

In addition, high tech companies should establish an accountability framework to encourage the support and use of these programs and policies. This will force managers to ensure that learning is not displaced by pressures for current results.

In addition to formal learning, the data would suggest that the opportunity to learn on the job is critically important to a substantial number of knowledge workers in the high tech sector. A number of indicators point to this conclusion. One in ten "key" employees said that they felt they had achieved career success because their job offered them the chance to learn. One in four "key" employees stated that the opportunities they had to learn new skills were, for them, the most rewarding aspect of working in high tech sector. Half of the "key" employees indicated that they would leave their current organization for a job that challenged them and provided them with the opportunity to learn. High tech companies should accommodate their employees' desire to learn from and be challenged by their work by implementing job rotation schemes (which would also satisfy the need for mobility), increasing employee contact with the client, and making more use of cross-functional and self-directed work teams.

While the ability to learn and develop new skills was very important to most of the study participants, the data would suggest that not all are able to turn to their organization for support in this regard. In fact, just over one-third of the interview sample stated that they had developed their careers by engaging in independent learning. The independent learning strategies described including reading books, trade magazines and journals. Technology companies can facilitate this kind of learning by making recent journal articles, trade magazines, learning CDs and the like readily available within the work setting.

Reimbursing employees for subscriptions to relevant trade magazines and journals would also be helpful.

Organizations that engage in a variety of strategies to support learning are likely to best satisfy employee development needs. Similarly, a variety of strategies are helpful in fostering a sense of accomplishment, providing stimulating work, and developing breadth amongst employees. While organizations may be tempted to focus on only a small number of development initiatives, this would be a mistake. Despite widespread agreement amongst knowledge workers that opportunities to experience a sense of accomplishment, challenge, and learning are important, there is significant variation in the specific goals knowledge workers seek to attain. One size does not fit all. To provide successful development for all requires a tailoring of strategies to meet the needs of quite different groups of employees. The next section examines some important differences between subgroups of knowledge workers.

Tailoring the Development Approach

Career goals and career development needs are affected by a variety of factors. There are significant differences, for example, in the career experiences of managers and non-managers, women and men, and younger and older employees. While the scope of this chapter does not permit an analysis of all of these relevant differences,[2] we want to examine two important differences that affect career development needs: differences in definitions of success and in career orientations.

Two Distinct Approaches to Success

The data from both the interview and survey studies suggest that there is no one common view of career success held by high tech workers. Nor do all knowledge workers have the same aspirations. The research indicates that approximately one-third of the study participants hold "traditional" definitions of career success while the rest espouse newer, more dynamic and holistic definitions.

Those with "traditional" definitions of career success define success in terms of career progress, upward progression, recognition (rewards, fame) and increased financial rewards. The aspirations of employees in this group are positional (e.g. want to be in a management or senior management position) and progression related (succession up the ranks, more responsibility). Employees in this group define satisfaction with career progress in terms of visible progress, financial rewards, and "getting the position they aspired to" (i.e. I'm where I want to be, I've proven that I can meet my goals by getting this job, I have influence, I make a difference in this position).

Those with more holistic views of career success define success in terms of satisfaction with the work they do, a personal sense of accomplishment, a chance to make a contribution,

---

[2] Those interested in gender, age, and job type differences should see Duxbury *et al.* (2000).

successful work-life balance and being able to learn and develop new skills. The aspirations of this group revolve around job satisfaction (i.e. want to be in a job I enjoy), feeling a sense of accomplishment, being in a position where they can learn something new, doing a job that makes a technical contribution and recognition from peers. Employees in this group define satisfaction with career progress in terms of personal accomplishment, self-esteem, learning, doing work they like, being challenged, and interacting with stimulating people who share their technical interests. Employees with holistic views of success feel rewarded when they experience a sense of accomplishment, a chance to make a contribution, challenging and stimulating work, positive interactions with colleagues and a chance to learn.

Supporting Traditional Definitions of Success

The data would suggest that those with traditional definitions of career success are more likely than their "holistic" colleagues to find fulfilment within Silicon Valley North. The data indicates that this sector seems to do a reasonably good job of satisfying those people who define success as increasing financial rewards, movement through positions of increasing responsibility and being in a position of authority. The data would, however, indicate that even some employees with traditional definitions of success are having difficulty fulfilling two aspirations: a salary that provides a comfortable life style (gap 24%) and influence over the organization's direction (gap of 32%).

Generally speaking, knowledge workers in Silicon Valley North appear to be well paid. The average survey respondent earned just under $68,000 (managers averaged $87,000 while non-managers averaged $59,000). Medical plans, dental plans, life insurance and vacation time were virtually universally available. Some employees also had available to them a company investment plan, bonuses, a stock purchase plan and tuition reimbursement. In the survey, 53% of respondents reported being satisfied with their salary. At the same time, 76% of those who had considered leaving their organization reported that a higher salary was one of the reasons they had considered employment elsewhere. One quarter of the "key" employees said that they remained in the high tech sector because of the compensation (good pay and benefits); the same group said that they would leave their current organization for better compensation elsewhere and that they could be induced to stay where they were by an increase in compensation (e.g. a raise, a bonus, stocks).

The data identified 3 groups of workers who are more likely to leave for increased compensation: non-managers, younger employees, and employees who do not find their job rewarding (i.e. no sense of achievement from work, work not challenging). These data would suggest that high tech firms need to review salaries for the non-management group to ensure compensation reflects market values and to ensure, in particular, that compensation reflects knowledge, skills and abilities rather than age or other demographic differences. For some employees, concerns with salary seem to reflect concerns about recognition and contribution. For this group, ensuring that they are appropriately challenged and recognized for their contributions to the organization may help to alleviate some of their dissatisfaction with salary.

The other major gap identified for those with traditional definitions of success was influencing organizational direction. For these employees, increased autonomy and involvement in the organization's decision-making process is important.

Supporting Holistic Definitions of Success

Career development practices in most organizations reflect traditional assumptions of success. Organizations in Silicon Valley North need to develop different types of career development programs to accommodate those with different definitions of success, career aspirations and career orientations. High tech companies need to redefine "career success" to include traditional and non-traditional career paths and career aspirations. This re-definition should include changes to the compensation system (i.e. compensation should be attached to breadth, mentoring, coaching, and specialization as well as upward progression) and greater employee choice of career paths.

Unfortunately, this research indicates that current high tech career development practices and work cultures do not satisfy employees with more holistic definitions of career success (the majority of high tech knowledge workers); nor do they help employees in this group meet their career aspirations. Gap analysis indicates that many employees in the holistic group do not feel that their job (as it is currently structured) provides them with a personal sense of accomplishment (gap 37%), offers them the opportunity to learn and develop new skills (gap 25%), provides a balance between their work and their family (gap 25%), or permits them to make a contribution to their field (gap 22%).

Employees with a more holistic definition of success measure their jobs by the degree of personal satisfaction they afford. For this group, experiencing a personal sense of accomplishment and the ability to learn are critical. The initiatives described above that support learning, lateral moves and recognition are all essential for this group. Their relationship with their immediate manager is also critically important. A manager who understands employees' abilities, interests and goals will be better able to provide challenge, learning opportunities, effective feedback and recognition. All of these contribute to the job satisfaction considered essential by employees with holistic definitions of success.

In addition to practices that foster a personal sense of accomplishment and support learning, those with a more holistic definition of success are likely to appreciate family friendly policies. Many traditional career development strategies (i.e. mobility, intensive training programs with residential requirements, long hours) conflict with desires for work-life balance. Career planning and development programs may be meaningless unless an employee's role as a family member is also considered. What can be done? The research literature in this area suggests several strategies. From an organizational perspective successful management of dual-career parents requires flexible work schedules, special counselling, training for supervisors in career counselling skills, and the establishment of support structures for transfers and relocations. Other strategies that have proved successful include job sharing programs and childcare assistance.

Making a contribution to their field is important to many of those with a more holistic definition of success. Challenging jobs with autonomy provide opportunities for employees to make a contribution and employee recognition programs help to validate those contributions. Facilitating employee contributions requires, however, that those opportunities are matched to employees' talents and aspirations. The data indicate that a diversity of career orientations exist amongst high tech knowledge workers that employers need to recognize and support.

Diverse Career Orientations

To assess their career orientation, interviewees were asked about their long-term career goals. When asked where they see their career ultimately, very few respondents (5%) described their ultimate goals in terms of money. Eight percent were unable to articulate an "ultimate" goal and 7% indicated that were already where they wanted to be. An additional 8% indicated that they expect to leave the high tech sector completely. The rest expressed goals, which were highly related to their definitions of career success. Four distinct career orientations were identifiable in the career goals of "key" personnel and the proportion of the sample that selected each of these paths was very similar. Of key personnel, 21% had a managerial orientation (they wanted to move up in management), 21% had a technical orientation (enjoyed being a specialist in a technical area), 17% had a project orientation (were looking for a series of challenging assignments), and 16% had an entrepreneurial orientation (wanted to own their own business). It is worth noting that only a minority (one in five) aspire to senior management positions even though a majority (63%) of the interview respondents are managers now and all have been designated by their companies as "key" personnel.

This diversity in career orientations parallels what other researchers have found. Three of these orientations are consistent with those found by Allen & Katz (1985) in their study of engineers and scientists. They identified managerial, technical, and project orientations. In their terminology, a managerial career orientation means the individual would ideally want to move into a management position, a technical orientation would represent a wish to advance upwards but into higher technical positions, and a project orientation refers to a wish to work on a series of challenging projects irrespective of whether this would involve a promotion upwards. They also reported that their respondents were distributed between these three groups as follows: 33% had a managerial orientation, 22% had a technical orientation, and 46% were project-oriented. Another study by Bailyn (1986) found that women were distributed approximately equally across the three orientations. The entrepreneurial orientation seems to be unique to Silicon Valley North.

The existence of substantively different career orientations amongst employees suggests that Silicon Valley North companies need to create alternative career paths. Career development programs need to accommodate these different orientations. As part of its career development initiatives, the high tech sector should provide dual career ladders so that employees whose goal is to make a technical contribution can achieve success and be recognized for it. A technical career ladder, which parallels the management career ladder, can provide the desired recognition and promotion for technical specialists. Project oriented employees should also be recognized for their increasing experience and breadth of knowledge through successively responsible assignments. Redesigned career paths, recognition and reward programs, and compensation systems will be needed to adequately meet the needs of these diverse career orientations. Recommendations specific to those interested in pursuing each of these career orientations are described below.

Developing Managers

A substantial number of knowledge workers in this sample see their ideal career path in terms of progress through management positions of increasing responsibility. For this group the key to retention and job satisfaction appears to be advancement, visible progress, the ability to influence the organization's direction, increased authority and recognition.[3] With respect to career development, high tech companies need to be cognizant of the fact that while one group of employees defines career success as having more authority (and sees progression up the ranks as a positive thing), another group (those who prefer the technical nature of their job) have more authority than they want!

High tech organizations should identify knowledge workers who wish to be promoted into a management position. Those who have the aptitude and talents for a management position (i.e. good communication and planning skills) should be:

- offered management development training;
- included in the organization's succession planning process;
- given a senior manager as a mentor;
- promoted regularly (these people will likely leave if you do not give them regular promotions).

By providing these career development experiences, not only will high tech companies retain employees with a managerial orientation, they will also develop a more effective pool of management talent.

Developing Technical Specialists

The data indicates that working with the technology itself is what approximately 20% of the knowledge workers in this sector find satisfying. In fact, one in five of the "key" employees defined career success as making a technical contribution — leading the field technically. The same proportion had career aspirations which involved working with the technology in some way or another (i.e. want to work in a more technical area, one that is more product related). One quarter said that for them the technical nature of the job was the most rewarding aspect of working in the high tech sector. Another 25% felt rewarded by that fact that they had contributed to their field ("I am on the cutting edge of technology"; "what we do here really makes a difference — advances the field").

The data also gives us an idea of what can happen when people with a technical focus are put in management positions. Twenty percent of the "key" respondents said that they

---

[3] The opposite of the things that will keep those, who love the technical nature of the job satisfied, with the company!

had taken a job that hadn't worked for them (I didn't like it; I wasn't interested in the work; wrong fit). Ten percent said that they were dissatisfied with their careers because their current job did not match their skills (not challenged, not working in an area I want). Nearly three-quarters of the survey respondents said that being recognized by their colleagues for their expertise was important to their personal definition of success. Unfortunately, only half of the survey respondents felt that they had encountered this type of recognition.

These data lead us to recommend that high tech organizations identify those employees who do not wish to be promoted into a management position and groom them to be technical specialists or technical troubleshooters. This implies supporting learning opportunities for in-depth specialization. It also implies providing recognition and reward for technical specialists, which does not involve promoting them into a management position (e.g. dual career ladders). Unless the same kind of prestige is afforded to "key" technical specialists as to 'key" managers, these initiatives will be unsuccessful and high tech companies will lose valuable human resources.

Developing Project-Oriented Personnel

A healthy minority of high tech knowledge workers (17%) have a project orientation. Their career goal is to work on a series of interesting and successively more challenging projects. Employees with this orientation are more interested in challenge than in promotion. Nevertheless many of them also value recognition. Critical to their development is a good understanding of their current skills and experience and identifying relevant challenges for their next assignment. Our recommendations regarding breadth are particularly relevant for this group. Specifically, organizations that want to retain these employees need to make it easier for them to make lateral moves by identifying some of the most likely lateral moves both within and between departments. This serves to validate lateral moves, which are often invisible and undervalued. In addition, organizations need to ensure that increasing breadth of experience is rewarded. Compensation needs to reflect project experience as well as managerial and technical experience.

Developing Entrepreneurs

The benefits of developing the entrepreneurs within their ranks may not be immediately obvious to high tech employers. Yet a significant minority of Silicon Valley North employees (16%) has business ownership as their ultimate career goal. To ignore the career development of this group would be to create a subgroup of dissatisfied, demotivated and underutilized employees. Some of these employees may be interested in business ownership because they see it as the only way to pursue their innovative ideas — ideas which may be of significant value to their current employer if their development were appropriately supported. Furthermore, many of these current employees, in pursuing their dreams, may someday become customers or suppliers of their original employer so fostering positive relationships may have future payoffs.

Many people who aspire to business ownership are motivated by a desire for greater autonomy. Providing employees with autonomy and input into decision-making processes may help organizations to retain them as committed employees. Many in this group may also seek management experience which will help to support their entrepreneurial dream so ensuring adequate management development opportunities may also help to retain employees with this orientation.

Developing Managers Who Develop People

Employees who report that their manager supports their career development are more likely to be satisfied with their jobs, committed to the organization and intend to remain with their current employer. From the data we can identify several attributes shared by managers who are perceived to be facilitating the career goals of their employees. According to the data, such managers are good communicators (good listening skills appear to be particularly critical) who are sincerely interested in learning about employees' career goals, informing employees about different career opportunities and helping subordinates to reach their career goals. They also appear to be very good at providing employees with the information they need to develop their careers (i.e. give good feedback, keep employees posted on trends, activities and opportunities) and at providing opportunities for their subordinates to develop new skills. Finally, employees appreciate a manager who helps them achieve their personal career goals by assisting them in their pursuit of breadth and visibility. Such managers also mentor their employees and help them scan the horizon. These findings correspond to research in this area which suggests the most important contribution a manager can make to the career development of his/her subordinates is to provide them complete information and honest feedback about their job performance. The data also indicate that employees appreciate a manager who gives them autonomy ("gives me directions and then trusts me to do a good job").

Unfortunately, the data would indicate that not all high tech managers are doing a good job with respect to employee career development. For example, almost 20% of the "key" employees sample said that their supervisor did "nothing" to help their career development. And less than one third of the survey respondents indicated that their manager supported their career development.

The data also suggests that it may be easier for managers to support the career development initiatives of their subordinates if they work in an organization, which has a culture that encourages and facilitates the communication of important information, focuses on people management and encourages training and career development. Best practice organizations have recognized that the organizational culture needs to support career development if initiatives and practices are to succeed. Measurement and accountability (at the supervisor, department and organizational levels) are necessary to effect cultural change in this area.

Since most career support comes from one's immediate manager, high tech companies need to help managers become better people developers. We recommend that high tech companies devolve responsibility for career development to the level of the employee's immediate supervisor. This will allow managers to tailor developmental opportunities to an individual's needs and values and avoid the "one-size-fits-all" approach to career development. Managers need to be provided with training, which gives them the business rationale behind career development as well as the skills and tools they need to be a career development "partner" with their subordinates.

In support of managers' responsibility for developing their subordinates, organizations need to keep managers informed about organizational priorities and future career opportunities so that they can communicate such information to their subordinates and provide career-counselling where appropriate. In addition, organizations need to provide managers with training on how to deal effectively with people (i.e. communication skills, negotiation, feedback, conflict resolution). Once training has been provided, managers should be held accountable for the career development of their employees.

To ensure management accountability, organizations should measure subordinates' awareness of, access to, and use of various career development initiatives and develop accountability around subordinate participation. Managers who effectively develop their subordinates should be recognized and rewarded. Departments also need to be held accountable for the career development of their staff using similar measures. In addition, managers should be assessed on their people management and people development skills. A 360-degree feedback system would be valuable in this regard. Finally, in support of this management responsibility, organizations need to adjust management workloads so that managers have time to support employee development. If it matters, and the research suggests strongly that it does, developing people should be assessed and supported like other management responsibilities.

Conclusions

The data lwead to numerous specific recommendations regarding career issues in Silicon Valley North; however, two overarching conclusions can be inferred. The first and most important is that career development matters. Organizations that provide effective career support to their employees enjoy higher levels of employee satisfaction and commitment, and lower turnover. Since these attitudes have direct links to productivity and costs, career development is not a frill — it is a bottom line issue. Effective career development can enhance recruitment, retention and rejuvenation, and all of these are critical to the health of organizations. Organizations need to include career development as part of their competitive strategy.

The second key conclusion to be noted from the research is that career development needs and experiences differ significantly by group. Standardized programs and practices will not meet employees' needs. The only way in which the various aspirations and abilities of a diverse workforce can be met is by individualized consideration. The kind of individualized consideration and support that is required to effectively develop employees' careers does not come from centralized programs — it comes from individual managers who are trained and rewarded for developing their people. Managers who develop their people help the organization to keep good people; managers who do not support employee career development undermine the effectiveness of the organization. Organizations need to recognize and support the critical role that managers play in career development if they want to maintain a vibrant workforce.

Acknowledgments

The authors would like to express their gratitude to the companies that participated in the research and to the employees within those companies who took time to complete the survey or participate in the interview process. We would like to thank Derry McDonell at Carswell for his assistance in publishing the original research. Finally we would like to thank our research assistants Linda Schweitzer, Sean Lyons, Shikhar Agarwal, Richard Brisbois, Donna Coghill, Carole Campbell and Karen Julien for their excellent work.

References

Allen, T. J., & Katz, R. (1985). The dual ladder: Motivational solution or managerial delusion? *R&D Management, 16*(2), 185–197.

Bailyn, L. (1986, February). Experiencing technical work: A comparison of male and female engineers. Alfred P. Sloan School of Management, MIT. Working Paper 1750–1786.

Bowlby, G. (2003). High-tech — two years after the boom. *Perspectives on Labour and Income* (Statistics Canada, Catalogue No. 75-001-XIE), *4*(11), 14–17.

Bowlby, G., & Langlois, S. (2002). High-tech boom and bust. *Perspectives on Labour and Income* (Statistics Canada, Catalogue No. 75-001-XPE), *3*(4), 9–15.

Cross, J. (1999). Back to the future. *Management Review*, February, 50–54.

Donnelly, K., LeBlanc, P., Torrence, R., & Lyon, M. (1993). Career banding. *Human Resource Management, 31*, 35–43.

Duxbury, L., Dyke, L., & Lam, N. (2000). *Managing high technology employees*. Toronto, Canada: Carswell Press.

Gionfriddo, J., & Dhingra, L. (1999). Retaining high tech talent: NIIT case study. *Compensation and Benefits Review* (Sept./Oct.), 31–35.

Gower, D. (1998). The booming market for programmers. *Perspectives on Labour and Income* (Statistics Canada Catalogue No. 75-001-XPE) (Summer), 9–15.

Granrose, C. S., & Portwood, J. D. (1987). Matching individual career plans and organizational career management. *Academy of Management Journal, 30*, 699–720.

Habtu, R. (2003). Information technology workers. *Perspectives on Labour and Income* (Statistics Canada, Catalogue No. 75-001-XPE) *16*(9), 15–21.

Hein, K. (1998). Programming loyalty. *Incentive* (February), 31–34.

Labour Force Survey (2003). Labour force for computers and telecommunications sector. Ottawa-Gatineau [Data file]. Ottawa, Ontario: Canada: Statistics Canada.

O'Grady, J. (2002). *Survey of IT occupations 2000, Part one: Employer survey*. Retrieved November 4 2003 from http://www.shrc.ca/lmi/index.html.

Software Human Resources Council (2003). *The Canadian IT labour market initiative: Labour force survey, May 2003*. Retrieved November 4 2003 from http://www.shrc.ca/lmi/lfs/pdf/lfs_may03.pdf.

Vaillancourt, C. (2003). *A profile of employment in computer and telecommunications industries*. Conectedness Series. Catalogue No. 56F0004MIE No. 9. Ottawa, Ontario, Canada: Statistics Canada.

Wolfson, W. G. (2003). *Analysis of labour force survey data for the information technology occupations*. Ottawa, Ontario, Canada: Software Human Resources Council.

Chapter 13

Can Technology Clusters Deliver Sustainable Livelihoods? Constructing a Role for Community Economic Development

Edward T. Jackson and Rahil Khan

Abstract

Can technology clusters deliver sustainable livelihoods? While social capital is crucial to technology-cluster growth, social inclusion has not been a sector priority. During the 1990s in greater Ottawa, low-income households and under-educated workers benefited only negligibly from the region's spectacular tech-sector expansion. This chapter discusses the potential for community economic development (CED) to "deal in" those on the outside of the sector and also help knowledge workers themselves cope with the inevitable volatility of clusters. Digital-divide bridging, customized training, work-life programs, mobilizing private philanthropy, multi-sector leadership structures, and community-owned science facilities are among the CED strategies considered.

Introduction

Can technology clusters deliver sustainable livelihoods? With the bursting of the "tech bubble" worldwide, and the consequent shedding of hundreds of thousands of jobs in recent years by major and minor companies in the global "new economy," this question is top-of-mind for many citizens and at least some institutions. The question also encapsulates the challenge faced daily by both employed and unemployed knowledge workers. Perhaps community economic development (CED) can help. In the past, this locally driven strategy has been applied to the economic margins, in underdeveloped and remote regions and in poor urban neighbourhoods. It may, in fact, be that CED offers one of the *only* feasible solutions for reducing the dysfunctional volatility of tech-cluster labour and business markets. Drawing on the experience of Canada's National Capital Region (Ottawa-Gatineau), this paper examines the limits and possibilities for CED strategies to be employed alongside the efforts of business and government to promote the growth of technology clusters.

Silicon Valley North: A High-Tech Cluster of Innovation and Entrepreneurship
Copyright © 2004 by Elsevier Ltd.
ISBN: 0-08-044457-1

Technology Clusters: An Ascending but Narrow Paradigm

In Canada today, as in most developed countries, technology-cluster growth has gained a privileged position in economic-policy discourse and practice (Industry Canada 2002a). It is an ascending paradigm with undeniable public-policy momentum. It is, above all, a concept underpinned by science and technology, and not by social dimensions. Fundamentally, technology clusters are seen to be driven by the commercialization of science and technology, and little else.

During the 1990s, a number of clusters grew in robust fashion across Canada. Nation-wide, information and communications technologies (ICTs) generated almost $60 billion in 1997, representing 6% of the total economy. Knowledge workers in this sector earned, on average, 50% more than employees in the economy as a whole. Vibrant ICT clusters emerged in Ottawa, Toronto, Waterloo, Calgary and Vancouver, among other centres. Other clusters are focused on biotechnology (Montreal), ocean and marine technologies (St. John's, Halifax), environmental technologies (Toronto), biopharmaceuticals (Winnipeg), alternative energy (Calgary), and fuel cells (Vancouver) (see ITAC 2002).

Social-science research has begun to highlight the pivotal role played by local knowledge and learning in growing clusters (Wolfe 2002a). A major multidisciplinary study, the Innovation Systems Research Network (ISRN) Project, funded by the Social Sciences and Humanities Research Council and government agencies, is underway to:

> investigate how local networks of firms and supporting infrastructure of
> institutions, businesses and people in communities across Canada interact
> to spark economic growth (Wolfe 2002b: 1).

Key to this interaction are networks of trust among different economic actors that combine to form a community's social capital. Studies suggest that regions that continuously engage stakeholders within a learning and action framework tend to succeed in cluster development (Wolfe 2002c). Such recognition of the importance of community-driven innovation is an important step forward in understanding how clusters can be grown. However, the prevailing framework is a limited one. First, it is primarily corporatist in character. The key economic actors are larger businesses, research institutions and governments. And, unless they are CEOs, successful entrepreneurs, venture capitalists, university presidents, senior government officials or major politicians, there is little role for ordinary citizens to exercise meaningful "stakeholder rights" in this process. Rather, the process of building local innovation networks is led by high-profile civic entrepreneurs from the companies and institutions with the greatest stake in cluster success (Henton *et al.* 1997).

Second, the role for civil society is thus circumscribed to those non-profit institutions with a direct interest in business and research and development, notably: chambers of commerce, professional associations, research agencies, think tanks and universities. Third, from a labour-force perspective, there is embedded in this framework a kind of knowledge-worker elitism that views employee recruitment and retention issues as *only* involving highly educated and well-paid software engineers, scientists, consultants and business managers. Public services — education, health, transport, policing, greenspace — that attract and retain these middle- and upper middle-class professionals are what is important, end of story.

That's who's in. Who, then, is *out*? Basically, low-income, less educated citizens and the non-profit organizations that serve their interests are invisible in cluster-development discourse. The list of organizations *not* on the radar screen of innovations systems policy and strategy is a very long one, indeed, and includes social-service agencies, community development corporations, non-profit housing programs, microcredit funds and many others. Because they involve tech-sector donors and volunteers, some social agencies, such as community foundations and United Ways, do remain vaguely on the screen. These latter groups are sometimes able to play a bridging role between tech and non-tech elements in the community, and have done so in several North American cities.

So, What's the Problem?

The general problem is that technology clusters seem to be capable of delivering sustainable livelihoods only for elite workers, and even then, only for a while, and, ultimately, only for some of them. It is well-known that the knowledge economy primarily hires highly educated and specialized professionals. Engineers, scientists, consultants and managers form the core of this elite group. It is true that busy supplier firms and consumer-spending multipliers (on houses and cars especially) create important spin-off jobs. However, overall, clusters are powered by a narrow-gauge labour market.

Almost by definition, then, there is no natural place in a cluster for under-educated workers, who often also happen to be poor. In labour-market terms, clusters are "gated communities" that keep the "haves" (in terms of education) in and the "have-nots" out. Left totally to market forces, there are few opportunities for low-education, low-income households to enter and benefit from clusters.

But even for the "haves," there is another serious problem undermining sustainable livelihoods. In North America at least, few technology companies have shown they have rational plans for laying off workers when, inevitably, booms turn into busts. Against a backdrop of often excessive executive compensation, and plummeting stock prices (translating into heavy losses for employees with big stock-option programs), major technology companies have demonstrated a singularly *irrational* approach to shrinking their labour forces. These factors have combined to cause employee motivation to "tank," at all levels, even among otherwise loyal senior managers. And, in many firms, employee trust in the corporation's leadership and strategy has hit bottom.

Moreover, the tension and dissatisfaction caused by labour-market volatility also finds its way home. Households coping with stress and uncertainty in the workplace must also deal with more inter-personal tensions within the family unit. Marriages are strained, or broken altogether. Children act out. Teenagers join gangs. Of course, these problems occur in other economic sectors that are restructuring or downsizing. The point is that the new economy is not immune to these "old" social dislocations.

Furthermore, there are community-level economic impacts. Large-scale downsizing triggers personal and business bankruptcies, a lowering of real estate values, and a general reduction in consumer spending on "big-ticket" items such as cars and homes. "Small-ticket" purchases, like eating out at restaurants, also decline.

The Search for Sustainable Livelihoods: The Case of the National Capital Region

One community that has seen both meteoric growth and stunning decline in the technology sector is Ottawa. And it is beginning to test CED as a way of addressing some of its challenges. The National Capital Region (NCR), which includes the municipality of Gatineau in Quebec, as well as metropolitan Ottawa, is presently home to more than 1,000,000 citizens and a labour force of almost 600,000 working age adults (Statistics Canada 2002). The region's modern infrastructure, clean air, low crime rate, extensive greenspace and many cultural institutions all contribute to a very good quality of life and a growing population.

In the last half of the 1990s, Ottawa's population, especially in the urban core, grew at a much faster rate (7%) than that of the country as a whole (4%). The population became more diverse in that period, as well. In 1996, 15% of Ottawa residents were members of visible minorities (Social Planning Council 2002). In 2001, one in five residents of Ottawa identified themselves as belonging to a visible minority (Tam 2003). One in five is also foreign born. It is also likely that the incidence of poverty in the National Capital Region, which had risen from almost 15% in 1991 to 19% in 1996 (Jackson & Graham 1999), continued to grow in the late 1990s. In 2002, 70% of the families on the City of Ottawa's waiting list for subsidized housing were immigrants (O'Connor & O'Neill 2003), reflecting, among other things, the large number of unemployed and underemployed foreign-born professionals in the region.

Traditionally, government and, to a lesser degree, tourism provided most of the region's employment. By the mid-1990s, however, public-sector spending cuts had eliminated 15,000 good government jobs in the NCR. Fortunately, a dynamic technology sector — powered by multiple clusters in telecommunications, software, photonics and life sciences — was able to replace those jobs in the latter half of the decade. By early 2001, the new-economy sector in the region reached a peak of 69,000 knowledge-worker jobs (Goff 2002).

Then the "tech wreck" hit. The lead players in the region's telecom and photonics clusters — notably Nortel networks and JDS Uniphase — announced a series of major layoffs (Bagnell 2002). In a dramatic reversal, between March 2001 and October 2002, the NCR's technology sector lost 15,000 jobs (Goff 2002). Ironically, though, this time the slack was picked up by government, which hired 13,000 new employees during the same period — many of them, in fact, "refugees" from the new economy (Galt 2002). Government contracts also kept many tech firms viable, a few even prosperous (Bagnell 2003). Expanded construction activity produced another 4,000 new jobs, especially those related to federal-government real estate projects (May 2003). And an estimated 400 technology start-ups were also initiated, many of them by engineers and entrepreneurs using buyout packages from their former employers (Goff 2002).

For this most recent tech downturn, then, it appears that the region was able to regain its economic equilibrium relatively quickly. But, without the federal government's spending spree, the economic and social damage would likely have been considerable. The region dodged a bullet. Moreover, the full impact of the technology meltdown has not really played out yet; more layoffs are pending, the startups have yet to prove themselves, and knowledge-worker households will have expended much of their savings and equity over the next few years.

The greater Ottawa region has, in many respects, been a textbook case for how to develop technology clusters. The technology sector's origins really began with government agencies and research institutions collaborating with the private sector on communications and computer systems in the early 1970s. The 1980s saw the growth of a number of successful homegrown firms (Mitel, Corel, Newbridge Networks) and units of U.S. companies (Systemhouse, EDS, Digital). In the 1990s, Nortel and JDS became global leaders in their fields and expanded in explosive fashion. Tech-sector leaders like Denzil Doyle, Rod Bryden, Michael Cowpland, Terry Mathews, John Roth and Josef Straus were lionized, with good reason. Ottawa's new economy became more visible, more confident and more globally-oriented (see also the chapter by Callahan *et al.* this volume).

Underpinning this success was a network of institutions that catalyzed and facilitated the learning and action of the sector (see Ghent Mallett this volume). Chief among these was the Ottawa Centre for Research and Innovation (OCRI), which connected business, professional, research, education, training and civic institutions in the region with each other and with external markets and policy agencies. Along with the municipal government of Ottawa and its former Economic Development Corporation (OED), OCRI and Centre members promoted labour-force programs to provide the clusters with the employees and training they needed, advocated policy reform and research to advance specific clusters, promoted better civic infrastructure in transport and housing, linked companies in the region with markets and partners in the U.S., Europe and Asia, encouraged the venture capital community to invest more heavily in Ottawa, and helped to steadily build the social networks and capital among these key actors in the sector (see also the chapter by O'Sullivan this volume).

As successful and impressive as the work of OCRI was, and is, its links to and concern for citizens and workers outside the technology sector have remain underdeveloped. In fact, OCRI and its allies did take on useful projects on opening labour-force opportunities to immigrant professionals and setting up "smart-sites" in community centres to democratize Internet access to citizens. Nevertheless, these initiatives were always positioned as subordinate to business imperatives, and their scale remained modest in any case.

Moreover, the role of social-sector leaders and agencies in the *governance* structures of OCRI and OED was negligible. This marginalizing of the social sector in OCRI's decision-making structures contributed, at worst, to mutual distrust between anti-poverty advocates and tech-sector leaders, and, at best, to a sustained disconnect. In particular, there was little interaction between OCRI and the Social Planning Council. The latter agency struggled financially through the 1990s, but stayed committed to and linked with organizations serving the poor, though the Council was also often perceived as anti-business. In another example, OCRI and OED gave only tepid support to the Ottawa Community Loan Fund, a non-profit microfinance program for unemployed and low-income microentrepreneurs.

However, one site of convergence, where technology leaders and social advocates could work together more frequently, was the Community Foundation of Ottawa (CFO). During the 1990s, the Foundation brought onto its board a number of tech-sector executives. Sector growth also translated into Foundation growth, as wealthy donors from the new economy made major gifts to CFO. At the same time, the Foundation began a decade-long process of moving towards a more asset-based community-development approach to grant-making with community groups, along the lines advocated by Kretzmann & McKnight (1993, 1999). Currently, the Foundation is cooperating with the City government and community groups to develop strategies to promote individual development accounts, affordable homeownership and microenterprise among low-income residents of the region (Brown 2002).

Other key players in the region, such as the United Way and social-science academics, are moving towards an asset-based approach, as well. In fact, the City of Ottawa's (2002) Human Services Plan for the next 20 years is heavily influenced by an asset perspective. The Plan seeks to promote human development across all economic sectors, including the region's technology clusters. With a consensus building on the merits of the assets-based approach, it will be interesting to see how all this plays out in the NCR.

For the most part, though, the experience of the 1990s in technology cluster growth in the National Capital Region was that it was largely irrelevant to the interests of poor and disadvantaged citizens. *While much social capital was built, little social inclusion was achieved.* What was achieved was a technology sector that created social networks, trust and learning *for itself.* This was necessary for sparking cluster growth, and impressive in its own right. However, it did not prove sufficient for generating sustainable livelihoods for the broader citizenry, or, for that matter, knowledge workers themselves.

Re-Visioning Possible Roles for Community Economic Development

Community economic development (CED) is an inclusive approach to creating economic opportunity that engages the broadest range of stakeholders, through non-profit structures, to generate economic opportunity for unemployed and disadvantaged citizens. Across North America, community development corporations, multi-stakeholder cooperatives, credit unions, microcredit programs, community foundations, and Aboriginal development corporations have provided technical advice, capital and social support services to enable unemployed and poor citizens to set up community, cooperative and micro enterprises in urban and rural areas alike (Bruce & Lister 2001; Favreau & Levésque 1999; Galway & Hudson 1994; MacLeod 1997; Perry 1987; Savoie 1999; Shragge 1999). CED is described by some commentators as one of the most promising areas of social and economic policy in Canada (Battle & Torjman 2002).

CED is, however, no magic bullet, no panacea. Used alone, it is a thoroughly inadequate policy tool. But applied in concert with other policies, from effective fiscal and trade regimes to fair and sustainable social programs, community economic development can make an important contribution to nation-building and to sustainable livelihoods for households.

Notwithstanding its limitations, as recent research by the Caledon Institute of Social Policy has shown, the CED sector has been characterized by a high degree of organizational innovation (Torjman & Leviten-Reid 2003). CED organizations (CEDOs) and their enterprises mobilize the resources and knowledge of all elements of the community: business, government and civil society. They have often engaged low-income citizens in designing, governing, managing and evaluating CEDOs and their businesses. Seeking to achieve success in two and sometimes three bottom lines — commercial, social and environmental — community enterprises demand more rather than less organizational learning and innovation than conventional businesses.

However, over the past 30 years, CED enterprises have been remarkably *low* in technology and science intensity. Until the full force of globalization hit local economies, it was often possible to create small, labour-intensive service and (less frequently) manufacturing businesses, employing low-income, low-education workers that could survive through a combination of commercial revenue and government grants. In successful cases, these workers would transit from unemployment insurance or social assistance to become productive, tax-paying citizens. Thus, the "return on taxpayer investment" via government grants was reasonably good. Today, however, globalization and technology have combined to create a hyper-competitive environment for small businesses. Without knowledge-intensity, *any* small business — community-owned or otherwise — faces severe and unforgiving challenges in the marketplace.

Perhaps it is time to "re-vision" what CED could bring to cluster development and what science and technology could bring to CED. Perhaps there can be a win-win "social contract" created for both sides. Perhaps the tech sector and the social sector can forge an alliance through the medium of knowledge-intensive CED.

More specifically, experience has shown that there are at least five roles that CED can play in the context of technology-cluster development:

(1) bridging the digital divide to ensure greater opportunities for new-economy jobs among the unemployed and underemployed;
(2) enabling knowledge workers to cope with technology-sector volatility;
(3) mobilizing the resources of corporations, wealthy individuals and governments to promote asset-based community development among low-income and economically marginalized citizens;
(4) creating multi-sector leadership structures that encode representation not only from business and the tech sector but also, substantially, from social-sector organizations, as well;
(5) promoting the growth of community-owned science and technology enterprises that generate benefits for the broadest range of citizens and businesses in the community.

It is worth looking more closely at how each of these roles can be operationalized (Table 1).

Bridging the Digital Divide

The digital divide is, of course, a global as well as a local challenge, especially in developing countries. "But," as the United Nations has observed, "the digital divide need not be permanent if technological adaptations and institutional innovations expand access" (UNDP 2001: 35). In Canada, in the late 1990s, the federal government supported a range of programs to expand internet access in schools, libraries and non-profits, especially in rural regions but also in poor neighbourhoods of urban areas. A new program to install broadband connectivity in rural and poor regions is underway, as well. Community

Table 1: Roles for community economic development in technology-cluster growth.

Role	Lead Organizations	Program Strategies
(1) Bridging the digital divide	Non-profit organizations	Public access sites (e.g. Smartsites)
For undereducated and poor citizens	Community centres	Broadband expansion
For rural communities	Libraries	Training Employment counseling Individual Development Accounts (IDAs)[a]
(2) Enabling knowledge workers to cope with sector volatility	Sector associations	Work-life balance programs
	Major companies	Employment counseling/networking
	Municipal governments	Targeted credit programs for mortgages, business loans ("Super IDAs") Social support networks Youth programs for children of knowledge workers
(3) Mobilizing resources for asset-based community development	Community foundations United Ways	Microfinance services Homeownership/options through non-profit and private projects Individual development accounts Volunteer leadership training Donor-advised funds Donor education programs
(4) Creating multi-sector leadership structures with substantial representation from both the technology and social sector	Leadership forums and roundtables with multiple sponsoring organizations	Rotating chairs Study groups/sub-committees on human resources, infrastructure, environment, etc.

Table 1: (*Continued*)

Role	Lead Organizations	Program Strategies
(5) Promoting community-owned science and technology enterprises	Community development corporations Non-profit organizations Municipal governments	Laboratories Super-computers Telescopes Museums Eco-tourism exhibits Specialized training institutes

[a] IDA programs seek to enable low-income individuals to save funds for home ownership, small business and education. Individual savings are matched, often on a 2:1 or 3:1 basis, by program funds to encourage asset building. However, Employment Insurance is taxable, while social assistance (welfare) is not, but provincial regulations limit the savings recipients can accumulate. Both these constraints must be addressed by IDA proponents.

development corporations, local associations and municipal governments can play a key role in engaging enterprises, citizens and social services to increase connectivity and internet access — and then to exploit these new tools.

In Ottawa, OCRI manages Smart Capital, an ambitious demonstration program to build "the world's most connected city." With 20 service providers, and 50 development partners, Smart Capital enables governments, schools, students, community groups, businesses and citizens at large to create and use efficient, low-cost online services, including training courses, counseling, database management, software applications, e-mail, webcasting and many other features. Smart Capital is implemented with federal, provincial and municipal funding (Smart Capital 2002).

Customized training in technology skills is another important strategy for bridging the digital divide. In Toronto, the non-profit Learning Enrichment Foundation (LEF), a leading community economic development organization, offers short courses in computer, networking, Internet and database skills to enable systemically unemployed workers to find entry-level jobs in technology companies. Through partnerships with companies like Microsoft, Novell and others, LEF continuously assesses market trends and the evolving needs of employers in the sector. The Foundation has experimented with different combinations of learning methods, including classroom instruction, self-study and experiential learning. As firm-level skill requirements become more sophisticated, LEF is moving to more advanced training to prepare their students for such jobs as help-desk and walk-around technicians. Federal and provincial grants, and private sector sponsorships and partnerships, support LEF's work (Khan 2001). LEF is currently leading a five-city demonstration project to show how targeted, community-based training can help overcome labour-market shortages in the new economy. The project uses extensive database man-agement, flexible funding for trainees, call centres and a collaborative network of trainers, counselors, "matchers" and corporate developers — all focused on matching the assistance needs of the unemployed or underemployed with the recruitment needs of technology companies (Valvasori 2002).

Between 1995 and 2000, the National Research Council operated Vitesse, a 16-month training program to move immigrants with traditional engineering skills into the technology sector as software engineers. Sponsored by companies, Vitesse students were trained for specific jobs (see also the chapter by Chhatbar this volume).

Another initiative of the late 1990s, the Compaq-Adeco project, trained single parents and new Canadians with generally low education levels to work in Compaq's call centre. The Partners for Jobs initiative funded 40–50% of the students on social assistance while Employment Insurance funded 30–40% of the students. By 2000, more than 300 people had been trained in the Compaq-Adeco project, with a 99% placement rate (Khan 2001).

There is also an urban-rural digital divide. One serious barrier experienced by small towns and rural areas on the periphery of urban clusters is frustratingly slow Internet access. Installing high-speed, broadband telecommunications infrastructure requires cooperation by all levels of government, the private sector and community organizations. Setting up citizen-oriented public access sites to the Internet, in libraries, schools and government offices in rural communities requires a similar type of cooperation. So too does promoting a culture of innovation and learning in rural schools, businesses and civic organizations. CED organizations are well-placed to animate these efforts, mobilizing resources and hosting projects, to extend the benefits and capacity of cluster-growth to non-urban areas.

Helping Technology Workers Cope with Volatility

There are many ways to help technology workers cope with the volatility of their sector. One important approach is for firms to provide generous layoff, buyout or retirement packages, all of which enable the exiting employees to leave their former worksites with dignity and go on to conduct job searches, retrain themselves, or invest in other businesses, often start-ups. Major companies, including Nortel and JDS Uniphase, have provided such benefits.

Another approach is active recruitment. When the initial rounds of layoffs were announced at software firm Corel, recruiters from other companies were waiting in the parking lot for the laid-off employees to emerge! Some former Nortel employees set up a website to market their services. In the first year of the tech meltdown, a large number of laid-off knowledge workers in the NCR found jobs with other firms. An equal or even larger number, though, moved over to the public sector. Others started their own small businesses.

One of the interesting, though to date minor, by-products of the technology downturn in Ottawa-Carleton is that some exiting workers have, in fact, made their way to the non-profit sector. In so doing, they have brought with them valuable skills in communications, computers, finance and management. For example, former employees of Nortel are now directing donor services at the Community Foundation, and human resources at the Mission, a non-profit providing food and shelter for street people. Other former tech workers have retired and work part-time or volunteer with such agencies as the Boys and Girls Club and the Children's Aid Society (Orton 2002). Following the bankruptcy of his company, one technology entrepreneur went to Nepal as a volunteer to teach computer literacy to kids with the non-profit agency, Child Haven (Pappone 2002). A more focused effort by local non-profits could multiply the number of high-skill technology professionals transiting to the non-profit sector, and match them with the social organizations that could best make use of their talents.

In the area of training, Ottawa's municipal government has maintained the Partners for Jobs Initiative, launched in the late 1990s to mobilize key stakeholders — "anchor" companies, universities and colleges, training institutes — to address the skill shortages in tech clusters in the region. The most recent incarnation of this effort is Talent Works, also run by OCRI. This project is overseen by a steering committee of the region's business organizations, and spins off new projects as skill requirements evolve. Talent Works has become the region's main non-profit "skill-filling" tool, engaging in and remaining active even in the tech sector's present diminished state, undertaking workforce analysis, municipal planning, and raising awareness of trades training, employee retention and employment for special-needs groups such as Aboriginals and the disabled. Federal, provincial and municipal funds support Talent Works (Talent Works 2002; see also the chapter by Paquet *et al.* this volume).

In the technology sector, work-time and workload expectations continue to cause work-family conflict, stress and burnout, especially among high performers. As with all sectors, there is a high cost associated with these problems to both households and firms (Carnoy 2000; Duxbury 1999; Dyke *et al.* this volume). With some exceptions, technology companies were among the worst in the 1990s in recognizing and dealing with work-family issues. And, even when programs were put in place, the industry's culture often inhibited employees from using such programs. One example, however, of a company that has taken this matter seriously is radiation-technology firm MDS Nordion. Assertively promoted by the company's President, MDS' award winning workplace programs include special parental leaves, flexible start-stop time, and work-sharing, supported by a regular employee wellness survey and an employee "climate metre" to assess program effectiveness (Khan 2001).

Community-based organizations can play an important role in lobbying technology companies to institute measures that support employees in coping with the demands of their current workplaces, or transiting to new ones. At the same time, community organizations can directly deliver training and counseling programs that enable tech workers to navigate amid sector volatility.

Mobilizing Private Philanthropy

Community-based organizations also have a role in mobilizing private philanthropy that can be used to promote asset-based community development among low-income and economically marginalized citizens. This is particularly important in Canada, where reliance on government resources to solve poverty-related problems is the "knee-jerk" traditional response. While government should, indeed, be substantially engaged in poverty reduction, the resources of the business sector and, more specifically, technology companies and their leaders, are required, as well.

During the boom decade of the 1990s, tech firms and executives demonstrated an ambivalent attitude toward philanthropy. True, there were spectacular examples of generosity and strategy in giving: Microsoft's Bill Gates set up the world's largest private foundation to promote international health and inner city education. In Canada, Red Hat's founder, Bill Young, used his proceeds from the sale of the company to establish a foundation and a non-profit, Social Capital Partners, to engage in venture philanthropy with urban social enterprises. However, self-interest and self-indulgence prevented many companies and individuals from doing more through philanthropy.

One notable exception, however, was that of community foundations. Offering a more targeted approach to giving and receiving, through their donor-advised funds, community foundations grew steadily in the 1990s in Canada and the U.S. These structures often benefited from those gifts that did originate in the technology sector. "Older" philanthropic mechanisms, like the United Ways, seemed to have less appeal for new-economy donors. In the U.S., the assets of Community Foundation Silicon Valley (1998) expanded in breathtaking fashion, benefiting especially from the generosity of younger managers and employees in the tech sector, prompting the foundation to work even harder at surveying and promoting corporate and individual giving and volunteering in that region.

The Community Foundation of Ottawa (CFO) experienced parallel success during the 1990s. CFO received a number of major gifts from tech-sector leaders, most of them anonymous and most in the form of stock. The Foundation's policy was, and is, to liquidate such gifts as soon as it receives them, at their present value. At the same time, the Foundation recruited new board members from among the ranks of technology executives, set up a range of donor-advised funds, developed new donor-liaison and education initiatives (especially for first-time givers), and began slowly to reorient its grant making to a more asset-based approach. The Foundation also often provided a voice for the social sector at gatherings of the technology sector. With the recent shrinking of Ottawa's telecom, photonics and software clusters, the Foundation has renewed its efforts to connect with the social sector and to prepare for the next round of tech growth (Khan 2001).

More broadly, the 1990s also saw the rise of venture philanthropy, a high-engagement approach to grantmaking that uses some of the techniques of venture capitalism, particularly business planning, board-level guidance, and follow-on investments in successful business models. Technology leaders were prominent among the American and Canadian venture philanthropists who emerged during this period. In recent years, however, there has been a realization among venture philanthropists that promoting social enterprise is not as "straightforward" as regular venture capitalism — and takes much longer to generate economic and social returns. And, as they have hit these programmatic "walls," many venture capitalists have gained a new appreciation of the skills and dedication of social-sector leaders and professionals (Byrne 2002).

Creating Multi-Sector Leadership Structures

One of the most innovative models for creating multi-sectoral leadership structures in Canada were the Leadership Roundtables set up under the Opportunities 2000 project in Waterloo, Ontario a few years ago. Involving business, all levels of government, foundations, educational institutions and social organizations, these structures enabled technology executives to interact directly with welfare mothers, for example, to try to understand each other better and develop a poverty-reduction plan together. This required strong professional facilitation skills, with an appreciation of the knowledge and capacity of all stakeholders — skills impressively possessed by the OP 2000 team. Subsequently, the Maytree Foundation set up the Tamarack Institute for Community Engagement, which, with the support of the McConnell Foundation, has embarked on a replication in 16 Canadian cities of the OP 2000 approach (Tamarack Institute 2002).

In Ottawa, the Partners for Jobs initiative, led by the City and involving other sectors, has probably been the most broad-based structure that involves both the social and technology sectors (Torjman 1999). There is an important difference between Partners and the OP 2000 model, though. Where Partners became primarily a training and labour-force initiative, OP 2000 was designed as a more comprehensive poverty-reduction effort, of which training was one component. And, while they run important and innovative programs, the governance structures of other organizations — OCRI and the Community Foundation, in particular — contain little or no permanent, *direct* representation of organizations serving the poor in the National Capital Region. This is unfinished business in an institutional sense in the region. Community economic development can serve as the framework to address this outstanding issue.

Promoting Community-Owned Science and Technology

There is something else that CED can do. It can promote community ownership of science and technology facilities. In turn, these facilities — laboratories, telescopes, super-computers, research museums, etc. — can generate sustainable local employment and business opportunities for the unemployed, underemployed and general labour force. In Lethbridge, Alberta, for example, a volunteer association manages astronomy — education and tourism programs associated with a powerful telescope located in the community. Nearby, a non-profit Aboriginal museum on the buffalo hunt draws tourists and conducts anthropological research on indigenous knowledge and culture, feeding this into the museum's programs.

In Cape Breton, a research chair at the University College of Cape Breton was instrumental in promoting the growth of high-tech start-ups on an island dominated, historically, by resource-extraction employment. There have also been some interesting twinning arrangements involving small technology enterprises and local CED organizations on the Island (Gurstein 2002). There are other good examples of smaller Canadian cities, or regions, building dynamic technology clusters: astrophysics and agrifood in the Okanagan Valley, agricultural biotechnology in Saskatoon, applied agriculture and biotechnology in Olds, Alberta, land resource management in Brandon, mining and forestry in Timmins, microelectronics and environmental technologies in Sherbrooke, bioactives for pharma/nutraceuticals in Charlottetown, and ocean engineering and marine communications in St. John's (Industry Canada 2002b). In each case, networks of public and private institutions, supported by universities, have served as important tools to grow these clusters.

Community organizations can also directly own and operate technology companies. Some 15 years ago, the West Prince Industrial Commission in Prince Edward Island set up Westech Agriculture, a biotechnology firm that used gene-splicing techniques to develop new varieties of crops, including wheat and barley. Westech created seven permanent and 50 seasonal jobs, in the process attracting several research scientists and technicians to permanently relocate to the region (MacKinnon & Peirce 1989). More recently, in Ottawa, the Social Planning Council used geographic information software to build a poverty-mapping capacity that has generated revenue through consulting and research contracts. There have been many other examples in both rural and urban settings where community development corporations, cooperatives and non-profits have mobilized science and technology to set up new businesses.

To succeed in these ventures, however, community agencies initially must build strong alliances with government laboratories and research programs. The role of the National Research Council's institutes on biotechnology in Saskatchewan and bio-diagnostics in Winnipeg was crucial in fostering technology cultures in those regions (Doern & Levésque 2002). Federal science and technology labs are themselves looking to form new alliances with NGOs and communities as they seek both to demonstrate their value to the public and to diversify their revenues (Doern & Kinder 2002). Finding ways to make public laboratories in government and universities more responsive to changing research needs and opportunities is a challenge common to all developed countries (OECD 2001).

What is needed in Canada, though, is a more comprehensive initiative to promote community-based science and technology. In poor urban neighborhoods and in towns and villages, public funds should be available for community organizations to test new approaches to generating jobs and businesses in knowledge-intensive fields. Linking these efforts to technology clusters in nearby regions would make sense, as well. Some communities would establish specialized laboratories and research centres, others would start up technology companies. All would seek strategic alliances with governments and the private sector. Most would target export as well as Canadian markets for their products and services.

Conclusions

It would appear that technology-cluster growth needs CED, and vice-versa. Technology clusters can only deliver sustainable livelihoods when knowledge workers have the opportunities and tools to cope with inevitable sector volatility, and when economically marginalized citizens are included in the new economy. "Smart communities" and customized training, plus rural broadbanding, to bridge the digital divide; "skill-filling" systems and work-life programs in the tech sector itself; mobilizing private resources; asset-based initiatives with the poor through community and venture philanthropy; multi-sector leadership structures with an authentic role for the social sector; and new forms of community-owned science and technology — these are all important strategies for optimizing the livelihoods capacity of technology clusters.

In Ottawa, some of these measures are underway. One crucial outstanding issue, though, is to restructure the region's economic-development governance structure to include an effective voice at the table for the social sector. With such broader representation, and its associated stronger links to the non-tech and poorer segments of the economy, regional institutions would be well-positioned to undertake a comprehensive study of how the

Ottawa cluster is surviving the present extended downturn, and how it could possibly reinvent itself to regain its growth trajectory. How the non-tech economic sectors, and civil society, are adjusting to these circumstances matters a great deal, as well, and should be examined in detail. Community economic development can serve as both a lens for understanding these dimensions of economic and social change, and as an instrument for taking action on what is learned.

A second issue relates to scale. In the NCR today, a large pool of public and private resources and organizations are devoted, and rightly so, to the labour-force needs of tens of thousands of knowledge workers. But inclusive training for those outside the sector has only, to date, reached hundreds of citizens. The actual need, in fact, is to reach *thousands* of these citizens. Addressing both key issues — governance and scale — will require substantial political will, through a coalition of non-profit, public and private leaders.

One of the most important tasks ahead, for Ottawa and for Canada generally, however, is to inject into community economic development activities much greater knowledge-intensity than in the past. Community organizations should set up research and development facilities, partner with government labs and private companies, capitalize small technology enterprises and commercialize scientific innovations. Linking these initiatives to nearby technology clusters, and supplying high-quality products and services to anchor firms in those clusters, will optimize the impacts and sustainability of these efforts.

Sustainable livelihoods is the goal. Knowledge for inclusion is the path forward.

Acknowledgments

An earlier version of this chapter was presented to the Annual Conference of the Association for Research on Nonprofit Organizations and Voluntary Action, Montréal, Quebec, Canada 2002. The authors are indebted to a number of individuals whose advice and assistance supported the preparation of the chapter, including George Brown, Jacques Carrière, Eric Leviten-Reid, Barbara McInnes, Lisa Naphtali, Larisa Shavinina, Norean Shepherd, Sherri Torjman and Sonja Vanek.

References

Bagnell, J. (2002, November 7). House of glass: Nortel's shattered legacy. *The Ottawa Citizen*, F2.
Bagnell, J. (2003, December 26). A fine balance. *The Ottawa Citizen*, F3.
Battle, K., & Torjman, S. (2002). *Social policy that works: An agenda*. Ottawa, Ontario, Canada: Caledon Institute for Social Policy.
Brown, G. (2002). Asset-based community development: As simple as ABCD? Presented to a seminar sponsored by the Centre for the Study of Training, Investment and Economic Restructuring. Ottawa, Ontario, Canada: Carleton University.
Bruce, D., & Lister, G. (Eds) (2001). *Rising tide: Community development tools, models, and processes*. Sackville, New Brunswick, Canada: Rural and Small Town Programme, Mount Allison University.
Byrne, J. A. (2002, December 2). The new face of corporate philanthropy. *Business Week*, 82–92.
Carnoy, M. (2000). *Sustaining the new economy*. Cambridge, MA: Harvard University Press.

City of Ottawa (2002). *Human services plan (Draft)*. Ottawa, Ontario, Canada: City of Ottawa.
Community Foundation Silicon Valley (1998). *Giving back: The Silicon Valley way*. Report. San Jose, California: Community Foundation Silicon Valley.
Doern, B., & Kinder, J. (2002). *The roles of federal S&T labs: Institutional change and challenges*. Research Report, Carleton Research Unit on Innovation, Science and Environment. Carleton University, Ottawa, Ontario, Canada.
Doern, B., & Levésque, R. (2002). *The national research council in the innovation policy era*. Toronto, Canada: University of Toronto Press.
Duxbury, L. (1999). *An examination of the implications and costs of work-life conflict in Canada*. Research Report. Ottawa, Ontario, Canada: Health Canada.
Favreau, L., & Levésque, B. (1999). *Développement économique communautaire: Économie sociale et intervention*. Saint-Foy: Université du Québec.
Galt, V. (2002, November 11). Many laid-off high-tech staff leaving field: Study. *The Globe and Mail*, B8.
Galway, B., & Hudson, J. (Eds) (1994). *Community economic development: Perspectives on research and policy*. Toronto, Canada: Thompson.
Goff, K. (2002, November 7). Ottawa's second coming. *The Ottawa Citizen*, A1.
Gurstein, M. (2002). Community innovation systems and the chair in the management of technological change. In: J. A. Holbrooke, & D. A. Wolfe (Eds), *Knowledge, clusters and regional innovation* (pp. 259–280). Kingston, Ontario, Canada: McGill-Queen's University Press.
Henton, D., Melville, J., & Walesh, K. (1997). *Grassroots leaders for a new economy*. San Francisco: Jossey-Bass.
Industry Canada (2002a). *Canada's innovation strategy*. Ottawa, Ontario, Canada: Industry Canada.
Industry Canada (2002b). *Creating new wealth: Improving the innovation capacity and performance of smaller Canadian cities*. Ottawa, Ontario, Canada: Industry Canada.
Information Technology Association of Canada (2002, November 8). Special supplement. *The Globe and Mail*.
Jackson, E. T., & Graham, K. A. (1999). Introduction. In: E. T. Jackson, & K. A. Graham (Eds), *Diversification for human well-being: Challenges and opportunities in the national capital region* (pp. 5–14). Centre for the Study of Training, Investment and Economic Restructuring. Carleton University, Ottawa, Ontario, Canada.
Khan, R. (2001). *Sustaining livelihoods in the new economy in the national capital region*. Unpublished manuscript, Centre for the Study of Training, Investment and Economic Restructuring. Carleton University, Ottawa, Ontario, Canada.
Kretzmann, J. P., & McKnight, J. L. (1993). *Building communities from the inside out*. Chicago: ACTA Publications.
Kretzmann, J. P., & McKnight, J. L. (1999). *Leading by stepping back: A guide for city officials on building neighborhood capacity*. Chicago: ACTA Publications.
MacKinnon, W., & Peirce, J. (1989). *The West Prince industrial commission: A case study*. Local Development Paper No. 7. Ottawa, Ontario, Canada: Economic Council of Canada.
MacLeod, G. (1997). *From Mondragon to America: Experiments in community economic development*. Sydney, Nova Scotia, Canada: University College of Cape Breton Press.
May, K. (2003, January 2). Why the boom is back in Ottawa. *The Ottawa Citizen*.
O'Connor, E., & O'Neill, J. (2003, October 11). Ottawa's changing face: A special series. *The Ottawa Citizen*, D1, D3.
Organization for Economic Cooperation and Development (2001). *Science, technology and industry outlook*. Paris, France: Organization for Economic Cooperation and Development.
Orton, M. (2002, December 26). Charity begins after Nortel. *The Ottawa Citizen*, F2.
Pappone, J. (2002, November 16). Lessons learned, lessons shared. *The Ottawa Citizen*, H1.

Perry, S. A. (1987). *Communities on the way: Rebuilding local economies in the United States and Canada*. Albany, New York: State University of New York Press.

Savoie, D. (1999). *Community economic development in Atlantic Canada: False hope or panacea?* Moncton, New Brunswick, Canada: Canadian Institute for Research on Regional Development, University of Moncton.

Shragge, E. (1999). *Community economic development: In search of empowerment*. Montreal, Quebec, Canada: Black Rose.

Smart Capital (2002). Website (www.smartcapital.ca).

Social Planning Council (2002). Ottawa: The people and their city. *Our Social Capital 2*(1), Special Issue.

Statistics Canada (2002). *Community profile: Ottawa-Hull*. Ottawa, Ontario, Canada: Statistics Canada.

Talent Works (2002). Website (www.talentworks.ca).

Tam, A. (2003, January 22). One in five Ottawa residents belongs to a visible minority. *The Ottawa Citizen*, A15.

Tamarack Institute for Community Engagement (2002). Website (www.tamarackinstitute.ca).

Torjman, S. (1999). *Reintegrating the unemployed through customized training*. Research Report. Ottawa, Ontario, Canada: Caledon Institute of Social Policy.

Torjman, S., & Leviten-Reid, E. (2003). *Innovation and CED: What they can learn from each other*. Research Report. Ottawa, Ontario, Canada: Caledon Institute of Social Policy.

United Nations Development Program (2001). *Human development report 2001*. New York: United Nations.

Valvasori, J. (2002, Autumn). A new role for the Federal Government in human capital development. *Making Waves, 13*(3), 9–13.

Wolfe, D. A. (2002a). *The Innovation Systems Research Network (ISRN) Project*. Unpublished Note. Toronto, Canada: University of Toronto.

Wolfe, D. A. (2002b, March 18). Give R&D a place to grow. *The Globe and Mail*, A13.

Wolfe, D. A. (2002c). Social capital and cluster development in learning regions. In: J. A. Holbrook, & D. A. Wolfe (Eds), *Knowledge, clusters and regional innovation* (pp. 11–38). Kingston, Ontario, Canada: School of Policy Studies, Queen's University Press.

Chapter 14

An Innovative Model for Skill Development in Silicon Valley North: O-Vitesse

Arvind Chhatbar

Abstract

The author describes a new and innovative approach developed in Ottawa through a partnership between NRC, local universities and industry to address the fast changing requirements of Silicon Valley North's technology sectors. The project, O-Vitesse, has become a success story in rapidly re-skilling highly qualified professionals to meet the demands for skills especially as business cycles become shorter and new technologies are rapidly introduced into society. With the growth of the knowledge-based economies and increased global competition, companies face the challenge of meeting new skills needs in compressed timeframes. The merits of the Vitesse Re-Skilling model as a solution are presented.

Introduction

At an Ottawa information technology industry "town hall" meeting, two years after the tech meltdown, executives from local high tech firms unanimously agreed that their biggest challenge will continue to be the insufficiency of qualified graduates being produced by local post-secondary institutions.

In a parallel development, a survey conducted by Deloitte & Touche (2001) predicts that genomics, biotechnology and health care firms are likely to be the biggest recipients of new investment in the near to mid term future. The province of Ontario, Canada's economic engine, in availing itself of the opportunities committed itself to make the province the third-largest biotech hotbed in North America. In doing so, the government at the time acknowledged that to do so will require a huge increase in the number of life-science professionals qualified in such areas as genomics, bioinformatics and molecular biology.

Silicon Valley North: A High-Tech Cluster of Innovation and Entrepreneurship

Concern about access to skills is not a new or transitory phenomenon. Nor is it unique to any one province or region. Since the mid-1980s, the shrinking pool of critical skills has been a source of concern to all Canadian firms whose ability to innovate and compete depends on access to leading-edge technical and scientific knowledge. This has been more evident during the high-tech boom, especially in Ottawa.

Increasingly, however, the growing shortfall in workplace skills has begun to impact the full spectrum of Canadian industry. In a growing number of occupations, from taxi drivers to hard rock miners, new technology is being applied to improve productivity and respond to quickening competition. As Peter Drucker observed, "the world is becoming not labour intensive, not material intensive, not energy intensive, but knowledge intensive" (Drucker 1992: 334).

It is virtually axiomatic, of course, that productivity and competitiveness ultimately depend on access to a skilled workforce. Ingenuity has always been the handmaiden of progress but it takes on even greater significance in today's knowledge-based economy. As the focus of economic activity shifts away from the exploitation of natural resources and traditional manufacturing to the creation of services and advanced technology products, and as knowledge and information become the key commodities in a global marketplace, a skilled labour force is vital to innovation and competitiveness.

Recognizing that global competitiveness in turn requires a climate that fosters innovation, governments at all levels in Canada are considering a wide range of measures intended both to encourage innovation and facilitate the more rapid transfer of technology from researchers and developers to industry. The success of these efforts, however, is predicated on industry's access to a workforce with the skills needed to assimilate new technologies and translate them into marketable products and services.

Unfortunately, a combination of factors is already having a dampening effect on Canada's ability to retool its labour force. According to research by the Conference Board of Canada, these factors will result in a shortfall of nearly a million workers by 2021 (Conference Board 2001a, b). As the sheer scale of the problem attests, the requirements of the knowledge-based economy are no longer confined to any one industry or sector. Every Canadian industry, from forestry and agriculture to manufacturing and financial services, now competes on the basis of skills and innovation.

Already feeling the strain, it is increasingly clear that Canada's educational system will not be able to meet the demand for skilled workers without significant assistance from other quarters. In 1999, only one job in six required post-secondary education but within the next two years, one in four jobs demanded a university degree. Between 1990 and 1999 there was an increase of 2.25 million in the number of job opportunities for Canadians with post-secondary education and a decrease of 800,000 for those with less than high-school education. Unfortunately, in many disciplines deemed critical by Canadian employers, university enrollments are either not increasing fast enough to meet demand or are relatively static. Indeed, in some high-demand disciplines enrollment appears to be declining (Conference Board 2001a, b).

Complicating the problem is the fact that almost half of the labour force needed by 2021 is already working and — by 2011 — virtually all-new entrants into the workplace will be immigrants. In both cases, past experience suggests that a huge investment in retraining and re-skilling will be needed, to simultaneously keep the skills of existing workers up to date and to upgrade the skills of new Canadians in order to prepare them for work in a North American context.

Admittedly, Canada's workforce is justifiably regarded as one of the best in the world, but there is a general consensus that it is falling behind in terms of its ability to ensure long-term productivity and competitiveness. According to most informed observers, dramatic improvements in both the quantity and quality of Canada's labour force skills are needed to maintain the pace of innovation.

In response to what is now generally perceived as a potential crisis, the government of Canada has focused on the skills challenge as a key element in its still emerging plan to strengthen Canada's capacity for innovation. The relatively recent release of discussion papers on the issue from Human Resources Development Canada (HRDC) and Industry Canada clearly signals that a solution to the skills problem is a key building block in the emerging innovation strategy and an important item on the nation's agenda.

As the authors of *Achieving Excellence* take pains to point out,

> to succeed in the global knowledge-based economy, a country must produce, attract and retain a critical mass of well trained people. The demand for high-level skills will continue to grow in all sectors, and competition for highly skilled workers will intensify within Canada, and between Canada and other countries (Industry Canada 2002: 8).

Nor will it be enough, they add, merely to increase the capacity of existing educational facilities.

> To remain competitive and to keep up with the accelerating pace of technological change, Canada must continuously renew and upgrade the skills of its work force. We must provide opportunities for workers to improve and upgrade their skills and acquire new ones to meet the changing skills demands of the new economy (Industry Canada 2002: 8).

Consistent with its goal to develop the most skilled and talented labor force in the world, *Achieving Excellence* outlines a number of key targets. Among them:

- Over the next five years, increase the number of adults pursuing learning opportunities by 1 million.
- Through to 2010, increase the admission of Master's and Ph.D. students at Canadian universities by an average of 5% per year.
- By 2004, significantly improve Canada's performance in the recruitment of foreign talent, including foreign students, by means of both the permanent immigrant and temporary foreign workers programs.

Clearly, the achievement of these targets will require a nation-wide effort involving a broad coalition of private and public sector institutions. New models, methodologies and approaches will be required.

At the Root of the Problem

Although demand for critical skills has been increasing for some time, it is only in the relatively recent past that the dimensions of the problem and its economic consequences have been fully appreciated — this was no where more evident than in Canada's Silicon Valley — Ottawa.

Three key imperatives underscore the need to focus on improved skills creation strategies at this point in Canada's development.

Skills in the New Economy

The emergence of a global knowledge-based economy is fuelling exploding demand for skilled and well-educated workers at every level of the economy. Revolutionary advances in information and communications technology have transformed the way in which people work, produce and consume. As a result, the skills required for many traditional occupations are changing rapidly and, in an economy, which is increasingly knowledge-based, many skills are in danger of obsolescence. At the same time, advances in science and technology are creating demands for entirely new disciplines.

As noted in *Knowledge Matters*:

> By 2004, more than 70% of all new jobs created in Canada will require some form of post-secondary school education and only 6% of new jobs will be held by those who have not completed high school. Canada is already facing structural skills shortages in occupations such as nursing, engineering and management. The Canadian Federation of Independent Business reported that in late 2000 up to 300,000 jobs were vacant because of a lack of suitable skilled workers (HRDC 2002: 2).

Shortages of both technical and cultural skills are particularly acute in such high tech industries as informatics, aeronautics, biotechnology and the life sciences. Firms operating in these fields have long noted that difficulty in identifying, acquiring and retaining critical skills is a significant constraint on their growth. In such industries, not only there is an absolute shortage of skills in a number of leading edge disciplines, but the pace at which new technology is transferred from the development laboratories and universities to the workplace lags well behind industry needs. The sheer velocity of technological change is such that failure to recruit and retain what, in some cases, may be a relative handful of well-trained knowledge workers in a few key disciplines may make the difference between survival and failure for many firms.

The Need for Continuous Learning

Canada shares the increasing intensity and relevance of technical skills especially those in emerging growth areas of the recent past and future such as those in information technology and biotechnology with many industrialized countries. Fundamental change in the nature of work as a result of changes in the national and global economies demand a higher level of technical content in the work environment which in turn underlines the need for lifelong learning and continuous training in the workplace. In addition, for Canadian industries to remain competitive, the country must continue to graduate even-greater numbers of people from post-secondary institutions and continue to train, and re-skill people throughout their lives. Unfortunately, after graduation, Canadians are poor performers in terms of continuing education opportunities. According to the Conference Board of Canada, training investment per employee in Canada is in the $800–$850 range annually and has remained so since 1993 (Conference Board of Canada, Training & Development Outlook 2001a, b). This poor performance confirms the ranking of Canada as 23rd out of 46 countries in employer supported learning (World Competitiveness Yearbook 2000).

Much of the continuous learning opportunities for today's labour force derive from the information workplace and on-the-job learning. Too often, however, industry practices in this regard are inconsistent, and given the mobility of knowledge workers from position to position and potentially from industry to industry (a feature of the new economy), these inconsistencies would not serve the overall goals of a nation in advancing towards global competitiveness. Industries have difficulties in developing competence-based learning systems and there is often little incentive for them to do so due to market failures such as "cherry picking."

It is clear that there will be a need for formal continuous or lifelong learning by knowledge workers and that need will have to be served by a model that is different from the current one that is being offered by educational institutions. Most of this is offered through what educational institutions have dubbed their "professional development" units or their adult learning or continuing education arms. These have proven to be dismal failures in meeting the needs of the knowledge-based economy as they are heavily reliant on the individual to engage in these processes often at the mercy of the educational institutions own legacy programs that cannot keep up the pace of change occurring in the economy (Mather 2002).

The Demographic Crunch

A steady, seemingly irreversible decline in Canadian birthrates along with shortfalls in skills-based immigration are conspiring to hinder the growth of Canada's work force. Certainly, there will be continued growth but at a much slower rate than in the past. The stark reality is that future labour supplies are unlikely to keep up with demand. At the same time, the overall population is aging and the next cohort of young workers will be significantly smaller than in the past. By 2011, in fact, federal officials suggest that all net labor force growth will come from immigration.

Unfortunately, Canada will face increasingly stiffer competition from other countries, both for skilled immigrants and for native-born talent. The so-called "brain drain" to the U.S., for example, has already led to skills shortages in a number of critical industries — especially health care and technology sectors.

Inherent Problems in the Learning System

Although Canada enjoys the world's highest level of participation in post-secondary education, it is increasingly clear that our learning system is not adequate to the task of meeting future skills and labor force demands. Unfortunately, as it was mentioned above, in many disciplines deemed critical by Canadian employers, university enrollments are either not increasing fast enough to meet demand or are relatively static. Indeed, in some areas enrollments appear to be declining (Statistics Canada, Education Indicators 1999).

Universities today are typically institutions defined in the 19th and early 20th centuries, which were geared to serve a developing industrial economy. The basic educational infrastructure remains unaltered despite the emergence of new technologies: tenured faculty, large investments in classrooms and laboratories, structured curriculum development process, and the length of degree programs irrespective of changing economic structure. Higher education institutions, and universities in particular, continue to be organized primarily along traditional disciplinary boundaries and faculties. The very nature of their curriculum building process means that formal recognition of a "new" discipline does not occur until a relevant industry has already achieved significant growth. Ironically, by the time political and financial support is forthcoming for new curricula, demand for critical skills is already in decline. The resulting time lag for the supply of new skills to catch up with employer demand is too long.

Inherent in the problem is the conflicting demands placed upon educational institutions to provide both education and training. Education provides knowledge and the preparation for lifelong learning, while training is concerned with the development of skills already in demand by employers.

The problem today is that our universities no longer serve industry or the economy as effectively as they used to. As we move from the industrialized to the new knowledge-based economy, Canada needs post-secondary institutions that are as dynamic, innovative and rapidly changing as the economy itself.

Despite some examples of innovative activity through science parks, incubation of firms and centers of technology transfer (see the chapter by Armit, this volume), universities in the new knowledge economy no longer have the field of knowledge production to themselves. Universities are simply one actor amongst many contributing to the flow of knowledge and information that propels the process of technological and economic innovation. It will be important for universities to rethink their relationships (and the implications for programs) with industry and governments, and other knowledge-producing institutions.

Universities are not currently structured and therefore not well positioned to address the needs of the new knowledge economy. Both the state of knowledge in contemporary times, as well as its growing value to diverse spheres of human behavior, is giving rise to a new form of knowledge production that is highly dynamic, trans-disciplinary, less reliant on single institutions for expertise and more socially responsible (Mather 2002).

As Mather points out, this fact is further complicated by the segmenting of academic programs to be core and non-core ones. Continuing education programs or the life long learning component fall under non-core categories. Yet, it is the continuing education units that are geared to serve the growing demands (and demographics) of knowledge worker population. This is particularly pertinent in Ontario at the current time, where there is a clear disconnect between recognition of the needs of Ontario's future labor force, and the role of higher education institutions in terms of training adult workers.

Clearly, it is increasingly important for universities to explore trans-disciplinary approaches across the range of academic programs as has been tried in some areas such as technology and business programs. It would be important for universities to be more in tune with needs of students who will make up the nation's knowledge labor force. Agile mechanisms are needed while a balance is being struck between the two. Such mechanisms should be capable of identifying new requirements early in the industrial development process and developing appropriate programs quickly and effectively.

At present, and perhaps in the foreseeable future, Canada's education and training establishment is inherently incapable of delivering new skills as quickly as they are needed in newly emerging and leading edge industries without a way to bridge the divide between industry and universities. The sheer velocity of technological change and the rapid emergence of entirely new disciplines is simply too great for traditional institutions to keep pace.

The Skilled Immigrant — An Undervalued Resource

New entrants into the labor market are being increasingly foreign-trained professionals who also need to be brought up to speed with new skills. According to Human Resources Development Canada, between 1991 and 1996 the Canadian Labor force grew by 608,000 individuals of whom 431,000 were immigrants. Furthermore, immigrants are expected to account for all net labor force growth by 2011, and for all net population growth by 2031 (HRDC 2002).

Clearly, a skills-based immigration program is a critical element in any potential solution. Unfortunately, despite policies intended to strengthen the labor force by admitting immigrants on the basis of educational achievement and technical training, the capabilities of many new Canadians are grossly under-utilized.

Paradoxically, at a time when industry is expressing growing concern about the difficulty of recruiting and retaining human resources, valuable immigrant skills — particularly the high-level technical and professional skills so much in demand — are being wasted. This is not, by any means, a new development. Immigrants have always faced difficulties integrating themselves into their adopted societies. In recent times, immigrants have complained of discrimination and the low value Canadian employers attach to overseas education and work experience. Accounts of foreign-trained engineers and doctors driving taxis, manning sales, or working as janitors, are deeply woven into the fabric of the immigrant experience. This is simply not an urban myth but a growing reality.

Even with higher education and better skills, immigrants are now less successful than Canadian born workers with equivalent education. It takes up to ten years for the earnings of university-educated immigrants to catch up to those of their Canadian counterparts (Reitz 2001). The reason for this "integration gap" is that immigrant skills are being discounted. In fact, the extent of this discounting has increased. While the mainstream workforce participated in the move toward the knowledge-based economy and the value of educational skills has increased, the relative value of immigrant skills has actually declined.

The significant disparity in income between native-born and naturalized Canadians is the result of several interrelated factors. These factors include the difficulties in assessing the equivalent value of a particular training and professional education, the reluctance of professional licensing bodies to grant credentials to immigrants trained overseas, and the inherent problems of determining the relevance of foreign experience to Canadian needs.

An increased emphasis on credentials in the labor market has changed the process by which immigrant skills are perceived and evaluated. The importance of credentials might be expected to enhance objectivity, yet immigrant credentials are not understood or recognized. Although there are a number of examples of this, even programs that aim to "fill the skills gap" such as the one being run by Vitesse in biotechnology showed that these immigrants could not on their own enhance their credentials by taking advantage of the "continuing education" opportunities without first going through a customized "safety course." For immigrants, the trend seems to be toward exclusion from the knowledge based economy.

A number of researchers have documented the trend, among them Jeffrey Reitz (2001). He analyzed earnings and income data from the 1996 census to demonstrate that immigrants receive smaller earnings premiums for formal education and work experience relative to native-born Canadians. Overall, Reitz (2001) suggested that, if immigrants received full compensation for their education and work experience, their annual earnings (based on 1996 data) would be fully 20% higher than they actually are. On this basis, Reitz (2001) concluded that immigrant skills are not only under-valued (and thus wasted), but far from compensate for the significant losses in human capital which result from foreign competition for skilled workers. This figure is estimated to be in the region of $15 billion!

As Reitz (2001) pointed out, measurement problems are a major obstacle. Where employers must choose between Canadian and foreign-trained applicants, the practice of discounting foreign qualifications may be seen as an effort to reduce risk — risk which directly results from the lack of metrics to evaluate the quality and/or relevance of overseas credentials. Reitz (2001) suggested that one of the best ways to overcome such obstacles is to devise a more effective "mutual orientation" for immigrants and prospective employers. In the normal course of events employers spend a good deal on the recruitment and orientation of new employees in any case. Accordingly, Reitz (2001) suggested that remedial educational institutions, professional associations and federal immigration authorities could also contribute to such an orientation process. In so doing, he concludes that helping Canadian employers deal with the very practical problems of using the new global workforce could be a low-cost way of improving returns from our investment in immigration.

The "integration gap" for immigrants into Canadian knowledge economy will have a long-term impact on Canada's immigration as a whole. Intensity of global competition to attract highly qualified professionals, especially to the U.K., Australia, Japan, Germany and USA, will put additional pressure on Canada. A new and innovative approach is required if Canada wants to attract the best and the brightest and use the pool of new immigrants effectively.

The Emergence of O-Vitesse as a Model Approach

In 1996, with the high tech boom catching a grip in Ottawa and with Ottawa beginning to use the term "Silicon Valley North" with greater confidence, the looming skills crises seemed to be the one issue that would prevent Ottawa — a cold northern capital from attracting skilled resources to meet its growing needs. The National Research Council (NRC), a federally funded Canadian government research institution, at about this time was itself going through a process of self-examination and grappling with the problem of finding ways to directly associate investment in research to economic activity, and thereby justify the large government funding for its research.

In an attempt to seek answers and suggestions for better linkage, the NRC embarked on an untried approach to create the first regional innovation office to build better ties to the local community. NRC was cognizant that with most of its research laboratories in the Ottawa region, any attempt at developing and building Ottawa's economic base could come under severe criticism as being a regional favorite. I was asked to initiate these discussions and to form the Regional Innovation Forum, a forum that brought together a cross-section of the community: local industry leaders, academia as well as economic development agencies and financial institutions. The Regional Innovation Forum's objective was to help in removing barriers to innovation in the region.

At the first Regional Innovation Forum Roundtable in 1996, the NRC Regional Innovation Office invited over 250 leaders from "Silicon Valley North" to identify these barriers to innovation. Much to the surprise of senior NRC executives present at the Roundtable, the industry leaders in Ottawa expressed not the need for increased technology commercialization efforts by government laboratories as was anticipated, but rather expressed grave concerns about the lack of skilled human resources needed for the growing high tech sector and in keeping with the reputation of being Canada's Silicon Valley.

As is generally the case in most discussions on skills shortages, especially for highly qualified professionals, the immediate response was to improve the system for faster processing of applications for new immigrants in categories that met the requirements of Ottawa and through it Canada's high tech sector. Fortunately, the discussions evolved to the realization that a number of recent immigrants and native-born Canadians, as well as spouses of recent migrants to Ottawa, possessed qualifications other than those relevant to the high tech sector but nonetheless were interested in seeking opportunities to transition to this sector given the lucrative job offers that were being made at the time.

In responding to this issue, a team was put together in my Regional Innovation Office to develop ways in which these highly qualified individuals could become the new source of skilled workers. Initially, there was considerable resistance from the two local universities, both indicating that they did not have the time or the resources to take on physicists, chemists, biologists and retrain them to become "software engineers." After much persuasion, the two universities agreed to take five candidates each from an incredibly large application pool of 450. With the assistance of Mitel, a local company, whose CEO was also the co-chair of the Regional Innovation Forum, the universities agreed to provide mentorship to these ten candidates.

The development of the pilot project, which came to be referred to as O-Vitesse (Ottawa Venture in Training Engineers and Scientists for Software Engineering) also faced challenges within Mitel even though its CEO was supportive of it. The technical managers at Mitel were overwhelmed with a heavy workload and were not too keen to provide mentoring support to a group of people that had little or no knowledge of computer science. However, when they were provided with a list of the potential candidates and their qualifications, their enthusiasm rose and they agreed to volunteer their time to mentor these candidates, permitting the launching of the O-Vitesse Pilot Project.

The program for O-Vitesse was designed to have an initial four months of academic training using existing courses in computer science at both the two local universities, Carleton University and University of Ottawa, followed by four months of mentorship at Mitel. This was then followed by another round of academic training and then a final term ending at the workplace. The key to the success of the program was the fact that the selection of courses for both the academic terms was done by the mentors and academic advisors rather than by the candidate. This approach ensured that the candidates were being re-skilled to meet the immediate needs of industry rather simply to acquire academic qualifications.

With the overwhelming success of this initial pilot program, a number of other companies joined in and a new not-for-profit corporation — Vitesse Re-Skilling Canada Inc. was formed to permit the use of this model in other locations and for other sectors.

The O-Vitesse Model demonstrated that academic credibility with respect to skills can be achieved through a targeted and shorter program in which industry is a key player. It also showed that individuals who possess qualifications in the any discipline of science or engineering are capable of rapidly acquiring new skills and transitioning to new knowledge-based sectors.

Growth and Expansion of the Vitesse Re-Skilling™ Model

Although the Model was initially only designed for technical skills, experience with participating Ottawa companies have suggested improvements in the model to incorporate soft skills as part of the re-skilling process. The underlying basic philosophy of the Vitesse Model is a cooperative approach to skills development that brings together highly qualified professionals, industry and academic institutions together.

The Vitesse model is based on an existing menu of course offerings provided by a variety of educational institutions with unique expertise in specific disciplines of interest to industry. Sponsoring firms can select courses from the menu to develop a program that is tailored both to their specific needs and the capabilities of selected candidates. Courses may be either classroom-oriented or self-study and each academic semester typically requires completion of five courses. Academic semesters alternate with work terms until training is completed.

During pre-program screening, candidates are matched with a sponsoring company. Sponsors cover both the costs of tuition and work-term stipend. During the work terms, students are assigned to a training-related project, which provides valuable hands-on experience. Students are assigned an in-house mentor from their sponsor company and an academic advisor. Together they identify key skills requirements and monitor student performance on the job and in the classroom.

Vitesse's role is to identify industry requirements, bring together all the key partners, and manage the overall process. Once a program is designed, Vitesse manages the recruitment phase of the process. Applicants are pre-screened by Vitesse's staff on the basis of pre-determined eligibility requirements. Final selection is made on the basis of a personal interview with the sponsor company.

The academic advisor and company mentor together assess the individual's existing skills and formulate a personal study plan designed to fit the sponsor's skills requirements.

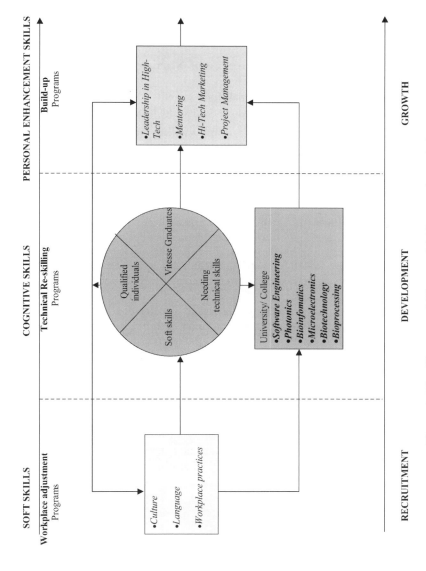

Figure 1: The Vitesse re-skilling model (the complete solution).

If these requirements change during training, the process is flexible enough to accommodate modifications in the training curriculum.

The advantage of this "just-in-time" approach (which is referred to as the *Vitesse-Triad*) allows the programs to respond very quickly to evolving industry needs, while at the same time ensuring that the student is equipped with leading-edge skills which are genuinely in demand (Figure 1).

Current Vitesse Programs — Evidence of Success

Since its inception, a total of 495 professionals have benefited from various re-skilling programs. These programs have included software engineering to biotechnology. The examples below illustrate the flexibility in Vitesse programs permitting re-skilling in various fields with industry as the key focus.

Vitesse Software Engineering Program

Vitesse's flagship offering started with the Software Engineering Program, a fast-track cooperative program designed to provide high-level IT skills to under- or unemployed science and engineering professionals in the Ottawa region. The program drew teaching resources from partnering institutions and is customized to suit the needs of individual employer sponsors. Courses are selected from the calendars of Carleton University and the University of Ottawa.

Candidates are screened and selected by Vitesse and placed either in a 16-month program which alternate between the university classroom and industry work term placements or an accelerated 12-month version.

Employer sponsors cover both the tuition fees and work term stipend for successful applicants and, in addition, provide a company mentor. In conjunction with a faculty advisor, the mentor's role is to ensure that students can immediately apply their newly acquired skills during work-term assignments and in subsequent full-time employment. The program has been offered seven times between the period 1996–2000 and attracted more than 1400 applicants, of whom approximately 65% were foreign-trained scientists and engineers. The program successfully re-skilled and placed 120 chemists, biologists and civil and mechanical engineers into IT and telecommunications firms in the Ottawa region.

Photonics Re-Skilling Program

Vitesse's Photonics Re-Skilling Program was pioneered at the start of the growth of the Photonics industry in Ottawa — addressing the qualitative skills shortages experienced by companies in the 2000–2001 period. The rapidly emerging science of photonics encompasses physics, materials sciences, electronics, chemistry and optics. Employed primarily in the telecommunications field, photonics technology can also be used in imaging, environmental monitoring and biomedical applications.

There were a number of similarities between Vitesse's Software Engineering re-skilling model and the Photonics one. In both cases, existing academic resources were used to provide the required skills. Industry participation was a key component of the model and re-skilled professionals provide an enriched environment in their organization.

Development of the Vitesse Photonics Re-Skilling Program was again in direct response to requests from industry and recommendations by the Ottawa Economic Generators Study to sharpen the competitiveness of what is rapidly emerging as a major growth opportunity for Canada.

Given the dynamic and multi-faceted nature of the emerging discipline, however, Vitesse quickly recognized that a "one-size-fits-all" solution was inappropriate and instead set out to create a series of opportunities tailored to specific industry needs. In so doing, Vitesse faced a number of challenges that were not a factor in the Software Engineering Program. For example, Vitesse's research confirmed that academic resources in the photonics area were virtually non-existent in the educational institutions in the Ottawa area and, since industry needs were urgent, a 12–16 month academic engagement was impractical and unsuitable for companies.

Accordingly, Vitesse put together a list of an international network of top-ranking university professors with the expertise needed to deliver the courses in the proposed Vitesse photonics curriculum. In response to industry requirements for a speedy solution, a series of condensed training modules were developed that matched employer content requirements and time lines.

The Program featured an intensive weeklong introduction to photonics and laser technology, with shorter multi-day programs in telecommunications systems. Specialized seminars provided more intensive instruction on specific subjects or areas in which sponsoring employers had a unique requirement. Where larger companies had the critical mass to support it, course modules were offered in-house.

This program became an important element for re-skilling of electrical engineers and physicists within companies that were making a quick changeover to photonics. The Photonics Re-Skilling Program re-skilled some 200 professionals.

Vitesse Bridging Program for Foreign-Trained Biotech Professionals

The program is targeting to re-skill, over three years, several foreign-trained biotech professionals for the Ontario biotech industry, without duplicating their existing education and experience. The program addresses the challenges facing foreign-trained professionals, namely, non-recognition of academic credentials, lack of Canadian experience, and technical skills gap and provides candidate with needed communications skills to effectively function in the Canadian workplace environment. This is an on going program funded by the Ontario Ministry of Training, Colleges and Universities, and is currently being developed by Vitesse in close cooperation with the interested stakeholders — universities, industry and professionals. A total of 27 people have benefited from the program in its first year that began in 2003.

The program features a modular approach to bridging the skills gaps of foreign-trained immigrants who come from a number of countries each with its unique set of academic programs and work experiences. The program provides for language and workplace skills modules scaled to meet the different requirements for each individual. It also features modules that allow for refresher courses, as well as skills to meet the Canadian companies' requirements in the diverse field of biotechnology. The program is unique in its design providing the maximum flexibility with the objective of ensuring that each professional is able to acquire all the necessary skills that would enhance the candidate's ability to work effectively in the Canadian workplace at the same level as any other Canadian trained professional.

Vitesse Bioprocessing Program

This program was originally designed to ensure that the investment by DSM Biologics, a Montreal based bioprocessing company will not suffer from any shortage of skilled professionals if it chose to expand its operations there. The Vitesse approach was to demonstrate that qualified biotechnology professionals trained with specializations in various different areas of biotechnology could easily be re-skilled to meet the specific human resource requirements of the bioprocessing industry.

The Vitesse Bioprocessing Re-Skilling Program was delivered in conjunction with McGill University as a Pilot Project that led to the development of a new curriculum to meet the specific needs of the selected professionals and the anticipated needs of the Bioprocessing industry. It included a "hands-on" component and was delivered during the summer term to allow for participation from industry and for a customized program to be delivered by McGill faculty.

These are only four examples of the various programs developed using the Re-Skilling model. Vitesse has delivered a number of other programs, which follow the same principles of flexibility, timeliness of delivery, meeting specific industry needs and using the expertise resident in existing educational institutions (Figure 2).

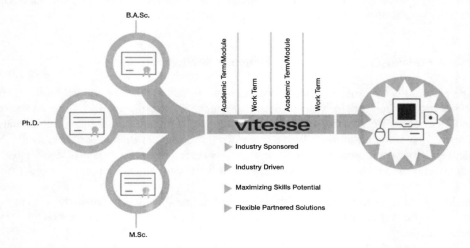

Figure 2: Targeted re-skilling.

Re-Skilling rather than Re-Training: A Silicon Valley North Innovation

The Vitesse Model demonstrates that the programs most useful to industry are those that provide *mutual orientation* (Reitz 2001) for both employers and professionals seeking to re-establish themselves in the labor market through the acquisition of new skills. Based on the experience in providing both training in specific skills and in developing programs aimed at making professionals workplace-ready, all the elements needed to deal with the skills challenge already exist. Ottawa has been a good testing ground from which to draw a number of conclusions.

First, that both the raw knowledge and technological know-how needed to sustain the new economy already exist within Canada's research and academic institutions. While Canada can certainly benefit from increased levels of R&D and from an infusion of new talent into many university faculties, we can achieve a great deal more with what we already have.

Second, while population growth may be slowing, we should not discount the fact that we have a large and well-educated workforce capable of absorbing new skills and revitalizing its existing knowledge base. In the short term, at least, we can respond to many skill requirements with appropriate "re-skilling" programs aimed at refreshing and upgrading existing technical skills.

Third, Canada has a large and growing inflow of skilled immigrants whose skills are not being fully utilized. In many cases, immigrants need "up-skilling" and "re-skilling" and some degree of "cultural reconditioning" — or training in so-called soft skills — to meet current industry needs.

Employers' reservations about recruiting immigrants are based in part on their lack of familiarity with Canadian business custom and management style. Training in such areas as oral and written business communication, presentation and interviewing skills, workplace practices, teamwork and self-management techniques are seen by industry recruiters as important prerequisites to employment. Both types of training, in soft as well as technical skills, can be delivered relatively inexpensively and in a much shorter time frame than presently perceived by most traditional educational institutions.

In providing a variety of tailor-made training vehicles to the high-tech sector, the Vitesse' Model suggests that the environment is both complex and dynamic demanding innovative solutions. Traditional methods of training and development are not always as effective or as appropriate in the fast-paced new economy. Accordingly, the Re-Skilling Model has consciously focused from the outset on the development of innovative training approaches and methodologies, which are both responsive to individual needs and employer requirements.

In so doing, it provides the template for a national re-skilling program, building on its regional roots. It requires no new infrastructure and, with relatively little adaptation, the model can be applied to a wide range of high-tech skill requirements. The Model has been applied to meet the new needs that emerged in 1998 for Photonics, and more recently for Biotechnology and Bioinformatics. New programs in Biophotonics and Nanotechnology and Wireless will add in addressing the needs of these emerging technology sectors.

The Vitesse Model and approach to the skills development challenge has a number of benefits, all of which are a "win-win" situation for those involved. Vitesse methodologies offer an enormously flexible and relatively inexpensive solution to current skills shortages and a model for long-term training and skills development. For industry, re-skilled graduates represent an invaluable addition to their human resource pool through a customized solution on a timely basis that can guarantee quality of output. Since training is closely monitored by the firm itself, quality assurance is enhanced with higher than normal retention rates.

On the academic front, the Re-Skilling Model enables both institutions and individual professors to forge a relationship with industry — but in a manner that does not compromise the overall objectives of university education. The Model prevents industry from being able to dictate the direction of education as it does not involve large-scale financial contributions and building of facilities that tend to have an industry bias. At the same time, this Model acts as a test-bed for the development of mainstream curricula and enables faculty to address industry needs without investing in new infrastructure. The end result is to enhance the responsiveness of the learning system to critical social and economic needs.

The most obvious beneficiaries of this Model are the professionals themselves. In applying their existing training and experience to the acquisition of new and current skills, they assure themselves of new career opportunities in industries that are on the cutting edge of the knowledge-based economy. Of all participants, foreign-trained immigrants are most likely to benefit. Since an important part of the Vitesse-Triad™ process is that previous education is reviewed and scrutinized by academic advisors, problems with credential recognition are virtually eliminated.

At the same time, the Re-Skiling programs eliminate another typical hurdle faced by foreign-trained professionals — the lack of Canadian experience. Because at the outset of the program there is a match between the individual candidate and the sponsoring firm, employers are able to determine the suitability of the candidate throughout the selection, training and evaluation process. Although there is no obligation on the part of sponsors to hire graduates on a permanent basis, there has been a 98% take-up rate by firms to date.

Figure 3: The partnership approach to re-skilling.

These programs also address the problem of Canadian cultural orientation for immigrants through its soft skills training modules (Figure 3).

Looking and Thinking Forward

The Vitesse Re-Skilling Model is an innovative model that involves the development of a "just-in-time" curriculum and program to meet the immediate needs at all times of industry while taking into account each and every professional's background, experience and qualifications. The trademarked Re-Skilling Model allows for optimum utilization of Canada's educational resources across different universities and colleges and relaxing the current "territorial" structure of education. Yet, it allows for a local and regional solution to the skills needs of any particular industry or technology cluster.

The model provides the necessary skills within a timeframe that is shorter than one year while at the same time provides the candidates with the necessary academic credit essential for recognition purposes. These credits could then be used, should there be a need by the company or the individual, to pursue the traditional degree or diploma programs. The Vitesse Model focuses on skills rather than academic degrees or diplomas yet it is not a vocational training programs offered by Colleges. It provides a transition opportunity, a true life long learning opportunity into a new career or field that is currently not possible or available through our educational system. It is therefore an effective mechanism for adjustment of shifts in labor demand as a result of changes in business cycles and a necessary tool to meet the needs of young and emerging sectors.

Canada has one of the highest rates of educated workforce. This statistic, however, does not distinguish the skills requirements in Canada's traditional sectors and those in the knowledge sectors and as such does not explain the shortages of skilled labor in the growth sectors. The Vitesse Model allows for re-skilling of the current workforce for a future need. It is increasingly clear that investment in workplace training and the refreshment of technical skills must increase if Canadian industry is to remain productive and competitive. The technology related knowledge sectors are especially vulnerable and yet these sectors provide the greatest promise for a new round of economic activity.

In contrast to many of Canada's trading partners and competitors, Canada spends very little on workplace training. Estimates of this spending is as low as 31% of firms providing training to their staff as compared to 75% in Japan and 80% in the U.K. The Vitesse Re-Skilling Model demonstrates that if there is an effective interface between industry and academic institutions, the investment in re-skilling need not be heavy. Most elements needed to ensure that future skills requirements are met are already in place. Nor is there a need to invest in costly new training infrastructure or facilities — other than those necessary to expand enrollment and research activities. What is required is an innovative delivery system that does away with the archaic "continuing education" approach so prevalent in universities today and replaced by more dynamic mechanism outside of the university system with which it can interface with a broader array of sectors and other educational institutions.

The Vitesse projects show that such mechanisms can easily be developed and that the skills gap issue that has been a matter of discussion for decades can finally be put to rest. The re-skilling methodology has proven to be effective in multiple sectors and in various regions. Skills development programs need not be encumbered by questions of jurisdiction as this model shows — it is free of any parochial or provincial restrictions and limitations as it is market driven and pervades those limitations and can serve as Canada's response to the skills crises.

References

Conference Board of Canada (2001a). Canadian outlook: Long term forecast 2001. Ottawa, Ontario, Canada: Conference Board of Canada.

Conference Board of Canada (2001b). Training and development outlook – 2001. Ottawa, Ontario, Canada: Conference Board of Canada.

Deloitte & Touche (2001). *North America technology fast 500 – CEO survey result – Fifth annual survey*, www.fast500.com.

Drucker, P. F. (1992). *Managing for the future: The 1990s and beyond*. New York: Truman Talley Bools & Dutton.

Human Resources Development Canada (1996). *The early careers of engineers and the accumulation of skills in the Canadian economy*, Applied Research Branch.

Human Resources Development Canada (2002). *Knowledge matters: Skills and learning for Canadian*. Ottawa, Ontario, Canada: Government of Canada, February.

Industry Canada (2002). *Achieving excellence: Investing in people, knowledge and opportunity*. Ottawa, Ontario, Canada: Government of Canada, February.

Mather, F. (2002). *The new knowledge labor force for global economic competitiveness: Do higher education institutions matter and can they respond*? Unpublished Ph.D. dissertation. Toronto, Ontario, Canada: University of Toronto.

Reitz, J. (2001). Immigrant skill utilization in the Canadian labor market: Implications of human capital research. Unpublished draft paper for the *Journal of International Migration and Integration*.

Statistics Canada (1999). Education indicators in Canada. Report of the Pan-Canadian Education Indicators Program. Ottawa, Ontario, Canada: Statistics Canada.

Notation

"Re-skilling" has been registered as a trademark by Vitesse Re-skilling Canada Inc.

Chapter 15

Ottawa's TalentWorks — Regional Learning and Collaborative Governance for a Knowledge Age

Gilles Paquet, Jeffrey Roy and Chris Wilson

Abstract

Ottawa is home to both technology clusters and public institutions and as a result, it must sustain a skilled and educated workforce. As Ottawa competes with communities throughout the world, improving access to skilled and adaptable workers has become a key priority. This chapter examines the formation of Talent Works, a unique initiative designed to orchestrate an integrative and collaborative strategy for workforce development. As a critical element of Ottawa's future as a locale for innovation and growth, Talent Works represents an important initiative and a revealing case study on the challenges of building collaborative governance.

Introduction

Ottawa is uniquely diversified economically across a strong presence of technology companies in the private sector and the headquarters of the Government of Canada in the public sector. This phenomenon is particularly important within the context of a knowledge-based economy given the reliance on knowledge and services across both sectors. As a result, the area must sustain a highly skilled and highly educated workforce. Just as many of the products and services generated in Ottawa must compete in the global marketplace, Ottawa must compete with communities and regions throughout the world to develop, recruit and sustain a highly talented workforce.

While Ottawa has an advantage of a highly educated workforce, business leaders report that the actual skills of workers differ from the qualifications demanded by many industries and employers in the region (TalentWorks 2002a). As the proportion of knowledge-based jobs in the area increases and the giant cohort of baby boomers approaches retirement, skill requirements will continue to rise. Therefore, improving access to skilled and adaptable workers has become one of Ottawa's highest economic and community development priorities (TalentWorks 2002a). The central element in addressing this priority is information.

As the child of *The Ottawa Partnership (TOP)* and the Ottawa Centre for Research and Innovation (OCRI),[1] *TalentWorks* is a unique initiative that has brought to the same table business, government, education and training and community leaders to facilitate broad community-wide dialogue and collaboration with the aim of both taking stock of Ottawa's workforce, including its existing strengths and weaknesses, and developing a set of mechanisms to better nurture the city's human capital. We define workforce development to mean the collective engagement of government, employers and the education and training providers in the development of skills programs that provide sustainable economic achievement for all segments of the employable population within a given jurisdiction.

Clearly, collaboration is difficult, particularly the transition from dialogue to action, as creating common ground, identifying resources and orchestrating concerted actions are all significant challenges. As a critical element of Ottawa's future success as a locale for technological innovation, entrepreneurship and growth, TalentWorks represents an important initiative and a revealing case study of the rising importance of collaborative governance for local success in a knowledge-based economy.

Collaboration, Learning and Competitive Advantage

Workforce development is a collective learning challenge for all sectors engaged in economic development. To better understand the local or regional determinants of learning, one must explore their learning dynamics.[2] A convincing body of knowledge points to the role of learning as a determinant of industrial competitiveness, product and process innovation, and collaborative capacities (Castells & Hall 1993; Florida 1995; Moss Kanter 1995; Paquet & Roy 2004a, b; Storper 1997). Thus, a region's social, technical and productive infrastructure is critical to the success of local firms, complementing their own individual activities and providing shared and positive externalities for all actors in the region.

The dynamics of learning and adaptation, central to the complexities of ecological systems, are increasingly used as an analogy to the collaborative relations between sectors in local systems of governance (Moore 1996). Our economies are developing a far richer ecology of institutions to co-ordinate economic activity, to generate ideas and translate them into products. In this new ecology a range of corporate, regional and personal

---

[1] The Ottawa Partnership is a local network of economic development agencies and private sector leaders who meet under the auspices of the City of Ottawa — and as such, this informal council is co-chaired by the Mayor of Ottawa and a prominent private sector representative. OCRI, one member of the Ottawa Partnership, is the City's leading economic development agency, a quasi-autonomous organization accountable jointly to the City and its membership. OCRI's primary mission is to facilitate multi-sector partnerships in a range of areas designed to strengthen local entrepreneurship and innovation in the economy, particularly technology-oriented industries (http://www.ocri.ca). OCRI houses the TalentWorks secretariat, coordinating resources and strategies, responsible to a steering committee of stakeholders. The recommendations discussed in this chapter have been prepared by a research team, including the authors of this chapter, at the University of Ottawa's Centre on Governance.

[2] For purposes of this chapter we assume "local" and "regional" to be inter-changeable terms, in reference to a territorially defined, primarily urban jurisdiction (unless otherwise defined).

networks will organize the most critical process: generating new knowledge that can be translated into products and services. Durable and dynamic networks are underpinned by reciprocity and mutual trust, which allow members to share information, risks and opportunities with greater ease (Leadbeater 1999: 148).

Therefore, the success of a region is determined, in large part, by their effectiveness in gathering and using knowledge. The ability to innovate depends on obtaining access to learning-intensive relations. Innovation stems from the interplay among the different institutions and individuals — firms, laboratories, universities and consumers. The result is a society composed of more network-based governance patterns (Stoker 1996), and as we shall see below this means that appropriate response mechanisms — such as those envisioned by the TalentWorks's initiative, will be increasingly horizontal, collaborative and multi-stakeholder.

Through these conditions and responses regions can contribute in a unique and significant way to an enterprise's flexibility, responsiveness and innovation (Keeble & Wilkinson 1999). In response to the growing pressures of globalization and new technologies, communities around the world have begun to sketch out the first drafts of "networked" communities — networks of individuals and firms linked and aligned in new social and electronic channels, and in new partnership arrangements. With regard to the formation of such arrangements, there is often an emphasis on economic agents, and their ability to learn through innovation, an approach best exemplified by Florida's "learning region" (1995). In short, within this market-centric perspective, organizational learning represents the internal dynamics of firm processes, while community-based learning represents the firm's web of external linkages.

Regional learning, however, cannot be purely market based. Henton's emphasis on civic entrepreneurship recognizes both the many faceted dimensions of learning and the multiplicity of actors who participate in building new forms of synergistic ties (Henton *et al.* 1997). The picture of learning that emerges is one marked by distributed governance across market, state and civic spaces (Paquet 1997), where even those most interested in the managerial consequences for firms point to fluid boundaries, new ecologies, and multi-stakeholder ties as necessary elements for competitive advantage (Moore 1996).

Building on the work of Storper (1997) in their investigation of the dynamics of an innovation milieu, Lawson & Lorenz (1999) suggest that collective learning is the product of linkages between tacit knowledge flows and the region's innovative capacity. In other words, production and innovation systems are interdependent elements of a form of learning that rests almost exclusively on mechanisms for knowledge management. Capello (1999) makes a similar claim on collective learning as a form of club good — with commonalities as the basis of shared externalities for all actors within the local milieu.

This emphasis on partnership implies that any inclusive template for collective learning will require an explicit governance dimension. The production externalities, innovation dynamics, and civic bonds that are all necessary and interdependent components of the region require coordination. However, coordinating these components is becoming an increasingly complex challenge, one that is a growing policy priority for governments, as well as a strategic priority for the private and community sectors.

This type of coordination is essentially a shared governance challenge, one in keeping with the realities of workforce development for any given region. As key elements of collective competitiveness and learning, since human capital is the key agent of knowledge generation that moves both within organizations and across them, skills training and education and the range of partnerships required to address all segments of a local workforce are all nodes across a shared strategy of improving the local talent pool. Attempting to coordinate the various dimensions to workforce performance is an emerging priority.

The Centrality of Workforce Development

An increasingly knowledge-based economy has been shown to be more focused on continuous innovation than previously more industrial eras — and as a result, it is highly dependent on what we might refer to as knowledge churn — a continuous cycle of generation and dissemination of knowledge within society (Capello 1999). While it is true that knowledge builds wealth, sharing knowledge can accelerate the creation of wealth in much the same way a fixed volume of money creates more wealth the more it circulates.

There are, in fact, business models in use today, such as open source software models, that base their entire success on giving away this precious knowledge resource in order to generate attendant services or establish competitive market standards (Tapscott & Ticoll 2003). And while innovation often leads to enhanced quality, the rate of innovation or time to market inevitably pushes organizations to work together to form complex partnerships and networks in order to deliver those innovations to consumers faster than anyone else (Tapscott & Ticoll 2003).

With knowledge as the principal resource and innovation as the key to global competitiveness, its flows and usages are not subject to the same ownership and control as the physical assets of the industrial age. Workers in the knowledge economy are increasingly mobile and that mobility demands that more attention be paid to what motivates them to move. Understandably, issues of talent supply — how to develop, how to attract, and how to keep top talent — have moved to the front of the economic and social agenda. In a recent report prepared for the U.S. National Governors Association the number one recommendation was to invest in systems that build workforce skills and promote lifelong learning to ensure a competitive workforce (National Governor's Association 2001). Florida (2000) has emphasized the surrounding geographic and cultural environment as key attributes in shaping the locational choices of an increasingly mobile class of knowledge workers — and as such, workforce development becomes widened to include the collective attributes of a particular city or country in not only nourishing their own labour force but also setting the conditions to harness a positive inflow of new talent and ideas.

A simplistic answer to questions of what drives the choices of workers, particularly the most educated, often begins with measures of financial compensation (i.e. "pay more money"). But in a competitive world if everyone pays more, then everyone ultimately loses, as much of the potential advantages of higher wages become thwarted by a collective, upward spiralling of costs. Moreover, there are many non-monetary factors that attract and motivate people like a good educational system, access to health care, affordable housing, safe and clean environments, a rich and diversified quality of community — that are not easily copied from one area to the next.

Wages and salaries may not even be the most central concern or motivation of knowledge workers. Factors such as the challenge aspect of work, the opportunity to interact with interesting people, the exposure to new technology, career opportunities, work environment, quality of life, and the opportunity for continuous learning may well be prioritized ahead of financial compensation (see also the chapter by Dyke *et al.* this volume). While the ranking of such factors no doubt varies for each individual the collective package of attributes and enticements represents a key resource not only for the single company, but also for the cluster and region as an integrative entity. As people make career choices, whether they are choice of profession, identification of preferred employer or preferred route for education and training, they do so within a context — and such a context is viewed, in part, as a range of factors that represent a community.

It is for this reason that today regions feel compelled to make a strong effort to sell their own jurisdictions as an advantageous place in which to live as well as work, the broad contours of which are presented on any municipal or civic website. A locally based quality of life is invariably marketed in direct juxtaposition with its career opportunities. While this may not seem significant to some, the increasing reliance of firms on people as both their principle resource and their competitive advantage, makes it incumbent on Ottawa-based employers to work hand-in-glove with community decision-makers to create a high quality living and working environment that is perceived to be competitive and desirable on a "world class" basis.

The reality that innovation drives our economy and that relentless change characterizes our society should not be thought of as an obstacle but an opportunity. Such change needs to be harnessed to maximize the advantages of Ottawa's knowledge economy, such as employment and wealth creation, and to redress the economic and social shortcomings of those who may find themselves displaced from this new economy. In this interdependent environment where decisions taken by either employers or community organizations may have significant influence on one another, there is a rising need for more shared forms of decision-making and coordination (see also the chapter by Jackson *et al.* this volume).

The first step in achieving effective collaboration will be for everyone to share what it is they are seeing as a problem so that a consistent pattern can emerge. TalentWorks, though the creation of a *Workforce Development Strategy*, will be creating a context for that kind of ongoing regional dialogue around a wide range of workforce issues (TalentWorks 2002c). The idea of a workforce development strategy is not new. Yet, along with intensifying competition what is most often lacking in many cities, including Ottawa, is a holistic portrait of the strengths and weakness for the workforce as a whole, along with a collective assessment and strategy for improving the entire range of skill sets, educational portfolios and employment opportunities that shape the pool of talent underpinning economic creativity and growth. Often, the first step is merely taking stock and gathering all of the pertinent information into a common lens.

Taking Stock — Information as the Foundation

An effective workforce development strategy must go beyond simply identifying common labour force data to gather information that better reflects those factors that are attractors and motivators of talent. These may be economic indicators, educational achievement levels or quality of life indicators; all of which, taken together, can help present a general picture of the community. We also know with the workforce markets as volatile as they are, static snapshots have a short shelf life. Often by the time a labour force study is completed, the economic conditions, which such a study may describe, will have turned around or altered in a dramatic fashion.

A workforce development strategy should therefore be dynamic, organic and able to respond to change. As well, it should be future-oriented and include information on educational and training opportunities for workers and their families. Furthermore, it should include information on innovation and change in the various economic sectors so that education and training providers can contribute to new developments through research and development activities and make timely adjustments to future skill sets.

The approach of TalentWorks has been based on the recognition that it is highly likely that much of the contextual information required by key community decision makers, job seekers and employers already exists, has already been produced by a variety of institutions and agencies around the region (TalentWorks 2002a). However, the information has not been integrated into a holistic picture of the region nor has it been put in a form that is readily useable by most citizens. After a series of regional consultation sessions with representatives from all major stakeholders across Ottawa, broad agreement emerged around the need to present workforce related information so that it would help inform the decision making of people, organizations and the community. The research compiled for TalentWorks collectively determined that a complete portrait of relevant workforce and education information required essentially nine dimensions (TalentWorks 2002a):

• Economic, cost-of-doing-business, innovation, and income dimensions which speak to the needs of organizations in the knowledge economy.
• An employment profile, workforce transitions, and access to technology dimensions which speak to the needs of people in the knowledge economy.
• A skills and education profile and community quality of life dimensions that speak to the needs of organizations, people and the community.

The economic data is crucial to help keep organizations abreast of market trends and Ottawa's relative economic performance. Obviously, if the overall economy is in recession or in growth, the focus of a workforce strategy will be more in the quantitative direction, whereas knowing whether the outputs of Ottawa's workforce are globally competitive will influence the qualitative direction of a strategy. The indicators in this group will suggest some of the key costs of doing business in Ottawa. This has relevance to both organizations and individuals in terms of the attractiveness of the area. Changes in labour costs will tend to have inverse impacts on organizations and individuals and so a balance must be achieved. However, increases in taxes, facilities and transportation costs will be clear disincentives for both.

As previously mentioned, success in the knowledge economy demands innovation. While directly measuring a subjective quality like innovativeness is not possible, one standard proxy for a region's innovativeness is the educational attainment level of its workforce. The assumption is the higher the level of education across a local economy the more innovative the workforce is likely to be (Capello 1999). Other indicators like R&D spending, venture capital investment and the number of new businesses tell us how creativity and ingenuity are being employed and how that innovation is being valued in the economy (Paquet & Roy 2004a). The innovative the region, the more it will attract innovative people and innovative companies which will increase the demand for well paid, high value-adding knowledge workers.

Given the increasing value contribution of knowledge to economic outputs, the data on income levels represents a proxy for the degree to which knowledge is permeating the workforce. Since low-knowledge, low-skill manual work is paid only minimally and high-knowledge, high-skill is well paid, the higher the average income levels the more knowledge is being utilized in the workforce, in general. However, if the average income is increasing due to an increasing gap between highest and lowest income levels, it would suggest more is required to upgrade the skills of the low-income group. The goal is not only to have as many people employed as possible, but also to have Ottawa's workers adding more value and being the most productive in the world so that they can enjoy the highest standard of living.

The employment profile will help assess where people are working and how employment patterns are changing relative to total population growth. Is Ottawa doing better at finding people jobs or helping them to create their own jobs? What parts of Ottawa's workforce needs attention? In any economy, firms are constantly changing. They are born, they grow and sometimes they die. People, too, do not remain the same and today they are unlikely to stay at the same job for long periods of time, especially knowledge workers. This workforce mobility implies that at any given point some people will always be in transit or unemployed.

As a community, there is a collective interest in assisting people as they make a transition from one opportunity to the next. As a cluster, this type of investment represents a shared and positive externality for all firms, and a particularly critical impetus for the ability of entrepreneurs to form and grow new business ventures. Consequently, we need to be aware of those who are temporarily or chronically unemployed, juxtaposing our options against the needs of the economy and the opportunities for knowledge and skill enhancement. The workforce transition measures help in this regard.

With the ubiquitous presence of technology in every economic sector, access to technology and technology training has become a prerequisite skill for employment. Technology reduces the time for the collection, manipulation and dissemination of knowledge and extends their reach. It is also the basis of much of the productivity gains that have been made in the last decades. Recent research has suggested that those with access and knowledge of technology are most likely to succeed in this economy and those without get left behind (Nelson 1998; see also the chapter by Thorngate this volume). The expression, digital divide, has been coined to describe this modern version of class distinction. Therefore a knowledge of general technology and technology training accessibility will be essential to ensure widest opportunity for employment and the highest quality of Ottawa's workforce.

The profile of skills and education tells us how our system of workforce development may be responding to the future needs of the economy. It will give us an indication of the size of the future workforce that will not participate in the knowledge economy because it will fail to meet the basic minimum standard of high school completion. It will also give us a distribution of post-secondary training at universities, colleges or in technical trades. It will also give a sense of the level of skill upgrading being undertaken by the private sector. Altogether this will give us a rough estimation of how current education and training efforts are shaping the future workforce. For employers, this will aid in forecasting future talent supplies and for job seekers or those wanting to advance their careers a sense of where opportunities lie.

The quality of life indicator group suggests the degree of regional attractiveness to workers. Recalling the significance of community quality of life (Florida 2000), firms may use this information either to attract new workers if they are already here, or perhaps relocate or expand to Ottawa from elsewhere. As suggested by Kotkin (2000) wherever knowledge workers cluster, whether in small towns or in big cities, that is where wealth will accumulate and therefore that's where businesses will want to be. Citizens and workers themselves can use this information to inform potential relocation decisions of their own or even to get a comparative evaluation of the lifestyle opportunities here in Ottawa.

Ottawa's Top Ten Workforce Priorities

Through a consultation process conducted by the TalentWorks research team,[3] including a survey of over 500 local area residents, interviews with over 60 key industry sector representatives and 12 focus groups involving more than 80 representatives from all of the major industry sectors of Ottawa's economy, data was systematically gathered, distilled, summarized and interpreted in order to present a collective and complete workforce profile (TalentWorks 2002b).

The research and analysis that led to the workforce profile became the basis for attempting to pinpoint the key issues and priorities facing Ottawa in its efforts to enhance workforce development team. From this analysis, and summarized below, are the ten most critical priorities likely to shape Ottawa's future potential in terms of attracting, retaining and nurturing a highly-skilled and adaptable workforce (TalentWorks 2002c):

(a) Insufficient linkages and partnerships
Despite common perception that Ottawa had evolved extensive networks between business and government, between these two and the community, between businesses and institutions of higher education, and between businesses and schools at all levels of education, the inadequacy of cross-sector linkages was a recurrent theme across discussions with local employers and educators. In particular, industry participation in helping to shape curriculum and guidance for young people in terms of skills and career choices was deemed inadequate.

The disconnect between the available education and training programs and the needs of Ottawa employers was often described in terms of networking failures: the failure of

---

[3] The TalentWorks research team includes the authors of this chapter and a number of additional contributors from the Centre on Governance at the University of Ottawa. A complete listing of experts and contributors is provided in each of the TalentWorks reports (2002a, b, c — referenced in this chapter and also available online via the Ottawa Centre for Research and Innovation at http://www.ocri.ca).

industry and education to exchange personnel; the inability to use industry input in the formulation of curricula; the failure to develop effective internships and co-op placement systems beneficial to both students and employers; and the absence of a widespread system for mentoring or training the trainer initiatives. While in Ottawa this sharing of industry and academic resources is being done through the National Capital Institute of Telecommunications and through Algonquin College's Bachelor of Information Technology program, a strong sentiment suggests that such ties must be both deepened and expanded.

(b) Lack of a single window for information on Ottawa's workforce demands and training resources

There is a lack of clear, timely and comprehensive information on Ottawa's current and future workforce demands, and on available training programs that might address these demands. Such information should be easily accessible to employers and employees, the unemployed, and potential new Canadians. There is a need for a "one-stop shop" of reliable information rather than a multiplicity of sources. An online solution should be included.

(c) The threat of a triple crunch (retirements, double cohort, and growing economy)

The need to establish a new and more effective system of workforce governance is strongly underscored by the coming together of three unfolding challenges. First is the demographic challenge presented by the retirement of a large segment of the senior professors, trainers and teachers in the workforce in the coming decade. Given that Ontario is also creating fewer Ph.Ds today than in 1990, we know that there will be fewer people, particularly at the post-secondary level, to provide the training needed.

Second, the next big wave of students, the children of the baby boomers, is currently moving through the post-secondary system. This trend, combined with the impact of the double cohort that began the fall of 2003 (the elimination of Grade 13 resulting in two graduating classes from high school the same year), will add significant demand to the already stretched resources of the post-secondary system. This spike in demand will last for five to eight years. The demands of a growing economy will probably siphon off specialists from the education system, as occurred between 1997 and 2001. The net result of this triple crunch is that just as the demand for talent reaches its highest point, the community's capacity to meet that demand will be significantly diminished. Last, the talent demand of the next wave of advanced technology growth will probably begin in the next two to three years.

(d) Insufficient career counselling

There is a clear need for significant reinvestment of time, money and people in career counseling across the region at the secondary, post-secondary and adult levels. This message is consistent from industry leaders, job seekers, placement organizations, and education and training organizations. The standard advice to clients from existing career services is to get a university education in order to get work in the advanced technology sector. Obviously, any community is built on more than one sector, and Ottawa is no exception. Career counsellors need to familiarize themselves with a wider range of career options, and they need more up-to-date information on where the job market is heading, what skills (both technical and employability) are required, and what education and training options will deliver those skills effectively. The need for more effective career counselling applies not only to youth, but also to all employed and unemployed people.

(e) Underutilization of foreign-trained professionals
Due to artificial barriers created by immigration policies, provincial regulations, and the regulations and standards of certain professional associations, foreign-trained professionals remain underutilized in Ottawa. Further, the lack of policy coherence among the federal government, provincial governments and the national professional associations creates a perverse situation: individuals are encouraged to come to Ottawa because of a talent they may never be able to use in Ottawa. The root of this incoherence stems from a lack of investment in the immigrant screening processes in the countries of origin, a failure to assess and recognize immigrant qualifications, and an insufficient amount of resources dedicated to immigrant skills upgrading (see also the chapter by Chhatbar this volume).

(f) Insufficient employer commitment to employability skills and failure of educators/ trainers to integrate employability skills in curricula
Despite an overriding recognition of the importance of soft skills such as communication and inter-personal relations, there is no long-term vision or commitment to the systematic development of these skills, backed by appropriate incentive systems. In today's job market, firms consider candidates on the basis of their technical skills but also select them on the basis of such softer skills — writing and communication, for example, are often critical determinants. When the job market picks up this is unlikely to remain the case and the bias towards technical skills may once again screen out many good potential candidates. Even though we have heard from those we surveyed and interviewed that technical skills are what you train for and employability skills are what you hire for (underscoring the importance of employability skills), education and training programs continue to focus more on technical skills and largely treat employability skills as a given (TalentWorks 2002c).

Education and training providers (private and public) are not integrating technical skills, business skills and interpersonal skills effectively. As a result, employees are frequently underutilized, because it takes time for them to acquire these skills and integrate them (to the benefit of their employer). The often expressed need for several years of experience (which is seen by many potential employees as a barrier to employment) is based on the assumption that, given sufficient experience, employees do develop the necessary business and personal skills and integrate these with their technical skills or they leave the industry. Since educators and trainers have failed to integrate these skills, employers must rely on employees graduating from the school of hard knocks (i.e. learning by doing).

(g) Insufficient mapping of industry skills and training requirements to aid transferability
Few industry sectors have developed a detailed map of the skills and training requirements of their sector: one prominent exception is the mapping conducted by the Software Human Resource Council, a body that has created the Occupational Skills Profile Model (OSPM),[4]

---

[4] http://www.shrc.ca/ospm/index.html.

designing it as a reference tool for Canadians interested in Information Technology. This model clarifies job definitions for software workers and describes the skills required for jobs in the software industry. The lack of this kind of skill mapping in other sectors limits skill transferability within sectors and makes it difficult for job seekers and employers to assess skill transferability across sectors. Ultimately this lack of knowledge reduces the flexibility of the workforce to adapt to the ups and downs of any particular industry.

(h) Need to reduce the lag time between skill identification by employers and the education/ training response
Educational institutions and government do not respond adequately to changes in skill sets and changes in skill demands. There is a significant lag time between the recognition of a skill need within an industry and the response by educational organizations. In the case of colleges and private sector trainers, that lag time may be nine to twelve months; at the university level the delay may be as much as three to five years. Closer ties between industry and the education/training sector are needed.

   In addition, given the increasingly technical emphasis of education, and therefore the short life span of the skill sets developed, educational institutions seem to be consistently preparing for the past. For example, there has been a considerable effort over the past few years to increase the scope of information and communication technology-based education just at the time when the demand for graduates has been cut in half (in light of the downsizing of many technology firms). At the same time, minimal attention is paid to the more universally required employability skills that have long life spans in a technology worker's career.

(i) Regular collection and publication of workforce performance data
There is a necessity for ongoing data to both gauge and benchmark progress on key aspects of workforce development. A strong consensus emerged from discussions with key stakeholders that the sorts of information generated in the TalentWorks profiles (TalentWorks 2002a, b) must serve as a common template — continually tracked and updated, serving as a public utility for all stakeholders to consult and use a basis for collective action and accountability. The issue raised in this recognition is who should be mandated to perform such a role, given the lack of collective architecture for such research, TalentWorks being an initial and non-permanent initiative. A response to this issue in the form of what is required next is outlined below.

(j) Need to revitalize trades education in secondary schools
There is insufficient coverage of the seven broad-based Technological Studies programs at local area secondary schools.[5] The schools over-concentrate on information and communication technology-related studies at the expense of other broad-based technologies such as skilled trades. Therefore, students are not being introduced to the full range of trades and technology opportunities. Compared with students in other school districts from across

[5] These seven programs are: communications technology, construction technology, hospitality services, manufacturing technology, personal services, technological design, and transportation technology.

Canada, the number of Ottawa students enrolled in the broad-based Technological Studies program is low. This imbalance, combined with the inadequate career counselling that is available to students, may deter students from developing career paths in the professional trades.

Coordination over Centralization — Building Collaborative Governance

To build a 21st-century workforce, an innovative and systemic approach is needed, but the reality of economic development today means that such an approach must be more horizontal and less vertical than traditional economic development approaches of the past. Thus, an important organizing concept for moving forward is some form of a regional human resource agency or department, with a shared and associational mandate to work collaboratively across all sectors. Such an entity would address issues of information gathering, recruitment, training, career development, counselling and support, policies, and funding.[6]

An effective workforce strategy must begin by creating the ability to bring people and resources from a variety of constituencies together to deal with challenges and opportunities as they emerge. It cannot focus only on increasing the number of engineers, or photonics researchers or waitresses or carpenters or automotive repair specialists — even if these occupations may be in demand today. By the time a community can act within the current structures to fulfill a particular labour demand in a given sector, the original need may have evaporated — as it did with computer and engineering specialists. Therefore we cannot be simply reactive; we must be proactive. However, we categorically state our belief that centralized labour planning has never worked, does not work now, and never will work.

The most important capacity required to improve Ottawa's workforce is that of helping people and organizations make better choices for themselves. Making better choices requires essentially two things — improving the quality of available information and removing any artificial or unreasonable barriers to people's ability to realize their choices. Providing better information and removing barriers underscore the basis for addressing the aforementioned priorities and challenges, a basis which become institutionalized in a more permanent format.

In addition, no single stakeholder in the community has the ability to deal with these fundamental issues on a city-wide basis: no one stakeholder has all the authority, the resources (human and financial), and the ability to consistently focus on these issues in order to address them. Therefore, one of the strategic recommendations put (TalentWorks 2002c) is the following: *TalentWorks create a regional Human Resources department for the city-region of Ottawa, which we will refer to as the Workforce Agency of Ottawa (WAO).*

---

[6] This is not to say that *all* such activities in the region would or should be coordinated in this way, but only those that are common among firms and that pose no competitive threat to each other, while benefiting from this type of consolidation.

The primary roles and aims of the WAO would be to:

- Help people make better choices with improved quality of information, whether they are job seekers or employers.
- Provide the services necessary to match skills with available work and encourage the development of the right sets of skills.
- Connect the people who need to change their skills with the programs that can help them do so.
- Provide lifelong learning within the context of current workforce conditions, tailoring programs to the needs of workers and employers.
- Create an altogether new capacity to account for the region's human capital.

Such an agency must be multi-stakeholder by design, with key workforce stakeholders on its board in order to raise collaboration to a very high and sophisticated level, allowing for more thorough integration of all aspects of workforce development. The aggregation of many workforce and human resource functions at a regional level would result in the elimination of many redundancies, in savings for organizations, and in improved quality of services (for instance, better training, improved career planning, and reduced costs for recruitment, retention and training). Most important, a regional entity would create sufficient scale and focus that its activities would receive the attention of a core business.

The biggest risk of creating such an entity is the complexity required to put it in place. For instance, the Province of Ontario and the Government of Canada are often at odds, unable to resolve their differences with regard to establishing a labour market agreement. As such, a WAO as a primarily local entity should be able to sidestep federal-provincial jurisdictional disputes. However complex, the consequences of not creating such an agency will continue to limit the community's ability to integrate resources and services and respond in a timely fashion to changes in the workforce environment. For example, without collaboration resolution of some key issues will remain highly unlikely, as in the case of career counselling and doing more to better integrate foreign-trained professionals — even when the basis of clear solutions present themselves. Mutual accommodation can be reached, but only if mechanisms for both dialogue and action are in place.

Governance Design

To operationalize the WAO, decision-making structures and accountability mechanisms must be established. This entity could potentially take many forms. It could be a function added to the municipal government. It could be a virtual partnership much like TalentWorks is today. It could be an independent institution mandated by the provincial or federal governments like the National Capital Commission. Or, as we believe, it can be an institution with a delegated temporary mandate that exists only for as long as the stakeholders who create it see fit to continue it.

Since regional workforce monitoring, matching, transforming, upgrading and inventorying activities are not central to any individual organization, the aggregation of many of these activities within a WAO could well save costs for organizations and improve the quality of services to individuals and organizations. Under the umbrella of the WAO, these efforts can be coordinated, and much duplication of resources, time and effort can be eliminated, resulting in larger impacts for existing resources, as well as better direction and more utilization. The WAO would have a coordinating and serving role, both from the client perspectives of citizens and organizations and from the perspective of the community at whose discretion it would function. The WAO would help people and organizations by performing the following functions:

- Provide capacity to address priority issues.
- Create an organic, fluid entity to anticipate human resource issues and proactively address local human resource issues.
- Provide cost savings through the reduction of duplication by area organizations.
- Ensure Ottawa's workforce development is an ongoing, continuous process continually realigned with the evolving demands of local citizens, firms and the city as a whole.
- Provide the community with the continuing capacity to resolve regional issues in a comprehensive holistic manner rather than piecemeal, as is the norm today.

The concept of a WAO may seem daunting, but specialists in large companies regularly deal with different functions, with different groups, and with services and business that have different cultures, values, needs and expectations. Therefore, the diversity of needs and interests in the region should not deter us. Caution, however, needs to be advised. The major risk in creating a new regional institution is that we may add to an already overly complex system. We say "complex" rather than "bureaucratic" because there exists no single, ponderous workforce authority in Ottawa. The space of workforce issues in Ottawa is a multi-stakeholder arena — and it must remain as such.

However, there may be the temptation with a WAO to over-engineer, micro-manage, or inadvertently obstruct the natural process of workforce evolution rather than truly nourish the workforce through the formation of full, rich, dynamic partnerships and connections whose outcomes cannot always be predicted in advance. Again, centralized planning is less than optimal as an approach when collective and dispersed partnerships are required to move forward on a city-wide basis. Although TalentWorks has evolved as an informal mechanism to achieve workforce coordination, it lacks direct access to resources and the authority to act assertively in multiple directions.[7]

The WAO would be an independent multi-stakeholder institution for resolving regional workforce issues, requiring formalized commitments (in funding and resources) from the three levels of government, businesses and the social sector. It would not be a controlling institution, but a workforce intelligence gatherer, an agent for workforce education and

---

[7] Moreover, Ottawa is not alone in requiring workforce coordination at a regional level. If the WAO were formed as a demonstration project to explore the viability of similar Workforce Agencies beyond Ottawa, it could benefit the other 26 metropolitan regions of the country that comprise just over 64% of Canada's population, or about 19,297,000 people. We propose, therefore, that the WAO have a mandate of five years, after which a review and evaluation be undertaken. The possibility of continuing the WAO experiment and exporting it to other regions of the country could then be explored.

training, an advocate for job seekers steering "clients" to relevant providers or agencies, and a coordinating body. The WAO would have the following characteristics:

- Guided by a multi-stakeholder form of governance to ensure accountability.
- Not mandated by any new authorities but operating as an agency from the bottom up (i.e. its authority would be derived from delegated authorities from its stakeholders).
- Not owned or dominated by any single level of government (federal, provincial or municipal), nor any particular industry sector or community organization.
- Residing *in* the city of Ottawa, but not *with* the municipality of the City of Ottawa (the government).
- Operating with an established budget adequate for its objectives, adequately staffed and appropriately housed.

The WAO Board would consist of representatives from the three levels of government, industry sectors, education/training institutions and community groups. From a corporate governance perspective, a good size for a board is 10–15 members. This facilitates manageability and effective learning. The WAO will eliminate overlaps and redundancies in human resource and workforce training-related initiatives and efforts across constituencies and institutions in Ottawa.

This point underscores the reason TalentWorks was originally created. Under the umbrella of WAO, these efforts can be more effectively coordinated, and much duplication of resources, time and effort can be eliminated, so that existing resources will have larger impacts, being better directed and more utilized. The WAO should be made to explicitly avoid additional bureaucracy. The make-up of the Board and the background variety of its officers (from governments, industries, education, etc.) will likely maintain a dynamic tension between them within the organization. While a uniformity of thought is not required of the Board members or group members, a willingness to engage in dialogue and consensus building is. In addition, its stakeholders, not stockholders or legislation, decide the mandate of the WAO. The proposed funding mechanism, its implementation and its disbursements also circumvent the formation of a big bureaucratic machine. What is required is the commitment to invest resources with appropriate public accountability.

Volatility, Leadership and The Costs of Inaction

Despite broad participation, considerable investments, and wide and shared support for the TalentWorks process, the initiative faces an impasse. To date, the City of Ottawa has not moved on the recommendations of the multi-stakeholder council (including the key aspects summarized in this chapter, notably the creation of a WAO), despite expressing support for its goals and a hope that in the future the makings of an integrative strategy for workforce development can, indeed, emerge.

Why this inaction? It appears to stem from an inter-related mix of economic volatility on the one hand, and fragmented and weak political capacities on the other. In terms of economic volatility, the well documented decline of the technology sector globally, and locally in Ottawa, may well be a factor, lessening the short term sense of crisis with respect to skills gaps and a now seemingly over dramatized (and distant) sentiment that technology companies cannot find enough qualified workers to hire. Moreover, the shifting market conditions also impact the attentions and priorities of companies, many of whom may well be less enthusiastic about supporting new multi-stakeholders endeavours.

The shaky economics of technology has also emerged in tandem with rising insecurity and a new focus on terrorism. Indirectly, this combination has both lessened revenues flowing to governments and shifted the spending priorities in terms of public sector action. For example, much heralded initiatives such as the Innovation Strategy and Broadband, seemingly sure bets for federal spending only a few years ago, are now more precarious and in stronger competition for limited financial resources. For Human Resources Development Canada (HRDC), a department of the federal government and a key stakeholder and provider of funds for TalentWorks, such forces have reduced the scope of discretionary spending and experimentation, resulting in a roadblock for TalentWorks and its future evolution into something akin to a WAO.

However, this seemingly necessary financial reliance on the federal government is more indicative of a larger problem facing Ottawa — and all Canadian cities, namely the weak fiscal, political and strategic capacities of municipal authorities in attempting to become more assertive and holistic in nurturing growth and designing governance and engaging communities to do so (Vielba 2001). Indicative of this problem is the fact that despite a widening recognition that cities are increasingly the central forum for clustering and the main engines of innovation, workforce development as a local governance function is practically non-existent, outside of provincial and federal interventions within their jurisdiction.

Indeed, what makes TalentWorks such a unique and important experiment is its localizing scope in terms of focus and coordinated action, and the willingness of both the provincial and federal governments to partner within a multi-stakeholder effort and collaborate rather than control, facilitating dialogue and local engagement rather than dictating and imposing prescriptions in a more traditional top-down manner.

The fiscal dependency remains, however, in an already tightening economic environment locally and the City of Ottawa faces a bind. Less prodded by a weakened private sector, organizationally struggling to foster a post-amalgamation set of structures and agencies for the single City of Ottawa, and financially crippled by a limited property tax base, the City is reduced to lobbying the other levels of government for help. Mayors across the country, including Ottawa's Bob Chiarelli, have been advancing the case for greater investments in Canada's cities.

As a political priority TalentWorks may lack profile and urgency, in comparison to other items requiring public spending — notably health care and transportation infrastructure. The latter is particularly central to Ottawa's Smart Growth Plan, wide-reaching and expansionary with buses and light rail envisioned as facilitators of less sprawl and smarter concentration, and completely dependent on forthcoming fiscal transfers from provincial and federal governments.

Accordingly, TalentWorks may well lack, in the short-term, political champions and economic leaders. More worrisome is the notion that TalentWorks may also reflect a weakness in civic capacities within Ottawa — specifically, a weakened ability to engage both the public and private sectors in not only identifying workforce development as a priority (which has been done), but also finding catalysts for further investment and action.

TalentWorks owes much of its existence and progress to date to civic entrepreneurs of the sorts found within OCRI, an organization whose mission in the past has been precisely to provide such a bridging and catalytic role. It may well be that OCRI's capacities are evolving as well, negatively impacted by a depleted private sector membership on the one hand, and greater control with less funding exerted by the City government on the other.

Yet, weakening market conditions and limited public resource cannot be mere excuses to justify community inaction. Even within California's Silicon Valley, the epi-centre of the high-technology meltdown, similar forces have not resulted in a lessening focus on people, skills and long-term learning. Conversely, such issues have risen in profile, prodded by a range of civic collaborative mechanisms, such as Joint Venture Silicon Valley Network, joining stakeholders across the community in precisely the manner that TalentWorks achieved in Ottawa (Joint Venture: Silicon Valley Network 2003).

It would certainly be wrong for local leaders in Ottawa to assume that the conditions stalling TalentWorks today are having similar impacts in other cities. The conditions and supports designed today will largely determine tomorrow's capacity for progress. In a fiercely competitive global environment, where people are rapidly becoming more mobile than companies themselves, workforce development is a critical variable at the heart of the growing nexus between innovation, quality of life and growth. TalentWorks has revealed the gaps in information and planning that should concern all economic sectors, as well as critical transitory difficulties faced by key segments of the Ottawa community, namely new immigrants (TalentWorks 2002c).

Unlike the visible and fully engrained multi-cultural fabrics of Canada's largest cities, notably Toronto, Ottawa is a city fighting to establish its diversity credentials. With growing evidence of the technology sector's global and local patterns of trans-national communities and the social capital created by ethnic ties, Canada is well placed to take advantage of such flows.

Conclusion

Three broad lessons can be taken away from the experience of TalentWorks and its recommendations. First, there is a need for a quasi-permanent function along the lines of our proposed WAO to serve as a critical voice and catalyst for workforce development in Ottawa, and on a holistic basis. Secondly, the primary role of such a new vehicle would be less about creation and more about facilitation. Many actors exist across niches of training, education, skills development — and employers themselves; yet; what is lacking is an overall architecture to coordinate these efforts, identify gaps and weaknesses (and strengths), and mobilize resources and efforts to address deficiencies. Finally, local governance capacities often remain weak and fragmented, struggling from a fiscal shortfall that favours federal and provincial governments at the expense of municipal authorities — and in the case of Ottawa, a weakened private sector has, temporarily at least, taken away the impetus for stronger attempts at corrective action.

Nonetheless, the emergence of TalentWorks in Ottawa, and the research and recommendations that have resulted, amplify the growing degree of recognition that knowledge and learning are shared processes that cut across industries, sectors and communities. While all organizations, private, public or civic, must focus on their own skill base and the capacities of their own workers, there is a basis for competition that is shared across all such organizations, as they share a local pool of human capital and compete in an increasingly open and global environment for the ability to retain and replenish such a pool. In short, workforce development is a key source of competitive — and collective — advantage for cities such as Ottawa looking to succeed in a globalizing and increasingly knowledge-driven economy.

References

Capello, R. (1999). A spatial transfer of knowledge in high-technology milieus: Learning vs. collective learning processes. *Regional Studies*, *33*(4), 353–366.

Castells, M., & Hall, P. (1993). *Technopoles of the world: The making of 21st century industrial complexes*. New York: Routledge.

Florida, R. (1995). Toward the learning region. *Futures*, *27*(5), 527–536.

Florida, R. (2000). *Competing in the age of talent: Quality of place and the new economy*. Pittsburgh, PA: Carnegie Mellon University.

Henton, D., Melville, J., & Walesh, K. (1997). *Grassroots leaders for a new economy*. San Francisco: Jossey-Bass.

Joint Venture: Silicon Valley Network (2003). *Regional index of Silicon Valley*. San Jose: www.jointventure.org.

Keeble, D., & Wilkinson, F. (1999). Collective learning and knowledge development in the evolution of regional clusters of high-technology SMEs in Europe. *Regional Studies*, *33*(4), 295–304.

Kotkin, J. (2000). *The new geography: How the digital revolution is re-shaping the American landscape*. New York: Random House.

Lawson, C., & Lorenz, E. (1999). A collective learning, tacit knowledge and regional innovation capacity. *Regional Studies*, *33*(4), 305–318.

Leadbeater, C. (1999). *Living on thin air: The new economy*. London: Viking.

Moore, J. F. (1996). *The death of competition — Leadership and strategy in the age of business ecosystems*. New York: HarperCollins.

Moss Kanter, R. (1995). *World class — Thriving locally in the global economy*. New York: Simon & Schuster.

National Governors Association (2000). *State strategies for the new economy*. Washington, DC: National Governor's Association.

Nelson, M. R. (1998). Government and governance in the networked world. In: D. Tapscott, A. Lowy & D. Ticoll (Eds), *Blueprint to the digital economy: Creating wealth in the era of e-business* (pp. 274–298). New York: McGraw-Hill.

Paquet, G. (1997). States, communities and markets: The distributed governance scenario. In: T. J. Courchene (Ed.), *The nation-state in a global information era: Policy challenges the Bell Canada papers in economics and public policy* (Vol. 5, pp. 25–46). Kingston, Ontario, Canada: John Deutsch Institute for the Study of Economic Policy.

Paquet, G., & Roy, J. (2004a). *Serving and value-adding: CIPO as a catalyst in the knowledge-based economy*. Forthcoming study to be published in *Proceedings of Industry Canada Conference* on Intellectual Property and Innovation in the Knowledge-Based Economy, May 23–24, 2001, Toronto, Ontario, Canada.

Paquet, G., & Roy, J. (2004b). Smarter cities in Canada. *Optimum Online, 33*(1) (forthcoming).

Stoker, G. (1996). Private-public partnerships and urban governance. In: J. Pierre (Ed.), *Partnerships in urban governance – European and American perspectives* (pp. 34–51). London, UK: MacMillan Press.

Storper, M. (1997). *The regional world: Territorial development in a global economy.* New York: Guilford Press.

TalentWorks (2002a). *Ottawa works – A mosaic of Ottawa's economic and workforce landscape.* Report I: Ottawa's workforce environment. Ottawa, Ontario, Canada: Centre on Governance, University of Ottawa.

TalentWorks (2002b). *Ottawa works – A mosaic of Ottawa's economic and workforce landscape.* Report II: Profiling Ottawa's workforce. Ottawa, Ontario, Canada: Centre on Governance, University of Ottawa.

TalentWorks (2002c). *Ottawa works – A mosaic of Ottawa's economic and workforce landscape.* Report III: Ottawa's workforce development strategy. Ottawa, Ontario, Canada: Centre on Governance, University of Ottawa.

Tapscott, D., & Ticoll, D. (2003). *The naked corporation – How the age of transparency will revolutionize business.* Toronto, Ontario, Canada: Viking Canada.

Vielba, C. A. (2001). Cities in transition: New challenges, new responsibilities. *Local Government Studies, 27*(1), 136–137.

Part III

Conclusion

Chapter 16

The Luster of Clusters: A Cautionary Tale

Warren Thorngate

Abstract

Communities seeking a recipe for developing their own high technology industrial cluster can find both hope and caution in the Silicon Valley North experience. The preceding chapters document many of the necessary ingredients for development. Less is said, because less is known, about how to find or combine these ingredients. Chance is likely to play a significant role in their discovery and combination. So too is the nature of emerging markets. It is more likely that successful future Canadian clusters will use existing technologies for new markets than will create new technologies for existing markets.

Introduction

Birds flock. Cows herd. Fish school. People affiliate. Industries cluster. The geographical concentration of a social species, a group of people or a set of companies with similar interests is as natural as evolution and circumstance allow. Humans gather in places called neighbourhoods, villages, towns and cities. Markets find their places in bazaars, shopping malls, the streets of Wall and Bay. So too do the companies producing what we go to the markets to buy. Northern England hosted the Industrial Revolution. Hollywood covered itself in film studios, Detroit in automobile plants. Airplane manufacturing proliferated in Southern California, insurance in Boston, publishing in New York, petrochemicals in Calgary, lumber in Vancouver, crime in Miami, culture in Montreal.

The long history of industrial congregation continues in the clustering of companies producing elevated technologies born of silicon, software or biochemicals in real or metaphorical valleys around the world. Those who visit the valleys notice that most generate or attract a lot of wealth. Houses are larger, communities cleaner and children more spoiled than those of the farmers who once sowed the valley soil. The correlation between the growth of high technology clusters and the economic success of their surrounding communities stimulates our Humean habit to infer a causal link between the two: high tech clusters cause economic success. This inference brings hope to poor communities wanting to enrich themselves. Following hope comes the desire for prescriptions, a recipe book, for cluster development.

The preceding chapters in this book reveal many of the ingredients important for developing Ottawa's high technology cluster. Some of the chapters also discuss how these ingredients were or should be combined in the development and maintenance of Silicon Valley North (SVN). Gleaned from the chapters is a long list of major ingredients associated with development of SVN. Included are pools of technical and entrepreneurial talent, easy access to venture or other capital, good industry-university relations, favourable government regulations, timely access to technical and market information, managerial styles that appeal to the nonmonetary desires of employees, innovative training and community development programmes, formal and informal social networks for deal making and knowledge exchange, and mutual respect, trust, and cooperation.

Such a list is likely to discourage those seeking a single, key ingredient for creating a high technology industrial cluster. No single ingredient is sufficient. All are necessary. So attention must be paid to the lot. Yet a list of necessary ingredients, however long, is only one part of a complete recipe. A recipe must also tell us how and when to mix and cook the ingredients. And to use the recipe we must also have the ingredients at hand. How can we recruit, train and retain relevant pools of talent? How can we attract venture and other capital? How can we develop informal networks or ensure trust, respect and cooperation? And how can all these ingredients best be combined?

Many of the case histories, surveys, prescriptions and speculations about Silicon Valley North discussed in preceding chapters address these and similar questions, but no detailed answers emerge. It is not the fault of the authors but of the complexity of interactions and influences among the major ingredients of cluster development, and of the paucity of data needed to determine what these influences are. Any detailed, instrumental, "how-to" knowledge in a recipe for high technology cluster development can only emerge after we analyse other successful high technology cluster development projects, then compare them to unsuccessful projects and to low technology ones. Still, there is no guarantee that the analyses and comparisons will bring us the detailed knowledge we desire. We might discover that several recipes are variously successful in different communities. We might discover than no recipe works beyond the community or era it describes. Such discoveries await future research.

In the meantime, there seems no harm in asking more questions about the complex links between the antecedents documented in the preceding chapters and the development of Silicon Valley North. My reading of the chapters leads me to ask three of them. First, how important is chance in the development of high technology clusters? Second, do clusters respond to some markets more or less favorably than others? Third, what might future clusters be?

The Likely Importance of Chance

One of the most sinful pleasures of historical analysis is "What if?" speculation. What if Kennedy had not been assassinated? What if Darius or Stanfield had won? What if the farmers had not sold the valley, or the Wired City had not been dismantled, or Matthews and

Cowpland had received their shipment of lawnmowers for MITEL? Thought experiments like these focus our attention to the possible importance of random events as "tipping points" of historical trajectories (Gladwell 2002). At least one thought experiment can lead us to wonder how much chance might play a role in industrial development beyond the boundaries of any recipe for high tech success (see Thorngate & Hotta 1995).

Consider Bingo, a simple game with simple rules. Each player pays into a common pool or pot for a Bingo card on which is drawn a 535 matrix with columns labeled B I N G and O. Under each column are five random numbers from 1 to 99, the numbers varying from card to card. The Bingo *caller* randomly draws balls on which are written various combinations of the five letters and 99 numbers, announcing each ball drawn one at a time: "B37!"; "N52!"; "G21!" and the like. As each ball is announced, players check their card, covering a cell if it matches the call. Eventually, one player covers five cells in a row, or five cells in a column or the five cells of the main or off diagonal. The first player to do so yells "Bingo!" wins the game and receives some portion of the pot (the rest goes to charity, the caller, or other interested parties).

Consider now a simple version of Bingo. Assume 100 people (or companies) gather to play as many games as they can, each continuing until he/she goes broke. Each player brings $5 to the gathering, and places $1 (think of monthly startup costs) in a pot to pay for a card to play a round of the game. The winner is given the entire pot of $100 (think of a lucrative contract or initial public offering). What can we expect to occur? Sooner or later, the first winner will shout "Bingo!" and receive the $100 pot. The winner will then have $104, and 99 losers will have $4. The 100 players will then ante up another $1 for Game 2. Though it is possible (a 1% chance) that the winner of Game 1 will also win Game 2, it is far more likely that one of the other 99 players will win. Result: when Game 2 ends, two players are most likely to have $103 and 98 players to have $3.

Fast forward to Game 5. Though it is possible the one or more people will win two or more of the first four games, it is far more likely that four different players will have won Games 1–4. These four people will each have $101; the remaining 96 players will each have $1. All 100 will ante $1 for Game 5. Only one will win it, most likely a fifth player. When game 6 begins, no fewer than 95 people will be broke and no more than five people will each have at least $100. Only the latter will have resources to continue the game. Of course, the pot will decline from $100 to $5. Yet, because so many other players were forced to drop out of the game, the chances of winning subsequent games will greatly increase: from 1 in 100 to 1 in 5. The combination of increased wealth and reduced chances of losing virtually guarantee that the remaining five players will continue the game forever.

Are the long-term survivors of this Bingo game more talented, educated, fit, motivated, entrepreneurial, networked or better managed than their unfortunate peers? Not at all. Only one thing distinguishes the survivors from the casualties in a Bingo game: *luck*. The rules of the game guarantee survivors, but provide only two possibilities for a player to improve the odds of survival. First, bring more money to the game than the other players do, hoping to outlast them. Second, reduce the chances of losing what one brings. One means of reducing the chances of loss is to pool resources with other players and share whatever winnings accrue (Thorngate *et al.* 1996). This gives potential advantage to a cluster or companies willing to pool resources and share their profits, much like farmer's cooperatives do. On the other hand, such a cooperative cluster only has competitive advantage if other players continue to play alone. If they too form clusters, the competitive advantage disappears, leaving only one possibility for increasing the chances of survival: wealth. The rich really do get richer in Bingo and analogous situations; it is a mathematical certainty. But it is hardly useful to prescribe that high tech companies should start with more money than their competitors in order to continue earning more money — a variation of the Matthew Effect (Merton 1995).

Is the development of a high technology industrial cluster in any way analogous to playing in a Bingo game? In many ways it is. Bingo is one example of a winner-take-all market, beautifully analyzed by Frank & Cook (1995). Many markets of high technology products show winner-take-all features, including markets that evolve to a single standard or format such as VHS (not Beta), Windows (Not Be) or MS Word (not Word Perfect) or Flash (not SVN). Often as not, the chances of a company surviving in a winner-take-all market have less to do with the quality of its products, the talent or education of its inventors, the social network of its managers or the efficiency of operations than with advertising (think of the Energizer Bunny), timing, habit, consumer caprice or the optimism of its investors.

There is a cautionary lesson here. It is insufficient to argue that following an Ottawa recipe, or any recipe, will increase the chances of future high technology industrial cluster success. We must also estimate the size of this increase. If an Ottawa recipe would increase the chances of success from, say, 10–80%, then it is probably worth following. If it would increase the chances from 5 to 10%, as is likely to happen in a winner-take-all or other luck-infested market, and then following the recipe might not be worth the bother. How can we estimate the increase? I don't know. But in light of our knowledge of the perils of winner-take-all markets, I would guess that other market features are also crucial to the success of an Ottawa or similar recipe.

Finding the Best Markets

Although many high technology markets show several analogies to Bingo and other winner-take-all situations, not all do. People unwilling to despair over the possibility that luck alone determines high tech success have good reason to argue that the ingredients of an Ottawa or similar recipe do make a substantial difference in high tech cluster success, at least in some markets. What are these markets and how do they differ from the winner-take-all? The question is important. The answer is unclear. However, it is probably safe to presume that alternatives to winner-take-all markets are those that distribute the wealth in some other way. One popular vision of an alternative distribution is this: Companies will capture their share of a market in proportion to the value of their products. Value, of course, is an exceedingly slippery term. But it does encourage the belief that factors influencing value will make a difference in market share. It is a short, compelling conceptual leap from this belief to the belief that success will follow a formula that looks like a simple linear equation, each ingredient making its independent, additive contribution to market share like bricks to a house or logs to a fire.

This additive belief is part of a philosophical perspective on life viewed as a series of tests offering rewards to those who pass each. The perspective is frequently instantiated in grade school where every student passing the tests of one grade is guaranteed entry to the next grade, and in the courtroom where there is no upper limit on the number of guilty or innocent judgments made. Those who pass or fail the same tests receive the same consequences, and the pool of rewards or punishments expands or contracts according to the number who pass or fail.

I know of no market that works this way, though some give the illusion they do while they are young and unsaturated. People rarely make decisions according to absolute judgments about value, and they rarely distribute their money across products according to such absolute judgments. That is why it is uncommon to hear someone say, "I rate these apples as a 5 on my 10-point value scale, and rate those as a 3, so I will buy 5 of these and 3 of those." Instead, people far more often compare values and buy only what they judge best by comparison. These comparative judgments point to the crucial difference between tests and contests. As noted above, *tests* require resources to be adjusted according to how many people or companies seeking them pass some minimum, absolute standard. *Contests* place a limit on the resources and distribute them according to who or what is better or best.

Markets are contests for the dollars of buyers, including markets in which the winner does not take all. More technically, they are adjudicated contests in which decisions to buy or not are the result of buyers' comparative judgments. We who dwell in the study of human decision-making know a lot about adjudicated contests and how they evolve (Thorngate 1988; Thorngate & Carroll 1987, 1991; Thorngate *et al.* 2002). Some of this knowledge is important to consider when evaluating a recipe for high technology industrial cluster development.

Suppose a local startup company or cluster is created to develop, manufacture and sell a wildly creative and wonderful new high tech gizmo, the HTG, that has a large potential market and no competitors. The stage is set for an exciting and hugely profitable venture, and as long as orders eventually flow, the start-up process need not be unduly formal or efficient. Yet with success, two consequences almost surely follow. First, the company or cluster must grow to meet market demand, which leads to formalization, structure, and the decline of spontaneity, play and fun that so often motivates creative endeavors. Second, the company or cluster will attract competitors eager to win a share of its new market. All competing companies or clusters are likely to be motivated to stay solvent by gaining or maintaining a profitable share of the market. To do so they must appeal to buyer preferences. Market research or trial-and-error will give each competitor a sense of what buyers want and value. If buyers want reliability, and judge the value of competing HTGs accordingly, then competing HTG companies must match their product reliability to stay alive. If buyers want low prices and judge HTG value accordingly, then HTG prices of competitors must head toward the lowest available. Competitors slow to adapt their HTG to these wants and values are likely to die.

As competing HTGs evolve to meet the wants of buyers, they afford buyers the opportunity to change their wants or to increase them (Helson 1964). Most buyers exploit the opportunity. Last year's highly profitable 3 mega-pixel, 32-port, 87 gram, two gigahertz, 40 gigabyte, 49-button, three-hour battery life, flip up, remotely operated, medically certified, ISO compliant HTG is sure to be copied or exceeded this year by more than one company, and its more profitable replacement duplicated or exceeded in following years. Rhapsodic economists often call this progress, or the miracle of the (buyer's) market. The miracle creates at least three problems for high technology companies. First, each escalating round of progress requires companies to invest increasing amounts of everything to stay in the market, leaving less to invest in other markets. Second, the market begins to saturate, slowing growth in sales. Third, as surviving HTGs become less distinguishable in their technical features, consumers increasingly turn to whimsy in making their buying decisions. As the turn occurs, the success of a high technology product comes to depend more on marketing than engineering. Colours, shapes, nifty knobs and branding do make the difference when all competitors have the same technology inside. When everyone's chips are fast and light and full of capacity, style triumphs over substance.

The lesson? Though it is sparsely documented in the preceding chapters, I risk a guess that the Ottawa recipe was successful in part because a high proportion of Silicon Valley North companies produced things that opened new markets rather than competed in established ones. When the famous atonal composer, Arnold Schoenberg, was asked why he wrote such novel music, he apocryphally replied, "Because I can't beat Beethoven at his own game." The rationalization might be echoed in Ottawa. Silicon Valley North companies, clustered or otherwise, are unlikely to beat Microsoft in the saturated markets it dominates, as Corel has found. But, like Schoenberg, the companies might profit from fresh markets with little or no competition, even modest ones, as Cognos has found. Where are these markets? My reading of the Ottawa business news indicates that the highest proportion of markets of Silicon Valley North companies are for new parts or components, hardware and software, of larger high technology products. It leads me to wonder if the success of Silicon Valley North has been less the result of high technology than of new technology. Contemporary business cant about industries of knowledge, innovation and ideas reinforces the belief that it is more profitable to be new than to be improved. And it prompts the question: Are there new markets beyond high technology that could be efficiently colonized by future clusters?

What Might Future Clusters be?

Communities wishing to home-bake their own high technology industrial cluster would surely be heartened by mention in preceding chapters of several different kinds: clusters of companies serving a telecommunication market, a photonics market, a genomics market, etc. The Millennium fall of the telecommunications market might lead communities to leave it for Ottawa and try something less settled or cultivated. Perhaps more fertile territory can be claimed first in high technology markets for remote sensing, health, robotics, alternative energy, agriculture, translation, computer or homeland security. Although the Ottawa recipe might tell communities what high technology industrial clusters must have to grow, it does not reveal where the growth is most likely to occur.

Is there a recipe for discovering or creating new markets? High-priced futurists, consultants and business gurus want us to think so, but a foolproof recipe has not yet been revealed. In its absence, we are left with common sense, and a little psychology. Markets are, to social psychologists such as me, wonderful manifestations of reciprocal problems solving. A problem is the difference between what someone has and what someone wants. A solution reduces or eliminates the difference. Whenever two or more people meet to solve each other's problems, a market is born. I want your houseplant more than my $20. You want my $20 more than your houseplant. We exchange your houseplant for my $20 to get what we want. Our market has solved two problems.

So the discovery of new markets is one step removed from the discovery of new problems. New problems occur either when we develop a new want for something we do not have, or when an old want is no longer satisfied by what we do have. Market research is sometimes successful in fathoming wants unfulfilled. So too is a regular read of the news and some thought about the trends the news reveals. Example: More Canadians are getting older, creating growth in wants to prevent, retard or compensate for the decline of sensory and cognitive functions that come with advanced age. Markets will thus emerge for preventatives, retardants and sensory or mental prosthetic devices, including those brought by biotechnologies of all kinds. Example: As news factories compete for public attention with increasingly homogeneous servings of escalating shock, the homogeneity will create a want for something different, be it a different kind of news or none at all. Web sites serving different fare are thus likely to attract more attention and perhaps dollars as well.

Problems, thus markets, can also be discovered by listening to complaints, those often-annoying statements of problems large and small. Many complaints can also be found in letters to editors. Others reside in flaming web sites or cynical joke books. Still more can be inferred from front-page tragedies that point to glaring system deficiencies. Consider, for example, all the markets that are beginning to emerge from the tragedies of crime, global warming or 11 September 2001. Of course, not all problems have a high technology solution; indeed, it is likely that only a small proportion do. It is also likely that more new problems can be solved, and hence more new markets can be developed, by finding new uses for recent technologies than by inventing new technologies. The most obvious example I know comes from my local video rental store. The high technology allowing consumers to watch DVDs at home will soon saturate its market. Yet public desire for new content distributed via the technology shows no signs of saturation and many signs of insatiable growth. India and Egypt have thriving entertainment industries, not because of they invent new technology but because they adapt current technology to their content. Faced with a choice of developing another high technology cluster or a new entertainment cluster, it seems reasonable to propose that smart Canadian money should find its way to the latter as quick as can be.

The next few decades will complete more of the story about high technology cluster development. Variations of Silicon Valley North are likely to emerge. Some are sure to be virtual variations, though their success is likely to be hampered until the virtual can sustain the levels of deal making and trust now found on the golf courses of Ottawa. A few will succeed. Many will fail. The Ottawa recipe will be modified according to emerging markets. And farmers, bless them all, will find other valleys to sow the seeds that feed us.

References

Gladwell, M. (2002). *The tipping point: How little things can make a big difference*. Boston, MA: Little Brown & Co.

Helson, H. (1964). *Adaptation-level theory*. New York: Harper & Row.

Merton, R. K. (1995). The Thomas theorem and the Matthew effect. *Social Forces, 74*(2), 379–424.

Thorngate, W. (1988). On the evolution of adjudicated contests and the principle of invidious selection. *Journal of Behavioral Decision Making, 1*, 5–16.

Thorngate, W., & Carroll, B. (1987). Why the best person rarely wins: Some embarrassing facts about contests. *Simulation and Games, 18*, 299–320.

Thorngate, W., & Carroll, B. (1991). Tests versus contests: A theory of adjudication. In: W. Baker, M. Hyland, R. van Hezewijk, & S. Terwee (Eds), *Recent trends in theoretical psychology* (Vol. 2, pp. 431–438). New York: Springer-Verlag.

Thorngate, W., Faregh, N., & Young, M. (2002). Mining the archives: Analyses of CIHR research grant adjudications. Canadian Institutes of Health Research, 44 pages.http://www.carleton.ca/~warrent/reports/mining_the_archives.pdf.

Thorngate, W., & Hotta, M. (1995). Life and luck: Survival of the fattest. *Simulation and Gaming*, *26*, 5–16.

Thorngate, W., Hotta, M., & McClintock, C. (1996). Bingo! The case for cooperation revisited. In: C. Tolman, F. Cherry, R. van Hejiwek, & I. Lubek (Eds), *Problems of theoretical psychology* (pp. 211–216). New York: Springer-Verlag.

Subject Index

275, 279, 282–285, 287–289,
297–299, 301, 302, 304, 305,
307–309, 312, 314–323, 325, 327, 334

University
  Carleton, 15, 16, 23, 33, 34, 38–45, 47,
    48, 50, 58, 81, 182, 203–207,
    211–220, 302, 304
  of Ottawa, 16, 40, 41, 50, 58, 61, 73, 81,
    153, 163, 203–207, 211–220, 302,
    304, 312, 318
Université
  du Québec en Outaouais (UQO), 245,
    248, 249

Venture capital (VC)
  investment cycle, 16, 26, 27, 61, 69, 98,
    110, 168, 172, 175–177, 180–182,
    188, 191, 194, 198, 317
  new venture financing, 173
Volatility, 7, 17, 227, 238, 275, 277, 281,
  282, 284, 285, 288, 325

Wired City Simulation Laboratory, 15, 33,
  34, 40–42, 47, 48, 51
Wired Scientific City network, 40, 50
Workforce Agency of Ottawa (WAO),
  322
Workforce performance data, 321